12

280396

No.

STATE OF MICHIGAN

PROBATE COURT

For the

COUNTY OF WAYNE

IN THE MATTER OF

ANNIE COHEN

AN ALLEGED INSANE PERSON

APPLICATION FOR

ADMISSION TO HOSPITAL

MAY 8 1940

Dr. Bolewick appt'd

3rd phys

ENTERED IN SHORT BOOK

INDEXED

May 20

June 10

ANNIE'S GHOSTS

ANNIE'S GHOSTS

A Journey into a Family Secret

Steve Luxenberg

New York

Library of Congress Cataloging-in-Publication Data

Luxenberg, Steve.
    Annie's ghosts : a journey into a family secret / Steve Luxenberg.
        p.   cm.
    Includes bibliographical references and index.
    ISBN: 978-1-4013-2247-2
    1. Luxenberg, Steve—Family.   2. Adult children of aging parents—Family
relationships—United States—Case studies.   3. Mothers and sons—United States—Case
studies.   4. Sisters—Family relationships—United States—Case studies.—5. Inmates of
institutions—Family relationships—Michigan—Case studies.   6. Family secrets—Case
studies.   I. Title.
    HQ755.86.L89   2009
    306.875'408740977434—dc22
        2008055661

Hyperion books are available for special promotions and premiums.
For details contact the HarperCollins Special Markets Department in the New York
office at 212-207-7528, fax 212-207-7222, or email spsales@harpercollins.com.

Book design by Jennifer Ann Daddio/Bookmark Design & Media Inc.

FIRST EDITION

1   3   5   7   9   10   8   6   4   2

THIS LABEL APPLIES TO TEXT STOCK

We try to produce the most beautiful books possible, and we are also extremely
concerned about the impact of our manufacturing process on the forests of the
world and the environment as a whole. Accordingly, we made sure that all
of the paper we used has been certified as coming from forests that are managed
to insure the protection of the people and wildlife dependent upon them.

To Mom and Annie, too late to be set free;

to "the 5,000," who still might be;

and to Mary Jo, who stands alone

{ CONTENTS }

FOURTEEN: One of the Thousands   227

FIFTEEN: The Ghosts of Radziwillow   247

SIXTEEN: Abandoned   265

SEVENTEEN: Dad's Secret   281

EIGHTEEN: Uncontoured Ills   299

NINETEEN: Always the Bridesmaid   317

TWENTY: Reinterpretation   333

EPILOGUE   351

          FAMILY MEMBERS AND
          RECURRING FIGURES   359

          AUTHOR'S NOTE   363

          NOTES   365

          ACKNOWLEDGMENTS   387

          INDEX   393

ANNIE'S GHOSTS

Spring 1995

The secret emerged, without warning or provocation, on an ordinary April afternoon in 1995. Secrets, I've discovered, have a way of working themselves free of their keepers.

I don't remember what I was doing when I first heard about it. If I had been thinking as a journalist rather than as a son, I might have made a few notes. As it is, I'm stuck with half-memories and what I later told my wife, my friends, my newsroom colleagues—and what they recall about what I told them.

Just as secrets have a way of breaking loose, memories often have a way of breaking down. They elude us, or aren't quite sharp enough, or fool us into remembering things that didn't quite happen that way. Yet much as a family inhabits a house, memories inhabit our stories, make them breathe, give them life. So we learn to live with the reality that what we remember is an imperfect version of what we know to be true.

What I know for certain is this: On that spring afternoon in 1995, I picked up the phone and heard my sister Sashie say something like, "You're never going to believe this. Did you know that Mom had a sister?"

Of course I didn't know. My mother was an only child. Even now, I can hear her soft voice saying just those words. *"I'm an only child."* She told that to nearly everyone she met, sometimes within minutes of introduction. She treated her singular birth status as a kind of special birthright, as if she belonged to an exclusive society whose members possessed an esoteric knowledge beyond the comprehension of outsiders.

She suggested as much to my wife, Mary Jo, during their first getting-to-know-you conversation. That was 1976, four years before Mary Jo and I were married. The two of them, girlfriend and mother, were sharing a motel room while I recuperated from an emergency appendectomy that had abruptly ended a weekend camping trip. (I still wince at the memory, and I'm not referring just to the surgery.) As soon as Mom learned of my plight, she hustled to the Detroit airport and found her way to rural West Virginia. During their evenings together in the motel, Mom made a big point about how she felt an unusual connection to Mary Jo, her fellow traveler in the only-children club. "I understand what it's like," Mom assured her. "I know how it is to grow up without brothers and sisters."

It never occurred to me that it was a little odd how often Mom worked those "only child" references into her conversations. I simply accepted it as fact, a part of her autobiography, just as I knew that her name was Beth, that she was born in Detroit in 1917, that she had no middle name, that she hated her job selling shoes after graduating from high school, that she would have married a guy named Joe if only he had been Jewish, that she was the envy of her friends because of her wildly romantic love affair with my Clark Gable look-alike father, that she was kind and generous and told us growing up to, above all else, always tell the truth.

A sister?

"Where did you hear that?" I asked Sashie.

Sash and I are close, although she is twelve years older. When I first learned to talk, I couldn't say her name, Marsha. What came off my un-trained tongue sounded something like "Sashie." The mangled pronunciation stuck. She is Sashie, or Sash, even to her husband and some of her friends.

As Sash would say, Mom was not in a good place in the spring of 1995. Her health, and her state of mind, were often topic A in the long-distance phone calls among her children. (Our family, like many, is a complicated one. My parents, Beth and Jack, married in 1942 and had three sons. I'm the middle one; Mike is seven years older, and Jeff is three years younger. Sash and her older sister, Evie, were my father's children from a first mar-riage that lasted seven years. The girls lived with my parents for a large chunk of their childhood, particularly Sash, who thinks of herself as having grown up with two families and two mothers—and double the worry when both moms began having health problems as they aged. Evie moved out just before I was born, so I never knew her nearly as well as I knew Sash, my "big sister"; Sash married and left the house when I was about eight, but our relationship remained close as we managed that tricky conversion from childhood to adulthood.)

My mom was still working at seventy-eight years old, still getting herself up every morning and tooling down one of Detroit's many expressways to her bookkeeping job at a tiny company that sold gravestones, a job she had been doing for more than thirty years. But her emphysema, the payoff from a two-pack-a-day smoking habit that began in her teens, had gotten worse. So had her hearing; she fiddled constantly with her hearing aid, frustrated that she could no longer understand the quick mumbles that punctuate everyday conversation, but also frantic to avoid the sharp whines that burst forth from the tiny device whenever it picked up a sudden loud noise, such as the shrieks of happy grandchildren.

On top of Mom's periodic trips to the ER for shortness of breath, her doctors believed that she was suffering from anxiety attacks. It was a chicken-and-egg problem: The shortness of breath made her anxious, and her anxiety triggered the feeling that she couldn't breathe. She emerged from a February hospitalization with a fistful of prescriptions and a fear that her days of good health were behind her. The Xanax made her less anxious at first, but within a few weeks, she was fingering the medication as the cause of her insomnia and jitters. "It makes me want to crawl out of my skin," she said.

As if that wasn't enough of a roller coaster ride, she was following doctors' orders to quit smoking. She called cigarettes her "best friends" in times of stress, and these were certainly stressful times, for her and for us. There was so much going on with her—the nicotine withdrawal, the reaction to Xanax, the shortness of breath, the sleepless nights—that it seemed impossible to find a way back to the equilibrium that had once ruled our lives. We bounced back and forth, thinking one minute that everything would work out if she would just give the medication a chance, and the next that, no, this was crazy, the medication was the problem, maybe everything depended on getting her doctors to switch her to some other magic pill.

She had been feeling so lousy that she didn't even want to drive. That was a bad sign. Henry Ford himself would have smiled to hear her talk about driving with my father during their courtship days, the feeling of flying along on the open road, your hair free in the wind, the sense that the world was yours for the taking as long as you had wheels. Not even Dad's sudden death in 1980, which sent Mom reeling like nothing else I had ever seen, had slowed her down. Her Chevrolet Beretta wasn't just a car; it symbolized her independence, her vitality, her youth, and her freedom.

But for several months now, Mom had left her car at home, relying instead on a counselor at Jewish Family Service, social worker Rozanne Sedler, to take her to various doctors' appointments. Rozanne had gotten to know Mom pretty well during their car rides and counseling sessions, and had urged her to visit a psychiatrist. Mom, who had always disdained psychiatrists and psychiatry, consented to go—another sign that she was not in a good place.

When I heard Sash's voice on the phone, I assumed Mom had landed back in the hospital. But a sister?

Looking back, it's startling to me that I can sum up all we learned initially about Mom's secret in just a few sentences. Mom had mentioned, at a medical visit, that she had a disabled sister. She said she didn't know what had happened to this younger sibling—the girl had gone away to an institution when she was just two years old and Mom was four. Rozanne was confused when she heard this; Mom had already informed her, during their many times together, that she was an only child. So Rozanne called Sash to resolve the contradiction.

That was it. So little information, so many questions. Institutionalized? For what? Was Mom's sister severely disabled? Mentally ill? A quick calculation: If Mom was four, then her sister went away in 1921. What sort of institutions existed in Michigan during that time? I had no clue. Was it possible that her sister—my aunt—was still alive? What was her name? Could we find her? Would Mom want us to find her?

Sash and I had long conversations about what to do. The dominant word in our discussions, as I remember them now, was "maybe." Maybe it wasn't so odd that Mom hadn't mentioned it. Maybe Mom called herself an only child because she never knew her sister. Maybe it wasn't our place to ask her about it. Maybe we should let her tell us.

So we decided not to press Mom about it. After all, we reasoned, Mom had chosen to hide her sister's existence all these years. She hadn't told any of us before, and even now, she hadn't told us directly. We weren't even sure that Mom knew that we knew. In fact, we were pretty sure that she didn't. Rozanne had only brought it up because she was perplexed by the discrepancy. She couldn't know that her simple query would land like a bombshell.

Besides, this wasn't the best time to probe Mom's psyche. Her anxiety level had reached a point of incapacitation. Mom's psychiatrist, Toby Hazan, had concluded that depression, not anxiety, was at the root of her problems. He wanted to take her off Xanax and treat her with an antidepressant that, in rare cases, could lead to respiratory arrest. Mom's emphysema increased the risk. Hazan didn't feel comfortable putting her on the medication at home; he recommended that Mom voluntarily enter a psych ward for a two-week treatment regimen, which would allow him to monitor her closely for any adverse side effects.

Naturally, Mom was resisting. Whenever I called her, as my siblings and I were doing almost daily, concern about her health trumped any curiosity about an unknown sister. It didn't seem fair to ask her now, when she was so vulnerable. Best to wait, I thought, for her return to the strong, self-sufficient woman we had always known.

Besides, she was as much in the dark about her sister as we were. It seemed pointless to ask her a lot of questions. She might feel betrayed if we revealed that we knew, and to what end?

That question hung in the air when Sash went to visit Mom several weeks later. Her report wasn't good. "I just spent the worst night of my life," Sash told me during an early morning phone call. Mom had sat on the side of her bed most of the night, moaning and groaning, Sash said, and yet didn't seem physically sick. She wasn't eating well, and she was too jittery to keep up with the cleaning, so the apartment wasn't in its usual spit-spot condition.

"You want me to come out there, don't you?" I said.

"Yes."

Sash has no trouble being straightforward; that's been her modus operandi most of her life. I learned long ago to deal with her no-nonsense style, and even to appreciate it. If nothing else, it simplifies decision-making that otherwise might drag on, to no one's gain. By early evening, I was sitting in Mom's apartment.

That night was a rerun of the previous one. Moans, groans, no sleeping for Mom, or for us. The following afternoon, in a hastily arranged meeting in Dr. Hazan's office, Mom reluctantly agreed to sign herself into the geriatric psych ward at Botsford Hospital so she could get off the Xanax and start taking the antidepressant.

It seemed the best of the options, and we needed to do something. We took Mom there the next day around 5 P.M., as soon as a bed became available, and left her there for the night. At 7:30 A.M., the phone rang. "Steven," she said, panic evident in her voice, "you have to come take me home. I can't stay here, Steven. You don't understand. This is not the right place for me. I made a mistake coming here."

I stalled for time to think, unwilling to say anything I might regret. Inside, though, I had plenty of sympathy for her reaction. I had seen the other patients on the ward; everyone was suffering from Alzheimer's or other forms of dementia. Grim was not too strong a word for what she was facing.

"Mom, we'll be there soon," I said. "We can talk about it then."

"You don't understand," she said. "They took away my pencils. I can't even do a crossword puzzle." That was bad. Finishing the daily crossword, she often said, was her way of proving to herself that she still had all her marbles.

"We'll be there soon, Mom."

If that earlier night had been the worst of Sash's life, then that Friday was the worst day of mine. On the way to the hospital, Sash warned me that Mom would put on a full-court press, begging to go home. Sash had already concluded that Mom needed to stay, but I was ambivalent. "If you decide to take her home," Sash said, with her usual directness, "I can't be a party to it." So the pressure was on me.

Mom wasted no time making her case. She was unrelenting. I can still remember sitting tensely in a chair, in the ward's bright and airy day room, with Mom draping herself over my back, cajoling, coaxing, crying, sweet-talking. "I can't stay here," she pleaded. "Steven, please, please. I'll do anything you say, if you just take me home." Our roles had reversed: She was the child, employing every manipulative trick to get her way. I was the adult, resisting, observing, comforting her as I tried to figure out the right thing— or at least the best thing—to do.

It took all my strength not to give in. I tried not to cry, and I failed. If seismographs could measure tremors in the human voice, I'm sure that mine registered a slight earthquake on the Richter scale. As gently as I could manage, I told her that we couldn't just go home, that she wasn't really able to take care of herself, that the hospital was the best alternative. I had no idea what else to say, and no idea that her obvious terror came from some place other than watching the demented patients around her. "I can't stay here," she repeated, like a mantra. "Please don't leave me here alone."

"It's two weeks, Mom, that's all," I said. "You'll be home in two weeks. We'll talk to you every day. You won't be alone."

I took a good, long look around, and what I saw depressed me, too: patients who couldn't feed themselves, patients muttering unintelligibly, patients exhibiting every form of senility I could imagine. Mom was the healthiest person there, by far, and it made me cringe to think that I would be leaving and that she would be staying. That vision of Mom, surrounded by dementia patients, trying to get a pencil so she could do her damn crossword puzzle, stayed in my head. I retreated to a nearby room to make some phone calls to other facilities, hoping to find something better. I found one with a much younger clientele, primarily teenagers who had tried or were threatening to kill themselves. What a choice: Suicide or senility—take your pick.

As soon as I returned to the day room, Mom resumed her campaign. "Please, Steven, please. I can't stay here." It went on for what seemed like hours. Late in the afternoon, the three of us—Sash, Mom, and I—met with Hazan in one last attempt to settle her down. Hazan's notes on the meeting are part of Mom's hospital record.

If you leave the hospital, Hazan asked her, what will you do?

"I have no plan, I just want to go out," Mom said angrily. "I don't think this is the right place for me. This is not home."

Home, Hazan bluntly reminded her, had become hell—sleepless nights, moaning, groaning.

"My mind tells me I should stay here," Mom conceded. "Rationally, I know I should stay here." Then, desperately, she turned to me. "Please, I just can't take it."

Sash couldn't take it either. She left the room. I looked at Mom. The sight was not pleasant. Her glasses magnified the tears in her round, expressive eyes. Her face, so striking when she smiled, sagged under the pressure of the long day and the exhaustion of several sleepless nights. Her blouse hung loosely on her bony shoulders. She had lost twenty-five pounds from her five-foot-six-inch frame over the past two years, so she now weighed less than one hundred. My heart went out to her, but my head told me that it would be a mistake to take her home.

"Mom, I think you should stay for a few days. As Dr. Hazan said, the law allows him to keep you for three. If you want to leave after that, even though he's saying that it's against his best judgment, you can sign yourself out."

I had abandoned her cause. Her son, her own flesh and blood, had gone over to the other side. Out of options, she gave up the battle, at least for that moment. The look of pure fear remained in her eyes, though—a fear that I wouldn't truly understand until much later, when I learn the truth about Mom's sister—and that's the image that stayed with me long after Sash and I exited the hospital and drove away in May's cool night air.

Two weeks later, her new medication working well, Mom went home. My older brother Mike flew in from Seattle to help her for a few days. A month later, she told Hazan she felt "fantastic." She had survived the ordeal; so had we.

While she was sick, it never seemed like the right time to ask her about her sister. Now that she was doing better, Sash and I thought she might reveal the secret on her own. But she never did. So we let it rest. Hard as it is for me to fathom this now, we never asked her about it; since she didn't know anything about her sister's fate, I guess I didn't see much point.

Mom went back to work, back to driving herself, back to the independent life that had once seemed gone forever. We cheered, even as we kept trying to persuade her that she might be better off moving closer to one of us. Then, catastrophe: On the afternoon before her grandson's wedding in September 1998, while smoking a cigarette outside the entrance to a non-smoking Seattle hotel, she was knocked off her feet by the automatic sliding door, breaking her pelvis and sending her into months of painful rehabilitation. Exhausted, she never quite recovered.

She died in August 1999, her secret intact, as far as she knew—until six months later, when it surfaced once more, unforeseen, uninvited, nearly forgotten.

This time, though, the secret had a name.

Spring 2000

Previous page: *The family album, circa 1960: Mom, with her arm around me; at bottom left, my brother Jeff*

"W ho the heck is Annie?"

My younger brother Jeff was on the phone from Boston. After Mom's death, he had taken on the unenviable task of dealing with her final tax return, her outstanding bills, and her forwarded mail. In March 2000, a solicitation arrived from Hebrew Memorial Park, the cemetery where Mom's parents, our grandparents, are buried. Spring was around the corner, and the cemetery was offering to plant flowers on the grave sites. Cost: $45 each.

Except the solicitation listed not two graves, but three: Hyman Cohen, Tillie Cohen, Annie Cohen.

Annie. Just one word and yet it made Mom's sister so much more . . . real.

The solicitation also should have raised doubts about Mom's claim of ignorance regarding her sister. Mom obviously had been receiving these letters for years. But strange as it seems, that didn't occur to me at the time. Still the trusting son, I thought instead: What a shame this didn't come to light earlier. Mom could have learned something about what happened to her long-lost sister.

"That must be the sister," I said.

"What sister?" Jeff asked.

As proof of how lightly the secret had skipped across the family surface five years earlier, Jeff had no recollection of ever hearing about it. Our memories conflicted. I could have sworn that Sash and I had told Jeff and

Mike about it at the time, even debated with them whether the story could be true, sought their views about whether to ask Mom. Jeff, however, said that it was all news to him. So did Mike, when he heard about the cemetery's offer.

Curiosity took over now, as I imagined what we might find out. I assumed that Annie must have died when she was quite young, and that my grandparents probably had decided not to tell their older daughter, believing that it was better for her to be in the dark about her sister's fate than to endure the pain of losing her entirely. That kind of thinking was typical of the older generations in my family, which seemed to have a collective amnesia about anything sad, tragic, or pre-American. So I grew up with only the fuzziest of notions about my family's origins. Mom's parents were Polish or Russian Jews, while Dad's came from somewhere in what is now northeastern Poland, and all of them, from both sides, had arrived before 1920.

Beyond that, it was pretty much a mystery. Our family tree had no branches older than our grandparents; we didn't know whether we descended from farmers or merchants or soldiers or rabbis. We didn't know if our grandparents had left behind relatives in Eastern Europe, and if so, whether they had survived or perished in the Holocaust. We heard no stories about life in the old country, and what's more, we didn't much care— we were a modern American family, looking ahead rather than back, determined to make something of ourselves, freed of whatever injustices or circumstances had held back our European ancestors. "Mom taught us to move on, to go forward," Mike reminded me. The past wasn't just past. It was irrelevant.

But for me, Annie was different. She belonged to my mom's generation; born here, lived here, died here, buried here. If we could find out about this unknown aunt of ours, why not try? If for no other reason, it seemed important for our kids to know the reason for her institutionalization, in case there was a genetic basis for whatever disability she had.

Jeff put a halt, temporarily, to my speculation. How did we even know, he said, that this Annie was Mom's sister? With the last name of Cohen, she could be Hyman's sister, or cousin, or some other relative. The reply Jeff sent to the cemetery office, even before he called me, had reflected his un-

certainty: "Beth Luxenberg passed away this past year. . . . Could you tell me
the relation of Annie Cohen to Hyman and Tillie Cohen, if your files so
indicate?"

Elaine Klein at Hebrew Memorial Park was only too happy to help. Several
weeks later, we had photocopies of all three burial records. Annie's consisted
of a single page, couched in the language of officialdom. Deceased's name:
Annie Cohen, of 3710 Richton in Detroit. Time of death: 4:30 A.M. Place of
death: Broadstreet Medical. Occupation: Nonc. Parents' names: Hyman and
Tillie Cohen. Martial status: Never married. Citizen: Native. Date of death:
August 7, 1972. Age at death: 53.

Here was conclusive evidence: Annie *was* Mom's sister. But beyond
that, I was more confused than ever. Fifty-three years old when she died?
Had she been in institutions for more than half a century? If that were true,
why did the burial record list her place of residence as 3710 Richton? That
was where my grandmother, my Bubbe, was living when she died in 1966,
six years *before* Annie's death. (I was nearly a teenager before I understood
that "Bubbe" wasn't her name but was Yiddish for grandmother, which also
explained why every other Jewish grandmother I knew was named Bubbe.)

My grandparents had moved to the Richton apartment in the mid-
1950s. Had Annie lived there with them at some point? That didn't seem
possible. Growing up, I had visited that apartment every Saturday for nearly
a decade—I took a weekly allergy shot at Dr. Bernstein's office close by, and
stopping at Bubbe's was a required part of the trip. I still remember the
sounds and smells of the place: the scary, creaky elevator with the heavy
accordion-like inner gate; the Old World scent that permeated my grandmother's furniture, her clothes, and her hair; the vanilla wafers that had a
permanent place on her kitchen table.

Dropping by Bubbe's wasn't my first choice for a Saturday activity; I saw
it as a detour on the way to an afternoon of basketball. But while I might
have been impatient about the visits, I wasn't oblivious—if Annie had lived
there, I would have known it.

The burial record raised still more questions: It listed the "informant"
for Annie's death as "Northville State Hospital Records." I vaguely recalled
that Northville was a place for the mentally ill. I turned the page over. On
the back, under "Survivors," there was a single, startling line: "1 sister—
Mrs. Jack (Beth) Luxenberg, 22551 Fargo."

If Mom had lost all contact with her sister, how had the cemetery—or was it Northville—known my mother's whereabouts?

I stopped thinking like a son and began thinking like a journalist. "I'm trying to figure something out from what you sent my brother," I told Elaine at the cemetery office when I reached her, a bit shaky at the implications of the question I was about to ask. "Can you tell from your records who handled the arrangements for Annie's burial?"

Elaine said she would check the file. I was at work, where I was supposed to be editing an article for the weekly commentary section of *The Washington Post*, which I oversaw at the time. Instead, my mind raced with the jumble of possibilities: If Mom knew about her sister's death in 1972, maybe she wasn't telling the truth when she said she didn't know what had happened to Annie. If she knew about Annie, did she tell anyone else? Did my dad know?

My mind drifted back to what I was doing in August 1972. I was home from college that summer. Had Mom managed to bury Annie without my knowledge?

Was I that clueless?

Elaine's answer was intriguing but not definitive. A rabbi had conducted a service of some kind; typically, the family would make that arrangement. But the file was old, she reminded me, and the cemetery didn't keep a copy of the payment. So she couldn't say for sure.

I didn't feel stymied, though—the burial record contained plenty of leads. I could check birth and death records, newspaper death notices, and old Detroit city directories, just the kind of detective work I relished during my investigative reporting days.

Later, the debate would begin. My siblings and I would talk about whether it was a good idea to unearth this information, whether the secret— whatever it was—should remain buried. After all, we had decided not to ask Mom about it when she was alive. Now that she was no longer here to add her two cents to the debate, was it right, or fair, to go ahead without knowing her views?

Those were tough questions, and ones that I would eventually have to confront before deciding whether to write this book. In the spring of 2000, however, a book wasn't on my mind. I had no idea what I was going to do with the information I was collecting. It just seemed like something we should know. Mom had a sister. We had an aunt. What could we learn about her?

A month later, I placed a call to the Michigan Department of Community Health, overseer of the state's mental health system. Unsure what to say or even whom to ask, I talked to several employees before landing in the hands of a woman who served as the traffic cop for this busy intersection of government in Lansing. Trying to be brief, I told her the bare bones: The family had recently discovered that our mom had a sister who might have been a patient at Northville. We wanted to find out more.

"You and five thousand other people," she replied.

What did *that* mean? I was well aware that state asylums had once held thousands of people, and that many had remained there for decades. But the deinstitutionalization movement had ended that era years ago, back in the 1970s. Why, I asked her, would so many people be seeking information about their relatives now?

"I get dozens of calls a month from people just like you," she replied.

Now I did start to take notes.

Who's making all these calls? I asked.

"Family members," she said, "who have just discovered that they have a relative they never knew about."

And what can you tell them? I said.

"I can't tell them anything," she said. "State law doesn't let me."

But I'm next of kin, I told her.

Doesn't matter, she said. You'll need a court order, and even then, you'll need a good reason, such as a concern about something genetic.

That doesn't make sense, I said. My aunt's been dead thirty years. What's the harm?

She laughed—sympathetically, I thought, if a laugh can be described that way.

"It's known as the Patient Protection Act," she said. "But sometimes we call it the Hospital Protection Act."

She seemed in no rush to get off the phone. She talked about how she had once helped a twin look for her deinstitutionalized sister by providing a key bit of information. The twins later reunited and sent her a photo of their reunion. I could tell she wanted to help me, if she could just figure out a way within her interpretation of the law.

"Do the Northville records exist?" I said. "There's no point in seeking a court order or suing to get the records if they don't."

"They might have been destroyed," she said. "The hospitals are supposed to keep them for twenty years after discharge, but there are so many records that they don't always get around to destroying them."

Would you be willing to check for me?

She said she had a friend at Northville she could ask. Trying to make myself into more than a disembodied voice, I gave her my address, and my home and office phone numbers. When I hung up, however, I thought pessimistically: dead end.

Several weeks later, she left me a voice mail. It took me half a minute to place the name. I called back immediately.

"No luck," she said. "My friend couldn't find any records."

Just accept it, I thought: A dead end, for sure.

A few days later, a hastily written note appeared on the fax machine at work. "My computer is down so I can't type this note," it said. "I just heard from Northville, and they did find Annie's file. . . . Her discharge summary is being faxed to me tomorrow and I'll fax it to you."

I arrived at the office early the next morning, the Friday before Memorial Day weekend, hoping to get a good start on the day's tasks. The promised fax was already there. I sat down for a quick look.

Disbelief.

On a sheet with the heading "Eloise Hospital" (what was that?), next to the line "Date of Admission," I saw, "4–26–1940." Directly below was Annie's date of birth: "4–27–1919." Couldn't be. According to this record, Annie wasn't two years old when she went to the institution. She was a day shy of twenty-one.

And Mom wasn't four.

She was twenty-three.

. . .

It's rare to learn something so head-snapping, so mind-altering, so frame-shattering. Annie: twenty-one. My mother: twenty-three. They had grown up together.

If each of us has a personal time line, then this new fact had no place in my mother's. She had told us so many stories about her childhood, and told them so often, that we had a standing joke when she repeated one. "Number 32," we'd chime, much to her good-natured annoyance. Sometimes, to drive the point home even harder, we'd go to three digits. "538," one of us would say. "Or wait, was that 422?"

I knew the stories so well that I had images to go with the text. There was Hyman, the tall, gaunt, junk peddler who rarely spoke, and whose English, when he did speak, made clear that he did not feel entirely comfortable in his adopted homeland. There was Tillie, the diminutive woman with kindly eyes, a permanent hint of sadness in her smile and a severely rounded back that made her look much older than her age. And there was Mom, the only child, living with her parents until well into her twenties, forced by circumstances to remain at home, struggling to withstand the ravages of the Depression. She and Hyman and Tillie, just the three of them, in their cramped walk-up apartment on West Euclid Street in Detroit.

Now, Annie. A fourth person. In my mind's eye of life on Euclid, I had no space for Annie, no idea where she fit. Accommodating her required more than revising the old stories. We couldn't just call them 538a and 422b. We needed to re-imagine, re-consider, re-interpret, rewrite.

At first, I could not imagine. I thought of Josh and Jill, my two children, also born two years apart. They weren't even out of high school, but already they had a lifetime of shared experiences, documented by our photo albums: the mundane and the memorable, the silly and the serious. Whatever their relationship as adults might become, could either one construct a world, a childhood, or a life in which the other didn't exist?

And what about Annie? What was her personal narrative?

I turned back to the faxed pages in my hands. Three of them came from the beginning of the case, standard forms that recorded biographical data at the time of Annie's admission to Eloise Hospital. The other three came from the end—they documented Annie's move to Northville in January 1972 and, after several months of evaluation, her transfer to a nursing home in Detroit. The final page recorded the nursing home's call to Northville on August 7, 1972, to report that Annie had died.

With my newspaper deadline looming, I could do little more than scan the pages. In May 1972, a social worker and a doctor at Northville, preparing for Annie's transfer to the nursing home, had summarized her history, her condition, and her chances for improvement. More than thirty years in institutions, compressed to fewer than a dozen paragraphs. The phrases, each more eye-opening than the last, flew by like a high-speed ticker tape: "52-year-old female patient . . . born with congenital leg deformity . . . leg amputated when she was 17 . . . attended special schools . . . although retarded, was an outgoing bubbling person . . . about a year before hospitalization, she became withdrawn, seclusive, dependent . . . patient's mother felt somewhat guilty about patient's illness and related that the sins of the parents are paid for through their children."

I put the pages down, aware that I was trying to catch my breath. "Sins of the parents"? Was this just an expression of my grandmother's guilt, or did this refer to some sin in particular? Almost reluctantly, my eyes went back to the doctor's notes, and his concluding words: "Patient has had no visitors in years . . . she remains being incoherent and irrelevant much of the time . . . final diagnosis (1) Mental Deficiency (moderate); (2) Schizophrenia (Chronic) Undifferentiated Type . . ."

Too much to absorb. Too much, too fast. And more on the way: My Michigan contact informed me that she had several other pages from 1940 to send, but the photocopies had turned too dark to be readable if she faxed them. She would mail those. Fine with me. I needed time to think about what I had just read.

In 1995, when the secret first emerged, I thought I had understood why Mom had never spoken of her sister. Mom was only four years old, she didn't know anything about Annie, she wasn't involved in her hospitalization, and her parents probably didn't like to talk about it. Her motivations for keeping quiet seemed obvious, to me and to others. Whenever I mentioned the secret to someone, the conversation often took a familiar path: sympathetic nodding, talk of "shame" and "stigma," comments about how back then we just didn't know what to do, we sent people to asylums, pretended they didn't exist, what a shame for the family, but now, things have changed, we know better.

Largely true, and certainly heartfelt. Ultimately, though, I found the shame and stigma explanation to be unsatisfying. Obviously both were real factors, but they seemed more context than explanation. Sure, if you grew up in a household of lowered voices and furtive glances, if you absorbed at a young age the idea that certain subjects were taboo, then yes, it's fair to say that shame lies at the root of the silence, promotes it and nurtures it. But that particular scenario didn't fit the facts as I came to understand them.

Annie wasn't a secret when she went to Eloise. She had spent twenty-one years in the neighborhoods where Mom grew up. Even if Annie had trouble getting around on her misshapen leg, she still must have accompanied her mother to the market, gone with her sister to the playground, talked to other kids on the street. People must have seen her, met her, known her. If Mom felt ashamed of her sister, she had lived with that shame for a long time. Keeping Annie a secret after twenty-one years—making her *into* a secret—wouldn't be easy. Had there been a moment, a specific time and place, when Mom made her decision? Or was it gradual, never actually decided, but a fait accompli that took hold as Annie's commitment to Eloise became permanent? Or was it not even Mom's decision, but rather the wish of her parents? Had they enlisted Mom in the conspiracy of silence, or had she enlisted them?

And what about my father? Had he kept the secret, too? Surely Mom had told him about Annie. But Sash said, no, I bet he didn't know. That was inconceivable to me. How could my parents have lived under the same roof for thirty-eight years without something about Annie landing unexpectedly in Dad's lap, just as the cemetery's letter had landed in ours?

Thinking about the strain of keeping the secret, I found myself with a certain admiration for Mom's ability to maintain the facade all those years. It required stamina and focus, yet surely it must have taken its toll. Had she wanted to tell us, to unburden herself? Or was it not a burden at all, but rather a projection on my part, the result of seeing too many movies and reading too many psychological novels?

· · ·

The other pages arrived the following week, six in all, a single document titled "Routine History" that told, in one narrative sweep, the devastating circumstances that led my grandparents, Hyman and Tillie Cohen, to seek the commitment of their youngest daughter to Eloise Hospital, an institution for the mentally ill operated by Wayne County, the county that includes Detroit.

The narrative was like a Rosetta stone. The more I studied it, the more information it yielded about Annie, her condition, my grandparents, my mom, the family's history. Much later, when I knew more, I would understand the richness of its detail. But on that initial read, what stood out were two sentences about Annie that flung me back to Mom's apartment in the spring of 1995: "She screamed during the night, kept wanting to get up, and seemed to think she would die if she stayed in bed. . . . patient was so difficult to manage that the family couldn't get any sleep and were 'all going crazy.'"

So Mom feared that she was becoming her sister. That was why, during that awful day at Botsford, she kept repeating to me, *I can't stay here. It's the wrong place for me. You don't understand.* Mom saw Botsford as her Eloise.

That didn't make sense, of course. Mom was only supposed to spend two weeks at Botsford. But panic isn't necessarily rational, and besides, we didn't know the circumstances of Annie's commitment. Maybe she was supposed to have gone home after just a few weeks, too.

Why didn't Mom tell us about Annie? By keeping the secret, Mom had walled herself off, suffered her fears alone. If only she had said, "Look, I had a sister, and I saw her fall apart to the point that my family sent her to a mental institution, and that's why I'm so scared right now," then she wouldn't have been reduced to saying "I can't stay here. You don't understand." We could have understood. We would have understood.

As I recounted the story to friends over the next few years, though, their questions made me realize that I really didn't understand. Gradually, it became clear to me: Just as Mom needed to keep her secret, I needed to find out *why* she kept it. Unless I understood the secret, how could I come to terms with the anguish of that day at Botsford, when I defied Mom's wishes and left her no choice but to commit herself to a psychiatric ward?

· · ·

"I'm leaving the documents on the table here," I announced, "if anyone wants to read them."

It was a vividly sunny day in July 2000, six weeks after the documents had arrived from my Lansing contact, and I had brought the envelope to a family gathering in the hills of southern Vermont. The reunion was a kind of tribute to Mom: At her funeral, we had talked about making sure all the children and grandchildren continued to get together, even though Mom was no longer around to provide the glue. We hatched the idea of renting a house for a week somewhere; the West Coast branch agreed to come east for this first round, and southern Vermont won the location lottery. Sixteen of us—siblings, spouses, and children ranging in age from eleven to thirty-one—signed up for the trip.

I had briefed Sash, Mike, and Jeff by phone soon after obtaining the Lansing documents, and I discovered that not everyone had the same level of interest. Sash and I were at one extreme, wanting to find out more; she thought I should chase all leads, wherever they went. Mike was skeptical, suggesting that the records offered more chance for misinterpretation than insight; he felt we could never know enough (or learn enough) to understand the choices that Mom made. Jeff was somewhere in between, curious but not quite as captivated as Sash. (When I talked later to Evie, who wasn't part of the Vermont group, she questioned the wisdom of digging around in the past, asking aloud whether we wouldn't be better off to leave well enough alone.)

After that round of phone calls, I wondered whether I should just leave the package at home. This was planned as a vacation, not a conference on family skeletons; if I wanted to share the records, maybe I should just mail everyone a set. But that felt even more activist, an intrusion rather than an invitation. Finally, I opted for openness. The contents of the envelope belonged to the family, not to me, and they should be available to anyone who wanted to see them—Sash, Mike, Jeff, their spouses, and their children. I would put the documents on the table, and people could choose for themselves what to do. This family was strong enough and close enough to handle the surprises.

The weather was too good to spend time indoors, so the envelope mostly made the rounds in the evenings. Some people read everything; some took a quick glance and moved on. Toni, Mike's daughter and a newly minted psychologist, spent the most time poring over the documents and giving me her thoughts about Annie's condition and Mom's motivations. She left Vermont wanting to know more.

I was pretty sure that her dad didn't agree. He didn't say much, and when he did, he seemed wary, almost pained. While we're seven years apart in age, Mike has never made me feel like his "little" brother. When he went off to the University of Michigan, he would invite me to Ann Arbor for weekend visits, and if his roommates ever complained about a thirteen-year-old hanging around their apartment, Mike never let on. He always watched out for me, and it distressed me to think that I was causing him any discomfort.

What I didn't expect, as the week wore on, was that the family would expand to take in a new member. But that's what happened. As people dipped in and out of the records, as the debates flew about what we knew and what we didn't and whether we should be digging around in the past, Annie gradually became a part of the family consciousness. She was no longer just a name on a hospital record. She was no longer just "the secret."

Attached to the photocopies of the records I had brought to the reunion was one last note from my Michigan contact: "Enclosed please find the information sent me regarding Annie Cohen. . . . It may help to know that there are many stories like yours where relatives were forgotten or ignored. I do hope this gives you some peace."

The note's kindness, its attempt to suggest that I was seeking "closure" and that the information in these pages would help provide it, provoked just the opposite reaction in me: I wanted to find out more. I couldn't write about all the "forgotten" people, but I could write about one. And in writing about Annie, about her life before Eloise and about her life at Eloise, perhaps I could give some of those other callers—the "five thousand," as I now thought of them—an idea of what their relatives had experienced.

Ever since I first heard about the secret, I thought the most interesting question was: Who knew? Now, as I reflected on the records in front of me, that seemed like the wrong question, or at least the wrong direction. Who knew was interesting, but not nearly as interesting as when and why and how Mom decided to make Annie a secret.

If I could recreate the world that Mom and Annie inhabited in the spring of 1940, I might have a shot at figuring out when Annie became a secret. And if I could understand that, I might have a shot at understanding Mom's reasons for hiding her. It was so unlike the woman I knew, or thought I knew. That woman, the one who had raised me, did not invent stories. She had no patience for lying or cheating. She had relished the investigative stories I had done; we had talked more than once about the burdens of secrecy, the unhealthy effects of guilt and deception.

But before I could reinterpret Mom's life, I needed to know more. If I could find people who lived in Mom and Annie's old neighborhood, if I could talk to Mom's friends from the 1930s and 1940s, if I could exhume any information on Annie's life at Eloise or track down anyone who knew her, I might have enough threads to re-stitch the narrative.

I had only a dim awareness of the intricacy of this tapestry. Without Mom or Annie to interview, I would need to rely on others to guide me; their suggestions on how I might understand the context for Mom's motivations and Annie's life would take me down many disparate and not always connected paths (as well as some blind alleys). Pursuing the secret would ultimately lead me back to the beginning of the twentieth century, through Ellis Island to the crowded streets of Detroit's Jewish immigrant communities, through the spectacular boom of the auto industry's early years and the crushing bust of the Depression, through the wartime revival that transformed the city into the nation's Arsenal of Democracy, through the Holocaust that brought a relative to Detroit and into my mother's secret, through the postwar exodus that robbed the city's old neighborhoods of both population and prosperity.

The secret also was bound, inextricably, to the history of Eloise. I somehow grew up in Detroit without any knowledge of this vast institution's significance. In 1940, at the time of Annie's admission, Eloise was a sprawling complex with more than nine thousand residents (not all of them mentally ill) and seventy-five buildings, as well as its own police force and fire department, a farm, a dairy, a cannery, and even a piggery. This was the grand age of massive public mental hospitals, the era when treating the mentally ill became a cause rather than an obligation, the era before the development of medications that fundamentally altered the mental health system. Eloise prided itself on being in the forefront of the profession's newest practices, but behind the ivied walls of the leafy campus, many thousands of patients languished for years, decades, even lifetimes, warehoused more than cared for.

Count Annie among them. She had lived at Eloise for more than thirty-one years—longer, I imagined, than anyone assigned to her care—and her time there straddled a revolution. When she arrived in 1940, the nation's public mental institutions were reaching the zenith of their influence in American life, with nearly half a million people on their wards; when she died in 1972, those institutions were dying, too, swept aside by medical advances, legal challenges, and another generation's moral reexamination of how best to care for the mentally ill.

What had Annie's life at Eloise been like? Had the staff been able to bring back the "outgoing bubbling person" of the year before Annie's commitment in 1940? Or did she remain "withdrawn and seclusive"? Did she really not have visitors for "years," as the Northville doctor noted in 1972, and what did he mean when he wrote that she remained largely—it was impossible not to wince at his word choice—"irrelevant"?

What about my grandparents? What had it been like for Hyman and Tillie to care for a child with a permanent disability, before Medicaid, before Social Security? What kind of toll did it take on them, to see their daughter's descent into paranoid behavior and then to give her up to strangers at a hospital eleven miles away? They owned no car to make such a trek; as far as I knew, neither ever learned to drive. A bus line must have served Eloise, but it would have been a time-consuming and complicated business to get there. My grandmother, in particular, always struck me as somewhat frail. How had she managed to see her daughter?

But, of course, I wasn't thinking of my grandparents as they really were, but as I remembered them. For me, they are like the image you see after pressing the pause button on the DVD remote: frozen, fixed in time. In 1940, my grandfather would have been fifty-three, younger than I am now. But I see him only as a lonely, broken man, unable or unwilling to engage in the world around him. I see my grandmother as a housebound Bubbe, her hair whiter than the snow that covered the ground during Detroit's icy winters. Could I capture a real sense of what they had gone through?

· · ·

A reinterpretation on this scale would not be easy, either logistically or emotionally. Daunting would be a better word for it: I would need to rewind the family tape, replay the stories that Mom had told, recover information that might well be lost to death or memory. Such an undertaking would require time and patience; I couldn't dabble in it. I would need to wait until I could concentrate the bulk of my energy on it.

I also would need family support. My search might take me places that I didn't necessarily want to go. Delving into families, and family secrets, has its perils. If the search—or writing this book—was going to cause a split, it wasn't worth it to me.

It helped that I wasn't seeking to settle any scores or revisit old arguments. Mom and I had been close for much of our lives. It was easy for us to be together, which is one reason why I found it so hard to deal with the neediness that she exhibited during her waning years. I can still see her: Her eyes would fill with tears, and she would look at me forlornly, and say, shyly, "Do you love me? Tell me you love me." Was her constant need for affection, her repeated requests to hear how much we cared for her, related somehow to carrying the secret?

Pursuing the mystery, I thought, might bring our relationship back into focus and help me to make sense of Mom and the choices she made. If I could do that, if I could understand why she followed a path so much in conflict with the advice she often gave me about life and how to live it, then perhaps I could once again make sense of the history that she and I had shared.

TWO

Looking for Mom

1943

Previous page: *Standing tall: Mom, at twenty-six, on a Lake Michigan beach*

It's the fall of 1964. I'm a skinny left-handed twelve-year-old with a decent curveball, and I'm nervously waiting to hear my name called at the annual banquet of the St. Eugene Little League, where I'm getting a pitching award. The church hall overflows with noise and sweat and the smell of mustard on hot dogs; sounds of backslaps echo across the crowded floor as fathers greet fathers one last time before gloves and mitts and uniforms go into storage until spring.

As I come to the front of the huge room to accept my trophy and shake the league director's hand, I turn to smile at my mom, the only mom I see—certainly the only Jewish mom—in the vast sea of several hundred male Catholic faces.

My mother does not exist before 1942.

How does a woman live for twenty-five years, and leave only the barest hints of her existence? That's what I'm thinking as I look through the papers that cover every square inch of my desk and much of the floor around it, the contents of a box that I had brought home after her death in 1999 and left untouched for more than six years. That box, and several more in my brother Jeff's attic, seem like the logical place to begin my hunt for Mom and the origins of her secret.

Why, I wonder as I rummage through the memorabilia that she left behind, aren't there any photos of her as a young girl? What did she do with the books she loved, the childhood letters she received, the souvenirs and trinkets that teenage girls treasure? Where are her report cards from school—or any evidence, for that matter, that she ever set foot in a class-room before receiving her high school diploma in January 1934?

It wasn't as if Mom went through life like a merciless tornado, unsentimentally hurling aside her possessions. After all, she had saved more than six hundred letters that she and Dad had written to each other during his Army days in World War II. She had preserved even the tersest of his telegrams ("I'm OK don't worry") confirming his arrival at bases in Texas, California, Illinois, and Washington State. She had kept every one of the schmaltzy "anniversary" cards they exchanged monthly during their early years of marriage, and yet not a single birthday card from her youth. She had lovingly put together several dozen photo albums chronicling the lives and times of her grandchildren, including a crayon scrawl from an industrious four-year-old's hand that might generously be called a drawing—and which she displayed as the early work of a future Van Gogh.

But the life and times of the young Beth Cohen? Nowhere to be found.

When we sorted through Mom's belongings after her funeral, we came across dozens of photos from late 1942 and the spring of 1943—glamorous poses of the newlyweds strutting for the camera, sprawling on beach blankets, leaning across the hoods of automobiles, walking arm-in-arm with Dad down neighborhood streets. She called him Duke, and sometimes called herself Mrs. Duke, and that's what she wrote in her neat, legible handwriting along the bottom of several black-and-white snapshots. But on most of the photos, much to my frustration, she recorded nothing except the year—including those that feature her friends. No names to give me a head start on my search.

I find one image of Mom particularly arresting. She's dressed almost entirely in white—white shorts that show off her long and graceful legs, a sleeveless white sweater pulled over a dark short-sleeved jersey that highlights the darker color of her long, wavy hair, which is pulled behind her so that what you see, at first glance, is the whiteness of her teeth and the radiance of her smile. She's standing on a beach chair, her right leg ramrod straight to stay balanced, her left leg slightly bent, her white outfit even whiter than the foam of the waves gently splashing against the shoreline behind her. She is slim, even elegant, and looks exactly her age—twenty-six years old, youthful but not young, a woman who seems to know herself and her place in the world.

I cannot see her as others might. I cannot separate this woman in white from the woman waving at me in the stuffy banquet hall at the St. Eugene Little League annual awards ceremony. Is she beautiful? I doubt that others would say so. Her chin is too long, her forehead too high, her cheeks too prominent, her mouth too wide. But Mom's sum always added up to more than her parts. She created an impression that lingered long after she had left a room.

So, too, with the photo of her in white. This image—more than the jaunty ones of her sporting a flower in her hair, or the formal ones where she's dressed to the nines in a new suit, or the silly ones where she's mugging for the camera—this is the image that makes me wonder why there are no shots of the teenaged Beth Cohen. She and the camera understand each other: She's not afraid to reveal herself to its lens, she's not the shy girl in the back whose face always manages to end up blocked by someone's shoulder, she's not the unfortunate girl in front whose eyes always close as the flash goes off. It's hard to believe that she acquired her photogenic qualities in her mid-twenties, that the camera didn't find her just as appealing as a teenager.

That's one reason why, as I sit at my desk on a blustery Baltimore day in March 2006, staring at the collection of images arrayed before me, I'm acutely aware of what's missing rather than what's there. Granted, my grandparents couldn't afford to buy a loaf of bread some days, let alone a camera and film. George Eastman's little Brownie brought affordable cameras to a mass market in the late nineteenth and early twentieth centuries, but it took a long time for that mass market to pull out those Brownies and snap everyday events. In the 1920s and 1930s, much more than today, photographs largely served as memories; for those clinging to the bottom of society's ladder, why remember the hardships of daily life?

Mom turned sixteen just six days after Franklin D. Roosevelt took over as president and announced his New Deal, declaring famously that "the only thing we have to fear is fear itself." My grandparents' fears made a longer list, and their worst days lay ahead of them. For most poor families like theirs, the idea of creating a photographic record of their lives, or their children's lives, was an unattainable luxury, beyond their reach as well as their imagination. So I suppose it's not surprising that I find no photos of

Mom sprawled on the floor, reading a book or playing with a friend. But what about the special occasions? Her birthdays? Her high school graduation? Her yearbook photo? Why weren't there any photos of the family together? Surely my grandparents had friends who might have taken a photo of the four of them at some event and given them a copy.

No, nothing like that. Of the dozens of old photographs that we found in Mom's apartment, only two predate 1942—a studio shot of Mom at four months old, dressed in a frilly, fluffy dress and lying on a shag rug that resembled an oversized bird's nest, and an undated one of my grandmother that appears, from her age, to come from sometime in the 1930s. That they exist at all, though, that they survived to the end of the century, is evidence that someone had thought them important enough to preserve.

But no shots of Annie. Discarded to keep the secret, or had they never existed in the first place?

The boxes contain only two documents suggesting that Beth Cohen had a life before 1942: her birth certificate and her high school diploma. To the unsuspecting (which once included my siblings and me), even those documents don't appear to belong to her. The birth certificate heralds the arrival of one Bertha Cohen. Not Beth, not even as a middle name. Just Bertha. The high school diploma makes the link between the newborn Bertha and the Beth we all knew. It proclaims that one "Bertha Beth Cohen" had completed the degree requirements of Detroit Northern High School in January 1934.

Even now, I smile at the memory of unearthing these documents in the days after her funeral. We had just come back from burying Beth, only to find out that she was . . . Bertha. Well, not really, I suppose. She had called herself Beth, so who cared if she neglected to mention that she had banished her birth name in favor of one she chose for herself? She wasn't the first child of immigrants to do that, certainly.

When I first saw the name Bertha on her birth certificate, I didn't think very hard about Mom's deception. Frankly, her motivation seemed transparently clear: What schoolgirl would want to be Bertha if she could be Beth? But now, going through the bits and pieces of the things she left behind, I wonder: If she got rid of her name, did she also get rid of her past?

Is that why there are no photos before 1942, no mementos, and no evidence of the life she shared with her sister?

My high school friends call me Steve, but my family calls me Steven, and sometimes I feel like two different people. It's Steve or Lux at school—except on the basketball court, where Coach has stuck me with the unfortunate Lefty—but as soon as I walk in the door, I'm Steven. I don't understand Mom's obsession with names, but if she had her way, she would eliminate every nickname on the planet, as if nicknames were some sort of identity theft to be stamped out. The only family nickname she tolerates is Sashie, perhaps because she's not Sash's birth mother and didn't name her Marsha in the first place. Michael is never Mike, and Jeffery is never Jeff, and God forbid, I'm never, ever, Steve.

"Why do they call you that?" she asks me, whenever she hears someone say Steve. "Do you introduce yourself that way?" She always says "that way," as she fears that uttering Steve aloud would cast a spell that would never be broken.

My ears burn, and I don't know what to say. Why does it matter so much, this question of identity? I like Steven; I like the sound of it and the extra syllable and that it seems a little less run-of-the-mill. But how am I going to stop people from calling me something else? (If I had that power, Lefty would be the first name to disappear, not Steve.) Beyond that, I'm not sure why Steve annoys Mom so much. But it does.

"If I wanted to name you that," she declares, bringing an end to the conversation, "I would have named you that. You're Steven, and as long as I live, that's what I will call you."

I reread the letter in the envelope marked "Do not open until after my death." Written on a yellow legal pad in 1984, and updated twice after the birth of grandchildren, it's a three-page document that says all Mom's money and worldly possessions should be divided equally among her children and grandchildren. There wasn't much of either, so it wasn't hard or complicated to comply with her wishes. She didn't list her possessions or give us any special instructions, with one exception: her half dozen paint-by-number canvases. "One request—the paintings on the wall are a part of me. I would like each of you to hang one somewhere," she wrote.

Guilt and memory collide. As directed, I had taken one of the framed canvases—a drab painting of an English lord's stagecoach making its way to a countryside castle, all dull grays and greens and browns—but I couldn't bring myself to actually hang the darn thing. For a couple of years, it rested against the bedroom wall, until I finally stored it in a closet, out of my sight.

I return to the letter. A theme runs through it. "Please live, love and enjoy for me," she urged in 1984. "Please remain close and watch out for each other." Then again in the 1989 update: "So I say again, remain close and take care of each other." And in 1996: "Fulfill my final wish and stay close and be good to each other."

"Watch out for each other"—what an interesting choice of words. Was she asking us to do what she didn't do, perhaps couldn't do, for Annie? What about me? Am I watching out for the family by investigating the past? Would my curiosity disturb the closeness that Mom so ardently desired for us?

As soon as I come into the house, the aroma of oil paint hits my nostrils, and I know Mom's been back at the canvas again. It's the early 1960s, which makes me ten or eleven years old, and Mom's paint-by-number projects have joined bridge and crossword puzzles as her primary leisure-time activities. After months of watching her at work, I ask if I can try it, if she will let me do a piece of the windmill (Was it that one? Or was it the portrait of the girl with the long golden hair?), and I'm thrilled when she says yes, thrilled that she trusts me enough to give me a chance.

She shows me how to hold the brush, how to dip the tip into the paint so that I don't get too much on the very fine bristles. I'm nervous, worried that I'm going to make a mistake, that I'll go outside the lines or put color no. 3 where color no. 8 is supposed to go, and that I will ruin the whole thing. I'm not thinking about why she might have taken up this particular hobby, whether it's some sort of therapy or escape. She's never been an artist, and I'm old enough to understand that paint-by-number isn't real art (although not quite old enough to understand that a real artist wouldn't touch a paint-by-number canvas except perhaps to whitewash it). But at this moment, none of that matters. All that matters is the brush and the paint and Mom sitting nearby, and the magic of making something appear out of nothing, of bringing to life what was hidden in the numbers.

. . .

Everyone has a way of coping with grief. Mine is to write.

On the night after Mom's death, I had found it cathartic, even pleasantly distracting, to plunk myself down at a computer in the hotel business center and pretend that deadline was looming as I banged out a draft of Mom's obituary for the two local newspapers. In truth, the *Free Press* obit writer had warned me that it was too late for the next day's paper, and besides, he said, an extra twenty-four hours would give the family a chance to find a suitable photo, get it scanned, and e-mail it to the paper.

Now I pick up the published *Free Press* version from the papers on my desk, and one phrase catches my eye: "the only child of . . ." How did *that* get in there? The *Free Press* reporter had wanted to put his own stamp on what I wrote, so he had selected the parts he liked in revising the rest to his taste. Had something gone awry in the handoff? I go hunting for my original, and find it: "A native Detroiter and the only child of immigrant parents . . ." No, I couldn't fault the *Free Press* for that bit of fiction.

I close my eyes, trying to summon up the memory of my night at the hotel computer. I have a vague recollection of thinking that we couldn't very well use Mom's obit to announce to her shrinking circle of friends that she had died and, oh, by the way, she had a sister. Mom had told everyone she was an only child, and her obit wasn't the place to argue the point. It was her obit. Shouldn't she have the last word?

But still, why did I use the unambiguous words, "only child"? Why not just avoid any mention of it? After years of deadline editing, I knew all the tricks for writing around a troublesome fact. I could have referred to her simply as "the daughter of immigrant parents," and left open the question of whether she had any siblings. Obits run every day that don't mention the deceased's brothers or sisters.

So why didn't I do that? I really don't know. Calling her an only child in print, if I knew it wasn't true, would have rubbed directly against my journalistic grain. So I wonder whether my use of the phrase is an indication that, as of August 1999, I hadn't truly embraced the notion that Mom had a sister. Since the 1995 phone call from Rozanne Sedler, we hadn't heard another word about the possibility. We didn't know whether Mom's sister had died young or was still alive, we didn't know the name of the institution that took her, we didn't know her name. Without a name, she was an abstraction, a wisp, a phantom; she resided in my consciousness somewhere between fact and fantasy, at that place where we put people and events that we do not know, have never had a chance to know, and cannot conceive that we will ever know.

On the day the obits ran, September 3, 1999, I ascended the dais at the modest chapel on the grounds of Machpeleh Cemetery, and looked out at the sixty or so people who had gathered to pay their final respects to Beth Luxenberg. They knew her as a mother, grandmother, stepmother, mother-in-law, friend—but not as a sister. Sister, of course, was never a part of our vocabulary when we talked about Mom.

"As we think about the last year," I told the crowd, "and how Mom's chronic lung disease closed in on her, making each breath so difficult, it is easy to forget that this was only one of her eighty-two years. This was not Mom's life. This was only her death."

Mike and Jeff chose to talk about the woman they knew personally, the one who lived by certain principles that she had instilled in us: the importance of family, education, hard work, honesty, and generosity. They described how she taught her children to act and think independently; she tried to make sure, as she put it, that "we could stand on our own two feet," that we could take care of ourselves. She saw our successes—in school, in work, in raising our own families—as proof that she had accomplished her mission.

I wanted to talk about the woman we didn't know, the one who had been alive for nearly three decades before any of us were born, the one we could only glimpse in old photographs or imagine from family stories. I thought if I could create a portrait of the young and vibrant Beth, before marriage, before motherhood, I could wipe away the final image we had of her. "I only knew Grandma as someone who was sick," my daughter Jill had said. I wanted to tell Jill and everyone in the chapel—particularly Mom's grandchildren—about the lively, lovely woman whose life lay ahead of her rather than behind her.

That life, as we all knew, hadn't been easy. "Growing up," I said, "she was acutely aware of her family's poverty, and it forever colored her view of herself and her aspirations. She once told me that she was ashamed of being poor; she felt that her schoolmates looked down on her and the way she dressed. It was hard for her to even talk about it. But she vowed that she would do everything she could to prevent her children from the pain of being poor."

I reminded the gathering that Mom loved to tell stories, and that she would have been delighted to hear those stories told once more as we closed the book on her life. "Mom desperately wanted to go to college," I said. "An uncle with some money offered to pay her way. She could hardly believe it. To her, it was a dream come true. But it never came to pass, and she said she never knew exactly why. It was more than a disappointment; it was a loss of innocence. When Mom told that story, and she told it many times, you could see in her eyes that the hurt and betrayal was still there."

I didn't name the uncle, out of ignorance rather than courtesy. I didn't know his name—Mom never mentioned it, and since I had never met any of her relatives other than my grandparents, I guess it had never seemed all that important to ask. Now I wished I had.

"There was a young man who wanted to marry her," I told the mourners. "His name was Joe, and Mom didn't mind the part of the story when she told us how ardently Joe had courted her. But there was a hitch. She told Joe, 'You know I can't marry you. You're not Jewish and my mother wouldn't hear of it.'"

I left out the part about how Joe (whose last name was also unknown to me) was so smitten that he offered not only to convert to Judaism, but to get himself circumcised.

"Then Mom met Dad, her beloved Duke. As she tells the story, and there's some dispute about the exact circumstances, she was at a wedding and saw him on the stairs, and said to a friend, 'That's the man I'm going to marry.' She got her wish, unlike Joe."

The rest of my eulogy depended on my first-hand memories. The crowd chuckled at my description of Mom's poker-table habits, how she would win all your money and then lend it back to you so that you could keep playing, saying teasingly, "You can pay me back. I'd rather have you owe it to me than cheat me out of it."

She always looked out for us that way, I said. I recounted a conversation from October 1998, when she was recuperating from fracturing her pelvis

and in so much pain that she couldn't believe she would ever get better. Talk
of death made its way into her conversation. "She told me, 'I can't die this
month, because it's too close to Mark's birthday, and I can't die in November because Daddy died on November 1, and it wouldn't be fair to you children to have us both die around the same time.'

" 'Well, Mom,' I said, 'you're in trouble. The family has birthdays and
anniversaries in almost every month. So you're stuck. You're just going to
have to wait for a while to die.'"

Emphysema, and more than six decades of cigarette smoking, had more
to do with the timing of her death than my flip comment, I told the crowd.
Congestive heart failure doesn't leave its victims much room for advance
planning. Nevertheless, by dying on the last day of August 1999, Mom made
sure that she would spoil no one's happy day.

On the family calendar of significant events, she has August all to
herself.

The vivid picture of Mom's youth that I had crafted for my eulogy doesn't
come close to the reality. Rereading it reminds me of how much I didn't
know then, and how much I want to know now.

Yes, I now know that Annie is real, yet she still seems like little more
than an apparition who has floated into our lives, without form or shape or
substance. But then, when it comes right down to it, couldn't the same be
said for the young Beth—or should I say Bertha—Cohen?

*I'm chatting with Mom at her kitchen table sometime in the late 1980s, if memory
serves, when the secret comes out.*

"I had an abortion," she says. Or something equally matter of fact.

*I wonder why she has decided to tell me this now, at this particular moment.
Maybe it's because abortion has taken center stage again in politics, and her personal experience has been on her mind. Or maybe it's because I'm a father now,
approaching my late thirties, and she thinks I can appreciate how agonizing this
must have been for her. Or maybe it was just impulsive, except impulse is not her
style. (Unlike guilt, which is very much her style.)*

Whatever her reasons, whether she's unburdening herself or merely revealing a powerful piece of her past, I feel good that she trusts me enough to confide something so private. A hundred questions pop into my head, but I stick with the conventional: When, where, what, how. Much later, I learn that I'm not the only one in the family to hear the story, so at some point, she must have decided she felt it was okay to talk about it.

She doesn't dwell on the details. It happened between Mike and me, which probably means the late 1940s, when Mom and Dad were still living in the tiny apartment on Euclid. Dad was struggling in the furniture business, had changed jobs a few times, and they didn't have enough money to pay the bills. Mom was overwhelmed, taking care of Evie, by then a teenager, and Marsha (not yet Sash), going on nine or ten, and little Michael, not yet in school. Dad's younger brother Billy was there, too, sleeping on a Murphy bed in the living room. Mom wanted another child, hoped for another child, but this was not the right time or the right place for an unexpected pregnancy. She despaired about what to do, and then she made her heartrending decision. Dad went with her.

Abortion was illegal in Michigan at the time, but like most other states, there were ways to have one. I ask where she went, how she found it. She says she doesn't want to talk much about that, except to say that it was traumatic and terrifying, the kind of place that deserved the back-alley label. Sometimes she thinks about how things might have been different, about the child who never was, but she says she doesn't regret her decision; she couldn't have coped, they couldn't have coped. She did what she needed to do. When she got pregnant again, she and Dad were ready, ready for the child who turned out to be me.

It doesn't occur to me to ask: Any other secrets you'd like to share? I have no reason to ask that. I don't think of Mom as a keeper of secrets.

As we were leaving the cemetery, after the ritual grasping of the shovel and spooning of a moundful of dirt onto Mom's coffin, I spotted two people among the departing mourners who were strangers to me—a man with graying hair, about my age, and an older woman, slightly stooped, with a smile and a stride that suggested she might have been a force to reckon with in her younger days. Shading my eyes in the bright September sun so I could see them better, I whispered to Sash, "Do you know them?"

"I'm pretty sure that's Mom's cousin Anna, and her son," Sash said.

"Mom's cousin?" I remember saying. "I didn't know she had any cousins. How come I've never met her?"

"I don't think they cared for each other," Sash said. "I'm not sure why, but I think they had some sort of falling out."

Sash wasn't sure of Anna's last name—Oli- something. I considered briefly whether to go over to them and thank them for coming, but they were already on their way, and I wasn't in the mood to chase after anyone for a bit of small talk.

In March 2006, as I begin my search for people who might have known Mom in her younger days, I go through the boxes in Jeff's attic and find the funeral guest book. "Anna and David Oliwek" reads the final entry. Anticipating that we might not be able to place the name, the writer had penned in "Cousin" directly above Anna's name. Well, that's a bit of good luck, much easier than combing through all the Oli- entries in the Detroit phone books.

I call Sash. Her interest in the secret has only grown since I started my detective work; I get the feeling that she wishes she could join me on the hunt. I tell her, "At the time of Mom's funeral, we still knew almost nothing about Annie, not even her name. We still thought she had been institutionalized when Mom was young. Now we know that isn't true. Do you think Anna knows about Annie?"

It's possible, Sash says, and then goes one step further. "I don't know why I'm saying this, but I'm wondering whether the tension between them had something to do with the secret."

The Rosetta Stone

It's 1964. I'm eleven. I wake up in the hospital, delirious from the anesthetic and believing that something has gone terribly wrong with the operation to remove a benign cyst near the corner of my left eye. I see nothing but darkness. I'm blind, I must be blind, this can't be happening. I cry out, and Mom goes off to grab the first doctor she can find. It turns out that blood from the surgery has congealed in my eye cavities, sending a signal to my brain not to bother opening my eyelids. "Very common," the surgeon tells Mom. "I should have warned you."

Mom can't contain her fury. "You should have warned HIM," I hear her say. "How could you do that to an eleven-year-old boy?"

I tell myself that if I just look hard enough at Mom's possessions, I will find some reference to Annie, some oblique clue that will make sense now that I know the secret. I'm like an archeologist on a dig, scrabbling through the rubble of a lost civilization, sifting for broken pieces that would fit together nicely if only I could uncover enough of them. But no shards reveal themselves, at least none that I recognize.

So I turn instead to the Rosetta stone, the "Routine History" completed by an Eloise social worker named Mona Evans in early May 1940, at the time of Annie's admission to the county mental institution. Here, in black and white on fading paper, is most of what I know about Annie. I study every sentence to exhume any nuance that might have eluded me the first few times through.

In my earlier reads, I had focused, inevitably, on the dramatic points of Annie's life—the leg that left her "so handicapped physically that she couldn't get around enough to go to school" until she was seven years old; the amputation at age seventeen; the prosthetic replacement that "never fitted right"; her deteriorating mental state at twenty, including her refusal to leave the apartment for two weeks at a time; the family "all going crazy" in the days before Annie's hospitalization on the eve of her twenty-first birthday.

Now, I find it disconcerting to know so much about her physical and psychic ailments, and yet so little about the most ordinary of things. What did she look like? Was she small, like my grandmother? Or taller, like Mom? What color were her eyes? How about her hair? Was it curly, like Mom's and mine, or straight, like my grandfather's? And what about her smile—did she smile?

The Routine History offers nothing so mundane, leaving me with just enough pieces to make out an image, but it's indistinct, a body dominated by a deformed leg, but no torso, no mouth, no nose, no eyes, no face at all.

Which is not to say that Evans's report is devoid of description. In her professional, dispassionate style, the social worker offered this account of Annie's entrance into the world: "The patient was born on 4–27–1919, the mother being confined at home. There was nothing abnormal about her birth except that the child's leg was bent and could not be straightened out. Patient 'didn't grow much,' and when she was seven weeks old weighed only four pounds and thirteen ounces."

Nothing abnormal about her birth except her bent leg? Perhaps there was nothing abnormal about the delivery itself, but if seven-week-old Annie Cohen tipped the scales at four pounds, thirteen ounces, she couldn't have weighed much more than four pounds at birth. I consult a medical reference book: It defines "low" birth weight as less than five pounds, eight ounces, and "very low" birth weight as three pounds, five ounces. Annie arrived with the odds against her: Low birth weight babies are at much greater risk for mental retardation and other birth defects.

It's hard to judge an infant's mental abilities, but everyone saw right away that Annie's right leg wasn't normal. When she was two, "Her mother took her to Children's Hospital Clinic, where an attempt was made to straighten the leg by stretching it out and putting it into a cast," Evans wrote. "From that time on she was in casts and braces all the time, but the leg didn't improve much, and failed to develop. Until she was 17 years of age, patient walked with crutches, and at that time she was able to walk a little with a brace." Then, for reasons not explained in the report, the amputation. "It was decided by Dr. Kidner that the leg should be amputated, and he performed the operation at Harper Hospital. A minor operation followed for the purpose of straightening the hip, and arrangements were made for the Welfare Department to provide an artificial leg."

I shudder to think of how my grandparents must have felt when confronted with the choice: Leave the leg alone, and doom your child to crutches for the rest of her life, or remove it, making her disability permanent and requiring her to accept a prosthetic limb that might improve her ability to get around but which would forever symbolize something lost as well as something gained. Not only did her new leg require daily cleaning and maintenance to work and fit properly, but it was just plain heavy, up to eighteen pounds of extra weight pulling on her shoulder and hips, every step a constant reminder that she wasn't normal, wasn't like those around her.

There was one benefit to Annie's leg problem, but the benefit is mine, not hers. A girl on crutches or in a brace until age seventeen meant a girl who stood out—at home, at school, on the bus, on the street, at the store, in the library. A girl on crutches or a wooden leg meant a girl harder to forget.

Surely someone would remember, if only I can figure out who that someone might be.

Evans's job wasn't to act as a family biographer, but she produced a more comprehensive and candid report than her counterparts today would write. I've shown her report to a variety of people who work in the current mental health system—social workers, psychologists, psychiatrists, therapists—and they all commented that Evans's style, once standard in the field, has gone out of favor in this age of lawsuits and political sensitivities. It is unlikely, for example, that a social worker in the first decade of the twenty-first century would begin her report this way: "On 5–3–1940, patient's mother, Mrs. Tillie Cohen, kept the initial history appointment . . . She is a poorly dressed, middle-aged Jewish woman. She talks in a complaining, whining voice, expressing a great amount of antagonism toward the Welfare, various hospitals, etc., with whom her daughter has had contact. She feels that if her family had money, the patient could have been made well long ago and the present mental disturbance would not have been manifested."

Others might bristle at Evans's language or dismiss her words as the defensive view of a jaded bureaucrat, but I inhale them as I think Evans meant them to be understood—as a matter-of-fact, even sympathetic, observation of her distraught client, a panicked mother defeated by her circumstances. The grandson may recoil at the social worker's unflattering portrait of his grandmother, but the reporter in me appreciates Evans's attempt to chronicle how Tillie saw the world, rather than how the world saw Tillie.

And what about Evans? What did she see? She saw a woman whose appearance and demeanor had changed drastically since her initial contact with the staff of Detroit's Harper Hospital in 1936, when she brought Annie in for an examination. "She was always well dressed, neat and 'proud,'" Evans wrote after interviewing Jean Powell, a social worker who met Tillie in 1936. "She appears to have aged considerably and has lost all interest in herself."

If Tillie could not escape the avalanche caused by Annie's downhill slide, what about my mother? Mom, of course, wasn't responsible for Annie, but as Tillie's oldest child, as the daughter who did well in school and could speak English without a heavy Eastern European accent, it's likely that my immigrant grandparents relied on her for help and support, if not advice. Did my mother resent her sister? That would be a normal reaction to a sibling who's getting all the attention.

The Evans report hardly mentions Mom, except to contrast her with Annie. "Bertha"—that's what the report calls her, so this is pre-Beth, or at least before Beth has asserted herself and banished Bertha from her life— "is said to be an unusually intelligent girl, popular with both boys and girls, and is normal in every way. She has had much difficulty finding work, however, and becomes very discouraged at times over this." (She and Annie had that in common, at least.) "She is said to be kindly toward and friendly toward the patient."

Said by whom? By Tillie, probably. Perhaps this statement was true—I want it to be true—but somehow I doubt Mom's feelings could be summed up so simply. In 1972, during the four months that Annie spent at Northville before going to the nursing home where she died, another social worker reviewing Annie's thirty-year history at Eloise wrote something that suggested Mom's attitude had changed over the years. "She admitted to Wayne County General that she hated the patient," reported social worker Jim Mulherin, apparently after reading some note in Annie's records from many years before. He didn't say when Mom "admitted" this, or the context in which she might have said it.

Hated the patient. The starkness of that statement makes me blink. I never knew Mom to hate anyone. She certainly could dislike people, particularly those who disappointed her, such as the doctor who had neglected to warn me that I would be temporarily blind after my cyst operation, or the uncle who had failed to follow through on his promise to send her to college. But hate? Not in her repertoire. Her face to the world was kindness—she preached it, practiced it, was fully aware of its power. She understood that people spoke well of those who were kind, and that kindness earned you points. So even if she did hate Annie, wouldn't she try to repress it? I want to know more about this "admission"—When did Mom make it? What were the circumstances?—but the 1972 report, much skimpier than Evans's, offers no details or documentation of this pronouncement.

What to believe?

I would have to find out on my own. Rosetta stones do not yield their secrets so easily.

Without really trying, I have become a collector of other families' secrets. Whenever I tell anyone about my detective work, the first question is invariably something like this: "Can you tell me the secret?" Sure, I say. The next question often is: "Want to hear my family's secret?"

No shortage of heirlooms line this attic: hidden affairs, of course, but also hidden marriages, hidden divorces, hidden crimes, even hidden families. I have heard so many secrets that I started a list. One of the most memorable: a man who learned, as a teenager, that his father was leading a double life—two wives, two houses, two sets of children, all two miles apart in a Detroit suburb. Perhaps it's a testament to the insular nature of suburban life that this master of deception managed to straddle these skew lines for more than a decade before his double life came crashing down around him.

Even when secrets do emerge, the reasons for the secrecy often stay buried. Families never learn the motivations, the circumstances, and the pressures that compel people to choose deceit rather than honesty. In this shroud of silence, the secret takes on the characteristics of an artifact—interesting to examine and exotic to behold, but mysterious and often impossible to fathom.

Families need not live their lives as open books, for anyone to read. Just as a cure can be worse than the disease, revelation can be more devastating than reticence. That's the fear that seems to drive many of us to embrace silence or deception. But too often, we're just telling one more lie, this one to ourselves.

Now that Annie was no longer a secret, now that Mom wasn't here, the revelation had lost its power to hurt anyone. Or had it? Would understanding Mom's reasons make me wish that I, too, had left well enough alone?

The question wasn't so much where to start, but which direction to go in first. Leads abound in Mona Evans's Routine History—file numbers, names of doctors and schools, my grandparents' addresses (including one on Medbury Avenue that went back to the 1920s), medical problems, and work history (such as it was—the report says that junk-peddling was my grandfather's primary occupation when he worked, which wasn't all that often after 1929 and the Depression's seemingly never-ending stay in Detroit).

Yet the report contains contradictions as well as clues. On the one hand, Annie can't walk well enough to go to school, "gets around with difficulty" as a teenager, and ends up with an ill-fitting artificial limb that means she "does not walk well" even though it is changed or repaired several times. On the other hand, "As she grew older, she went everywhere by herself, not allowing herself to be deterred by the difficulties of getting on and off buses, etc."

What to believe?

Was Annie a girl "who does all the housework she is able to, relieving her mother of a good deal of responsibility"? Or was she the girl who "took advantage of her physical affliction to demand special consideration," and "insisted that her family wait on her hand and foot"? Is it possible to be a girl of "poor intelligence" who might be better off in an institution for the feeble-minded, and yet possess enough insight and self-awareness for Evans to conclude that "in the last year or two, she has come to realize that many of the normal activities of other people will be necessarily forbidden to her, and she has become depressed over the impossibility of ever being independent, becoming more desperately determined to locate work and more and more dejected when she failed"?

Perhaps these weren't contradictions at all, but merely the normal twists and turns of one girl's troubled life. Evans wrote her report from a wealth of information but limited first-hand knowledge; she had to rely primarily on Tillie ("our informant," as my grandmother is called frequently in the report), and on hospital charts, social service records, and social worker Jean Powell, the family's primary contact at Harper Hospital for the four years before the crisis that sent Annie to Eloise.

The dominant voice is my grandmother's, that "complaining, whining Jewish woman" whose antagonism toward "the Welfare" and the hospital mixes with her guilt and anxiety to produce . . . more contradictions. On the one hand, Tillie wants to get help for her ailing daughter and escape the unrelenting anxiety that has made her family into virtual prisoners of Annie's behavior, so she portrays her daughter as very sick, so sick that she and Hyman cannot possibly help her, sick enough to justify sending Annie to a hospital for the mentally ill. This is the Tillie who says she "realized quite early that Annie 'didn't learn as she should,'" and tries, unsuccessfully, to place Annie in the state's home for the feeble-minded.

At the same time, Tillie is a proud woman, and she does not want the world, as represented by Mona Evans and all those people at "the Welfare," to think that she and her family have done anything other than their best, or that her younger daughter is defective beyond repair. This is the Tillie who tells Evans that Annie "always" liked to read (spending a great deal of time with fairy books, Evans noted), that Annie loved to sew, embroider, and knit, that she had been "very much interested" in millinery until her problems began the year before. This is the Tillie who asserts that Annie "has always enjoyed mingling with the other children, was very happy in school, participating fully in all the activities there, and being deliriously happy going to the Grace Bentley Camp"—a camp for disabled children—"the past two or three summers."

What to believe?

. . .

The central mystery in Evans's report revolves around Annie's state of mind. Here there is no contradiction—everyone agrees that she has undergone some sort of transformation and that life in apartment 203 at 2205 West Euclid Street has become a nightmare—but there is no agreement about when it happened or why. For the first two decades of her life, as far as anyone knew, Annie showed no signs of mental illness. Her leg problems made her a candidate for the Leland School for Crippled Children, spending five years there before moving up to junior high school at the Oakman School for Crippled Children, where she lost ground academically. When she finally graduated from the ninth grade in June 1937, at age eighteen, she "was given a diploma because it was felt that this would encourage her, not because she had actually completed this level of work."

This faux diploma capped a difficult year. The fall of 1936 began with the amputation of her right leg, and the next six months brought rehabilitation and readjustment as Annie learned the ups and downs of walking with an artificial limb. More setbacks followed graduation from Oakman: A stint at the Girls' Vocational School, where she went to learn the basics of millinery so she could get a job, ended prematurely because the high school's administrators felt she was "too disturbing" to other students.

Disappointment turned to discouragement, then to depression. "During the winter of 1939 and 1940," Evans wrote, "patient seemed to be suddenly overwhelmed with the realization that she would never be able to live a normal life like other girls have. She began to display interest in boys and yet she could not look forward to marriage . . . She began to lose all interest in activities inside and outside the home, no longer finding consolation in books, in sewing, or attending movies, or listening to the radio, and would spend all her time sitting in a chair, refusing to even go out of the house. At first, the family had to coax her to eat. She would not take a bath unless she was continually reminded" to do so.

Annie's interest in boys worried her mother, Evans wrote. "It was our impression, as the mother talked, that she was alarmed over the patient's very evident interest in the opposite sex and has done everything she could to repress any expression of these interests." Bertha described her sister as "boy crazy," and told Evans that Annie "likes to talk to strange men."

There is one startling claim in the report, stated but also discounted, that might explain Annie's withdrawal from the world in the winter of 1939 and her fear of anyone outside her family. No one gave it much credence at the time, and I have no basis for giving it greater weight now. Knowing the impact of these words, and the scant evidence to support them, I even find it hard to repeat them.

In November 1939, Annie said, she was sexually assaulted. "The patient tells the story that she met a strange man on the street and he took her into an alleyway, assaulting her," Evans reported, under "Psychosexual History." "There seems to be a good deal of doubt among the members of the family as to whether this event actually took place."

That's all Evans wrote. She didn't describe the severity of the assault, or whether Annie told her family about it right away, or whether the family reported the attack to the police. Evans didn't say whether a physical examination was done or contemplated. Maybe she didn't think those details mattered to the psychiatrists reading her report; what mattered was describing Annie's state of mind, what Annie believed.

But what do I believe?

On March 19, 1940, something happened at the Harper Hospital clinic that sent Annie's state of mind tumbling from fearful to something worse. Or maybe nothing much happened—maybe my family, mystified by Annie's accelerating decline and looking for an explanation for the inexplicable, fastened on a minor incident and gave it significance beyond its meaning, perhaps because they had not known how much significance to give Annie's account of being sexually assaulted.

The Evans report supports either possibility. It describes how Annie went by herself to the clinic, as Jean Powell had been encouraging her to do. Tillie had made the appointment, concerned that Annie, who suffered from bouts of severe constipation, had gone a week without a bowel movement. Tillie was reluctant to allow her daughter to make the trip alone, but bowing to Mrs. Powell's desire to promote Annie's sense of independence, Tillie stayed home, and "has blamed herself ever since."

Why did Annie agree to go? What forces, internal or external, convinced her to give up the familiar confines of her chair, the one where she had been holding herself hostage, refusing to eat unless coaxed or bathe unless asked? Did she resist? Ask her mother to come with her? If she did any of these things, the report doesn't say so. In fact, it says nothing at all about Annie's journey to the clinic, as if such a trip were as routine as, say, eating or bathing.

Annie arrived at the clinic to find a long line of patients. "It was necessary," Evans wrote, "for her to remain in the waiting room for an hour or two, and during that time, she made every effort to call attention to herself, particularly by pulling up her dress to show her artificial leg. Then she fainted."

That must have caused quite a stir, a young woman with a wooden leg collapsing in a crowded waiting room. Whatever the cause of her swoon—"it was later determined that she had come to the clinic without eating breakfast"—Annie "had to be put to bed for several hours." The staff examined her, found nothing alarming, and sent her home.

When she showed up, hours later than expected, she was, in the words of her family, "an entirely different girl." Evans put these words between quotation marks. Not just different, but "entirely" different? Different how? Different from the girl who had been refusing for months to eat? Different from the girl who wouldn't leave the house? Different from the girl who wouldn't cross the street?

Evans does not attempt to calibrate the difference. She merely reports the family's alarm at Annie's altered state—she appeared pale and sallow, believed that "the world was a different place," and said "everyone was laughing at her, wishing to see her in her grave." She even asked her mother what kind of casket she intended to buy for her. "She thought no one could see it as she did," Evans wrote. "She screamed during the night, kept wanting to get up, and seemed to think that she would die if she stayed in bed."

She insisted, though, that she wanted to live. She wouldn't let "them" get her.

No one could say what, if anything, had happened to her, including Annie. When Bertha saw her sister after that clinic visit, she immediately called Jean Powell, saying that Annie was "out of her head" and acting "crazy." Bertha was so upset that Powell arranged for Annie to see Dr. Stephen Bohn, a neurologist at Harper, who issued a diagnosis on April 4: "Congenital cerebral anomaly." Translation: brain damage at birth.

How that diagnosis related to mental illness is yet another mystery to pursue. Evans's report does not say what name the Eloise doctors gave to Annie's condition. The 1972 report from Northville, offering a "final diagnosis," gives two: "Mental Deficiency (moderate) and Schizophrenia (chronic) Undifferentiated Type." Was she also regarded as moderately retarded in 1940? Was schizophrenia the initial diagnosis as well? Did that word, schizophrenia, describe the same symptoms in 1972 or 1940 as it does now?

Equally puzzling was Bohn's recommendation about what to do next. According to Evans, Bohn thought that Annie "should be placed in an institution such as Lapeer and that she should be hospitalized at Eloise in the interim." The interim? I didn't know much about the Michigan mental health system, but I knew enough to wonder about the logic of this recommendation. Lapeer served the "feeble-minded"; Eloise treated the mentally ill. Two different problems, two different populations. If Bohn saw Annie as a candidate for Lapeer, why send her to Eloise? And if he meant for her to stay there "in the interim," how did that interim turn into thirty-one years?

Almost in passing, the 1940 report mentions that Bohn's course of action required the family to file a petition seeking Annie's commitment to Eloise, and that when Annie was "served notice of the court hearing," she insisted that she wasn't insane.

A court hearing. It hadn't occurred to me that there might be an official record. Perhaps it would shed light on why Annie's claim of sanity had failed to keep her out of Eloise. But did the court record still exist? All I have is Annie's name—no file number, no date, no judge's name. Would that be enough? And even if the court could find it, would they let me look at it? Are involuntary commitments an open record? I know, from my inquiries in 2000, that getting access to mental health records is never easy.

Back then, when my Lansing contact told me that Michigan's 1974 mental health code—the "Hospital Protection Act," as she had sarcastically called it—did not allow me access to Annie's medical records without a court

order, I couldn't believe it. Thinking there must be other options for a surviving next of kin, I consulted a former director of Michigan's mental health
department (someone I knew slightly), who consulted a friend in the attorney
general's office. Sorry, the former director reported, but it was true, I needed
a court order; under Michigan law, nephews don't have the same rights as
spouses or direct descendants. At the time, I wasn't prepared to go that route,
which promised legal hearings, lawyers, family drama, traveling back and
forth to Detroit, and a significant investment of time as well as money.

Like many legal debates, both sides have their points, and neither side
is wrong. Openness destroys privacy, but privacy prevents openness. The
rights of individuals and the rights of family members aren't the same, and
favoring one can undermine the other. Still, in the matter of Annie Cohen
vs. the State of Michigan, I can't see how the state's position has much to do
with Annie or her privacy. She's dead, as are her parents and her sister. But
the family's genetic heirs are alive, blood relatives who might benefit from
knowing something about the origins of Annie's ailments. Mona Evans's
report had yielded some clues, including the hieroglyphic "congenital
cerebral anomaly" diagnosis. Was there a genetic basis for that? Maybe it's
impossible to get a definitive answer, but without more information, we
wouldn't even know that.

Beyond that, there's this question: How can we, as a society, overcome
the shame long associated with the mentally ill if state laws mandate that
their history be kept in the shadows?

On a bleak day in March, I visit the National Archives and the Library of
Congress to make a list of every family living on the same block as Mom and
Annie in the 1930s, using census records and Detroit city directories. I'm on
the lookout for a few names that I found in Mom's effects, including a woman
known to me only by her first name: Faye. Mom had written Faye's name in
the margins of several photos from 1943, giving her a status not shared by
other friends. If I can find Faye, perhaps she will be my guide to the life that
Mom and Annie had before Eloise. But I'll need to move quickly—if Faye (or
anyone else from Mom's crowd) is still alive, she'll be in her mid-eighties at
least, older if she was born in the same year as Mom.

It's my first visit to the Archives, and I'm surprised that the entire collection of microfilmed census rolls, all the way back to the first set from 1790, fits along one wall in a large room, millions upon millions upon millions of names housed in just thirty-five cabinets of eleven drawers each. By federal law, original census records—the handwritten collection sheets with every street address, and every person living there—become public seventy-two years after the count. Unfortunately for me, that means the census clock stops at the Fifteenth Census in 1930; the 1940 census, the one that would list all of Mom's neighbors in the very month when Annie is "going crazy," won't be released until 2012.

I scan the microfilmed pages, column after column listing "place of birth" as Russia or Poland and "mother tongue" as Yiddish or Polish or Russian, and I spot a dozen Fayes. Which, if any, is her? I know almost nothing about her, nothing that helps me distinguish one from another. Without other identifying clues—the first name of a brother, her father's occupation—this search isn't just time-consuming, it's time wasted.

I also don't see my grandparents' name. Do I have the wrong address? Did the census-taker miss them altogether, another immigrant family uncounted? Then I see the problem: Enumerator Henry J. Lingohr had written "Hyman, Hyman" for the family living at 1026 Medbury and then, realizing his error, crossed out the first Hyman, but failed to substitute any last name. How appropriate. Without the Medbury address, gleaned from Annie's Eloise records, their entry would have remained invisible to me as well.

I peer through this window into the past, thinking how simply it reveals what my mother sought so assiduously to hide: Hyman, 42, Tillie, 39, Bertha, 13, Annie, 10. A family of four, not three; two sisters, not an only child. Seeing Annie's name is no surprise at this point, but it's still a relief, another confirmation of her existence.

What I don't expect, what makes me stop and readjust the microfilm reader's focus, is a fifth name at 1026 Medbury: Nathan Shlien, boarder, age 34. Who's that? Mom never mentioned anyone by that name. He must be Tillie's relative; Shlien is a close spelling of her maiden name, Schlein. Maybe he was visiting for a few days, and happened to be there when the census-taker made his rounds. Nathan would be dead by now, but maybe he had children, and maybe I could find them to see if they knew Mom and Annie.

Find them? What makes me think I can find anyone? I can't interview

Mom, or Annie, I don't know Faye's last name, I don't know where to start looking for Nathan Shlien's children, or even if he had any children. Am I pursuing a fool's errand?

As I leave the Archives, I smile ruefully at the inscription on a statue that stands sentry at the researchers' entrance: "What Is Past Is Prologue."

Not in my family. Not yet.

FOUR

Unlocking the Door

Previous page: *Mom and her "Duke": Ft. Lewis, Washington, 1944*

It's the 1960–61 school year. I'm in trouble with my third-grade teacher at Alex Dow Elementary, although I don't know it. Whenever I finish my classwork ahead of time, I'm supposed to occupy myself by choosing a book from the "library" shelf in our portable classroom, a trailer set up on the school's gravel playground to deal with the baby-boom enrollment bulge. But it's February now and I've read all the good ones—not so much because I'm a fast reader, but because the shelf doesn't hold that many books; for months, the teacher has let me take them home to finish them.

With no books left to read, I'm following the teacher's instructions for what to do when I have nothing to do: I'm sitting quietly at my desk, arms folded, lips zipped, unaware that my teacher thinks I'm lying about my reading progress and mocking her by assuming the folded-arms position. She complains to the principal, who calls Mom, who questions me casually, never letting on that she and the principal have been conferring. What am I reading? Mom asks me. Do I read a lot in class? What do I want to read next? Oh, my, really? You've finished all those books? Have you told your teacher? You did?

A few weeks later, we get a new teacher. I never learn what happened to her predecessor.

S   ash tells me to call her aunt Medji in California. Medji, she says, knows something.

Medji, now in her seventies, comes from Sash's other family—she

and Sash's mom, Esther, are sisters. Medji is the youngest of the three
Golde girls; Esther was the oldest. Sash had been telling Medji about Annie,
and my detective work, and Medji remembered something from long ago,
a few words overheard while babysitting for Mom in the mid–1940s. Sash
cut short the conversation, mindful of my concern about creating false
memories by telling people too much of what we already know.

"Call her," Sash says. We're at her kitchen table in Pennsylvania, scru-
tinizing Mom's photos, trying to remember who's who. "I told her you
would want to talk."

"I'll try her now," I said.

Medji enjoys a reputation as a fount of family lore, but it's not *my* family's lore, and I haven't seen her in years. Medji caught the West Coast migration wave early, moving to California in 1953, not long after I was born.
Whenever she came into my orbit, her feistiness and her eccentricities—to
my youthful eyes at least—made her stand out in my somewhat staid uni-
verse. Plain and simple, she was a bit of a character.

The raspy voice on the telephone is just as I remember it.

"Your mom called me to come over and babysit, some sort of an emergency," Medji begins. "She didn't say what the emergency was."

When was this? I ask.

"I was maybe thirteen or fourteen," Medji says.

A quick calculation puts us sometime in the fall of 1946. Medji was born
in 1932, and she was babysitting for Mike, who was born in June 1945.

"That's right," Medji says. "He was about a year old, I think."

Medji's family lived a few blocks from the apartment where Mom and
Dad had moved after Dad's return from World War II, and Mom often called
on Medji to babysit. A reliable fourteen-year-old girl was a godsend to a
woman with a year-old baby, a part-time job, and (by late 1946) two step-
children, Evie and Marsha, ages ten and six, old enough to be a handful but
not old enough to take care of their baby brother. The girls had spent the war
with Medji's family, and that's how Mom and Medji got to know each other—
Medji, then about eleven, would usually be around when Mom picked up
Evie and Marsha (as everyone called her in those days) for Sunday outings.

Medji was surprised to see Mom's parents when she arrived. "That was
unusual," Medji says. "Her parents were in the bedroom, and the door
wasn't closed. There were a lot of legal papers on the bed."

Leaving Medji in the living room, Mom rejoined her parents behind the bedroom door. Medji couldn't make out what the three adults were saying, and she got the distinct feeling she shouldn't ask. The conversation was hushed, the tone urgent. "Your mom had to take some papers somewhere. She seemed pressed for time. She had to get somewhere by five," Medji recalls.

Medji says she wasn't trying to listen to the muffled voices, but several times, a name floated from their lips to her ears, something like "Chana"—the pronunciation was Yiddish, with a hard "h" at the beginning.

"Do you know Annie's Hebrew name?" Medji asks.

"No," I say, "but it's on the burial record. Hold on."

I pull out the folder, and the name soars off the page.

Chana.

Finally, a shard—more like a flake—but Medji's story had enough substance, enough specificity, to call it evidence. What she had overheard is the first confirmation that at least by 1946, Annie's condition, perhaps Annie herself, had become a topic to be discussed in private—provided, of course, that the Chana of that urgent conversation was, in fact, Annie.

Medji is recalling events sixty years past, events that she says she hadn't thought about for decades. I want to embrace her account, but the archeologist needs to test the data.

"Tell me about the apartment," I say. "How many bedrooms did it have?"

Medji describes what she remembers: one bedroom for the children, and a converted sunroom where Mom and Dad slept. (That also squares with Sash's memory.)

"What else did you see in the room?"

"Papers were being unfolded and folded on the bed. There was a metal box, big enough to store the papers," Medji says.

"What did you think they were talking about?" I ask.

Medji says she could only guess. "I thought someone was sick. I didn't hear anyone refer to a sister, but I assumed it was a sister of either your grandparents or your mom, because why else would they be so upset? They called her 'she' and 'Chanaleh.'"

"Chanaleh?" I reply, puzzled.

A diminutive, she says, not a nickname exactly, but a term of affection for a girl named Chana. "The only time I ever heard about Chanaleh was that day. Your mother was heartbroken, your grandmother was heartbroken."

That poignant image opens the door to a sensitive question. I ease into it. "You had a good relationship with my mother," I say, "even though you were fifteen years younger. That's what I always thought."

From the other side of the continent, I could see her nodding. "Your mom and I had a special relationship, based on understanding and compassion," she says. "I begged her to come to California, and she wanted to, but it never worked out. But we stayed close. She was a very private person, but she also was an angel. Once when my mother was sick, your mom took a day off work and stayed with her all day and night."

"So if you were close," I ask, "why didn't you ask my mom about Chanaleh?"

She doesn't answer right away. Maybe she hasn't thought about it; maybe it's hard to put her thoughts into words. Then she says, "I guess I felt I had heard something I wasn't supposed to hear. I didn't think your mom wanted to talk about it." She hesitates. "I was fourteen. It never came up again. I didn't think it was my place to bring it up."

Not her place. Mom didn't need to recruit members to the cone of silence. The culture did the job for her.

"What about Eloise?" I say to Medji. "Do you remember hearing any talk about Eloise that day?"

"No," she says. "But that doesn't surprise me."

Why's that? I ask.

"Having someone in Eloise was a double shame," she says. "You had a relative who was mentally ill, and everyone knew you were poor. Eloise was where the poor went. You would hide your head in shame because it was a disgrace. A terrible disgrace."

Shame. Stigma. Disgrace. How often those words closed a conversation about Annie and mental illness, how quickly they came to the surface when I mentioned to friends or strangers that I was trying to understand why my mother had made her sister's existence into a secret, and why she had not only kept that secret, but guarded it, nurtured it. Was shame at the root of it? Perhaps it was. Perhaps Mom had grown up with such profound feelings of humiliation that when Annie went to Eloise—a departure that Mom could not have predicted—Mom decided to put as much distance as possible between herself and those feelings, if not to exorcise them, then to conceal them.

Medji's story, however, suggested that something more than shame was at work here. Secrecy could be maintained by speaking in Yiddish or in whispers; the rules of polite conversation allowed adults to have discreet conversations. But if Mom were hiding her head in *shame*, wouldn't she want to meet with her parents in secret—at their apartment, which was nearby, rather than in her own apartment, in front of Medji?

On the other hand, maybe I was assuming too much. Maybe this "emergency"—or whatever had caused Mom's urgent call to Medji—didn't leave time for careful arrangements and private meetings. Or maybe my grandparents had received something that had alarmed them—a phone call, a letter—and had descended on Mom's apartment unexpectedly. But what could have caused such urgency? Why did Mom need to deliver papers some-where by 5 P.M.?

I remember from the Eloise records that in the mid–1940s, Annie had spent time at a hospital in Sault Ste. Marie, in Michigan's Upper Peninsula, for reasons that weren't stated in the documents. Looking at the file, I no-tice the date of Annie's return to Eloise: October 3, 1946. Was that the "emergency," or just a coincidence?

Another lead to pursue, another reminder of how important it was to obtain the rest of Annie's records.

Eloise closed the door of its psychiatric hospital for good in 1979, another casualty of the mental health revolution that emptied most of the nation's public mental hospitals, and the county has been dismantling the place ever since. By 2006, only four of its seventy-five buildings remained, and its signature smokestack with the letters E-L-O-I-S-E marching down its spine—the backbone of a decaying corpse—had a date with the demolition ball as well. It's hard enough to get my head around a hospital that was home to nine thousand mentally ill, infirm, and homeless people at the time that

Annie was admitted, but getting my arms around a ghost town seems even harder.

Eloise's legacy and history rests in the hands of a tiny band of preservationists, former employees mostly, who call themselves the Friends of Eloise. Jo Johnson, chairman of the Westland Historical Commission and the engine that keeps the Friends running, tells me on the phone that the group meets on the third Tuesday of each month. I tell her I'd like to attend; I'm hoping the group will provide a route to finding someone who remembers Annie, or perhaps cared for her.

"I'll put you on the agenda," Jo says.

We agree to meet an hour before the Friends arrive so she can show me the small museum of Eloise memorabilia on the ground floor of one of the remaining buildings, now used to house several county offices. She is distressed at the county's lack of interest in taking care of an institution that was such a landmark in the lives of so many people. "It's all about money," she says. "It's cheaper to knock it down than to preserve it."

Even their monthly meeting takes a hit. "We start at six P.M., but we have to be out by seven because that's when the security guard's shift is done," she says. "The county doesn't want to pay him to stay later."

She says I'll want to see the 1982 history of Eloise written by the hospital's personnel director, Alvin C. Clark, as well as a book of photos collected by a former nurse at the general hospital, published in 2002. Jo cautions me that she doesn't have any patient records. I'm well aware of the state's laws by now, and how hard it is to get those records. Nonetheless, this also distresses her. "When people like you call about a relative, I want to be able to help them," she says. "Sometimes, if the person died at Eloise, I can find the name in the list of death records. But often, I have to tell them that I can't help them, and it breaks my heart."

At Sash's kitchen table, we're brainstorming about who else could have known, and who had the opportunity to know. It helps to think about Mom's life as divided into four distinct eras: before Annie's hospitalization in 1940; the war years, when Mom goes from single woman to wife, while still living with her parents; the postwar years, when Mom and Dad strike out on their own, eventually buying a house in the deepest corner of Northwest

Detroit, as far away from the old neighborhood as you could get without actually leaving the city; and after 1950, when Mom became a fixture in her new neighborhood and Annie became a fixture at Eloise.

The period from 1940 to 1943, immediately after Annie's hospitalization, seems like a crucial one. In those first few years of Annie's treatment, there must have been a possibility that she would improve, that the Eloise staff would declare her well enough to be sent home. As long as that possibility existed, it would be hard for Mom to pretend that Annie didn't exist. It wouldn't work anyway—too many people in the neighborhood knew the truth. Finding these people, the ones who knew Mom and her family before Annie went to Eloise, is my top priority.

Also on my list: people who should have known, given their close relationship with Mom or Dad. That category included Fran, a woman who worked at the shoe store with Mom during the war, and who later married Dad's first cousin, Hy Donofsky. Fran and Hy own the title for the most photographed couple in Mom's collection from 1943 and 1944, when the young couple was still dating. Hy had died years ago and I didn't know Fran's last name, but I had found an old phone number in Mom's address book and, with that clue, had tracked her to Michigan's Upper Peninsula. Even if Fran didn't know about Annie, she might be a path to some of Mom's other friends.

Then there was Dad's side of the family. He had a sister and two brothers, all three alive and all in relatively good health. They were spread out around the country—Texas, Oregon, North Carolina. I couldn't imagine one of them didn't know something; if they didn't, that would be evidence of just how tightly the secret was held.

Who knew? Who didn't? Both questions needed to be answered for a complete portrait. The artist's challenge was mine as well: To get the composition right, I had to master the negative space as well as the positive, to paint what was absent as well as what was present.

"I was thinking we might see a ball game," Dad says.

A ball game? He has never taken me to one, or even suggested it. We just don't do those sorts of father-son outings. We don't ride bikes or play catch or go camping. Heck, we hardly go anywhere, except sometimes to Kensington

Lake for the day, and we always get there late. A ball game? Now that I'm four-teen and taking the bus downtown to Tiger Stadium by myself, he wants to take me to a ball game? What's this about?

A more typical teenager's reaction might be irritation or indignation, but I'm too surprised to say anything other than "Gee, Dad, thanks, but are you sure you can get the time off?" Getting time off was always the issue, not whether he wanted to be close or loved me. Dad's hours at the furniture store didn't exactly mesh with the baseball calendar. He worked Saturdays and Sundays, every week; those were his big days, the days when he could sell enough to make his commission for the week, and if he didn't make commis-sion, he didn't make any money.

This was the fifties and sixties, the era when day games still ruled on week-ends. When 1:30 arrived and the first pitch headed toward the plate, I cheered for my heroes by tuning into WJR radio and Ernie Harwell, the fatherly voice of the Tigers. Ernie took me to the game before I was old enough to take myself; it never, ever, crossed my mind that Dad should be taking me instead. What did cross my mind? That whatever I did when I grew up, I wouldn't be on commission.

We don't go to that ball game together. Dad doesn't bring up the idea again, and neither do I. Instead, several months later, he proposes a father-son activity that gives me a front-row seat at the game he plays. "I'd like you to keep a record of my sales and commissions," he says. He wants me to keep a ledger so he can see if he's making his commission. This is strange, crazy—and better than a ball game. Any dad can take his kid to the stadium, but my dad is inviting me into his secret world.

I have no memory of how long I kept that ledger, or what use Dad made of it. I learned a little about the furniture business, and a lot about why we had so much trouble making ends meet. Whether my work truly helped him, or whether it was merely a ruse to spend time together, I never figured out. Whatever his mo-tivation, for a short time when I was fourteen, I felt grown up, valuable, trusted. No one else knew what I knew.

It was our secret.

Back in 1995, when Rozanne Sedler called to ask if Mom had a sister, I could say without hesitation that I couldn't have been more in the dark, or have been caught more unaware, than when I read about the CIA's assassination plots against foreign leaders, or John F. Kennedy's assignations with Marilyn Monroe, or the Reagan administration's secret Iranian arms deals. If there was a loop, I was out of it, as were Mike and Jeff.

Evie and Sash, however, say they had an inkling. As the older sisters, they had a history with Mom that went back to the 1940s. What did they know? Sash finds it hard to say. "If you had asked me before Rozanne's call if Mom had a sister, I would have said no," Sash told me. "But once I heard it, I had this feeling—call it a buried memory—that I knew of a sister once, a long time ago."

A buried memory? What does that mean? Perhaps she or Evie saw or heard something, but were too young to make sense of it. Or perhaps they saw nothing, but growing up in the apartment with Mom, absorbed a sense of secrecy—a stealthy conversation, adults switching to Yiddish when the girls entered the room, an evasive answer to a child's innocent question.

But Sash doesn't remember that happening. She's certain that the knowledge predated 1946 and her permanent move to her father's home. "I never heard any mention of it after we went to live with Mom and Dad," she says. "It would have been earlier, when I was really young, which is maybe why the memory is so buried."

For her, the secret was so well disguised that she didn't know there was a secret. "What surprised me," she says, "was not that Mom had a sister, but that she was alive until 1972. If you had asked me, I would have said she died long, long ago." She had no idea Annie was at Eloise, and neither did Evie, who, like Sash, says she had some vague memory of hearing that Mom might have had a sister. Evie can't put that memory into any framework, but she's convinced that if she heard something, then Dad must have known, too. Like me, she finds it hard to believe otherwise.

Evie was eight when Dad returned from the Army in September 1945. Sash was five. Sash is unearthing a memory that has been buried since then. How did it get there in the first place? We make a run at figuring it out.

"What about your mom?" I ask. "Could she have known? I mean, they all lived in the same neighborhood, so even after the divorce, she could have picked up something."

When I was growing up, I heard the "divorce story" many times, but always from Mom's point of view—how Dad had wanted custody of the girls, but according to the custom of the times and the wisdom of the legal system, that honor had gone to Esther, who deposited the girls with her mother and left town for Florida, where she found a job and didn't come back for a couple of years.

In Mom's retelling, this was the Cinderella story in reverse. As the good stepmother, she saw the girls often during the twenty months that Dad was in the military, taking them to the park or a movie on Sundays, bringing them home to the Cohens' apartment for an occasional sleepover. Esther . . . well, Mom didn't like to speak ill of anyone, but she made an exception in Esther's case.

Of course, as a charter member of Beth's camp, I didn't get to hear Esther's side of the story, except I knew that she had one. I might say there was no love lost between the two women, but that's not possible because nothing resembling love existed in the first place. Yet they remained yoked together throughout their lives, bound by a cord that encircled them and their daughters. Mom never really accepted Sash's view that she had two mothers; as far as Mom was concerned, Esther had forfeited her maternal ID card when she left the girls with their grandmother.

Sash walked the tightrope between them, somehow managing not to fall. Her balancing act meant, however, that she saw the best and worst of both women, and she feels certain that Esther must not have known about Annie. Given the tension between the two women, Sash says, Esther would have felt no obligation to keep Beth's secret. "If my mom knew," Sash says, "she wouldn't have held back."

Before I leave Sash's house, I retrieve a box containing about half of the six hundred letters exchanged by Mom and Dad during the war. Sash tried to read them a few years ago, but gave up because they reek of cigarette smoke and mold. At some point, I plan to brave the mustiness and read through them all.

If I had to bet on what I'll find, I'd put a lot of money on negative space— at least when it comes to Annie.

The woman who answers the phone somewhere in Michigan's Upper Peninsula says that Fran isn't available right now. When I identify myself as Beth Luxenberg's son, her pretense fades without apology. I explain that

I'm doing some research on my family, and that my questions might seem mysterious at first, but if she could bear with my roundabout approach, all would become clear. I want to make sure that if she knows about Annie, she tells me before I tell her, so that I capture her spontaneous memory first.

Among Mom's letters, I had found several from Fran, written in late 1944 when Mom was living for a few months in Tacoma, Washington, near the Army base where Dad was stationed. I offer to send her the letters; it's an unexpected present for her, and I'm glad to be able to make the offer, because it allows me to give as well as take, something reporters can't often do. It's also a good way to win trust.

I lead her into a general discussion of Mom's family—how well she knew Tillie and Hyman, whether she spent much time with them, what she observed of Mom's relationship with them. I'd much rather be interviewing her face-to-face than over the phone, where the chemistry is all voice and no eye contact, but the more we talk, the more warmth I feel. Mom came into her life at a critical time.

They met in late 1943, when seventeen-year-old Fran Rumpa applied for a job at the Boston Shoe Shop, the downtown store where Mom worked as manager and saleswoman. Mom, nine years older, became big sister and friend. With Dad away in the Army, the two women frequently went out on the town together, often returning late enough that Mom invited Fran to sleep over. In the morning, they would take the bus to work together. "We were good friends for a good many years," Fran says, wistfully.

Dad's cousin Hy, who would come by the store to see Mom, met Fran there. When they started dating, Hy's mother, the imposing Tante Hinde (who scared me when I was young), made known her displeasure. Fran wasn't Jewish, and Tante Hinde blamed the whole situation on Mom. After all, Hy and Fran had met at Mom's store, so it stood to reason—at least, to Tante Hinde's reason—that it was Mom's fault.

So Mom and Fran were close, not just coworkers, not just family (after her marriage to Hy), but warriors who had met Tante Hinde in battle and forged a friendship. Surely Mom had told Fran about Annie?

No, says Fran. "I didn't know there was a sister. There was nothing said about a sister. You say her name was Annie?"

I'm surprised, and yet I'm not. Fran met Mom in 1943, three years after

Annie's hospitalization. This negative space is revealing: It tells me that the secret was in place by 1943, and that Mom was hiding her sister from her closest friend at the time.

"What about Mom's other friends?" I ask. "Can you remember their names?"

No luck there, either. "She didn't have many friends," Fran says, almost apologetically. "She was kind of a workaholic, you know."

What about someone named Faye? I say. That ring any bells?

"No," Fran says. "Afraid not."

Preparing for my first foray into Detroit, I phone David Oliwek, the son of Anna Oliwek. I'm wary of calling Anna directly, in part because I know nothing about her or her health, and in part because of what Sash had said about Anna's rocky relationship with Mom. I've been having trouble finding a good phone number for David, and even now, I'm not sure I have the right one. A message I left on an answering machine a few days earlier hasn't been returned. This time, though, a man picks up.

"Hi," I say. "I'm Steve Luxenberg, Beth Luxenberg's son. I think we're related."

Without missing a beat, David says, "We sure are. We're cousins. My mom is a Schlein, and so was your grandmother."

Excited as I am to finally reach him, I tiptoe around my reason for calling, not wanting to let go of the secret until I understand more about why our two families, living within a few miles of each other for so many years, didn't have any contact. I tell him that I'm interested in talking to his mom, and he says that she's away.

Will she be back in a few days? I ask.

"Well, not exactly," he says, hesitating. "She's in Chicago most of the time."

I'm confused. "She's not living in Detroit right now?"

"It's a long story," David says.

He gives me the brief version: His mom and an old male school friend from her hometown in Eastern Europe—the same town, he says, where Hyman and Tillie had come from—had struck up a relationship after all these years. Both had lost their spouses. Three months ago, the widow decided to move to Chicago to live with the widower. "Can you believe it?" David says. "She's eighty-two years old!"

I ask the name of the town in Eastern Europe, and David tells me, but it's so foreign to my ear that I can't even figure out how to write it. Only later, when I see it in print, do I put the spelling with the pronunciation: Radziwillow (or Radzivilov, depending on the era and which country is running the show). And only when I have the spelling can I find it on a map—in present-day Ukraine, in the far western province once known as Volhynia, just a few miles northeast of the old Austro-Hungarian border. The town has gone back and forth between Poland and Russia, but in my grandparents' time, it sat on the fringe of the Russian Pale of Settlement, subject to the tsar's laws and whims, not a comfortable place for Jews to be in the late nineteenth and early twentieth centuries.

David and I spend a few minutes climbing around the family tree, filling in the branches with the names of brothers and sisters and cousins, which gives me an opening to slip in my question: Does he know about my mom's sister?

The clarity of his answer astounds me.

"Absolutely," he says. "My mother used to go visit her at Eloise all the time. She would drive Tillie there, and she took me along once."

"You saw my aunt?" I say, hardly able to get the words out. "How can that be? I never even knew she existed until a few years ago."

"No," he says. "I was too young to go in. Hospital rules. You know, that was such a horrible place. I can't blame your mom for keeping her a secret."

"How old were you?" I ask.

"I don't remember exactly, probably ten or eleven," David replies. He was born in 1950, so that would put this visit in 1960 or 1961, a new window on Annie's life.

"You have no idea how amazing this is to me," I finally say. "I grew up not knowing Mom had a sister, and you grew up knowing all about it. How can that be?"

By the time the conversation ends, I know exactly how that could be. But first, I learn a bit about Anna's life, an amazing tale in its own right: A Holocaust survivor who didn't arrive in the United States until 1949, she lost her entire family in a Nazi massacre and then avoided their fate by pretending to be a German, even securing a job as a translator for the *Wehrmacht*. It's quite a story, David says, and his mom will want me to hear it. As it happened, she was going to be in Detroit during the ten days that I planned to be there, and David would arrange for us to get together.

"How did she end up in Detroit?" I ask.

"Her uncle," David says. "He sponsored her—well, my mom, my dad, and my older sister, who was born in Germany."

What was her uncle's name?

"Nathan Shlien," he says.

"I know that name," I say. "Nathan Shlien was living with my grandparents in 1930, according to census records I've seen from that year."

That's how Anna found out about Annie—from Nathan, not my mom. She arrives in the United States, with her husband and her baby, and Nathan tells her about her American family—Hyman, Tillie, my mom, and Annie in Detroit, other relatives in New York. This is clear proof: The biggest threats to Mom's secret were the people who knew Mom and Annie *before* Annie's hospitalization. They were outside Mom's circle, like free electrons, uncontrolled and in their own orbit.

David confirms something else: There was bad blood between the cousins, Anna and Mom—and the secret stood at the center of it.

FIVE

Missing Pieces

Previous page: *The "only child": a mother-daughter outing*

My city is on fire. From our house in far northwest Detroit, more than ten miles from the heart of the riots at Twelfth and Clairmount, we can see the ashy, angry billow of smoke rising from the blocks around Mom's old neighborhood. It's Tuesday, July 25, 1967, the day of my fifteenth birthday, but there's no place to go, and there is certainly no thought of celebrating.

It all began two days before, in the wee hours of Sunday morning, with a routine police raid on one of Detroit's so-called "blind pigs"—unlicensed, after-hours drinking clubs serving home-made brews, primarily to the city's black population. We didn't yet understand how a few arrests at a blind pig (one of four raided that night) could be the spark for one of the worst urban riots in U.S. history, leaving forty-three dead and two thousand buildings destroyed or damaged by the time it was over. On Monday night, all we knew was that the overwhelmed police force had lost control to looters and arsonists, and those in authority—the mayor and the governor—were asking us to stay at home until order was restored.

The previous week, the TV had brought Newark's urban conflagration into our living room, but those flames felt distant, otherworldly. Now my city is on fire, and I'm full of questions as I watch the seemingly endless supply of images emanating from the twenty-six-inch Philco: Is it possible for so many buildings to be burning? Where are the fire trucks? Why are they called blind pigs? Do police raid them all the time? What do pigs have to do with drinking? Who came up with such a stupid name, anyway?

Together, Mom and I maintain a TV vigil. My brother Jeff, three years younger, must have been there, but I have no memory of him, or of my dad, who was probably at the furniture store, open as usual until 9 P.M., you never know, people might want to buy that loveseat right now, the riots are nowhere near the store, that's Twelfth Street for you.

The TV camera pans a street of burning buildings, leaping flames, and black-gray smoke against the humid night sky. Mom stares at the screen, cigarette in hand, but her mind is somewhere else, a different time zone, a different planet, a different year. Wherever she is, she's too far away to hear me.

"That's my building," she says. "That's where we lived."

"Where?" I say. "Which one?" I never lived in the old neighborhood, so I don't recognize the buildings. Could it really be the same one? The thick smoke makes it hard to see much, anyway. From the stories she's told us, though, I have this crystal-clear image: Mom, the only child, living in her third-floor apartment on Euclid with my grandparents, walking to school by herself.

Mom doesn't reply. She's still elsewhere, in a time and a place I don't know.

"Gone," she says. "All gone."

E ven the streets don't exist any more: The block of Medbury Avenue where my grandparents lived for seven years of Mom and Annie's childhood? Obliterated in the 1950s to make way for I–94, known to my generation as the Edsel Ford Freeway, one of a half dozen that criss-cross and encircle today's Motor City. The Leland School for Crippled Children? Now loft apartments. The building where Mom lived after she and Dad married? Demolished after the riots, replaced by a vacant lot of weeds and broken glass.

In the lengthening shadows of a spring afternoon in 2006, I stare at the barren ground where the apartment building once stood, thinking: I go looking for clues to the past, and what do I find? Empty space. A blank. Even the ghosts have no place to live.

I am a native of this city, but on this visit, I feel as if I'm seeing it for the first time. My search is taking me to unfamiliar places and buildings, but even the familiar haunts don't look the same. It takes me a while to realize why: reinterpretation. Where once I saw only Mom, now I'm imagining Annie, too. Cruising through Mom's old neighborhood, studying the old photos to identify any landmarks still standing, I revise as I go: Here is the street where Mom (*and Annie*) lived. Here is the corner where Mom (*and*

Annie) waited for the trolley. And there, that must be the apartment building where Mom and her parents lived *(after Annie went to Eloise).*

I leave the neighborhood and turn left at Woodward Avenue, Detroit's
main street. Woodward slices diagonally through the heart of the city, the
dividing line between the east and west sides, a broad ribbon of road that
travels from Detroit's beginnings at the Detroit River, crosses the northern city limit at Eight Mile Road, and ends thirty miles away in the far
northern suburbs. Woodward is a metaphor for the city's evolution—an
entrance for thousands of newcomers and then an exit route during the era
of white flight that began in the 1950s and accelerated to warp speed after
the 1967 riots.

A half dozen blocks up Woodward, the classical columns of Northern
High School, Mom's alma mater, come into view. In the school's library,
where the polished wooden bookcases and desks hark back to a pre-
Internet age, I ask the librarian if she has a 1934 yearbook. I want to see
Mom's photo.

The chief librarian, Shirley Britton, disappears into a little room where
the yearbook archive is kept under lock and key, and a few minutes later,
I'm holding the black-bound January 1934 edition of the *Viking.* I flip
quickly to the Cs—but there's no Bertha or Beth Cohen pictured. "Are you
sure she graduated in 1934?" she asks.

I extract Mom's diploma and check the date: January 1934. "She must
not have been in school the day they took photos," Britton says. "That happens, doesn't it?"

No, she must be here somewhere. But there's no sign of her in the group
photos of clubs and sports teams. She seems to have gone through high
school just as she went through the rest of her life before 1942: furtively,
leaving no footprints.

Finally, at the end of the graduates' photos, on a separate page with the
headline "Following is a Continued List of the Graduates," I find her: Bertha Beth Cohen, one of fifteen grads with no picture. Shirley Britton puts
into words what I'm thinking.

"She probably couldn't afford one," she says. "Not everybody could, you
know."

• • •

I still need names. If I want to understand Mom's world as she saw it, I need
to find one or more of her friends from the 1930s, before Annie's hospitalization, someone who's not gone. My leading clue comes from the Eloise
records: Jacob Robinson. At the time of Annie's admission to the hospital,
my grandparents didn't have a phone, so they listed Jacob Robinson, their
next-door neighbor, as the person to call in an emergency.

I know from census records that the Robinsons had two daughters,
Irene and Sylvia, born around the same time as Mom and Annie. I'm hoping that Robinson's obituary will give me the daughters' married names,
which is the only way I will find them. I remember what a researcher at the
Library of Congress told me one day as we commiserated about the difficulty of tracking women born long ago. "If I were in charge of the world,"
she joked, "I would forbid any woman from changing her name when she
marries. It just makes our job so much harder."

Success: As luck would have it, Robinson held prominent court and
labor union jobs, and his 1954 obituary, pasted on a yellowing index card at
the Detroit Public Library, tells me that I'm looking for daughters Irene
Doren and Sylvia Pearce. But then, disappointment: The only women with
those names and approximate birth dates have been dead for some time—
Sylvia Pearce in 1991 and Irene Doren in 2001.

Gone . . . all gone.

Edward Missavage proves the old adage that it's better to be lucky than good.
I find Missavage—stumble across him would be more accurate—when I ask
a librarian at the Detroit Public Library's main branch if she can help me
find material on the old county hospital known as Eloise. "You should talk
to the man doing his own research in the microfilm room," she says. "He
was an Eloise psychiatrist for years."

I practically sprint to where her finger is pointing. There, in the dark, I
ambush a bearded man with bifocals as big as coasters and the bushiest natural eyebrows I've ever seen. I lower my voice to library levels, explain that
I'm working on a book, and pepper him with questions. "Annie Cohen?" he
repeats, then shakes his head. "Doesn't ring any bells, I'm afraid."

It turns out that Missavage didn't have much to do with female patients
during his nearly thirty years as a psychiatrist at Eloise. He spent most of

his time working in the male division, rising to chief eventually. By the time Missavage arrived at the hospital in 1948, Annie had already been there eight years and Eloise had shed its name in favor of something more descriptive of its various missions: Wayne County General Hospital and Infirmary. But like everyone else, Missavage still called the place Eloise. For the next thirty years, except for a brief interlude to serve in the Korean War, Missavage and Eloise remained partners; he left in 1977 as it became clear that Eloise was about to close.

I thrust Mona Evans's Routine History report into his large hands, hoping that it would trigger some memory or give him enough clues to lead me to someone who treated or cared for Annie. He takes a quick look. "Where are the clinical records?" he grumbles. "I could tell you a lot more if I could read her clinical records."

"I wish I had them," I say. "I don't know if they exist. I'm lucky I have these."

He grunts, and squints again at the documents, which are barely readable in the pale glow of the microfilm machine's lamp. He fires a second volley: "Eloise treated thousands of schizophrenic girls over the years. Why do you think anyone would care about this particular twenty-one-year-old from 1940?"

His question seems stonehearted, the sort of dismissive attitude that makes some people wary of the medical profession. I tell him he hasn't heard the whole story, and he doesn't know about the "five thousand," those families just now discovering the existence of relatives hidden away in mental institutions. Besides, I explain, this book isn't just about Annie. It's about why my mother kept the secret, and the consequences of that choice.

In the microfilm reader's light, I can see his demeanor soften. He takes my number and promises to contact a few people. Two days later, just before 9 A.M., he phones. "You're a devil," he says. "You got me all stirred up. I've made some calls for you and I've got some ideas."

An abrupt change in plans: I had made a tentative date with David Oliwek to meet his mother for a first interview, but as I'm leaving the library, I pick up a cell phone message from Anna saying that she's not feeling well and won't be coming to Detroit after all. It's the first time I've heard her voice. "I'm in Chicago," she says on the message, pronouncing the first syllable with the hard "chick" sound of someone with an Eastern European accent. "I'd love to talk. You're in Detroit, right? How long you going to be there? Okay, call me back."

David had told me a bit more about his mother's move to Chicago and his mother's new beau, a man named Sidney whom she knew from her childhood in Radziwillow. It seemed sweet, the two of them, in their eighties, getting a second chance at romance, even if it did complicate my attempts to see her.

I dial her number.

"Hi, Steven," she says, using my full name, just as Mom would want. Now that I've got her on the phone, I'm tempted to dive right in, but I restrain myself. I want to be looking at her face when I hear about her falling-out with Mom, not sitting in a car as dusk is falling, worrying about whether the cell phone signal will take a vacation in the middle of the call.

Instead, I just tell her that I hope she feels better, and we agree to meet in Detroit the following month, when she's supposed to come for the Jewish holidays. "I can't wait to see you," she says. "I haven't seen you since you were a little boy."

Since I was a little boy? I wasn't aware that we had ever met.

As I pull into the nearly empty parking lot, the decaying smokestack of the old power plant comes into full view, the vertical letters that spell "Eloise" still visible in the brickwork. I climb the curved stairs of the seventy-five-year-old building that once served as the hospital's administrative center, and find myself face-to-face with Eloise herself, or at least her life-sized portrait, which greets visitors to what is now called the Kay Beard building.

The painted Eloise is young, no more than five or six years old, decked out in a Victorian ruffle dress, left arm draped over the back of her beloved dog, a strapping St. Bernard who is nearly as tall as his winsome companion. Eloise's father, Freeman B. Dickerson, was both Detroit's postmaster and, for two years, head of the Superintendents of the Poor, the board overseeing the mental institution, known in those days as the Wayne County

House and Asylum. In 1894, when an impasse developed over what to name the new post office being built to handle the growing bounty of mail destined for the facility, the Superintendents suggested Eloise—without chairman Dickerson's knowledge, according to the 1982 history of Eloise that Jo Johnson had mentioned in our first phone call. "The name was at once accepted by the Postmaster General" in Washington, the history says.

The power of the post office in shaping the local geography soon became apparent. If letters and packages now went to a place called Eloise, then it was only a matter of time before the new name showed up on road maps, train timetables, and the Michigan Central Railroad station that sat on the asylum's grounds. "The word became of such general use," the 1982 history reported, "that the Board applied it to the entire institution." On August 18, 1911, the asylum officially adopted the Eloise name.

Inside the five-story Beard building, I spend an hour wandering through the Eloise Museum, a dozen or so glass cabinets that line the first-floor hallway. The jumbled collection of memorabilia opens a variety of paths into Eloise's history, and into the history of mental illness in the early twentieth century. Here in one cabinet are the tools of the trade, including bulky leather arm restraints; here is a pair of shoes like those furnished free to male infirmary residents, with "Eloise" stamped in the sole to discourage them (so the story goes) from selling the shoes for liquor at the nearby Eloise Inn; here are milk bottles, dinner plates, and coffee mugs inscribed with the "Eloise" label; here are packages of home-grown tobacco provided to patients from the Eloise drying shed, marked "Luxury, Pipe and Cigarette Tobacco, Wayne County, Eloise, Mich."

A scrapbook in one cabinet displays a yellowed July 1945 news clipping about the institution's name change to Wayne County General, and describes the facility, authoritatively but perhaps not altogether accurately, as "the largest of its kind in the world." Eloise was certainly one of the nation's larger mental hospitals in the early 1940s, when its psychiatric population hovered at 4,000 patients. Maybe, if you added the infirmary residents—mostly homeless men whose numbers swelled the infirmary's rolls to 7,000 in winter before declining to 3,000 in summer—it conceivably could be called number one, because so few institutions had this dual mission.

If nothing else, the news article's grand statement stands in contrast to

the museum's modest size. There's no admission fee or onsite staff person;
the job of curator falls to Jo Johnson in her role as head of the local historical
commission. Her efforts to preserve Eloise's history, at least what's left of it,
have become a nearly full-time occupation. It's not a passion she expected to
be pursuing in her seventies, but it's a passion that she pursues with the vigor
of someone half her age.

The country lilt I heard in our phone conversation turns out to belong
to a bespectacled, gray-haired sprite of a woman with glinting eyes and a
determined set to her chin. We climb the stairs to the large conference
room where Jo chairs the monthly meeting of the Friends of Eloise. As
promised, Jo has put me on tonight's slate of speakers so I can ask the preservation group for help in tracking down anyone who knew Annie. I make
my brief pitch to the dozen or so Friends—no one knows my aunt, but they
all promise to ask around—and then Martine MacDonald and Andrea Irwin
have the floor.

Martine and Andrea represent the Downriver Council for the Arts, a
local organization with a small budget and a big idea. To commemorate the
former Eloise patients buried in a potter's field near the hospital, the council wants to invite poets, musicians, and visual artists to contribute to a
one-time show. The project has a dual focus: creating opportunities for
local artists and celebrating a forgotten part of Eloise's past—yet more
ghosts, I find myself thinking.

The show's proposed title echoes my thought: "Resurrected Voices."

If keeping a secret is hard, burying one must be even harder. Yet when Annie
died in August 1972, between my sophomore and junior years in college,
Mom managed to arrange for her burial without any of us suspecting a thing.
I was home from college that summer, painting giant lathes in an auto parts
plant and flirting with a girl who boarded the same bus as I did every weekday
morning, so perhaps my attention was elsewhere. Still, it's no mean feat to
pull off a stealth burial; the American way of death isn't a quiet one. Mom
must have received several phone calls and probably made several of her
own; maybe she went to Hebrew Memorial to choose a coffin.

Beyond that, there must have been an emotional toll. Whatever she felt
about her sister at that moment, or about herself for keeping Annie a secret

for so long, Mom had too much invested in her notion of family not to feel something about the loss of the last direct link to her parents and her childhood—whether it was relief, sadness, anger, defiance, or embarrassment. Whatever her emotions, she hid those, too, just as completely as she had hidden Annie.

Knowing Mom, and thinking about how naturally compassion came to her, it amazes me to think that she could have handled all that the burial involved and not alert any of those around her. But until my visit to Detroit, I didn't know how amazing it was.

At the office of Hebrew Memorial Park in the Detroit suburb of Oak Park, Elaine Klein agrees to dig a bit deeper into the files. I want to know who paid for the funeral. Was it the state of Michigan, because of Annie's status as a mental patient? Or Mom? Was there any evidence that Dad was involved?

When I arrive, Elaine is beaming. She slides another copy of Annie's burial record across the counter, the same as the one she sent us in 2000, but with the following handwritten notations added:

"8/7/72—Religious Rites—Gratis

Rabbi Milton Arm—$20.00

Death Certificate—9.00

Cement Frame—30.00"

Religious rites? Mom hadn't just buried her sister. She had arranged for a service, with a rabbi officiating. But why? Mom wasn't particularly religious, and while we celebrated the Jewish holidays at home when I was growing up, we rarely attended synagogue services, even on the High Holy Days of Rosh Hashanah and Yom Kippur. Yet I always had a sense that Mom believed in the rituals of our faith, so perhaps this service for Annie came from some deep reservoir of familial duty—Mom's attempt to do what her parents would have done, to give their daughter a proper Jewish funeral.

Or maybe it was something deeper—guilt or penance, Mom's way of saying to Annie, "I'm sorry for all those years that I didn't visit you, all those years of keeping you a secret."

The state of Michigan, apparently, had paid for the coffin, the biggest expense, and Mom had paid the rest. No sign of Dad's involvement. Elaine

couldn't say why Hebrew Memorial hadn't charged for use of its chapel to
conduct the rites. "Maybe your family couldn't afford it," she ventures.

That night, I phone Rabbi Milton Arm at home. Now in his mid-eighties
and long retired, he says, understandably, that he has no specific memory
of presiding at a service in 1972 for someone named Annie Cohen, but hold
on, he has records and he can check.

A few minutes later, he's back. "Yes, that's right, I did the service," he
says, and reads me the details—date, place, name of deceased.

"Does your record say whether it was in the chapel or at the graveside?"
I ask.

"It doesn't say graveside," he says. "I'm sure it wasn't. Otherwise, I
would have made a note that it was graveside only."

"Do your records indicate who hired you?"

"No," he answers. "But it must have been the family. Otherwise, why
would there have been a service?"

Good question. Other than Mom—and Dad?—who else would know that
Annie had died? And if no one knew about her death, who would be there
to mourn the end of her difficult and painful life?

Fred Garfinkel is wondering why I'm being so mysterious. I had phoned my
mom's former boss at the monument company earlier in the day, explaining that I was researching some family history and that I hoped he could
help. "Give me a hint," he says, but I tell him that it's better if I ask him all
my questions at once so that I can get his freshest memory.

"Steven, come in, great to see you," he says. He always calls me Steven,
like he's part of the family—which, in a way, he is. He and Mom worked
together for thirty-six years, almost as long as Mom and Dad were married.
After Dad's death in 1980, Fred probably spent more time with Mom than
anyone else on the planet. For that reason alone, he makes my short list of
people to interview.

Fred's wife is out for the evening, so we sit at his kitchen table, without distractions or interruptions. After hearing me mention family history on the phone, he collected all the burial records for Mom, Dad, and
my grandparents. "I didn't know if you had those, so I called around and
got them," he says, handing me a folder. It's a typically Fred thing to do,

eager to be helpful, anticipating the customer's needs. I glance at them to make sure there's nothing I don't already have, and my lack of reaction only serves to heighten his curiosity, so I leave the folder in my lap and make the leap.

"Do you remember a time when Mom needed to leave the office in a rush, to take care of some sort of family problem?" I ask.

He isn't expecting this line of questioning. He thinks about it, finally gives up. "No, nothing comes to mind. Why?"

Fred's in his seventies now, and like me, his hair retreats a bit more every time I see him, but otherwise he looks healthy. I've known him most of my life—through high school and college, marriage and children—and in the long stretches between the family visits that would bring me back to Detroit for a few days, Mom kept Fred abreast of her children with a running narrative that I occasionally found embarrassing. But now it has an unexpected payoff—he understands what writers and journalists do, and he trusts me enough to indulge my enigmatic approach.

Fred once joked to me that he's never forgiven Mom for dying, but on one level, it's no joke. Mom's been dead seven years and Fred never hired a replacement. He's now the sole owner and employee of Monument Sales Corporation, the small gravestone company that his brother-in-law Sid Frumkin started in the early sixties. On the scale of family businesses, this one couldn't get much smaller: After Sid's death in 1997, Fred and Mom soldiered on themselves, Fred selling the stones and Mom keeping the books.

Like many family businesses, this one didn't draw much of a line between family and business, and Mom had her feet on both sides of the divide. She worked for Sid and Fred, she played bridge with Sid's wife, Marilyn, and Sid's sister, Ann Black, and she occasionally socialized with Fred's wife, Barbara. When we had a family celebration—Jeff's bar mitzvah, Mike's wedding—the Frumkins and the Garfinkels were on the guest list. When Mom's health took a downturn in the mid-1990s, Fred went beyond an employer's duty, visiting her at home and in the hospital, occasionally driving her to doctor's appointments, alerting us when he thought that Mom might be telling her far-flung children less than we needed to know.

"Does it help," I ask, "to say that I'm talking about 1972, around August, and that it involved the death of a relative?"

He knows my family well, so the part about the death of a relative throws him.

"You're talking about thirty years ago . . ." he says. "No, sorry." He spreads his hands in the universal gesture of defeat.

"The relative was a sister. Does that help?" If this didn't go anywhere soon, I would put him out of his misery and tell him the story.

Still no hint of recognition. Then his eyes light up, a snatch of memory, and he points his finger at me. "She was handicapped."

Wow. I hadn't mentioned anything about Annie's leg.

"What kind of handicap?" I ask, cautiously.

"I don't know. Physical, I think. I don't remember when we were talking or why, but it just came to me—she told me she had a sister who was handicapped, who lived in a group home or a halfway house or something like that."

I press him for details, and his brow creases in concentration. Finally he says, "It was just something your mom said in passing. She didn't even say what kind of handicap, or if she did, I've forgotten that part." He pauses, trying to recover more of this fleeting conversation. "It wasn't one of those things where she was confiding in me. She didn't say, 'I want to tell you something . . .' I got the impression that her sister's death was years before, that it was in the past, just one of those sad things."

"Did she ask you not to talk about it?"

His eyebrows lift in surprise. "No. Like I said, it was just something she said in passing." He can't even begin to guess when this conversation took place. "A long time ago. Probably the eighties."

It isn't much, but it's still a breakthrough—an indication that as tightly as Mom controlled the secret, she did volunteer some information to someone close to her, even if she omitted or invented facts to control how that information might be understood, telling Fred that her sister was handicapped but not mentally ill, saying that Annie had lived in a group home rather than in a mental hospital, describing her death as long ago so that Fred might naturally conclude that Mom was very young when Annie died. It fit the pattern of 1995, when Mom had said she was just four years old, and Annie just two, when Annie was institutionalized. In both cases, she put the information out there, but in a way that shut off questions rather than provoked them.

I'm planning to give Fred a full account of what I've learned so far, but first . . .

"Fred, did Mom tell you her sister's name?"

His brow furrows again. "Not that I remember. What was it?"

"Annie," I said. "Annie Cohen."

The day dawns blustery and gray, perhaps not the optimum conditions for visiting Annie's grave. The sun tries, timidly, to dent the cloud cover, and a few rays make it through before the gray wins out again. The Hebrew Memorial Park cemetery occupies a large expanse in the far eastern suburb of Clinton Township, a good half-hour's drive from the Hebrew Memorial Park office and the northern/northwestern suburbs that have become the dominant centers of Detroit's Jewish community.

Dave Tomlian meets me near the cemetery's front gate. He's the superintendent ("and foreman, and grave-digger, and whatever else needs to be done"), one of four full-time employees. He's standing next to a pickup truck with its snow plow still attached, but he's dressed for warmer weather: plaid shirt, no jacket, no gloves. It's cold enough that I find it hard to take notes with my numb fingers.

Dave has worked at Hebrew Memorial for more than twenty years, going back to summers during college. "We've got about twenty-five thousand buried here, and room for another twenty-five thousand," he says, pointing at a grassy vacant area toward Fourteen Mile. "The summer is the busy time. We put on twenty workers to do cleanup, planting, etc."

"How many burials a day this time of year?" I ask.

"One, maybe two," he replies.

The rows each have metal signs, embossed with the section number, letter of the row, and the gravesite numbers. He escorts me to Section 19, Row J. A single headstone lies between my grandparents' side-by-side plots. On the headstone's left side, it says, "Beloved Mother, Tillie, 1891–1966." On the right, it reads, "Beloved Father, Hyman, 1887–1964." This is the first time I've seen it, I think; looking at it now brings back no memory of an earlier visit.

As we walk over to Annie's resting place in Section 18, Row B, he explains why Annie isn't buried next to her parents: "There was no provision made for her at the time that her parents died, so our records show that we put her as close to them as we could."

I have no expectations as I approach her grave, but I'm still unprepared for what I see. The site is unmarked, a simple cement frame containing a smoothed-over rectangle of earth where the flowers could be planted later in the spring. I feel the chill wind as I stare at the vacant space, acutely aware that it says nothing, reveals nothing. No gravestone to match the one I just saw, no "Beloved Daughter, Annie, 1919–1972."

Anonymous in life, and still anonymous in death. Mom, if you could have a rabbi bid her farewell, why not a headstone that says, if nothing else, "Annie Cohen"?

But perhaps it wasn't that simple. The gravestone business was a small world, and if Mom tried to order a headstone through one of her contacts, she would inevitably be asked about the deceased. Sympathy was a reflex in her line of work; I could even imagine the conversation: "So sorry about your loss, Beth. And just how are you related to the deceased? A distant relative? What shall we put on the headstone? Just 'Annie Cohen.' Nothing else? You sure?"

No, if the secret was paramount, better not to raise any eyebrows. Anonymous in life, so why *not* anonymous in death?

Still, why continue to keep the secret at all? Now that Annie was dead, did it really matter anymore? Of course it did. By 1972, I'm certain, the secret had become larger than Annie, had taken on a significance that went far beyond shame and stigma. Having pretended all these years to be an only child, how could Mom now explain herself to her unknowing friends and family? Burying Annie did not mean that Mom could now banish the secret, consign it to a grave of its own, not unless she was willing to bare her soul, and that she obviously wasn't prepared to do. *Mom, I wish you had. We wouldn't have loved you any less.*

Dave interrupts my reverie, reading a part of my mind. "I could make a temporary sign, put her name on it," he says.

I'm touched, and I tell him so. But somehow, a temporary sign doesn't seem appropriate, either. I tell him I'll think about it, but I know that's not what I want to do.

As I make a few notes in the car, I get a cell phone call from my twenty-year-old daughter, Jill. I describe to her what I've just seen. "I think we should put a marker of some kind on Annie's grave," I say. She immediately responds: "I think Grandma would like that."

I laugh out loud at the very idea. "Why on earth would you say that?" I ask.

"Remember Grandma's last wish?" Jill says. She's talking about the letter that Mom left behind, the one we opened after her death. "She told us that what she wanted, more than anything, was for all of us to stay together. This is something we can do together, as a family, and that would make Grandma happy."

It's a nice thought—no, it's more than that, it's a kind thought, a charitable thought—and I wonder if there's any harm in thinking that it might even be true.

SIX

Actually Insane

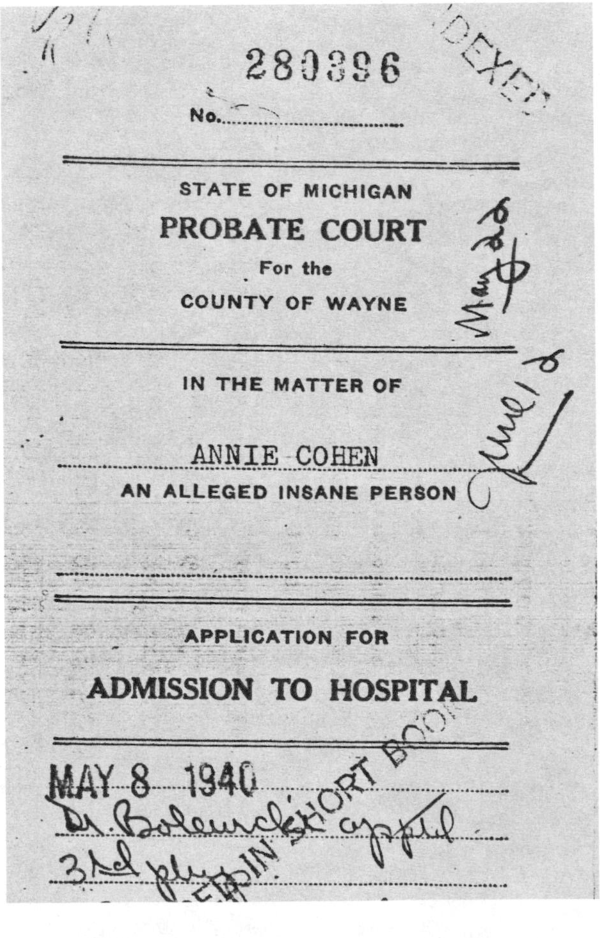

280396

No.

STATE OF MICHIGAN

PROBATE COURT

For the

COUNTY OF WAYNE

IN THE MATTER OF

ANNIE COHEN

AN ALLEGED INSANE PERSON

APPLICATION FOR

ADMISSION TO HOSPITAL

MAY 8 1940

The records office of the Wayne County Probate Court, on the thirteenth floor of the downtown Coleman A. Young Municipal Building, could serve without much modification as a movie set for a modern-day version of *Bleak House*, Charles Dickens's novel about an endless lawsuit in the English probate courts—the stained linoleum floors, the worn counter tops, the crowded hallways, the weary faces of the people waiting, numbers in hand, to file papers in this estate or that.

Eurick, a tall, fresh-faced clerk, frowns when I tell him that I'm looking for a case from 1940. I know that look: It means that I represent trouble. Finding ancient cases can be time-consuming and costly. Sure enough, Eurick tells me that files from that long ago must be retrieved from a warehouse, supervised by a private contractor that charges the court for each search request. If I'm lucky, and the file can be found, it will take at least two weeks before it's available to read.

First things first, though: Eurick cheerfully says he can't request the records without a case number, so he takes my yellow request slip with "Annie Cohen" written on it and disappears, murmuring something about needing an index upstairs. I can't go with him—the inner workings of the public records department are off-limits to the public. Half an hour later, he returns, my request slip in hand. Across the back, he has scrawled three file numbers and names: Anne Cohen, Ann Cohen, and Annie Cohen.

"Which one do you think is yours?" he asks.

I don't answer immediately. I'm mesmerized by the words he's written next to the third name.

"Annie Cohen, #280396, 4/13/40, Insane."

A week later, aided by a friendly supervisor who had agreed to expedite the search, I take the three legal-sized folders for Ann, Anne, and Annie Cohen and find a vacant desk in one of the Probate Court offices. I take a deep breath and open the thinnest one, the one marked "Annie Cohen Insane."

There's no docket sheet or index, just a dozen pages, none later than May 1940, primarily affidavits from five physicians attesting to Annie's state of mind, and a standardized "Application for Admission to Hospital of Alleged Insane Person," dated the 12th day of April 1940 and signed in a shaky hand by "Mrs. Tillie Cohen."

My grandmother's petition consists of a single page, but it speaks volumes about the process. It provides four lines for recounting the facts of Annie's alleged insanity, less than the space devoted to the section for the required signatures and notarization. Someone used a typewriter to complete the form, which means that someone helped Tillie to fill it out, because my grandmother had no access to a typewriter and no clue about how to use one. I'm not surprised that she received assistance; Evans's Routine History makes clear that the petition idea came from discussions with Dr. Bohn at Harper Hospital about Annie's increasingly bizarre behavior.

The typed words of explanation sound more like those of a medical person than a mother. "Patient imagines that someone wants to do her bodily harm. She talks to herself. She laughs and cries for no apparent reason. She cannot carry on a coherent conversation. She assumes one position for long periods."

Those thirty-six words triggered a whirlwind of legal activity, evidence of the speed built into the process once a petition had been filed. The next day, Wayne County Probate Judge Patrick K. O'Brien appointed two doctors, Benjamin W. Clark and Howard W. Peirce, to examine Annie. Three days later, a sheriff's deputy arrived at 2205 West Euclid Street to serve Annie and her father with a copy of the petition and notify them of a hearing date in May. When sheriff deputy John Marshick presented Annie with the petition, Annie insisted that she wasn't insane, according to what Mona Evans wrote in her Routine History.

Within a week, both Clark and Peirce had visited Annie to decide that question for themselves. By April 22, both had filed their reports. Like the petition, the physicians' form was short on facts and long on brevity, providing just eleven lines of space for the doctors to justify their findings, the opposite of the robust evidentiary detail I'm used to seeing in legal proceedings.

Clark used just seven of his lines to concur, in the form's preprinted words, that Annie was "actually insane" and required "care and treatment" in a mental institution. Annie, he wrote in his fifty-five-word explanation, "is an adult white girl, 21 years of age, physically deformed with an artificial right leg. She is oriented normally but has many vague fears and ideas of influences. She feels that people and things are conspiring against her and she places phantastic interpretations upon the simplest things about her. I would recommend commitment."

Peirce reached a different conclusion. "This young woman of 21 years has had an inferior complex due to a deformed (shortened) leg," he wrote. After amputation, she "has had difficulty getting a proper fitting wooden leg and has had difficulty learning to walk with it. She has also been unable to procure employment. Although she finished the ninth grade, she was slow in school and a mental test in November 1937 gave her age as 5 years, 11 months. Since being picked up by a man last Nov., she has been very nervous, has crying and screaming spells, disturbing the neighbors. Parents say she is afraid to be left alone." At this point, he ran over his allotted space, so he scrawled his last and perhaps most important sentence in between the lines of the next section: "While this girl is feeble-minded and extremely nervous, I do not believe her actually insane."

"Since being picked up by a man last Nov." Why did Peirce treat the alleged assault as fact? Did he have other information not contained in the Routine History? Or had Annie told him about the assault during his examination? And why did Peirce describe her as having a mental age of 5 years, 11 months, at age 18? Nowhere had I seen that specific test result before. That would be considered, then and now, severe retardation. Was it accurate? Mona Evans had noted Annie's "poor intelligence" and her difficulty in

school, but Evans had also described Annie's desire for a job and the independence that came with it, as well as her fears that she would never get one. Did that sort of insight, that level of sophistication about how the world works, square with a mental age equivalent to kindergarten or first grade?

To underscore his unambiguous view of Annie's mental state, Peirce penned the word "not" in two places, modifying the form to state that Annie "is NOT actually insane," and that her condition "is such as NOT to require care and treatment in an institution." Only then did it strike me: The form *presumed* insanity. This was the usual presumption turned inside out—insane until proven otherwise.

Peirce's contrary conclusion temporarily derailed the fast-moving process. Michigan law required two certifications of insanity before commitment to an institution, so until a third physician could examine Annie, the case was stuck in limbo. But Annie and her family weren't in limbo, the documents suggest; they were still in their nightmare on Euclid Street, where Annie's fears and paranoia, her screaming and crying, were driving the family crazy.

Sometime over the next four days, between Peirce's examination of Annie on April 20 and the morning of April 25, something must have happened, perhaps something dramatic, to change that. The scene shifted from Euclid Street to Detroit's Receiving Hospital, a downtown facility that served, in those days, as the city's first option for emergency psychiatric care and the place where police would take someone behaving erratically. There, on April 25, under court order from Judge O'Brien, two more physicians examined Annie.

Annie's file doesn't say how she ended up at Receiving, but when Dr. David Leach and Dr. Ivan Berlien arrived to evaluate Annie, they had a different mission than Clark and Peirce. Their job was to decide whether Annie needed to be confined immediately, on what the law called a "temporary detention"; if they concurred that she was insane and in need of treatment right away, then she would be transferred to Eloise and remain there, pending the outcome of her case. For the moment, the disagreement between Clark and Peirce about Annie's sanity had no bearing on her status.

Leach and Berlien had no such dispute, and no legal obligation to explain their unanimity. The temporary detention form they signed, certifying Annie's insanity, didn't even offer a space to explain their conclusions. Later that day, O'Brien ordered that "Annie Cohen be removed to and restrained in Eloise Hospital" to await the examination of yet another physician, Wayne County Court psychiatrist Peter E. Bolewicki, appointed by O'Brien to resolve the Clark-Peirce stalemate.

By the time Bolewicki met with Annie on May 13, she had been at Eloise for eighteen days, away from her family and the tense atmosphere on Euclid Street. On May 3, Mona Evans had interviewed Tillie at the Eloise Parole Clinic, and the "poorly dressed, middle-aged Jewish woman" with the "whiny, complaining voice" had provided Evans with information for her report—which Evans was still writing when Bolewicki had his session with Annie, so he couldn't have seen it.

Given the stakes, Bolewicki's report seems most notable for its hedged observations. Unlike Clark, Bolewicki pointed to no particular symptom or behavior to justify a finding of insanity. If he saw any evidence of the fears that Tillie cited in her petition or the paranoia described in Clark's report, he took no note of it. He suggested that she suffered from depression, but on balance, his evaluation seems as positive as it does negative.

Annie, he wrote, "is a fairly well developed young lady about 21 years old. She appears somewhat moody and self-centered. She is fairly well-oriented as to time, place and person. But she does not take an active interest in life. She is now at Eloise Hospital and wants to get well here. She likes to live by herself and shuns company. She does not care to mingle socially. At times, her imagination works faster than her mind. Her calculations are fair."

Moodiness and shunning company? Imagination working faster than her mind? That describes about a half dozen people I know.

Bolewicki's recommendation? "A little treatment in an institution may help her somewhat."

A little treatment? Might help her somewhat? What would Bolewicki think if he knew that on the basis of that tentative judgment, Annie would spend the next thirty-one years as a resident of Eloise?

I'm also puzzled by what's not in the file: There's no final order from O'Brien, no piece of paper changing Annie's status from temporary to permanent, and no transcript or summary of what was said at her hearing—in fact, nothing to show that a hearing took place at all, or that O'Brien had committed her permanently. There is only a cryptic notation on the outside of the original petition that says "Eloise or Ypsi Public" (a reference to the state-run hospital in Ypsilanti), along with O'Brien's initials and the faint stamp of a date, "June 12, 1940."

It strikes me as strange that the paper trail ends there. Wouldn't Annie's case have gone back to the court at some point? Is it really possible that she spent three decades at Eloise with no outside review of her status, not even a report about whether the "little treatment" recommended by Bolewicki had done her any good?

I grab the other two folders, one dated 1944 and the other 1946, thinking they must be continuations of Annie's original case. But the folders have nothing to do with Annie; instead, they offer a glimpse into the lives of two other troubled women with their own stories and journeys through the probate court system. No, what I'm seeing, according to the probate court staff, is Annie's complete file.

I didn't have any doubt, even after my visit at the probate court, that Annie was severely ill. The Routine History, and Tillie's description of Annie's behavior—screaming all night, waiting on the curb for an hour before crossing the street, refusing to eat or bathe, asking what sort of casket Tillie intended to buy for her—had persuaded me of that. But I was having a hard time getting my head around the notion of insanity, and the vastly different views of Clark, Peirce, and Bolewicki. I'm living in 2006, and Annie was living in 1940, and I need to understand better how her doctors saw her in their time, with their understanding of mental illness. Whether she displayed symptoms of paranoia or depression or schizophrenia, was she truly insane? What did the word mean?

Whatever insanity meant to me, that wasn't the meaning that mattered. Like most legal proceedings, the court case that sent Annie to Eloise would not turn on a layman's understanding. Michigan's rules about insanity had evolved from a set of laws and court rulings going back to the nineteenth century, and that record shows that in calibrating this particular scale of justice, the state legislature put a heavy finger on the side of the courts, the medical profession, the asylum, and the family.

Under the law in effect in 1940, "The father, mother, husband, wife, brother, sister, child, or guardian" could petition the court to have a family member declared insane, but the legislature didn't stop there. It specifically allowed a sheriff, a superintendent of the poor, a "county agent," or anyone that a judge deemed a "proper person to make such a petition" to come before the court and swear that a fellow citizen was "mentally defective"—insane, or "feeble-minded," or epileptic—and needed to be confined in an institution. Presented with such a petition, the judge's course of action was clear: The law required the appointment of two "reputable physicians," who did not need to be psychiatrists or neurologists, to do separate examinations. The judge then had to hold a hearing and collect evidence—"take proofs," as the law put it—but the patient could be prevented from attending the hearing, had no right to a lawyer, and no opportunity for remaining at home while appealing a judge's ruling (not that the law mentioned anything about a right of appeal or how an appeal might be made).

As if the courts and doctors didn't have enough power, the Michigan Supreme Court ruled in several cases during the 1930s that some judges were skipping the part of the law that called for the taking of evidence, and were relying instead almost entirely on the two physicians' findings. After several scoldings from the high court, the legislature stressed in a 1937 revision of the law that judges had to base their decision on facts and not opinions. But the procedures themselves remained much as before, and therefore, so did the outcomes. In essence, if both physicians certified someone as "actually insane," then most judges would take the next step prescribed by the law and "immediately issue an order for his admission to the proper hospital, home or institution." Worse, once the judge had issued that order, patients remained insane in the law's eyes until another pair of physicians, also appointed by the court, had certified their return to sanity.

If the process seemed more in keeping with a criminal proceeding than a medical emergency, that was no accident. The law still reflected concepts of insanity from the nineteenth century, concepts that Eloise and other hospitals no longer embraced. In 1940 legal parlance, the patients were still the "accused" in court, they were "inmates" at the mental hospital, and they were "paroled" on discharge. Today, the pendulum has swung in the other direction, with patient rights so strong that someone who is mentally ill—and whose judgment is impaired—can often refuse treatment altogether. But at the time of Annie's admission to Eloise, someone charged with a crime in Michigan had more rights than someone alleged to be insane. Not even God, I thought as I read through the law and the court rulings, could help a patient who protested to the judge that such a system was, so to speak, insane.

On a pleasant spring morning, I make a house call. Sandra Peppercorn Ellison, a therapist in suburban Detroit and a friend of my wife's cousin, is expecting me. As part of my quest to better understand what happened to Annie and my family in April 1940, I've decided to consult a variety of psychiatrists and therapists and ask them to help me interpret what I find as I go along. My first consultation is with Sandy, a small, dark-haired woman in her mid-sixties, whose bright eyes and round face give her an elfin look that only temporarily masks her intense curiosity and direct questions.

I had given her a copy of Annie's records, including the Routine History. After setting a cup of tea in front of me, she dives right in. "Some of my thoughts might be upsetting," she says. "I just wanted you to know before I start." I urge her to go on, but I can feel my throat tighten a bit.

She points to a sentence in the Evans report that I hardly remembered, even though I had thought I knew almost every word by heart: "Annie suffered with severe constipation all her life and had to take medicine constantly for it." I knew that Annie's constipation was one reason for her frequent visits to the Harper Hospital clinic, but I didn't attach any particular significance to it. Sandy, however, thinks it might explain a lot. For a teenager, she suggests, going to a hospital clinic for enemas and other invasive treatments can be profoundly upsetting. She speculates that Annie sexualized these procedures, and that she may have found them both disturbing and pleasurable. "It's one thing when you're small, and your parents are doing the enema at home," she says. "But when you're a teenager, and it's a stranger . . ." Her voice trails off.

"If the sexual assault happened, what effect do you think it had?" I ask.

"That's hard to say," she says. "It could have been profound, but I wouldn't describe it as the trigger. It was just one more thing, out of so much that went wrong for her. She had no personal boundaries by that time; starting with her leg, then the constipation, then the amputation, this was a girl who was poked and prodded almost from birth. She was treated more as a specimen than a human being."

In other words, even if no sexual assault occurred, this was a woman whose personal space was violated constantly.

"What about the final diagnosis, undifferentiated schizophrenia?" I ask, pointing to that phrase in the 1972 document. "What does that mean?"

"It's a catch-all phrase," Sandy says. "In 1972, and in 1940. It means they don't know exactly what to call her condition." Sandy is skeptical that Annie was schizophrenic, at least at the time of her admission, and she's certain that if the twenty-one-year-old Annie were alive today, no one would diagnose her as schizophrenic. The definition, she says, has gotten narrower as our understanding of schizophrenia has improved.

Nor, Sandy says, would anyone today suggest confining Annie to a hospital. Not only do today's laws make it difficult to commit a patient who insists she isn't insane but, Sandy points out, there are a range of treatments to try before taking such a drastic step, as well as community-based residential programs where Annie could live while learning a skill that might allow her to achieve some measure of the independence she craved.

I write a note to myself, and underline it: "Born at the wrong time."

"What do you think about Annie's level of retardation?" I ask. "What would have led Bohn to think that Annie belonged at Lapeer, an institution for the 'feeble-minded'?"

Sandy shakes her head, vigorously. "I don't think Annie was that retarded. She probably had a low IQ, maybe 80—the classic 'slow' learner. But she could read, and she seemed to be able to carry on conversations."

Now it's Sandy's turn. "Why are you doing this?" she says. "What are you trying to learn?" I give her my usual journalistic answers—fascinating detective story, unknown history of thousands of mentally ill patients, the challenge of finding Mom's friends from long ago, figuring out why Mom had clung so hard to the secret.

"That's what you're *thinking*," she says, stressing the last word and fix-ing her bright eyes on me. "What are you *feeling*?"

She's in full therapist mode, but I don't mind—it's a question I should be able to answer. I've asked myself similar questions, not so much what I'm feeling, but why do I want to make this journey, why is it important to me, not just as a journalist (that seems clear enough), but as a son? Family and friends had warned me that I was likely to find out things that I might prefer not to know, that it could upset the family equilibrium, that no one emerges unscathed from disturbing the ghosts in the family attic. Yet I push on. Why? Sandy's the first person to quiz me about this directly, and I'm interested in my spontaneous answer.

I tell Sandy that I want to understand how the secret affected Mom, whether it helped explain why she seemed so needy in the waning years of her life, why she had to be constantly reassured that we loved her and wouldn't abandon her. "It was sad that she couldn't reveal her secret. It might have brought me closer to her," I say. "Instead, I found her neediness in those last years annoying, so I put more distance between us."

Sandy doesn't say anything, the therapist waiting for me to go on. I sense that she thinks I'm ducking her question, that I'm talking more about Mom than myself. *What am I feeling?* I try again.

I find myself talking about pain, the pain that Mom endured in the last years of her life, both emotional and physical: her hospitalization for de-pression in 1995; her broken pelvis from the fall at the family wedding; her agonizing and lengthy recuperation at the Seattle rehabilitation center; her decline once she returned home. I know it's silly, I tell Sandy, but I feel guilty because I was the one who made it possible for Mom to attend the wedding. I had brushed aside her excuses about how she didn't feel well enough to go, I had flown to Detroit and rented a car to escort her to the airport, I had made all the arrangements so that all she had to do was pack her suitcase and get on the plane. "I know it's not my fault," I say, "but if I hadn't interfered . . ."

I describe the night I spent in the Seattle ER, with Mom screaming in pain as I coaxed her to hold still for an MRI, and I feel my voice catch. "I'll talk when my tears stop," I say, partly to let Sandy know that I'm not embar-rassed to show my emotions.

She doesn't try to comfort me. Instead, the therapy session in full swing, she pushes me. "I think you have a lot of pain, too," she says. "I think you feel a lot of pain about your mom."

I consider this. I'm conscious, as I wrestle with the implications of what she's saying, that I don't believe that the project is my way of dealing with that pain. It's more complicated than that—isn't it?—and I can't separate my motivations, as a journalist, as a writer, as a son, into nice, neat packages. Finally, I say, "I feel pain *for* my mom—her loneliness after my dad died, her neediness, her guilt about Annie."

Sandy picks up on the last part. "I'm sure your mom was suffering from depression for a very long time," she says, "and having a psychiatrist tell her in 1995 that she needed hospitalization, even for a short stay, undoubtedly scared the hell out of her, given what she knew about Annie."

I nod, remembering that day in 1995, remembering Mom pleading with me to take her home, remembering my guilt about leaving her there.

"That day at the hospital was awful," I say. "I think that this"—my pursuit of the secret, and trying to discover my mother's reasons for creating it and keeping it—"is helping me to put that day in its place."

Copies of Annie's court file in hand, I knock on the door of Ed Missavage's house, eager to show my latest find to the former Eloise psychiatrist. The house is a split-level, like so many others built in the 1950s and 1960s in the northern suburbs where Missavage lives, but that's where the similarity ends. It's a dramatic glass-walled fort that looks like it belongs in Miami or California or an architectural seminar on modern design. But I can see evidence of wear and tear, as well as Detroit's wet weather; years of condensation has left its mark here and there, and from the inside, mist on the glass often obscures a clear view of the lush terrain surrounding the house. Missavage's wife's death in 1999 left him to fend for himself, and he admits to waging a losing battle against the accumulating clutter of daily life.

Time has taken its toll on Missavage as well, or at least on his body. He moves slowly, his lungs damaged by years of smoking and his legs swollen from circulation problems, and he shuffles more than walks. But his large kitchen table suggests no slowing of his voracious appetite for research and reading; the stacks of papers and file folders leave no place to put the cup of coffee he graciously offers me.

He has promised me some ideas, and he makes good on his pledge. He's been calling around to find out how I can get the rest of Annie's medical records, and he says there's a simpler route than I've been led to believe. As Annie's next of kin, I could open an estate in her name, and obtain something called a Letter of Authority from the Probate Court that entitles me to see her medical records. I'm dubious—why hadn't anyone told me this back in 2000?—but I'm thrilled to hear that there's another door to try. I leave him with copies of Annie's court file, which he agrees to look over.

The next day, back at the Probate Court to pursue Missavage's suggestion, I discover a hitch. Michigan law does not consider me to be next of kin. That title still belongs to Mom, even though she's deceased. I'm astonished, but a Probate Court examiner patiently explains that because Mom outlived Annie and was the lone surviving relative from the immediate family, she's the next of kin in the law's eyes—and with Mom dead, Mom's estate has inherited the next-of-kin title.

Even from her grave, Mom still controls access to the secret.

Discouraged, I get ready to leave, but the examiner, a woman in a blue pin-striped suit, is thinking out loud. "There might be another way," she says. She tells me that as Mom's next of kin, I could open an estate for her, and if my brothers consent, I could have myself declared Mom's personal representative, which would give me the power to act in Mom's name. Then, armed with that authority, I could open an estate for Annie—thirty-four years after her death—and this would entitle me, as Annie's legal representative, to seek her medical records.

It's a double-bank shot, with no guarantees, but it couldn't help but improve my legitimacy in the eyes of Michigan's mental health system. I'd have two Letters of Authority, signed by judges, giving me certain rights on behalf of both Mom and Annie. My head is spinning. What am I getting myself into? Two estates? Two appointments as personal representative? It's so complex, so legal, so *Bleak House.*

But in a way, I'm glad for the complications and even the formality of getting my brothers' consent. Nothing focuses the mind like a legal document. It would give me a reason to talk with them in greater depth about what I was doing, and it would give them the chance to object if they wanted to. I know that Jeff's more fascinated than concerned, but that Mike still has some misgivings. Later that week, I call him. We have a somewhat awkward conversation, with both of us trying hard to respect each other's point of view, but eventually, we make our way to the heart of the matter.

Mike tells me that he's fine with signing the waiver, but he doesn't really understand my quest. "I don't see the point in digging this up," Mike says. "It's done with. We can't stand in their shoes."

"But that's what is fascinating for me," I say. "I want to understand what they did, and why, and how it affected them."

He's not persuaded. "I wouldn't do what you're doing," he says, "but this is your project, so I'm glad to sign the waiver."

I ask him about his misgivings. "I'm not worried about what you might write," he says. "I'm a little concerned that you might find out things that will be painful for you." I tell him I'm willing to take that risk.

Even though the conversation verges on uncomfortable at times, I'm delighted—because we're talking about the issues, not avoiding them. We're engaging, not concealing. We're not Mom and Annie.

A week later, signed waivers arrive from Mike and Jeff. A few weeks after that, I open the estates and have the Letters of Authority in hand. Immediately, I make two inquiries about how to request Annie's records, one at Wayne County for the Eloise files and one with the State of Michigan for her Northville stay. I'm pessimistic about Northville in particular; when the hospital closed in 2003, state law dictated the destruction of all patient records older than twenty years. But I want to know for sure.

And now that I am Mom's representative, I can also seek access to her medical records, and find out whether she had told her secret to any of her other doctors—and if so, what she might have said.

Several months later, I receive an unexpected gift from Jamie Soliman, a Wayne County Probate Court employee who had gone out of her way to help me navigate the system there. I had asked Jamie, whose curiosity and enthusiasm make her a valued species in the bureaucratic jungle, if she could gather all the involuntary commitment cases from April 1940, so that I could get a sense of how the process worked, not just in Annie's case but in general. When I arrive to review the files, she tells me excitedly, "I've found something I think you'll be interested in."

She hands me a letter about Annie, signed by Eloise superintendent Thomas K. Gruber and sent to the Probate Court in April 1940. Jamie had discovered it, misfiled, in another case folder from that same week. In the letter, Gruber invoked his authority, under Michigan law, to keep Annie from attending the hearing on her sanity—a power given to mental hospital superintendents, in a spirit of paternalistic concern, to protect severely impaired patients from a process that might make their condition worse.

"In the matter of Annie Cohen, a patient in Eloise Hospital under a temporary order issued by your court, alleging that this individual is insane," Gruber's letter began, "I hereby certify that it is improper and unsafe for the above mentioned patient to appear in your Court at the time of the hearing regarding the alleged mental disease."

The document itself is more telling than Gruber's actual words. It's a form letter, with "Annie Cohen" typed in where the name should go. When I look at the half dozen other involuntary commitment cases that Jamie had collected for me, I find three other Gruber form letters, all identical except for the name of the patient. Apparently, it was routine practice to keep Eloise patients from attending their own hearings.

Gruber cited no other information to support his immediate declaration about Annie's condition, so there's no way to know why Annie's doctors believed that it would be "unsafe" for her to go. Gruber's letter was dated April 27, 1940, the day after Annie's admission to Eloise. Within twenty-four hours of her arrival, with her hearing date still two weeks or more away, Gruber or his staff had already decided that she would be too sick to attend. Did anyone at Eloise have any second thoughts after Bolewicki, two weeks later, found Annie to be "fairly well oriented as to time, place and person" and found "her calculations to be fair"? Had the psychiatrist treating Annie even seen Bolewicki's certification?

Somehow, after everything I had read, it seems safe to say that the system wasn't geared to either reconsideration or appeal. The court had given Annie her day in court, even if she wasn't there to witness it. From now on, the doctors and staff at Eloise would decide Annie's future.

Welcome to Eloise

"In the practice of medicine, whatever the branch may be, there is no better teacher than that form of experience usually called Hind Sight."

—Eloise psychiatrist Milton Erickson, in a speech to doctors
in training at the hospital, April 24, 1940.
Two days later, Annie is admitted.

On the cool, clear morning of April 26, 1940, armed with the temporary detention order that Judge Patrick O'Brien had signed the day before, Wayne County deputy sheriff John McLean arrived at Detroit's Receiving Hospital to take Annie from the life she knew into a life unknown. What was she thinking during the fifteen-mile drive to Eloise? Did she even look up to see where she was heading when the gatehouse attendant waved them through the finely wrought iron gates with "Eloise" in the arched grillwork at the top? Whatever was going through her head, it's safe to say that she had no idea her temporary commitment to this unfamiliar place would never end. How could she? Everything had happened so fast. It had been only fourteen days since her mother had signed the petition that had led, unavoidably, to this moment.

The attendant probably paid little attention to the bewildered young woman, one day shy of her twenty-first birthday, as she passed him on her way to D Building, the starting point for all admissions to Eloise. Two or three new patients arrived almost every day, often in the company of a sheriff's deputy; three times a day, departing patients—or parolees, as they were still known—went through the gates and back into the outside world. To call Eloise a busy place in 1940 was to engage in gross understatement; it was as large as a small city, with more than ten thousand people—patients and police officers, doctors and custodians, nurses and engineers, farmers and firefighters, butchers and bakers. For several dozen employees, Eloise was both home and office; they lived on the grounds, either alone or with their families.

The ancient Greeks called ten thousand a myriad, and feeding this particular myriad amounted to a feat of epic proportions. Unlike today's hospitals, Eloise produced a large quantity of its food, from field to table. In 1940, Eloise's herd of cows sent more than 120,000 gallons of milk to Eloise's state-of-the-art pasteurizing plant; Eloise's slaughterhouse furnished 110,000 pounds of pork, 4,000 pounds of beef, and 2,500 pounds of veal to Eloise's kitchens; Eloise's cannery processed 65 tons of fruits and vegetables a month during the growing season; Eloise's new ovens turned out 1,800 loaves of bread an hour, powered by electricity from the dynamos in Eloise's own power plant.

All these enterprises combined to produce a level of noise that one employee would describe to me, years later, as a kind of constant hum, like the idling motor of a car. Early in the morning, the aroma of fresh bread would lure the Eloise employees' children to the bakery, where Mr. Prosser, the baker, might reward them with a treat. Ed Missavage lived in N Building, near the dairy, and he remembers the pungent odors of hay, manure, and silage wafting through the large apartment that he and his wife (a psychiatrist he met at the hospital) shared the summer after their marriage in 1950.

Like any small city, work and play went on simultaneously. During the day, at any given moment somewhere on the vast grounds, Eloise's more capable patients might be repairing drapes in the sewing room, or folding sheets in the huge laundry room, or reading a book in the Eloise branch of the Wayne County Library system, or watching a movie in the new audito-

rium, or attending one of the group therapy sessions that noted Eloise psychiatrist Ira Altshuler had started three years before, or undergoing the
grueling ordeal of insulin shock, prematurely described in a 1937 Eloise
annual report as a "remarkable new treatment" for schizophrenia. (Eventually, Eloise and other psychiatric hospitals would abandon insulin shock—
a labor-intensive therapy that required a large commitment of staff to make
sure the convulsions didn't send patients from temporary comas into ir-
reversible ones—as too expensive and too erratic in its effectiveness.)

Many patients, unable or unwilling to engage in the world around them,
rarely strayed far from their ward. Like Annie, the vast majority had been
committed involuntarily, and if they wanted to leave—and certainly some
did—they were not free to go, not until their doctors said so. Locked doors
kept them from wandering off the wards without permission, while inside
those doors, privacy was next to impossible. A photograph of a female unit
from the time shows four rows of 12 beds each, not even a few feet apart, in
the "open" style of the era. With every bed occupied, the sheer mass of humanity generated a buzz that faded only when the lights went out, and
sometimes not even then.

More aggressive patients lived in seclusion rooms on the ground floor
of several buildings, while the "Red Star" ward in N Building housed the
hospital's most dangerous patients, about sixty or so designated as sexual
deviants or homicidal. Superintendent Gruber had created this special segregated ward in response to a public outcry over the horrifying murder of
an eleven-year-old girl. Her killer had a previous record of attacking young
girls; twice, after police had arrested him, he was sent "for observation" to
Ohio's institution for the criminally insane and then released. In 1938, as
the legislature debated a new "criminal psychopathics" law, Gruber directed the hospital staff to stamp any such patient's records with a large red
star, "designed to alert hospital personnel to the need for special vigilance
and maximum security measures," in the words of one scholarly study.

All this activity swirled around Annie, but from her vantage point in D
Building, she saw little of it. Within a month or two, she would be assigned to
one of the eight buildings that housed female psychiatric patients, but for the
time being, with her state of mind in question and her legal status unsettled,
she would stay on D5, the female admissions ward, giving the psychiatric and
social work staffs ample opportunity to evaluate their new patient.

This is where she first saw Mona Evans and where, on May 13, she would meet with Peter Bolewicki, the psychiatrist assigned by Judge O'Brien to provide the tie-breaking opinion in her case. Until Bolewicki delivered, she was merely a temporary Eloise resident, patient number 17205, the latest in a line that stretched back to a previous century and a history that makes the evolution of Eloise all the more remarkable.

Her name was Bridget Hughes, but everyone knew her as Biddy, and on March 22, 1841, she became patient number 1, the first person registered as a "crazy person" on the rolls of Wayne County's poorhouse and thus the first officially insane person in the young state of Michigan, admitted to the union only four years before.

Biddy was anything but fortunate to be there. Alvin Clark's 1982 official history describes the second Wayne County poorhouse as "the only excuse for an asylum in the State of Michigan . . . In those days, the only division of the patients was by sex. Otherwise, babies, children, old men, blind people, the idiotic, the rational and the crazy were all huddled together in a miscellaneous unit. The Keeper and his wife, assisted by two or three attendants, often used chains to segregate the 'crazies' from the rational people—the only recourse left to them."

Perhaps the best thing that could be said about the second County House is that it wasn't the first. The first County House, a rickety two-story wooden structure on farmland a few miles beyond the city's northeast boundaries, began operation in January 1833; within a year, it "had become almost uninhabitable and the inmates greatly neglected," according to Clark's history. On March 4, 1834, under pressure from prominent citizens and a Catholic relief organization, the county's board of supervisors created a new authority with the apt, if paternalistic, name, the Superintendents of the Poor, to take over the operation and its fifty or so "inmates."

By 1838, the Superintendents were searching for a site to build a new and larger poorhouse, and Superintendent Ammon Brown urged them to consider land near his home in rural Nankin Township, nearly a day's ride from the city center, on the main stagecoach route between Detroit and Chicago. In early 1839, the Superintendents agreed, buying 280 acres and the Black Horse Tavern, a log cabin on the property that served travelers on the Chicago Road. The single-story tavern became the keeper's quarters, while the inmates of the first County House found themselves in a hastily constructed addition.

But not all the inmates—in fact, not even most of them.

"Records show that 35 persons were transferred," Clark's history reported, "while 111 refused to go to that 'awful wilderness.'"

The Superintendents made no pretense that they were doing anything for the insane in "that awful wilderness" other than housing them. As early as 1843, the Superintendents implored the state legislature to create an asylum exclusively for the insane, a call that other states, particularly in the East, were hearing as well. The 1848 legislature finally agreed, but it took another ten years for the first state asylum to open its doors in Kalamazoo, in the far western part of the state.

This was the dawn of the so-called "golden age" of asylums, the result of a reform movement that had its roots in the pioneering efforts of Dorothea Dix. Horrified by the conditions in the poorhouses and jails of Massachusetts, Dix campaigned to remove the mentally ill from their chains and cells. Other reformers expanded on Dix's work, pushing for new institutions in bucolic settings, away from the unhealthy influences of urban life. Fresh air was their mantra, and asylum was their concept, a place of peaceful refuge where the mentally ill might regain their balance.

The superintendents of these new institutions saw themselves as engaged in a more enlightened enterprise than their predecessors. In 1844, thirteen of them came together in Philadelphia to form an organization of mutual support. They were a distinguished group, all physicians and all dedicated to the idea that sharing their experiences would lead to improvements in treatment. They chose an unwieldy but descriptive name, the Association of Medical Superintendents of American Institutions for the Insane (forerunner of today's American Psychiatric Association), and the inclusion of "Medical" was no accident. They wanted to emphasize that their institutions had nothing to do with the poorhouses of the past, that only treatment rooted in medical and scientific principles had any chance of helping those suffering from these mysterious disorders of the brain.

At first, only asylum superintendents could join, which meant that
Michigan, which had no asylum until 1858, had no representative. But the
association had a significant impact on Michigan nonetheless; the Kalamazoo asylum was built to the specifications of the Kirkbride plan, named for
one of the association's thirteen founders. Thomas Kirkbride, a Philadelphia physician and superintendent of the Pennsylvania Hospital for the
Insane, believed so strongly in the curative powers of fresh air and sunlight
that, in 1853, he incorporated those principles into a building design that
served for the rest of the nineteenth century as the model for the public
asylum. Dozens of Kirkbride-influenced buildings, including some architectural showpieces with extensive grounds, sprouted up on farmland
throughout the United States. Among them was the Western Michigan Asylum for the Insane, in Kalamazoo.

Anticipating that the population of insane people would grow, Kirkbride and his colleagues at the association sought to limit the size of new
asylums, arguing steadfastly for a ceiling of 250 residents. But in 1866, after
New York expanded the capacity at the State Lunatic Asylum in Utica to
six hundred, the association's board adopted that larger number as its
standard—only to look on in dismay three years later, when New York, determined to empty its dreadful county poorhouses, opened the fifteen-
hundred-bed Willard Asylum for the Insane. It would not be the last time
that one humane goal would require the sacrifice of another in the pursuit
of better mental health treatment.

The Kalamazoo asylum, while adhering to the Kirkbride plan, was too
distant and too small to do Wayne County and Detroit much good. Not only
was the facility on the other side of the state—largely inaccessible in that
pre-automobile era—but the asylum keepers also restricted admission to a
limited number of "curable" patients. There was no place in the Kalamazoo
asylum for a long-term resident like Biddy Hughes. In 1868, the Superintendents of the Poor decided that Wayne County had no choice but to
construct an asylum of its own. As Clark put it in his 1982 Eloise history, "If
the State of Michigan had provided ample quarters for the insane at the
Michigan Asylum in Kalamazoo, the Wayne County Asylum would never
have been built." But built it was, and Wayne County would stay in the asylum business for the next 111 years, long past the time when those duties
had become a state responsibility nearly everywhere else in the country.

. . .

The patient records from those 111 years, at least the ones that still exist, reside today in a Detroit warehouse, managed by a company called Iron Mountain. As I began my reporting in 2006, Iron Mountain seemed as impregnable as Fort Knox. On a cool spring day, I take a ride to the public entrance to the fortress, which is not the warehouse itself, but a nondescript county building where Patricia Waterman has her office.

Waterman is the Wayne County Department of Health's record information management consultant, and the gateway to the Eloise records. She looks at my Letters of Authority and immediately we're at odds. She challenges the letter, telling me that by putting "Obtain medical records" under the "Restrictions/Limitations" section, the court has restricted me from obtaining medical records. She says she wants to refer the matter to the department's lawyer.

"Don't do that, please," I say. "There's no need to get into a legal battle." If an ambiguity exists, I say—and for the sake of clearing it up, I'm happy to concede that one does—why not just call the Probate Court for clarification?

But try as I might, I can't persuade her to make the call. If I had to read her mind, I would say that she doesn't want to get backed into a corner from which she can't escape. Would she be willing to talk with someone at the court, if I can reach someone? She hedges, but doesn't say no.

I make the call, and hand Waterman my cell phone. She takes it and soon an agreement is struck: The court will fax over a new letter confirming and clarifying my authority to seek medical records. Meanwhile, I fill out the necessary paperwork asking to see Annie's file, and Waterman says my request will be reviewed. In a month or so, I'll get a letter informing me of the department's decision.

Eager to leave as good an impression as I can, I tell her a bit about my detective work, but it's not helping. Trying to determine how long it might take to retrieve any existing records, I ask her about the warehouse's location. "I can't tell you that," she says. Then, confirming my fears about what she thinks of me, she interjects, "I hope you're not planning to go there."

Right, I think to myself. I'm going to break into the warehouse, *Mission Impossible*–style, to find one patient's file out of, what, forty thousand? Fifty thousand? More?

But I don't say that, of course. "No," I say politely, "I was just curious. Please let me know as soon as you can if you have the records."

The newly built asylum that became home, in 1868, to Biddy Hughes and her fellow inmates—somewhere between sixty and seventy, as best as I can determine from available records—was no Kirkbride model. The two-story structure was made of brick rather than wood, but the keepers' philosophy about the insane hadn't changed much from the poorhouse days, as proved by the shackles built into the new asylum's walls. The main purpose was to keep the insane segregated, not to give them a better life or make Dorothea Dix, Thomas Kirkbride, and their fellow reformers proud.

The Wayne County asylum didn't take long to achieve the same dark reputation as the poorhouse. An 1878 editorial in the *Detroit Lancet*, a medical journal, castigated the asylum for "sickening circumstances of inhumanity." But change was on the way, in part because articles like the one in the *Lancet* reflected a growing discontent in the medical community with the asylum system, nationally as well as locally. In 1881, the Superintendents of the Poor voted to require the asylum's keeper to have a medical college degree; soon after, the first of those professionally certified physicians, Ebenezer O. Bennett, "permanently removed the chains, shackles and dim cells in which the patients had been housed," according to the 1982 history.

By the time Biddy Hughes died in 1895, after fifty-four years as a ward of the county, the Wayne County asylum had grown to more than a dozen buildings, including an infirmary, a power plant, an icehouse, and a new administrative headquarters for Superintendent Bennett and his staff. This modest building boom, however, would soon be dwarfed by the remarkable transformation that would turn the modest-sized asylum into a leviathan-sized complex with too many patients and too few places to put them.

In late April, a week after my visit to Patricia Waterman's office, a form letter arrives at my house, informing me that my request cannot be processed because "we find no record of the above named patient receiving treatment at this institution for the date(s) requested." I'm floored. I realize that it's just bureaucratese for "we can't find any records," but somehow, the form letter's wording seems appropriate. Not only was Annie a secret, but the county that ran the institution where she lived for thirty-one years had no official record that she was ever there. I could find out more about Bridget Hughes than I could find out about Annie Cohen.

By the end of the nineteenth century, asylums and their superintendents were under attack from inside and out, and in a very public way that would have a profound effect on the evolution of mental health treatment in the United States. Neurologists, members of that relatively new branch of medicine, were challenging the essence of what the superintendents were doing, accusing them of making life worse rather than better for asylum patients. The neurologists saw most mental illnesses as curable, and they saw themselves as the scientists who would discover the physical causes that would lead to those cures. They regarded the superintendents, and their asylums, as impediments to progress.

To be fair, the neurologists were competitors as well as critics. They had ambitions of their own, and one goal was to break the stranglehold that the superintendents had on treatment of the insane. The neurologists, without a place for themselves in the asylum world, had formed their own association in 1875, barring the superintendents from membership. Criticism of the asylums soon appeared in the neurologists' new publication, the *Journal of Nervous and Mental Disease*, and this "open warfare" (as one historian called it) continued until 1892, when the superintendents voted to open up their asylum association to new blood. To reflect the change, the superintendents adopted a hybrid name: the American Medico-Psychological Association.

To celebrate the new openness, the superintendents invited a leading neurologist, S. Weir Mitchell, to give the keynote speech at the association's fiftieth annual meeting in 1894. The attendees had hardly settled into their chairs in the Philadelphia ballroom when Mitchell let everyone know he had no interest in a cease-fire. "Once we spoke of asylums with respect; it is not so now," he informed the crowd. "We neurologists think you have fallen behind us, and this opinion is gaining ground outside of our own ranks, and is, in part at least, your own fault."

Mitchell was just getting warmed up. His rhetoric now turned prosecu-
torial: Where, he asked, were the asylums' scientific reports? Where was
the internal give-and-take that characterizes any scientific endeavor? "You
live alone, uncriticized, unquestioned, out of the healthy conflicts and honest rivalries which keeps us up to the mark of the fullest possible compe-
tence," he said. "The cloistral lives you lead give rise, we think, to certain
mental peculiarities. . . . One is the superstition to the effect that an asylum
is in itself curative. You hear the regret in every report that patients are not
sent soon enough, as if you had ways of curing which we have not. Upon my
word, I think asylum life is deadly to the insane."

Asylum life didn't die that day, and wouldn't die completely for another
sixty years, but it's fair to say that Mitchell's speech marked a significant
moment in mental health history, a kind of dividing line between the old
ways and the new. Over the next thirty-five years, research and science became the new buzzwords of the psychiatric profession, medical schools created departments of psychiatry, and some of their most promising graduates
joined the quest to understand the human mind. Psychiatry came out of the
asylums and directly into the American consciousness.

In 1933, as part of Eloise's one-hundredth-anniversary celebration, Eloise
superintendent Thomas Gruber put his pen to paper and offered his thoughts
about extraordinary changes that had taken place since the founding of the
first Wayne County Poor House. Gruber, a big-eared, square-jawed native
of Ohio who presided over Eloise from 1929 until his early death of a heart
attack in 1949, waxed enthusiastically about his hospital's growth, as might
be expected, but his main focus was on something bigger.

"Within the last hundred years," he wrote, "science and the useful arts
developed more than during all the preceding centuries. . . . Railroads span
the earth, palatial lake and ocean steamers sail into every port. The automobile industry has changed the mode of living. . . . Vast dams have im-
pounded hundreds of millions of gallons of water for power and irrigation.
Medicine and science have had a new birth. . . ."

For all Gruber's fervor about science's advances, however, there was
one field he did not mention at all in his exuberant report—psychiatry.
This was not false modesty. It was possible to brag at length about ad-

vances in the physical sciences; the mind, however, was still the great mystery, in many ways as much of a mystery in 1933 as it had been a hundred years before.

Freud's psychoanalytic theories, as influential as they were, had no particular relevance in the treatment of serious mental illnesses such as schizophrenia. Major changes were coming, though: By the end of the 1930s, medical research underway in Hungary, Austria, Italy, and Portugal would bring forth experimental treatments for schizophrenia, including shock therapy and lobotomies, that would alter the practice of psychiatry at nearly every mental hospital in the country for the better part of two decades, including Eloise, although not necessarily for the better. Meanwhile, Eloise psychiatrists Milton Erickson and Ira Altshuler would soon make names for themselves with less invasive treatments for lesser disturbed patients—Erickson in the field of hypnosis, and Altshuler with pioneering work in music therapy.

But in 1933, Thomas Gruber and his staff were treating their patients with essentially the same tools, with much the same outcomes, as the previous generation had. That didn't mean, of course, that nothing had changed at Eloise. A visitor to the hospital in that year would see two major differences between the asylum of the nineteenth century and its successor, and both were significant: first, the hospital's stated commitment to treating its patients humanely; second, the sheer size of its population.

The two were inextricably intertwined. Being humane, in the view of psychiatrists of this era, meant not leaving the mentally ill to languish in jail or poorhouses. It meant giving them the best treatment available, in comfortable surroundings—not just a warm bed with a roof over their heads, but in well-equipped, well-staffed facilities, with access to books, music, movies, and other diversions.

Psychiatry had become a growth industry in the early twentieth century, and the ever-larger insane asylums—they would soon lose the asylum label in favor of ones that would emphasize that medicine was now the mantra behind the asylum walls—were proof of the boom. Few institutions were booming more than Eloise. "The past 24 years have experienced an evolution so phenomenal as to be really startling," Eloise's bookkeeper, Stanislas Keenan, wrote in 1933, when he updated his 1913 history of the institution. "This expansion has not been a wish of the Board, but a compulsion."

Unlike the shabby, slapdash construction of the nineteenth-century expansions, Keenan wrote, "the buildings erected during the period out-class in every way those of earlier times. They are massive, substantial and beautiful." Even accounting for the built-in bias of the beholder, "beauti-ful" could be defended: The classic brick-and-column facades of the new buildings looked like they belonged on the cover of a catalog for a New England college, while the interiors borrowed elements from the most elegant of the grand hotels, with columns and floors of yellow Verona marble—many tons of Verona marble—that the designers had imported from Genoa, Italy.

These massive buildings matched the style and thinking of the era. They were more than residences—they were monuments, shrines to the philoso-phy that a society is judged by its treatment of its most vulnerable citizens and that this generation, unlike the last, was determined not to fail the test.

Yet at many institutions, including Eloise, comfortable surroundings could not change the uncomfortable reality that many patients would still languish for years, decades, even lifetimes, just as they had before, with no outside review of their cases, trapped in a system that would soon experi-ment with a variety of risky and questionable treatments in a desperate at-tempt to cope with the rising numbers of "inmates."

Annie's status as a temporary Eloise patient must have ended sometime after June 12, 1940, when Bolewicki filed his tie-breaking report suggest-ing that "a little treatment might help her somewhat." If I could find out where she went to live among Eloise's many lettered buildings, I might be able to narrow the search for someone who knew her. Wayne County might have no surviving record of her, but surely the Census Bureau would have one.

The 1940 census took place early in April, before Annie's arrival on April 25, but she must have made it into the 1950 census. Although the ac-tual enumeration sheets remain closed until seventy-two years after the census is taken, I learn that, for a $65 fee, the Census Bureau will search for an individual family member and extract the information, once it has proof of the family relationship. I mail off my Letter of Authority, and several weeks later, I tear open an envelope to find that, yes, Annie Cohen was a resident of Eloise in 1950. But no, there's no indication of what ward she lived on, or in what building, or of any address at all.

I phone the Census Bureau's office in Indiana, and a helpful researcher says the full sheets for Eloise did not list specific buildings or ward numbers, reinforcing Annie's anonymity, her near invisibility. As far as the outside world was concerned, Annie had no fixed address. She wasn't Annie Cohen, of I or J or L building. She was a patient at a mental hospital named Eloise, and that's all the world needed to know.

Except, of course, that very few people even knew that.

Like other public institutions with roots in the almshouse and the asylum, however, Eloise remained a home for society's outcasts—not just the mentally ill and the homeless, but also those who suffered from some infirmity: the blind, the deaf, and the senile. When Gruber took over as superintendent in 1929, he reviewed a ten-year expansion plan that his predecessor had left behind and declared it inadequate. He sent a new one to the Superintendents of the Poor, calling for $12.1 million in improvements, a hefty sum in those days, equivalent to more than $150 million in today's dollars. But Gruber didn't have much choice: He was looking at Eloise's annual increase in population—a steady 10 or 11 percent—and wondering where he was going to put all these patients.

Then, in 1930, with Eloise's indigent population ballooning and welfare lines growing longer every day in Detroit, Gruber told the Superintendents that plans for a new infirmary, on the books since 1927, had to be cast aside in favor of a much larger facility. Within a few months, a new proposal emerged for a dormitory with a capacity for more than 5,000 residents and total floor space of approximately 382,000 square feet, more than twice that of the U.S. Capitol building.

This new behemoth was N Building, the latest addition to the alphabetical list of residences at Eloise, home to the infirm and the newly homeless, mostly men who would later come to be known as the POGIEs, the "Poor Old Guys in Eloise." Many were auto workers who had ended up on the streets after the Depression brought a majority of the assembly lines to a screeching halt.

In just 16 weeks during the summer and fall of 1930, construction crews of 350 worked almost around the clock to finish the first 2,600-bed phase. Despite this speed, the building couldn't be completed fast enough to take care of the need. N Building filled to capacity and beyond as soon as the last nail was hammered; with Michigan's winter temperatures regularly below freezing, beds were placed anywhere and everywhere as Eloise tried to cope with the crisis.

In 1931 and 1932, expansions doubled the number of beds as well as the size of the kitchen, which was thought at the time of completion to be the largest institutional kitchen in the country. To produce enough coffee for N Building's battalion of residents, the kitchen installed six eight-gallon urns that sent an almost continuous flow of the brew into a two-hundred-gallon reservoir. That meant a supply of 3,200 cups of coffee on hand—a staggering amount but, remarkably, not enough to go around in April 1933, when the infirmary rolls showed 7,441 patients, including 1,500 residents who were "blind, crippled or otherwise infirm" and wouldn't be leaving when the weather turned warm. That summer, and most summers during the Depression, the infirmary population routinely topped 4,000.

Inside the superintendent's office, Gruber couldn't quite believe the pace of change at his institution. In 1913, when Stanislas Keenan's first history of Eloise was published, the institution had 1,400 residents. "Now, there is almost 9,000 and during the acute Depression, over ten thousand," Gruber wrote for Keenan's 1933 update. (Gruber arrived at the 10,000 figure by adding the 4,000 psychiatric patients and the 6,000 infirmary residents.)

The workforce had expanded at an even faster pace. "The employees then numbered 140, and now there are over ten hundred," Gruber wrote. (On Gruber's handwritten manuscript, now in the Michigan State Archives, Keenan penned in the exact number of employees, 1,632, above Gruber's "ten hundred.")

Among those 1,632 were six social workers who, while small in number, represented the vanguard in Eloise's changing attitude toward the mentally ill. When the social work department opened in 1923, "the science of hospital social service was in its infancy," Clark wrote in his 1982 history. "There were very few traditions to be followed because mental hospitals up to that time had been largely custodial institutions and less interested in the patient's welfare than in keeping them removed from society. The Social Service Department helped make the transition from 'asylum' to 'hospital' due to its emphasis on the causes of the patient's illness" and personal history.

The aim was admirable, but the workload was impossible. In 1923, Eloise's mentally ill population had reached 1,700; ten years later, it had more than doubled. How could a handful of social workers delve into the personal history of that many patients? The social service department had to grow if the hospital expected it to accomplish anything, and grow it did, but never enough to keep up with the exploding psychiatric population. With nearly a thousand new admissions annually, each social worker was expected to produce detailed personal histories (like the one that Mona Evans did on Annie) on more than 130 patients each.

Gruber, as the product of the generation that had brought mental illness out of the nineteenth-century almshouses and placed it firmly into the medical arena, saw Eloise's annual increase in population as a phenomenon without end. He could be forgiven for writing in 1933 that "it is quite certain that the expansion will continue indefinitely, for as Wayne County expands, so will Eloise." He could not imagine, trapped in his time and place, that in fifty years, his institution would be emptied out, abandoned, and left to rot.

And it was unimaginable. The nation's mental hospitals had more patients than ever, partly the consequence of new definitions of what constituted a mental disorder. During the first thirty years of the new century, the number of mentally ill residents in hospitals soared from 142,000 to 365,000, an astounding 163 percent increase, far exceeding the country's population growth rate, which itself rose an impressive 65 percent (from 76 million to 125 million).

If big wasn't necessarily better, it matched the tenor of the times, as one historian noted in a 1944 retrospective, a book of essays called *One Hundred Years of American Psychiatry*, published by the American Psychiatric Association to mark the founding of its predecessor organization. "This has been the era of big things," wrote Samuel W. Hamilton, a mental health adviser with the U.S. Public Health Service. "Restraint on the size of institutions was thrown to the wind. Some able men uttered the dictum that it makes no difference how large an institution may be, that it is all just a

matter of organization. California and Illinois deliberately planned institutions for six thousand patients. New York already had one of those and
planned one for ten thousand. . . ."

Eloise's stated goal, appearing frequently in documents of the era, was to
return patients to a useful life outside the hospital; every year, Eloise paroled as many as one-third of its population. That meant the hospital was
sending about 1,200 people annually back to their homes and communities. Annie was not one of those 1,200. Why?

During one of my many interviews with Ed Missavage, I ask him for his
best guess as to why that might be. "There are a variety of factors at work
here," he says, peering at me through his oversized bifocals. "First, we would
look at her mental stability. Is she improving? Then, we would look at her
family. Do they want her home? Are they able to take care of her? Finally, we
would assess her ability to make it outside the institution on her own."

He pauses, searches among his papers for a reference work, and continues when he can't find it. "We're talking about the first few years, in the
1940s, before medication came along. Right off, there would be a question
about her mental stability, and you've got her mental retardation and her
wooden leg problems. So there's a question about whether she could make
it on the outside. Then there's her family. They don't know what to do about
her, so there's probably no pressure from them for a parole."

I look up from my note taking.

"Your family wasn't asking for her to come home, right?" he says.

Her records suggest that's probably the case. "Right, as far as I know,"
I reply.

"So from our point of view," Missavage continues, "she's a custodial
patient from the outset. She's the type we don't ever think is going home."

EIGHT

I Am Family

Previous page: *Family ties: Anna Oliwek's postwar identification card, showing her maiden name (courtesy of Anna Oliwek)*

The homework assignment seems clear enough: Do a family tree. I turn the paper sideways, and in no time at all, I've filled Dad's side with brothers and sisters, aunts and uncles, first and second cousins, more than two dozen names from Michigan and elsewhere. I've met them all at one family gathering or another, so I can jot down their names and draw the lines without asking Dad or Mom for help.

On Mom's side, though, I've reached a dead end after just three names—Mom, Bubbe, and Zayde. I've heard Mom mention an uncle, but I don't know his name or where he lives, or whether he's related to Bubbe or Zayde. And did Mom once say something about a cousin, or am I making that up?

I didn't save that flimsy family tree, and try as I might, I can't recall what happened when I attempted to fill the gaps in it—no memory of whether I asked Mom for the name of that uncle (I must have) or that cousin (did she dodge my questions?) or whether I was inquisitive enough (I can't imagine that I was) to delve into my grandparents' roots in Eastern Europe and the family they had left behind.

How old was I? I'm not sure, but eighth or ninth grade seems about right. Nevertheless, the exercise must have left its impression, because I can remember saying later to my college friends, in one of those where-does-your-family-come-from sessions, that I didn't have much family on my mother's side and that we just didn't know anything about the place where my grandparents' relatives lived in Eastern Europe.

Now, in a suburban Detroit restaurant, I reach out to hug one of those relatives, this cousin of my mother from the place called Radziwillow. I study Anna Oliwek's features, searching for a resemblance, and I'm not sure I see one. Anna is eighty-two years old, and has lived in the United States since 1949, but she has that Eastern European look that never seems to fade completely from the faces of some older immigrants, no matter how long they live in their adopted homeland or what fashions they embrace. Her broad forehead, her roundish cheeks, the continuous curve of her jaw-line, all combine to suggest that she hails from that vast expanse between the Rhine and the Volga, the only geography I can summon to mind as I kiss her remarkably unlined face. Her accented English only serves to confirm my first impression.

"I've had my hair done for you," she says. I think: *That's what Mom would have done, too.* I tell her I'm flattered, and slide into the chair next to her. She and David, her fifty-five-year-old son, are midway through dinner. On this cool April evening, I've come for coffee, maybe some dessert, and to hear, at last, Anna's story of her falling-out with my mother.

I ask how she's feeling, and she says better, although she's having some trouble with her diabetes—her blood sugar won't settle down and she's feeling a bit jittery. *That makes two of us,* I tell myself. "I haven't seen you since you were a little boy," she says. "And now, you're so big."

I smile. People say this all the time to my kids, but it's been years since someone has said it to me, and now that I've reached the solid middle age of fifty-four, I find it endearing rather than annoying. "I don't remember meeting you at all," I say. "How old was I?"

"You were so little, with that head of blond hair," she says. She's still shaking her head, amazed that, after fifty years, I've come back into her life, although that blond hair is a dark brown now, with flecks of gray.

David chimes in. "I remember going to your house. We played together." He's almost two years older than I am, so I suppose that explains why he remembers and I don't. He still has his boyish looks, with a thick head of curly, salt-and-pepper hair, the kind that I bet would draw envious glances at his high school reunions. His bushy mustache reminds me of Groucho Marx, probably because a playful smile seems part of his natural state of being.

I'm sorely tempted to stop right here and ask why I never saw either of them again, but I'm not quite ready, not until I learn a little more about this resurrected cousin of mine. "I saw you at my mother's funeral," I say, apologetically, "but I didn't know who you were, otherwise I would have said something. How did you hear about Mom's death? You weren't in touch with my mother in the years before she died, were you?"

"No," she says. "I guess I saw the notice in the paper, or somebody did."

I look at David. He shrugs. No help there.

"David told me that you came to America after the war," I say.

She nods. "Me and my husband and Bella, who was just a few years old then. Uncle brought us over. We lived in Chicago first."

"Uncle? You mean Nathan Shlien?" I'm eager to know more about this man who was living with my grandparents in 1930.

"Yes, Nathan," she says. "And that's how I met Tante Tillie and Chaim"—using the Yiddish word for aunt and my grandfather's original Yiddish name.

"*Tante* Tillie? I thought you were cousins."

"Oh, we were," Anna says, pronouncing the "w" with that slight "v" sound of Eastern Europe, so it comes out closer to "*vere*." "But that's what I always called her, Tante Tillie, because she was so much older."

Anna sighs. "And that child, that poor child. It wasn't her fault."

No going back now.

Anna pauses, and I switch on the digital voice recorder that I bought just for the interview; I'm still learning how to use it and I'm worried about the restaurant's ambient noise level, which is so loud that my own ears are having trouble hearing her. *Great*, I think—*I'm about to interview someone who has actually talked with Mom about the secret, and I'm fussing with a machine.* But the recorder's noise cancellation feature seems to be working well enough to pick out our voices amid the din, so I place it upright and give my full attention to Anna. More than two hours later, she still has it. By then, the restaurant's noise level is no longer an issue.

We're the only table left.

Stories rarely begin at the beginning, but every storyteller has to begin somewhere, and Anna chooses to start this story with shame. When I prompt her to tell me about "that poor child," as she had just called Annie, she replies: "Your mother, she was ashamed of her sister. But it wasn't the sister's fault. She was born that way."

"What was she ashamed of?" I ask.

"She was ashamed that people will find out that she had the sister."

I pursue. "How do you know that? Did my mom tell you that?"

"Her mother told me."

"You mean Tillie?"

She nods. "Tillie."

I want more than that, more than hearsay. This is the first time that I have talked with a witness to Mom's preservation and nurturing of the secret, someone who has first-hand knowledge that Mom actively took steps to keep Annie hidden, someone who can go beyond Medji's babysitting experience of overheard conversations and unasked questions. I want to know what Mom said, not Tillie.

I don't have to wait long.

"When I met your mother, she was very friendly to me, invited me to dinner and everything else," Anna says. "I come to your house." That's the house of my first eleven years, the small two-story brick bungalow on Houghton Street in Northwest Detroit that my parents bought in 1950. Sash had the upstairs, and Mike and I shared a first-floor room until Jeff came along, and Mike vacated his spot for a corner of our wood-paneled basement. Our neighborhood was one of Catholics and cops, and it remained that way long after Detroit's white flight began, largely due to the city's residency requirement for municipal employees. The suburbs were the next stop, across the northern city boundary of Eight Mile, a street name that always amused me and confused newcomers, since it's not eight miles from anywhere now other than one of the city's long-ago borders.

"When was this dinner?" I ask.

Anna can't remember the year, but she thinks it was before I was born. That would make it no later than 1952. At some point, Anna recalls, Mom took her aside for a private talk. Anna had an idea what was coming, because Tillie had already told her that Mom was keeping Annie a secret. Still, it came as a shock to hear it directly—except that in Anna's re-telling, indirect might be a better description. "She said to me, 'Anna, I would appreciate it, this subject in my house, my home, I don't want to hear it.'"

I want to shout "Subject? What subject?" But just then the waitress interrupts to offer more coffee, and when Anna picks up her narrative again, she returns to the same sentence and removes all ambiguity. "Your mother says, 'You're welcome in my house only if you do not speak about my sister.'"

This is a case history of the difficulty with reconstructing long ago events, of the intricate patterns of trouble caused by time and memory. Here I am, reinterpreting my mother's life, trying to replace the distorted picture that I grew up believing with the part that had been airbrushed out, and now I have two versions of this key moment when Mom is declaring to Anna her desire for secrecy. While I have no doubts about the crux of Anna's story—I know, after all, that Mom did keep the secret—which version comes closest to how Mom actually expressed that desire? Was she elliptical and polite, *"I would appreciate it . . . ,"* as Anna's first version suggests? Or did she issue the equivalent of an ultimatum, *"Anna, you are welcome in my house only if . . . ,"* as her second version implies? And even if Mom's exact words had been imprinted somehow in Anna's memory, what about Mom's inflection, her demeanor, her body language? Was she stern, or sad, or nervous, or demanding—None of the above? All of the above?— when she branded Annie as a taboo subject in her house?

Those nuances lie beyond my reach. I cannot wrest them, undistilled or unvarnished, from Anna's memory. Fifty years later, this is the best my cousin can do.

Whichever it was, request or ultimatum, Anna says she went along with Mom's wishes. That didn't stop her from wondering how far the secrecy extended: Mom's children and friends for sure, but what about Mom's husband? Was it possible my father was in the dark, too? That didn't seem possible to Anna, but then, none of it made sense to her, not even the shame. She couldn't comprehend it, couldn't stomach it, really. "It hurt me," she tells me. "The sister was still her sister. I know she's sick, but she couldn't help it." But there was nothing Anna could do, and she had no outlet for her simmering anger—until one day, months later, when Tillie came to her with a special request.

For years, Tillie had been riding the bus by herself to visit Annie ("Chaim wouldn't go, he couldn't take it," Anna says) and she was finding the hour-long trip harder and harder to make. Tillie couldn't get Mom to take her—not only did Mom have two small children and no car of her own, but she couldn't just disappear for most of the day without telling someone where she was going and why, which was as good as shouting her secret from the rooftop.

After Anna learned to drive in 1953, an almost mandatory act in the Motor City, Tillie asked: Would you take me to Eloise? Anna says she was happy to do it. "Tillie said, 'I'd like to see my child.' Sick or not sick, it's her child, she wants to see her. Your mother didn't want any part of it, so I take Tillie there at least once a month."

"Tell me," I say, "about the very first visit."

Tell me what Annie was like. Tell me about my aunt.

She was short, like my grandmother, not quite five feet. She had curly hair and that wooden leg, and she often was wearing a drab housecoat when Anna saw her. She lived on an open ward with five or six other women, and when she saw Anna that first time, she shrank back, afraid, unsure what to do or say. She clung to Tillie, to her mother, and told Anna to go away.

"I was a stranger. She was frightened," Anna remembers. "She was frightened about everything, but not for her mother. She hugged her. She kissed her. She wrapped her arms around her mother's legs, and wouldn't let go." Another image pops into my head: *Mom in the hospital, hugging me and pleading with me, Steven, please, you don't understand, I can't stay here.* Family history, repeating itself.

Tillie had hoped that Annie would take to her cousin, that kinship would overcome Annie's suspicion and distrust, but Annie wanted nothing to do with this newcomer, this interloper. "She wouldn't look at me," Anna says, sadness evident in her voice. "Tillie would tell her, 'This is Anna, she's your cousin,' but it didn't matter. Nothing helped."

"How did she act? Did she talk?" I ask. The Annie described by Mona Evans and by the court-appointed doctors appeared to have no trouble holding a conversation. Had thirteen years in confinement changed that?

"Oh, she talked freely, but only to her mother," Anna says. "She wouldn't talk to me. I'm a stranger."

"It must have gotten better as you visited more," I venture, more out of sympathy than conviction.

"No," Anna says, emphatically. "It never did. Tante Tillie, she would always cook something special and bring it to her. Annie would sit right down on the floor and eat there. She wouldn't sit in a chair. And she would look at me, no matter how many times she saw me, and say, 'Who are you? I don't know you.'"

"She sat on the floor? Why?"

"I think because if we went to the table, she was afraid that I would come, too. And she didn't want me there. She didn't want to share her mother. One time, she even attacked me, tried to choke me. After that, Tillie told me to stay outside, that it was too upsetting for Annie."

So their routine changed: Anna would walk Tillie up the steps of the building, and then find a place to wait so that Annie could have Tillie to herself. But then one day, Annie was watching from a second-floor window when they arrived, and she saw Anna escorting Tillie up the stairs, holding her by the arm. When Tillie returned from the visit, she gave Anna new marching orders—no more escorts. Tillie would get a nurse to help her so that Annie didn't have to see Anna at all. "She was jealous," Anna says, with a look of amazement, almost bewilderment. "She was jealous that I'm so good with her mother. So I had to stay in my car."

If I had to guess, I tell Anna, I'd add one more reason for Annie's jealousy: If Annie could not bear to watch Anna escorting her mother up the stairs, she must have been in agony watching Anna take Tillie away again. No matter how often Tillie came to visit, no matter what kind of food Tillie cooked for her, no matter how much love and affection Tillie showered on her, Annie must have known that at the end of the visit, Tillie would go home with Anna, while Annie had to stay behind, patient and prisoner in the place where her mother had put her.

These Sunday trips were no secret within the family, Anna says, so it didn't take long for Mom to learn of them. Tillie would have told her. "One day Beth says she wants to talk to me. She asks me about it, and I said, yes, I'm taking her, I'm not working on Sundays, and I have the time. She was mad.

She went on and on. She told me, 'You have no right. You have no right to mix in the family.'

"I said, 'I am family.'"

As Anna tells it, Mom wanted the trips to end. Anna refused. As she narrates her memory of the exchange, I can hear the edge in her voice, I can see the anger right at the surface. We might as well be back at the house on Houghton, only instead of Anna telling Mom how she feels about being told to stop the trips to Eloise, Anna is telling me, and her voice is rising. "Don't forbid me. I'm too strong. I'm too strong. When I want to do something, I do it." She kept driving Tillie, she says, "but I don't tell Beth nothing. She's not stupid, though. She knows. But she doesn't say nothing, she doesn't call me, nothing. I know why. Because she don't want to know what's going on."

Their relationship, awkward from the start, never recovered. The dinners stopped, the two families saw less of each other and, eventually, Anna's phone calls went unreturned. "Your older brother would answer. He would say, 'She's out,' or 'She's playing cards.' I'm not stupid. I realize, she don't want me. Nothing I can do."

"Did she call you?"

"No, because I was against her, I was against her will, what she wanted," Anna says, in a tone mixed with equal amounts of pride and defiance.

But if Anna could withstand Mom, she couldn't hold back time. In the early 1960s, as Tillie's health deteriorated, the Eloise visits grew less frequent and then stopped. Anna doesn't remember exactly when—she guesses that if they hadn't stopped before Hyman's death in December 1964, then they certainly ceased after that.

Patient has had no visitors in years. I had always wondered about that line from Annie's 1972 Northville records, and what "years" meant; now I knew that it must have been close to a decade.

"Did Tillie ever say she wanted to bring Annie home?" I ask.

Anna shakes her head vigorously. "She couldn't. She couldn't take care of her. She was a wonderful mother, but she couldn't bring her home. She's a sick woman herself. She started shrinking, she shrinks real badly. She had the bone sickness."

"Scoliosis?" I say. That was what we always thought of Tillie's rounded shoulders, so pronounced in her later years that she almost looked like a hunchback. Either that, or advanced osteoporosis.

"Something with the bones," Anna says. "Anyway, she couldn't take care of her. Then her husband dies . . ."

I decide to ask a different question, even though I'm pretty sure I know what Anna will say, and by now, how she will say it.

"Did my mother ever say she wanted to take her mother to Eloise?" I ask.

"No," Anna says with some vehemence. "Never. She never went there. She never wants to take her mother. She never wanted anything to do with it."

Anna's words reverberate, like a lingering drumbeat: *Don't forbid me. I'm too strong. I'm too strong. When I want to do something, I do it.*

There's something formidable about my cousin, a steely resolve and strength of will that probably goes a long way toward explaining how she managed, before her nineteenth birthday, to survive the extermination of Jews in western Ukraine. I can only imagine the combination of skill and luck it must have required to stay alive, first by fleeing Radziwillow amid rumors of an impending massacre and then by deceiving a Nazi major into believing—or at least not questioning—her bogus account of how she happened to end up in a city far from her own, without her family, without anyone.

She's eager to tell me her story of survival, and I'm eager to hear it, but I'm wary of throwing open that door right now. It's late, and I'm tired, and I know from my earlier conversations with David that her narrative is too complex, too dramatic, and much too personal to appreciate amid the clinking and clattering of a suburban restaurant near closing time. I propose that I come to Chicago for a separate interview, after I've had a chance to do some research on the Radziwillow massacres, which I think will help me understand her story better. She's pleased, I can tell, and so I don't feel quite so selfish for concentrating on Mom and Annie during this first meeting.

"As long as we're talking about Radziwillow, though, I'd like to figure out exactly how your parents are related to my grandparents," I say. "Can we do that?"

We try, but we can't. The three of us spend about fifteen minutes trying to construct a family tree; just like I did for school, I write down a lot of names and draw a lot of lines. Anna can go back several generations on her Schlein side, but we're missing some of the crucial connections that we need to leap from her branch to my branch. I do learn that Anna is related to both my grandparents—her father was a Schlein, like Tillie, and her maternal grandmother was a Korn, like Chaim.

I try another route. The Routine History of Annie's admission to Eloise, I tell her, says that Hyman had two brothers in New York City and that Tillie was one of ten children. "Is that right?" I ask. "Do you know any of them?" I explain that if I can find some of them—or, more realistically, their offspring—it might open an entirely new avenue. As I had already learned from my first conversation with David, Annie was my mother's secret, not my grandmother's, and for twenty years before her hospitalization, Annie wasn't a secret at all.

David chimes in. "Wow, one of ten? I never heard that."

Neither had Anna. She thought maybe Tillie had a sister in Israel, but she doesn't know her name. Another dead end.

Anna senses my disappointment, and begins an apology. "You know, I lost all my family," she says, blinking back tears. "I was so young . . ." She doesn't finish, but she doesn't need to. I can imagine what she means. She was eighteen years old when she fled Radziwillow, too young to have learned all the family names and relationships, too young to know about those cousins in America who left Radziwillow before she was born, too young to envision a day when she would meet relatives who would call her homeland the *old* country rather than *their* country. In that way, we're alike. When I was eighteen, I didn't know a thing about my overseas family, either.

In fact, I hardly knew anything about my grandparents.

It's a Saturday morning sometime in 1963, and I always spend Saturday mornings the same way—in the car, with Mom, on the way to Dr. Bernstein's for my weekly allergy shot, then to Bubbe and Zayde's for a visit. It's a routine, and I hate it. No, that's not right, it's not the routine I hate. I'm used to the shots by now, I've

been getting them since I was six, every Saturday morning for five years, but I hate
that I need them, that I have these allergies that won't go away, that I keep having asthma attacks when I'm allergic to something, and I'm allergic to plenty—
apricots and almonds, shrimp and shellfish of all kinds, broccoli and brussels
sprouts (which seems like a favor from the gods, as if they're giving me a break in
return for saddling me with this defective body).

   In my memory, the smell of the doctor's office—the antiseptic aroma of the
waiting room, the swab of alcohol on my arm—mingles with the scent of my
grandparents' apartment. For years afterward, a visit to a doctor's office would
remind me of the doilies on the back of the couch, the sugar cubes that Bubbe
plunked into her tea, and Bubbe herself, her wispy gray hair, those rounded
shoulders, her quilted housecoat. When I hug her, I worry that she's so small, so
frail, that I'm hurting her.

   I don't hug Zayde. He has a gaunt, defeated look about him, and I instinc-
tively keep my distance, as if I'm afraid that his dourness is catching. Maybe I'm
following Mom's lead—I can't remember seeing her give him more than a perfunc-
tory hug or peck on the cheek, nothing like the tenderness she shows toward Bubbe.
He doesn't talk much to anyone, and he says even less to me. Like Bubbe's, his
English isn't easy for me to understand. He's a tall man, several inches over six
feet, and slender enough that I can see the outline of his ribs under the thin
undershirts that he wears.

   Lately, it seems that Mom is constantly worrying about their declining
health and whether she can deal with their descent into old age. More than once,
Mom has rushed out of the house to attend to some emergency that sends one or
the other to the nursing home for a while. Occasionally, on our Saturday morning rides, Mom says something about it, about how all the responsibility falls on
her, how hard it is to care for aging parents all by yourself. I can't remember her
words, except for these: "I don't ever want to become a burden to my children,"
she says.

   I can't imagine Mom—young, vibrant, independent Mom—being a burden
to anyone. It's not fair, I think; if she weren't an only child, she wouldn't feel
so alone.

"She was a wonderful woman, a wonderful wonderful woman." Anna is
singing my grandmother's praises again, telling me how Tillie maintained

her dignity in the face of all the adversity that the world threw in her direction. "She was a good soul. There wasn't a thing she wouldn't do. As poor as she was, she would do anything for you." She also has admiring words for my grandfather. "Chaim, he would split the wood for us and bring it over so my kids wouldn't freeze. He was a good man, a kind man."

This isn't the grandfather I remember. The grandfather I knew was lost, sad, withdrawn. Anna is talking about a time that's ten years earlier, so maybe the wood-chopper had changed. But no, I think, this isn't the man described in Mona Evans's Routine History, either, and that was written a decade before Anna met him. In her 1940 report, Evans portrays him as sickly, discouraged, and "willing to leave all decisions to his wife." The report says he "peddled spasmodically" for a living until 1933, when an injury in an automobile accident caused two years of frequent fainting spells and he landed on the city's relief rolls in 1934. A doctor at the city's welfare office concluded that he was suffering from "poly-arthritis and old healed varicose ulcers." He was just forty-seven years old, eight years younger than I am now.

"Let me ask you something else about Hyman," I say.

Anna waits.

"I'm wondering what brought him to Detroit, and how Tillie ended up here, too." I mention the census record, which shows that Hyman emigrated to the United States in 1907 and that Tillie followed him in 1914. They married a year later, in Detroit. "Do you have any idea? Do you think Hyman was in touch with people in Radziwillow?"

Her reply is so startling that I ask her to repeat it: "Well, Tillie was his cousin, so that's probably why."

His cousin? My grandparents were cousins?

And if that weren't startling enough, she adds: "First cousins, I think."

Her words sink in. Anna sees my reaction, and realizes this is news to me. "Are you sure?" I say. "First cousins?"

"That's what I always heard," Anna says, although I can tell that my reaction has introduced some doubt in her mind.

First cousins? All sorts of thoughts flood into my head, but here's the one that pushes its way to the front: Was this one of the "sins" that Tillie was talking about when she told the hospital staff that "the sins of the parents are paid for through their children?" I had been puzzled about that sentence

ever since I first read it, but I had never thought about this particular possibility. Was Tillie saying that she committed a sin by having children, because the children of first cousins run a greater risk of birth defects? Or was
she saying it was a sin to have married Hyman in the first place? Was it a sin
under Jewish law for first cousins to marry? I wasn't sure. And whether it was
a "sin" or not, was it legal as far as the state of Michigan was concerned?

None of us knew the law, but David reminds me that it was more common
in those days for cousins to marry. Whatever sins Tillie had in mind, he says,
he's sure that this wasn't one of them. Anna agrees. "They were poor. That
was the sin," she says.

I ask Anna whether Tillie had ever said anything to her about sins.
Anna shakes her head. "She did say she feels guilty about putting Annie in
Eloise," she says. "But I told her, 'Tante Tillie, you can't blame yourself.
The girl was sick.'"

Sin or not, was it even true? I rummage through my mind, trying to
remember whether I had ever heard that Tillie and Hyman were related,
and suddenly I'm aware that I honestly don't know what I remember, that
now that this powerful possibility has entered my consciousness, I cannot
say with any degree of certainty what I knew before Anna's revelation and
what I knew after. Like a computer's hard drive, my memory has been over-
written with the new information. I was confident that I had never heard
anyone say my grandparents were first cousins. But what about distant
cousins? Had I heard that, and just forgotten it?

There's only one certain way to know whether it's true, and that would
be to examine the Radziwillow birth registry. But David has already done
some genealogical sleuthing, and he's had no luck in finding the Radziwillow records from that era. For the moment, and maybe forever, I'm left to
wonder as we say good night: Is this just another family secret?

Lost and Found

Gasping for breath, I scanned the bleachers, trying to see if Mom could tell that I was on the verge of an asthma attack, the kind that might have caused her to take me to the emergency room in my younger days. In three years of playing basketball for Henry Ford High School, I had kept my asthma under control and under wraps. But now, in my senior year, I was having trouble in the middle of a game, in front of hundreds of fans and my coach, who was undoubtedly wondering why the hell one of his starting players was so winded that he needed a substitute and was doubled over, gulping air. He was looking at me as if to say, it's midseason and you're that much out of shape?

Coach had every right to wonder, because he didn't know about my asthma. At least, he didn't know it from me. That was my secret, probably not a smart one to keep, but I wanted to play varsity basketball more than anything in the world, and I thought telling him I had asthma was as good as hanging a sign around my neck that said, "Damaged goods. Do not play." This was the late 1960s, before comprehensive physicals and lengthy questionnaires replaced the more generic permission forms, so I could keep Coach in the dark, running extra laps to boost my conditioning and finding excuses to leave the floor during practice if I felt a wheeze coming on—which, fortunately, rarely happened as I grew older and better at managing my asthma.

I didn't tell Mom that the coach didn't know, because I couldn't risk the possibility that she would intervene. So I had two secrets, and I had to enlist a few of my friends (who knew about my asthma) to help me keep both. I told myself that I wasn't exactly lying, that a lie was different than an omission, and that since I

*truly believed that I could control my asthma, that it was so infrequent a problem,
everything would be okay.*

*Until the infrequent happened at the most public of times, and exposed my
deception. I cursed whatever allergen had brought on the wheezing, but I knew
that I couldn't just stay on the court and wait it out. I couldn't run, or even pretend to run, and Coach could see that this was more than a case of fatigue. As best
as I could manage, I wheezed out the truth: Coach, I'm having an asthma attack,
but don't worry, it's probably not serious. I just need a breather and I'll probably
be fine.*

*Afterward, after I recovered (no emergency room necessary), Coach did what
coaches do, expressing both his anger about my immaturity and his hope that I
wouldn't suffer any repeat episodes during the rest of the season (I didn't). Mom,
however, didn't quite know what to say. Beyond feeling betrayed, she couldn't
seem to believe that I had put my varsity dreams before common sense and my
own safety.*

*I've forgotten her words—aided no doubt by my wish to forget the whole em-
barrassing episode—but I remember her message: It's okay to keep some things to
yourself. But not things that can hurt you.*

D avid answers my knock. It's a few nights after our lengthy restaurant session, and I've been invited to meet the rest of the Oliwek
clan—Bella, the oldest at fifty-nine, and Dori, the youngest at
fifty-one—at the house in suburban Detroit where they all grew up, and
where David now lives by himself. I'm particularly eager to talk with Bella,
who accompanied Anna on some of her Eloise trips, and was old enough to
have some memory of the glimpses she caught of Annie.

"Where's your mom?" I ask David.

"In the kitchen," he says. "She's a little woozy. Her diabetes."

Dori arrives a few minutes later, prompting hugs and kisses all around,
and concern for Anna, who's looking less lively than she did at the restaurant. I pick up some tension between Dori and David over Anna's eating
habits, and whether David is being too lax in monitoring her meals. They
spar over the cold cuts that David has bought for a light dinner ("Corned
beef and pastrami aren't good for her," Dori says. "She can eat the turkey,"
David replies. "She doesn't like turkey," she shoots back). Dori decides to

sit with Anna as she tests her blood sugar. David escorts me into the dining room.

The house has the glass-and-chrome style common to suburban ranchers of the 1950s and 1960s. The dining room table, laid out with the cold cuts and a salad, looks out on a large sunken family room with enough couches and chairs to accommodate another dozen family members. "Plenty of room if we discover any more cousins I don't know about," I joke to David.

I'm glad for the few minutes alone with him. I want to ask him what he thought of the interview the other night, especially Anna's uncompromising view of my mother. "Your mom didn't seem to like my mom much," I say.

"I was surprised at some of what she said, or rather, the way she said it," David replies. "She didn't miss many opportunities to criticize your mom."

"Most of it rang true," I say. "But some of the quotes didn't sound like her."

I didn't say what else I was thinking—that I felt somewhat trapped between the roles of son and journalist. I had spent much of the day transcribing my notes from our first interview, and there were moments when I could have risen to Mom's defense by challenging Anna on this point or that, but my goal was to get the best and most complete account I could, not to act as Mom's advocate. Also, I was at a disadvantage—I didn't have Mom's version of these conversations. The best I could do was offer up logic and a few facts that didn't quite match up with Anna's memory.

Pointing out minor discrepancies didn't prove anything, of course—some fuzziness around the edges is to be expected when someone is recounting conversations from fifty years past. (Sash and I have slightly different memories of the day at Botsford when we forced Mom to stay in the psych ward, and that was in 1995, not much more than a decade ago.) But that's just it: Anna's account of those conversations wasn't fuzzy. If anything, she recounted them with a clarity both notable and dramatic. That clarity was proof of the effect of these conversations on Anna, how she had absorbed Mom's words, translated and compacted them, so that when she told the story, she was expressing the *essence* of what she remembered and what she felt about Mom—and what she felt was disapproval and anger. When the right moment comes, I want to ask her about this disapproval.

Dori and Anna join us. If I had seen Dori across a crowded room without knowing that she was Anna's daughter, I wouldn't have connected the two. Her face is long and thin, with that healthy outdoor look more common to a sunnier clime than Michigan—maybe California or Arizona, which is where she lived for eleven years, I soon learn. Her clothes suggest that she didn't leave the Southwest entirely behind when she moved back to the Detroit area—she's dressed in the denim style of Santa Fe or Sedona, her home during her time in Arizona.

Bella arrives a few minutes later. As the sisters greet each other, I'm again struck by the difference rather than the resemblance. Partly, it's style: Where Dori is decidedly casual, Bella's clothes, hair, and makeup give her an au courant look. Neither Dori nor David has any children, leaving Bella and me to spend a few minutes talking about ours. That provides a natural segue into asking about her trips to Eloise when she was a kid.

"Do you remember what Annie looked like?" I say.

"Her hair was real frizzy," she says.

"And she wasn't too skinny," Anna chimes in.

"No," Bella agrees, "and she had this housecoat on."

"You were how old, like twelve?" I suggest, doing the math in my head.

"I don't want to lie to you," Bella says. "I really don't know. I think I might have been younger than that." She seems a bit agitated, and I soon discover why.

I turn to Anna. "Do you have any memory of when you took Bella?"

Anna shakes her head, and the conversation lapses momentarily, allowing Dori a chance to say good-bye. She's doing some dog breeding, and has to get home to take care of a new litter.

I focus again on Bella. "From a kid's perspective," I say, "what did you think was wrong with Annie?"

"What my mother kept telling me . . ." Bella begins, but before she finishes her thought, we hear Dori calling, asking Bella to move her car, which is parked behind Dori's. As Bella grabs her keys, Anna jumps in, turning the subject back to my mom. "Your mother never went there," Anna says. "She didn't want to see it. She didn't want to know. She didn't want nobody to tell that she has a sick sister. She said, 'I don't want my kids to know.' I drove her mother there. She said, 'Anna, you take her.'"

She can't let it alone. This is the third or fourth time tonight that she's taken the conversation back to Mom when we were talking about something else. Then I think, wait a minute: In our first interview, Anna had told me that Mom had gotten angry at her for taking Tillie to Eloise, seeing it as interference. Now she's telling me the opposite, that Mom was encouraging her to take Tillie?

I ask which it was. Anna hesitates, trying to sort it out. Finally, she says that it was both—Mom didn't like it, but she couldn't stop it, so she resigned herself. Besides, Anna said, "She was afraid I was going to say to someone that Beth had a sister. Better to let me take Tillie."

Bella returns, and picks up right where we left off, with my question about her view of Annie's illness. "Should I tell him?" she asks, looking directly at Anna. I'm not sure what's coming, or why Bella needs her mother's permission.

I glance at Anna. She shrugs.

"Okay," Bella says. "I used to ask why Annie was there, and my mom would say, 'Because she never got her period.' "

Bella shoots Anna a look that can only be classified as a glare. What's that all about, I wonder? Why aren't they laughing about the kind of little white lie that a mother tells a young daughter, trying to protect her from the more awful truth?

"Do you remember saying that?" I ask.

"Oh, yeah," Anna says. "Tante Tillie told me that."

I'm too surprised to say anything at first. This couldn't be true—there was no mention of it in the Routine History, and Mona Evans surely would have included it in her catalogue of Annie's various problems. So was that Tillie's usual explanation for her daughter's mental illness? Or was that the story she adopted as Annie's stay at Eloise went from temporary to long-term to permanent? Or—and I couldn't discount this possibility—was this pseudo-biological connection something that Tillie actually believed, or came to believe, perhaps her way of coping with her pain and guilt?

It did explain why Bella had insisted earlier that she was younger than twelve when she first went to Eloise—she had to place the visit before her first period. I didn't take the next logical step, though; I didn't realize how a premenstrual girl might react to this explanation. Bella helped me out.

"I worried about it for months," Bella said, "So when I finally got my period, I thought, 'Thank God, I know I'm not going to go insane.' "

· · ·

On Friday nights, the beginning of the Jewish Sabbath, my grandparents often went to the Oliweks for *Shabbos* dinner. We didn't celebrate the Sabbath at my house—we didn't light the candles just before sundown or say the traditional prayers or attend synagogue services on Saturday—and I wasn't aware that Hyman and Tillie were particularly observant, either. Sash traces our lack of religious involvement to Mom's frustrations as a teenager, when the family's poverty meant that they had no money to pay for tickets to the High Holiday services, and Mom would make the rounds of several congregations, pleading her case. She found it humiliating, made worse by her bottled-up indignation at the inferior role that women had to endure at nearly all synagogues in those days. Why should she beg to attend services that gave women short shrift or, in the more traditional congregations, made them sit separately from the men? (I wouldn't call her a feminist, exactly—more of a firm believer in equality and opportunity.)

Growing up, I had no idea that just past Eight Mile Road, in the suburb of Oak Park where the Oliweks lived, Friday nights were kind of a weekly reunion for the Schleins of Radziwillow. The 1950s dinner table often included Chaim and Tillie, Anna and her family, and Nathan—or "Uncle," as Bella, David, and Dori called him. He was their great-uncle, but they regarded him as the grandfather they never had, especially after he came to live with them for good in the mid-1960s, following his retirement from Ford Motor Company.

Uncle Nathan. Was this the uncle my mother often talked about, the one who had promised to send her to college and then reneged? Some facts fit, and some didn't: Mom described *her* uncle as living in Chicago (which Nathan did off and on, but he spent the bulk of his adult life in Detroit, according to Anna) and as well-off enough to pay her way (which sounds like a stretch for Nathan, an auto worker paying child support and alimony to his divorced wife in Chicago during the 1930s).

But most important, Nathan wasn't Mom's uncle. He was Tillie's cousin, and therefore Mom's cousin once removed. Was it possible that everyone called him Uncle, just as Anna called my grandmother Tante Tillie, even though Tillie wasn't her aunt? That seems unlikely. During the 1930s, when this mysterious uncle made the offer, Anna was still in Radziwillow. There was no one in America yet who would consider Nathan to be an uncle.

I ask Anna if she has any idea of the identity of Mom's uncle. She's sure it must be Nathan. David thinks so, too. "I don't know of any other uncles," he says. "In all the genealogy I've done, I've never found any other uncles."

As a result of these Sabbath dinners, the Oliwek children probably spent more time with my grandparents than I did, and their memory of them is very much the same as mine, except that David adds an adult-level twist. "They must have been traumatized by something," David says. "Chaim, he almost never talked."

That brings an emphatic second from Bella. "He didn't talk. He was silent. He was nonverbal. He really was."

"He didn't talk much," Anna concedes, "but he was a fine man."

No one endorses that view, or contradicts her.

"When I was young, I remember thinking about Chaim and Tillie, 'These people are so old,' Bella says. "They aged long before their time. Tillie was so small, so shrunken."

"And if you think about it," David says, "when we knew them, they were younger than we are now."

That wasn't quite true—my grandfather was already in his sixties by the time David was born—but I understood his underlying point: Hyman and Tillie didn't have an easy life, and anyone who met them could see that, even a child.

Before we call it a night, I show them some of the records I've collected on Annie, Mom, and my grandparents. "Wow," David says, several times, in reaction to the nightmarish weeks leading up to Annie's hospitalization, and "Unbelievable" when I read aloud about Annie's refusal to bathe or let her mother leave the house. I'm wondering if hearing some of the specifics might cause Anna to express some sympathy for what Mom was living through, but Anna remains silent until she hears the part about Annie crying when anyone visited the family. "Just like when I saw her," she murmurs.

We spend a few minutes sifting through some of Mom's photos from the early 1940s. Anna spots one, a shot of a young couple unknown to me. I had brought it just in case Anna could identify them. "That's Millie and her first husband," she says.

"Millie?" I say.

"Nathan Shlien's daughter."

Again, a link to the mysterious Nathan. "Were Millie and my mom close?" I ask Anna.

"Not too close. Millie lived in Chicago, but she came to Detroit occasionally."

But close enough for Mom to keep her photo all these years.

Anna lingers over a photo of my parents on their wedding day, November 1, 1942, taken outdoors before or after the Sunday ceremony—given their poses, I would guess that it's after. Dad, in a gray suit and unbuttoned overcoat, a silk scarf dangling from his neck, has his left arm around Mom, who's wearing a short-waisted coat made of something furry but nothing around her neck at all—a carefree poke in the eye of the November chill. Both have grins as wide as Woodward Avenue. On Dad's right is Mom's friend Faye; on Mom's left is Tillie, looking a bit grim in a dark coat and pillbox hat. She and Mom are holding hands, but Tillie's not smiling, and if I didn't know that this was a day of celebration, I'd say her expression is one of worry.

Looking at the snapshot, and Tillie in particular, spurs Anna to speculate at the mixture of emotions Tillie must have felt on the day of her eldest daughter's wedding. She would have been happy, relieved, and concerned all at once, Anna says.

Anna explains: In Eastern European towns like the one where she and Tillie and Chaim grew up, it was commonly thought that if one family member were "crazy," then future children might be crazy, too. So parents of a mentally ill child also worried about their other children. Would anyone want to marry them? If they did marry, would their offspring be mentally ill, too? These fears led some families, not surprisingly, to avoid any mention of a "crazy" ancestor. It was harder to conceal the behavior of a living relative, especially a living sister or brother.

But not impossible, especially in a bigger town such as Detroit. Had Mom told Dad about Annie before their marriage? Did she tell him afterward? Like so many of my questions, I had to believe that the answers were out there, and that with the right combination of luck and determination, I would discover them. But sometimes, I felt like someone rummaging through a lost and found: You go there looking for one item, and then you come across something else you didn't even know was missing.

As I drive away from the Oliweks, I can't get Anna's phrase from the other night out of my head. *I am family.*

Sash had been right about the rift between Mom and Anna, and yet I still hadn't come prepared for Anna's animosity toward Mom. Now I understood that these two women couldn't have come from two more different places.

Anna had lost everything to the Nazis. They had killed her mother, her brother, her sister—her sister!—and Anna herself had avoided certain death only by posing as one of them, as a German, the very people responsible for murdering her family and destroying her way of life. She survived, but at some psychic cost: Her deception worked so well that she ended up working as a translator for the *Wehrmacht*'s military police, and later for a German construction company aiding the Nazi war effort.

Then she comes to the United States, where she discovers that she hasn't lost quite everything, that she has a family after all, and that family includes Nathan, Tillie, Hyman, and a cousin named Beth, who's engaged in a pretense of her own—that *her* sister, part of Anna's precious new family, doesn't exist. Is it any surprise that Anna disapproved of my mother or her decision?

From Mom's point of view, Anna wasn't just a threat to the secret; she also was standing in judgment of Mom's choice. Whatever reasons or rationalizations Mom had for choosing to hide her sister's existence, whatever scars she carried from listening to Annie scream night after night, how could she explain any of this to this newcomer, this Holocaust survivor, this woman who had lost her mother, brother, and sister?

Their falling-out had inevitability written all over it, but I think it went far beyond the secret itself. Mom had asked Anna not to talk about Annie, and Anna had gone along. They continued to see each other, with no particular problem, until Anna agreed to act as a kind of surrogate daughter, to do something that Mom could not do, or would not do: take her distraught mother to see Annie at Eloise. Then Anna comes along and steps into the role that rightfully belonged to Mom, if only she had felt free to play it.

You have no right to mix in the family. That's what Anna had quoted Mom as saying. Whatever her exact words, maybe what Mom meant was: *You have no right to take my place.*

Two very different women, two very different backgrounds, yet both adept at keeping secrets.

"Have you ever heard that Hyman and Tillie were first cousins?" I ask Sash, as soon as I have a chance.

"First cousins?" Sash says. "Where did you hear that?"

Her question echoes the one I asked her back in the spring of 1995, when she phoned to say Mom might have a sister. Family history, repeating itself, again.

"Anna Oliwek. Although it may be more in the rumor-than-fact category," I tell her. "She's not sure of the family relationships in the generation before Tillie and Hyman, so without finding the birth records in Ukraine, there's no way to know for sure."

"Well, it's news to me," she says. She reminds me, though, that she didn't know my grandparents that well—that while she felt like she had two mothers, her dual world stopped there. "I didn't see Hyman and Tillie very often. I know Mom didn't like her father, and didn't like to talk about him."

"Or about her uncle." I repeat what Anna had said about Nathan Shlien, that she thinks he must have been the uncle who had pulled the rug on Mom's college hopes. "From what Anna says, Nathan saw a lot of Hyman and Tillie. How could we know nothing about him?"

Sash has a good time with that comment. "Do you really need to ask that at this point?"

"Want to hear something else weird?" I say. "Do you know who lived in the same neighborhood as the Oliweks in the 1950s? Uncle Billy." Bill was Dad's younger brother, married to Lil. His family and the Oliweks weren't just neighbors, I tell her—their kids played together and the families socialized. "Anna says she doesn't remember talking to Bill about Annie, but I suppose she might have," I say. "He's on my list of people to interview, so I guess I'll find out."

When I reach Mike and Jeff, they're just as surprised to hear about the first cousin story. "Do you think it's true?" Jeff asks.

"I really don't know," I say. "Often there's some truth to these things. Maybe they were cousins, just not first cousins."

But even if it is true, how could I ever know if it's one of the "sins" that Tillie felt she had visited on her children? Only Tillie knew what she meant when she said it, and as social worker Jim Mulherin wrote in his 1972 Northville report, "Apparently no one had noted just what sins mother was referring to."

I'm able to confirm one fact: In 1915, it was illegal for first cousins to marry in Michigan. The state is one of twenty-four that still prohibit first cousins to marry, a ban that originated in the moral view that such unions came close to incest and the scientific view at the time that the genetic risk for children was unacceptably greater. Recent studies have suggested that the risk of birth defects for the children of married first cousins is not as significant as previously believed; it's slightly higher than the rest of the population, about the same as the risk faced by a woman who gives birth at forty rather than at thirty.

The main question, though, is what my grandparents thought. Assuming they were first cousins, they may have been surprised to discover, when they applied for their Michigan marriage license, that they were violating a law by marrying. In the Europe of their birth, not only were first-cousin marriages legal but, in some cultures, they were encouraged as a way to preserve property. European royal families particularly favored the practice. And, as David had pointed out, Jewish law has no prohibition against it.

But I don't know one key fact: When did my grandmother make her declaration that "the sins of the parents are paid for through the children"? Not in 1915, when she married. Not in 1919, when Annie was born. Not in 1940, because the statement doesn't appear in the Routine History. She probably made it sometime during Annie's long tenure at Eloise, probably during some sort of meeting with the Eloise staff about Annie's progress. Then, in January 1972, when social worker Mulherin is reading Annie's records to assess whether she can be deinstitutionalized to a nursing home,

he discovers Tillie's statement and is so struck by it that he includes it in his report.

So what was the context? At the time Tillie made this statement, she had lived in the United States for a long time, long enough to be aware of the widely held view that first cousins were taking a big risk by marrying and bearing children. (Marriage itself was not the problem, which is why some states allow first cousins to marry if they agree to receive genetic counseling.) Annie's problems seemed like proof of that risk: Deformed leg, perhaps some retardation, and then her mental illness. So it's entirely possible that by the 1940s or 1950s or whenever Tillie made her statement to the Eloise staff, she has become convinced that she had committed a sin by marrying Hyman and having children.

But somehow, I don't think so. I don't think my grandmother was speaking about a particular set of sins, or even a particular action. I think she was talking about guilt, not sin. (If I were telling a joke, the punch line would be: After all, she was Jewish, not Catholic.) She was blaming herself for everything that had happened, for giving birth to a daughter with two strikes against her, for not being able to take care of her, for allowing her to go alone to the clinic (whether the sexual assault occurred or not), for sending her to Eloise, for the shame that it brought the family. Who knows? Maybe in some twisted way, Tillie felt responsible for putting Mom in the position of wanting to keep Annie a secret. If Annie had never been born, then Mom wouldn't have needed to hide her.

Did Toby Hazan, Mom's psychiatrist, know anything more about Mom's secret? Now that I have legal authority to seek Mom's medical records, I feel more comfortable asking Hazan to dig out his files on Mom from April 1995, when Rozanne Sedler surprised us with her question, "Did your mom have a sister?"

I've never been quite clear on the events that led Rozanne to make that call. I had always assumed that Mom must have said something to Hazan during their initial meetings, but if so, what, exactly? I was hoping that Hazan's notes might offer some clues as to why, suddenly and inexplicably, she had chosen to mention that she had a sister. Was it a small crack in the facade, evidence that she wanted to shed her burden, but couldn't bring herself to let the wall of secrecy just crumble?

Hazan phones back a few hours after I leave a message with his office, instantly reminding me of why I had always liked him: During the four years that he treated Mom and monitored her medication regimen, he was attentive and unfailingly helpful whenever any of us called to find out how Mom was doing. I mention that it's been seven years since we last talked, and I ask him jokingly what he's been doing in the meantime. He banters right back: "Waiting for your phone call."

Hazan once told me that Mom spent more time in her sessions with him talking about her children than about herself, so I'm not surprised that he remembers what I do for a living, asking, "How's life at *The Washington Post*?" That provides a perfect opportunity to explain that I'm on a leave of absence, working on a book about Mom's secret and her sister.

Hazan doesn't say anything right away. I assume that he's wondering how much he can tell me without violating doctor-patient confidentiality, so I mention my legal authority, but that's not the primary reason for his silence.

"I don't think I knew that your mom had a sister," he says.

That's the last thing I expected to hear. How could that be? All these years, had I been operating under a false impression? No, that wasn't possible. Rozanne had made that call to Sash (there was no doubt about that), and if she knew, how could Hazan not know? Even if Mom had mentioned having an institutionalized sister to someone else, Hazan was the doctor in charge, and he would have been told. He must not remember. After all, it's been years and he . . .

As if anticipating my thought, he says, apologetically, "I have a lot of patients." But he seems genuinely puzzled when I tell him about how the secret emerged and what happened afterward—the phone call from Rozanne, my discussions with Sash about whether to ask Mom about it, my subsequent conversation with a Botsford social worker.

"I'll check my records and get back to you," Hazan says, "but you know, we never talked about her childhood. The focus of our conversation was never on herself, always on someone else. She liked to talk about you children. We never went that far back in the past."

Now that did make sense. Hazan's focus in treating Mom was to bring her out of very present depression, not to explore her past. He wanted to get her off Xanax, which he thought was doing more harm than good, and replace it with an antidepressant that would give her a long-term shot at returning to self-sufficiency. After those awful months culminating in her hospitalization at Botsford, we wanted the crisis to be over, we wanted the moaning and groaning to stop, and we wanted Mom back. In the short term, at least, weekly therapy sessions exploring her childhood weren't the route to stability.

I remember that Hazan had suggested to Mom that such therapy might do her good, but her aversion to psychiatry and psychiatrists had made that suggestion a non-starter. I didn't think much about that at the time—after all, some people regard therapy as equivalent to a root canal—but it didn't occur to me that her disinterest was itself a diversionary tactic. Looking back at that period, I wonder whether she was engaged in one final mighty struggle with herself—should I tell? I must tell, no, I can't tell—over whether to shed the burden that she, alone, now carried.

Would revealing the truth to Hazan, or to us, have prevented her depression? I can't say I believe that. Eased her guilt? I have no trouble believing that. Given her peace? Set her free? Those were the great unknowns. Until I could reveal the past that she so skillfully avoided talking about, I wouldn't know what I believed.

Castles in the Air

It's the early morning of November 1, 1980, and Dad isn't going to make it. The day before, he went into cardiac arrest during a triple bypass operation that was supposed to prolong his life of sixty-seven years, and now the surgeon at William Beaumont Hospital is talking in terms of hours, not weeks or days. Dad hadn't wanted to have the surgery in the first place—he was scared to have his chest cracked open—but the surgeon had said that there wasn't much choice; his previous heart attacks served notice that his clogged arteries couldn't do their job any longer and that the bypasses offered the best shot at a decent quality of life. "Ninety-seven percent" was how the surgeon had put it—"You look like one of the ninety-seven percent who are good candidates for this surgery, based on what we can see."

What they couldn't see, what they discovered under the bright lights of the operating room, was that he belonged to the other 3 percent, the category of poor candidates with overwhelming odds against them. That's what the surgeon is telling us now, in the waiting room, all of us gathered around Mom, our vigil now twenty-two hours and counting, twenty-two hours since we squeezed Dad's hand and told him we'd see him after the operation, twenty-two hours since his gurney had disappeared behind the double doors.

Mom can't believe the worst has come to pass; she's crying nonstop, but she still manages to focus on something larger than the moment. "He can't die today," she moans. "Not on our wedding anniversary. I'll never forgive him if he does that to me."

She never forgave him, not really. How could she? She had made November 1, 1942, into something so large, so significant, so monumental, that she couldn't just retire it to a box in the attic, like a wedding dress or a beloved quilt. For the first thirty-nine months of my parents' marriage, they even treated the annual event as a monthly one, giving themselves thirty-nine opportunities to shower each other with telegrams, flowers, gifts, and the elaborate Hallmark-style cards that Mom adored. For May 1 in 1944, Mom had a military watch engraved to "Duke," with the date and "18th," and mailed it to Dad at the Texas camp where he was struggling to complete his basic training. This monthly tradition couldn't sustain itself, but we all grew up with the understanding that every November 1 was a sacred day, and woe unto any of us if we failed to call.

Before 1980, a call to the two of them on their anniversary was a happy affair, but after life's brutal twist of fate, I would pick up the phone on November 1 with dread, sometimes wondering whether it was better not to call, whether it was better not to trigger Mom's tears and hear her hollow voice on the other end of the line. But I always concluded that the only thing worse than calling was *not* calling. Yes, it would be painful, but that was more my problem than hers. The anniversary already made her sad, and she would be sad even if I didn't call. Hearing from her children would make her less lonely, and loneliness became Mom's primary companion after her partner of thirty-eight years was gone.

Now Mom's gone, too, and I sit alone, reading the letters that she and Dad wrote to each other during World War II, looking back into that past that she had sought so hard to protect. I have all the letters now, including the ones that Evie took home after Mom's funeral, and I read each one carefully, afraid I'll miss a reference or a clue, so at best I can only make it through two dozen or so a day. In some ways, the letters are better than interviews; I don't have to worry about the haze of memory. The stories are fresh, the words have an immediacy akin to a tape recording, the correspondence has an intimacy derived from the very fact that it takes place out of public view.

It's also dangerous, all too easy to read something between the lines when maybe nothing but innocence lurks there. When Mom writes on June 1, 1944, *Tomorrow, our anniversary of the day we met, June 2, the day I began to live,* is that merely a war wife's lovesick way of telling her soldier how much she loves him? Or does she mean just what she says, that she was reborn on June 2, 1942, with the implication that Dad had liberated her, given her an escape route from all that had defined her before, including her mentally ill sister? If I had read this letter before I knew about Annie, I would have smiled at the melodramatic overstatement, but now, I cannot read that sentence without seeing a deeper meaning, without engaging in reinterpretation.

My mother does not exist before 1942.

And here is Mom saying it herself: *June 2, 1942, the day I began to live.*

How often we had heard Mom's story of that day, how she looked down the staircase during a friend's wedding and spotted the dashing, dark-haired young man with the unforgettable streak of white hair at the edge of his forehead, like a splash of lightning against the darkened sky. His name, she would soon learn, was Julius Luxenberg, but he preferred Jack for its more American sound. Mom proclaimed to her friend that she would marry this man, this stranger she had never laid eyes on before, like Cinderella and Prince Charming, without the hassle of a glass slipper. It was so poignant, so magical, so enchanting that I embraced it as true, and believed it to be true, and therefore it became true. Now I wonder, in this time of reinterpretation, whether it will prove to be more fairy tale than fact, that my image of that day—was there such a day?—will dissolve like so much cotton candy, just another confection created for public consumption.

. . .

"I'll never forget the first time I saw you. And wasn't I the little hussy. Did I ever flirt with you, and am I ever glad. I knew even then, for didn't I say, 'That's the boy I'm going to marry.'"

—June 2, 1944, Mom in Detroit, writing to Dad at Camp Wolters, Texas

This fairy tale turns out to be real.

In their war letters, written for their eyes only, the story she and Dad told each other matched the romantic story she had told us all those years. She must have loved that story, because bits and pieces of it appear often in her letters, sometimes to remind Dad of happier days, sometimes to tease him, sometimes as a balm for their shared wartime loneliness. In the wee hours of Sunday, March 19, 1944, after yet another Saturday night without him, she conjured the scene once more: "When we met, I knew then standing on that stairway looking down you were my husband. How? Well, you just know." A month later, after an evening with Dad's cousins, brothers Hy and Hank, both soldiers and in town on furloughs, she wrote that their presence only heightened his absence and brought her back to their first night together: "Remember that little girl who looked down the staircase and flirted so brazenly—and said that's the man I'm going to marry—and she did."

She was twenty-five at the time, eight years out of high school, and yet her life was pretty much on permanent hold. She still lived with her parents in their third-floor apartment, still stuck in low-paying jobs with uncertain prospects, still wondering when, if, or how her luck would change. Then, suddenly, her Prince Charming came along, and everything was transformed. The world waged war that summer of 1942, and the news from Europe and North Africa could only be described as grim, but in the world that Mom inhabited, the news couldn't have been better. In their letters, Mom and Dad often revisit those first months of courtship—long drives on country roads in Dad's maroon Pontiac, excursions to Mount Clemens just for coffee, a dreamy week in a lakeside cabin in Traverse City, painful sunburns from a day at Ohio's Cedar Point amusement park on Lake Erie, dancing the night away to the big band sounds at the popular Eastwood. As their summer of love ended, they set a date to marry; they had known each other less than three months.

Love may not conquer all, but it sure did overpower Mom. How else to explain her relentless pursuit of a man like my father? It was one thing to declare impetuously in the heat of a June moment that there, on the stairs, was the man she was going to marry. It was quite another to stick with that declaration after learning that her Prince Charming was two months separated from his wife of eight years, that he had two girls younger than six, and that his employment history had as many ups and downs as the Cedar Point roller coaster. For a woman so resentful of growing up poor, he didn't exactly represent economic stability: Three weeks after he and Mom met, he filed a financial statement in his divorce case that listed his assets at $600 (his car) and his debts at $475. As a salesman for Manor Furniture, he was making $50 a week before taxes, but his ordinary expenses nearly exceeded his weekly income. If he cut out his laundry and dry-cleaning costs (estimated at $5), he had $3 in his pocket once he paid for rent, food, gas, interest on a bank loan, and the $15 he owed in child support for Evie and Marsha. Dad may have been a catch, as Mom's girlfriends kept telling her, but was he a keeper?

According to Mom's letters, she never had any doubt. But if she never wavered in her belief that matrimony was their destiny, Dad was not so sure. With the wedding date only weeks away, he surprised Mom with a suggestion of a trial separation to test the relationship's strength. "Remember the 'scene' as you called it, when you wanted to postpone it," she wrote him on January 19, 1944. "Aren't you happy now you didn't—wasn't everything as I said it would be—You always said test me to see, a separation would tell—well I didn't need it, I always knew you loved me."

As romantic as their courtship was, in both fact and memory, there must have been other factors at work that contributed to my parents' haste in getting married, factors that weren't apparent to me when I was growing up. For Mom, marriage represented a clean break from the past, not just from the many disappointments in her life but also, I now believed, from Annie and all that she represented. For Dad's part, he might have been worried about his draft status: As a married man with two children, he qualified for the coveted Class III-A deferment. But his imminent divorce meant that he would soon join the ranks of the unmarried just as the draft eligibility rules were changing, opening the door to the induction of single men with dependents. In the summer of 1942, the newspapers were full of talk about ways in which the Selective Service might further limit Class III-A eligibility. (The Selective Service abolished the III-A deferment on October 1, 1943, saying the need for fresh troops had become too great to allow ten million able-bodied men, out of the sixteen million registered, to stay home.)

On August 13, 1942, when Dad's divorce decree became final, it wasn't at all clear what would happen to the III-A exemption. For the moment, as a father, Dad was safe as long as he continued to pay child support for Evie and Marsha, but all the uncertainty surrounding the III-A classification would certainly have made Dad nervous. It probably wasn't the best time to be untying the knot; one bit of insurance might be to marry that girl he met on the stairs, and why not? They were in love. Haste made them both happy. On November 1, 1942, Miss Beth Cohen became Mrs. Beth Luxenberg.

Toby Hazan sounds sheepish when he phones. The psychiatrist has found his file on Mom, and when he tells me what Mom said and how she said it, I'm no longer surprised at his failure to remember that she had a sister. He was taking her through a list of routine questions during their first meeting, and Annie came up when he asked Mom about her family. "It was just so matter-of-fact, it didn't make much of an impression, I guess," he says, apologetically.

He read aloud: "The patient states that her sister was born with one leg and was institutionalized. There is the possibility that the sister may have suffered from an emotional disorder. She was deceased twenty years ago."

Born with one leg? That wasn't true. I ask Hazan whether he thought Mom had exaggerated Annie's physical condition—born without a leg rather than with a bent one—to leave the impression that this was the reason for Annie's institutionalization and to divert attention from her sister's other problems. "It seems so," Hazan replies.

Whatever Mom's motives, her circumlocution worked: Hazan says that his notes from their initial meeting on April 19, 1995, contain no other references to Annie.

We arrange to meet in Detroit after I've reviewed all his records on Mom, which he agrees to send me, as well as the files from Mom's two weeks at Botsford's psych ward, which I'll need to go to the hospital to see. "I'm sure I'll have new questions," I say, telling him that I'm also reading all her war letters to see what she might have said about Annie. In the meantime, I offer to send him copies of Annie's hospital records.

"I'd be interested in knowing your reaction," I say.

"I'd be interested in reading them," he replies.

Mom's life might have begun anew when she met Dad, but her wedding didn't change her address. The newlyweds returned from their honeymoon in Chicago and took up married life in the Cohens' apartment, sleeping in the same bedroom that Mom had occupied before the magic date of November 1. It wasn't what Mom envisioned, but until the young couple could make some money and figure out whether they could persuade Esther to give them custody of Evie and Marsha, it made sense.

This wasn't the apartment that Annie had called home before her commitment to Eloise. The Cohens had left the place on Euclid sometime in 1941 or early 1942, and moved to a similar sized apartment on Pingree, just two blocks away. Still, if Dad didn't know about Annie, it seems hard to imagine that he wouldn't find a trace of her in the Cohens' apartment; after all, her commitment to Eloise had taken place only two years before, so surely some hint of her remained—if not a photo, then some of her clothes, or some of the medical equipment she once used, or the fairy books she once read.

But perhaps not. If it looked like Annie might not be coming home, the move from Euclid to Pingree certainly provided the opportunity to discard her belongings, re-arrange the furniture, start over. I suppose it's possible that a newcomer to the apartment on Pingree, where Annie had never lived, would see nothing to suggest that this family of three had once been a family of four.

Possible, yes, but still hard to believe.

· · ·

"I'm ashamed to say this darling. I'm not making a very good soldier. It's getting me down dear and I'm going to pieces. I just can't take it . . . It's impossible to take all that's dished out. They just don't seem to have any heart. I'm being worked 18 to 20 hours a day, and every nite lying in bed I shed a tear. I just can't help it. Perhaps I'm not a man — at least in the army way . . . I doubt whether I'll ever be the same where and if I return to you.

"Precious, if it's at all possible in any way regardless of price — get me out of this — if I stay much longer I'll be in the insane asylums. I know I shouldn't be saying this — I can't help it. I know now once and for all that I won't be able to take 17 weeks of this Hell. Please, darling, do whatever you can — I really don't know what you'll be able to do — do something — please — please. Don't get upset as I know you probably will be — control

yourself as much as you can and try and see if there is any way for me to
get out of this mess. Even if you have to write the President — I mean it ..."
                    —February 2, 1944, Dad at Camp Wolters, writing to Mom in Detroit

My father, I often heard growing up, was a particularly lousy soldier. Some men, I guess, have the personality, and the body type, for the rigors of combat and the shock of war. Dad was not one of them, as he was all too quick to tell you. He literally didn't have the stomach for it—in his second month of basic training, he landed in the hospital with some sort of gastric distress. He was beyond miserable. "I cannot do this," he wrote Mom from Texas. "I am letting everybody down, but I'm sick all the time."

Training draftees for war is a daunting proposition; they come in all shapes and sizes, and there's no automatic way to tell at the outset who will be reliable on the battlefield and who will be a risk. After married men and fathers lost their III-A deferment in early October 1943, Dad had hoped that his finicky stomach and his age (thirty) would be enough to keep him out of the service; he was older than the Army's announced target group (men younger than twenty-six) and others in their thirties had received deferments based solely on age. His hopes undoubtedly rose even higher when the director of Selective Service ordered the nation's nearly 6,500 local draft boards to "first exhaust the pool of available unmarried men, and next the pool of married men without children, before fathers would be called." But the luck Dad often had in card games failed him in this lottery; when the first batch of 13,330 induction notices went out to fathers in the weeks after the exemption's end, Dad's name was among them.

On October 27, 1943, he was inducted; less than two months later, on December 17, he was on his way to basic training, leaving Mom in tears at the train station. On Christmas Day, he wrote to her from Camp Wolters in Texas, his first letter home: "I miss you, will write soon as possible don't worry love I am in the infantry Duke." Soon, she was vowing to join him. "No Army, no mileage, can keep us apart," she wrote.

Before the week was out, he sent her an SOS. "This cycle, which is 17 weeks, is too much for me. I can't take it. I didn't want to tell you this, but I guess I have to. I don't know how to get out—somehow it seems impossible. If you know of any way at all, try to see what you can do. This is worse than jail." He complained that his stomach was acting up. "Try and help me . . . answer immediately."

I never knew much about Dad's military service. When he talked about his war, he didn't talk about the Philippines, where he had served for several months in 1945; he talked about his ailing stomach and aching back. It didn't matter to me; I was proud that he had served at all. When my friends and I swapped stories about what our daddies did in the war, I was part of the club, and as a Jewish boy growing up in a largely Catholic neighborhood, belonging was more of a challenge than standing out.

But it wasn't until I began to read his letters that I came face-to-face with the raw depths of his unhappiness. The Allies won, but he failed—at least, that's the feeling that oozes from the letters he wrote during the winter of 1944. If I found them hard to read, I can only imagine what Mom felt, particularly that February 2, 1944 letter: *If I stay much longer I'll be in the insane asylums.*

Even if Dad meant it as hyperbole, it must have hit Mom like a shockwave to read those precise words. So she did what any woman concerned about her man would do: She did everything she could to break his melancholy, buck him up, boost his ego—to bring him home in as sound a condition, both body and soul, as she could.

. . .

"I have been elaborating on our plans for our house. Remember the one we drew up — I've been thinking I want two sets of couches, what do you think; also I think we ought to have a juke box in the recreation room so Evie can jitterbug — don't say it sweetheart — building castles in the air is very beautiful, as I sit here and write I can feel you beside me discussing our home. What seems a foolish fancy today becomes a wonderful reality tomorrow, and tomorrow always becomes today eventually . . ."
—January 24, 1944, Mom writing to Dad at Camp Wolters

She dreamed for both of them.

The war raged on, endless in her mind, her new husband more than a thousand miles away at basic training, wretched in his new life as a soldier, and still Beth Luxenberg managed to dream. She had no illusions about the likelihood of her dreams coming true—"*don't say it sweetheart, building castles in the air is very beautiful*"—but in her letters to her beloved Duke, now Pvt. Jack Luxenberg, #36891866, she tried hard, sometimes desperately hard, to keep up his plummeting spirits.

When he hinted darkly after a month of basic training that he might go AWOL, she cajoled him: "Don't feel badly — stronger men than you haven't been able to make it." When he begged for help, she haunted the Red Cross office in Detroit, urging the agency to investigate his medical condition and determine whether anything could be done to get him out. When his repeated bouts of diarrhea and stomach pain sent him to the hospital with a suspected ulcer, she got herself on a train to Texas to stand by her man in person. After tests showed no ulcers and a psychiatrist declared him fit for active duty, she told him to do his best and "not be ashamed to complain about your stomach again."

He left the hospital with a special dispensation that excused him from the most arduous basic-training exercises—the fifteen-mile marches, the five-mile speed hikes, the fully loaded pack—and then lucked out with an assignment to a new medical hospital still getting itself organized for overseas deployment. He would spend the fall at a base outside Tacoma, Washington, rather than with an infantry unit on the bloody fields of Europe. But when he learned that his medical unit training would include several more weeks of field maneuvers, he adopted a new strategy for survival. "Every hike or speed march that we have, I'm falling out — they can stand on their head, I'm not taking them."

To distract him, Mom often wrote about the future—about the house they might buy, the furniture they might own, the furniture business they might start together. She shared their entrepreneurial ideas with her boss at the shoe store, and reported his enthusiastic endorsement to Dad. "We rode home on the bus together and were talking of post-war days. I told him how much we'd like to be in business for ourselves — the furniture business. He thinks it's a marvelous field."

The war had disrupted everyone's life and everyone's spending patterns, and this offered a wonderful opportunity for a smart entrepreneur. "Darling, I wonder if you can visualize how wonderful," she wrote. "When peace comes, furniture will be their first item, plus of course electrical appliances — refrigerators, radio, etc. Darling, God only help us to have the money. We could fall into a fortune — the right spot!"

California loomed large in this future. They dreamed about joining the exodus to that state, especially after Dad visited Hollywood on his way to a base near Monterey. "Honey — Hollywood for you and I after the war — and I don't mean perhaps — it's the most loveliest place — ideal for you and I — real paradise."

. . .

"People sure have money like mad in this town — prices are ridiculous — the streets are jammed — restaurants have lines outside — and you should see the line-up for buses — boy oh boy this lousy war can never end too soon for me — they can keep all the money — Just send me home my baby, and I'll live in Traverse City on $20 a week."

—May 16, 1944, Mom writing to Dad at Camp Wolters

She sent him something—a note, a letter, a card—nearly every day, except for a two-month period in late 1944, when she took an apartment in Tacoma, about fifteen miles from where he was stationed at Fort Lewis. After several days of reading her daily letters nonstop, I felt as if I had taken up residence in wartime Detroit; I could see the people in the crowded streets and feel the economic hustle and bustle that brought the city out of the Depression for good. The assembly lines had ramped up to a level of work not seen since 1929, manned by workers from other Midwestern states and the South. The migration significantly and permanently changed Detroit's racial makeup, as the black population boomed along with the rest of the city. "You know baby," Mom wrote Dad on April 23, 1944, "I think there are 1,000,000 more people in Detroit — everywhere you go there are crowds — more crowds — shopping is a nite-mare — every entertainment place is filled to the gills — even the 30% Federal tax on liquor has no effect — people have money to burn."

Money to burn, but not necessarily places to spend it. Money alone couldn't buy rationed items like shoes or sugar or film. Movie theaters did a landmark business, though, for two reasons: People needed to laugh as they followed the often harrowing news from Europe and the Pacific, and no one needed a ration stamp to take in a show.

At the downtown shoe store where Mom worked as a manager, business had extreme highs and lows. At times, the store had so few customers that she wondered why she had opened at all. Then a shipment of "unrationed" shoes would come in, and she would have to hire extra help to handle the hordes. After the arrival of seven thousand unrationed pairs in January 1944, she had to work fourteen-hour days to keep up with the demand for the shoes, on sale for $3 each. "What a day," she wrote Dad on January 22. "We chained the doors to keep the customers out — shoes thrown all over the place . . . women yelling oh nuts . . . I was wrapping shoes so fast I couldn't breathe." She arrived home near midnight, giddy about the extra commission money she had earned from selling $75 in shoes, and so exhausted she could hardly muster the energy to take a shower.

But she had one last task to complete before she fell into bed. Taking several sheets of thin, government-rationed airmail paper from her drawer, she wrote her nightly letter to Dad, all the while staring at the photo that she kept on her bedside table.

· · ·

"Please believe me darling I want to know everything good or bad. If you can't tell your wife, who can you tell? I know what a terrible time you've been having and it's nothing to be ashamed of."
                        —January 24, 1944, Mom to Dad at Camp Wolters

The letters, of course, aren't just a narrative of life in Detroit or a running conversation between two lonely people separated by circumstances beyond their control.

They are also love letters.

Mom, in particular, had a fondness for the mushy, and by the time I reach March 1944, I've become quite familiar with her terms of endearment and euphemisms. One phrase, which she often uses to close her letters, stands out; it is not part of the usual lover's vocabulary: *my savior.*

In my head, I have my own running conversation with her:

"It's okay for me to read the letters, isn't it? Otherwise, why did you save them and leave them for us?" I ask.

"I don't mind you reading them," she replies. "Just be careful."

"Careful?" I say. "Careful, how?"

She hesitates. "We were in love."

"I know that, Mom."

"Love is what matters," she says.

"Can I ask you one question? At the end of many letters, you call Dad 'my sweet baby, my savior.' What was he saving you from?"

No reply.

I'll have to imagine the answer for myself.

The letters are making me sick. I had scoffed when Sash warned me that she couldn't read the letters because they reeked of mold and cigarette smoke after more than thirty years in Mom's small apartment. After several days with them, I can feel the musty smell settling in my throat, and my itchy nose tells me that my allergies are acting up. But I keep reading, looking for leads. Unfortunately, Mom's not writing to assist a reader sixty years later. As might be expected, she refers to friends by first name alone, and doesn't mention any identifying details, such as where they're living.

I wearily take out the envelope for December 1, 1944. And there it is:

Sylvia Pierce had all the girls out to her house — you know the one that lives on Steele. There was — Irene, Faye, Julie, Molly and Sandra — by the way Sandra is pregnant again, that's Goose's wife — she's in her 8th, that's no. 3. We had a nice time — oh well as good as can be expected. I don't enjoy much without you.

Sylvia *Pierce*. Not Pearce, as the obit in the Detroit Library had spelled it. I jump on the Internet, and discover that this is the right Sylvia Pierce— and that she had died just two weeks earlier, at the age of eighty-six. I'm disconsolate. Why hadn't that obit writer at the *Free Press* gotten her name right back in 1952? But at least I've cracked the circle. I've got a specific name to pursue.

I dial the home of Sylvia's daughter-in-law, Connie Pierce. I apologize for bothering her, and tell her I'm sorry about Sylvia's death. I explain that my mom and Sylvia were friends from long ago, and that I'm trying to trace others in their group for a book I'm writing. Connie tells me that Sylvia probably couldn't have helped me if I had found her earlier—Alzheimer's had taken possession of her memory in the last year.

I tell Connie about coming across Sylvia's name in Mom's letters. She's caught up in the detective hunt. "If I read you a paragraph from December 1944," I say, "can you tell me if you know any of these other women, and whether they're still alive?"

As soon as I finish, Connie says, "Yes, I know them all—all except your mom. What did you say her name was?"

There's one question I'd like to ask Mom as I get deeper and deeper into the letters. Where's Annie?

Her first letter is dated January 1, 1944. Her last is postmarked September 5, 1945. So far, I've made it to the end of March 1945, when Dad ships out to the Philippines and their correspondence goes on hiatus during his five-week voyage. Thousands of pages of prose exchanged between them, and not one sentence about Annie.

The letters pick up again in early May, which means I still have another four months' worth, a week of reading at least, but I decide to take a break, grateful that Connie Pierce has given me several promising leads to pursue. When I started my marathon reading sessions, I had hoped that I would find some reference, some allusion, even if it were just Mom telling Dad that, oh, yes, by the way, Annie's still the same, there's no change, or guess what, Ma (as she called Tillie) went to see Annie and she's doing a little better. But at some point, I can't really say when, I realized that my expectations had reversed, that I now assumed that I would consume every word of every letter, all the way to the final onion-skin page, and that Annie wouldn't be there. One afternoon, after extracting one letter after another from their musty envelopes, I even muttered out loud, "C'mon, Mom, *something* must be going on with Annie."

I couldn't imagine that nothing of significance had happened to her sister during those eighteen months that Dad was away. By 1944, Annie had been living at Eloise for more than three years. Maybe it was clear by then that she had become a permanent Eloise resident, but even permanent residents make progress, or take turns for the worse. I was pretty sure, based on what Anna Oliwek had said, that Tillie visited Annie periodically during the 1940s. Annie might have been gone, but she wasn't forgotten.

I couldn't understand Annie's absence in the letters. Maybe Sash was right—maybe Dad didn't know about Annie. Or maybe Dad knew all about Annie, but Mom had declared the subject, painful and embarrassing as it must have been, off-limits. That certainly seemed possible. Mom had no reason to inform Dad about Annie's progress; after all, Annie was Mom's sister, not her daughter, so Mom wasn't responsible for her. Eloise was taking care of Annie, and Mom's job was to take care of her despondent soldier-husband, who had more than enough on his mind. No need to worry him about a mentally ill sister-in-law whom he had probably never met.

But if he didn't know about Annie, then what to make of this sentence from Mom's letter on August 5, 1944, a sentence that concluded with a long description of her anger at Esther, who has come back to town and disrupted Mom's Sunday outings with Evie and Marsha? "I have been avoiding saying anything for I didn't want you to know how I felt," she wrote, "but then we never keep things from each other."

Never?

ELEVEN

The Old Neighborhood

Marsha + Bert

Previous page: *Girls' day out: Mom and Marsha, age two, Pingree Street, 1943*

"Sylvia Pierce had all the girls out to her house — you know the one that lives on Steele. There was — Irene, Faye, Julie, Molly and Sandra . . ."

All it takes is one—one name, one address, one correct piece of information—to wipe away weeks of frustration. Within a few days of talking to various members of the Pierce extended family, I'm able to piece together a working list of every one of the women mentioned in Mom's letter. According to Connie, the entire group had remained friends throughout their lives, all except Mom.

"Faye" was Faye Levin, almost certainly the Faye from Mom's photos, and she had married someone named Emmer. "Molly" was Faye's sister, and I knew from Mom's letter that Sylvia had "all the girls out to her house" to celebrate Molly's wedding, but Connie doesn't remember Molly's married name. Sandra was Sandra Goose, already married to Dave Goose and expecting her third child. Irene and Sylvia were the Robinson girls, whose family had lived next door to my grandparents on Euclid during the late 1930s. Irene had married David Doren after divorcing her first husband, so the *Free Press* obit from 1952 had been right on Irene's married name.

And Julie: Her maiden name was Julie Reisler or Reisner, the only one still alive as far as anyone in Connie's circle knew. Julie was somewhere in California, but Connie didn't have a phone number or any clues about how to find her, and there seemed to be some confusion about her current last name.

While I'm hunting for the elusive Julie, Laurie Brodie Green, another Pierce relative, suggests her mom, Millie, might be worth a call. Millie Brodie was Irene's and Sylvia's first cousin, and spent a lot of time at the Robinsons' apartment when she was young. Laurie says she'll call her mom to see if she remembers my mom.

"Tell me your mom's maiden name again," Laurie says.

"Cohen. Beth Cohen."

The following day, Laurie calls back. "At first she had no idea who I was talking about. 'Beth Cohen, Beth Cohen,' she kept repeating. Then I mentioned her sister, and her wooden leg. That did it. She laughed and said, 'Oh, you mean *Bertha*. She changed her name to Beth later. That's why I didn't remember.'"

"You speak such beautiful Hebrew."

I plaster on a smile and say thank you to all my well-wishers—thanks a lot, I'm glad you liked it, yes thanks, no I'm not studying Hebrew right now, sure, thanks again. I don't know what else to say and it isn't just because I'm sixteen and awkward about compliments. It seems rude to tell them, sorry, I'm a fake, I actually don't know a word of Hebrew, all I did was memorize these lines and I borrowed this tallit (the traditional prayer shawl) for the ceremony so, please, stop shaking my hand and giving me kisses and telling me how well I speak.

It's 1969, and at Mom's request, I had agreed to recite an aliyah at Jeff's bar mitzvah, a traditional role for family members to play at this Jewish rite of passage. I didn't want to do it—I remember telling Mom that if she wanted me to stand at the Torah and chant a blessing, at least let me be honest and say it in English. Unlike Jeff and Mike, I hadn't gone to Hebrew school, I hadn't studied the language, and I didn't have a bar mitzvah when I turned thirteen.

Mom saw it differently. Where I saw a charade, she saw an honor. It was a privilege to say an aliyah, to be called to the Torah. Please, she said, could you just do this for me? I found her request somewhat mystifying—we weren't even regular members of the congregation—but it seemed important to her, so I took the short transliterated passage and did my best to make myself sound as if I had some idea what was coming out of my mouth.

Why did it matter to her? I didn't know. I had heard her lament that I was the only one of her three sons not to attend Hebrew school (something to do with one of Dad's many job changes and the family's finances at the critical moment of enrollment), and the only one who didn't stand for a bar mitzvah. (My reaction, meanwhile, was to say a private prayer of thanks to God for relieving me of the obligation to spend three afternoons a week waiting for the Hebrew school bus so I could sit in yet another classroom.) Maybe the aliyah was Mom's way of saying, see, it's okay, he turned out to be a good Jewish boy after all.

What if an authentic Hebrew speaker had said to me after the aliyah, "Good job for a beginner" or "Did it take long to memorize that?" With no pretense to protect, I could have said something close to the truth: "Not long, and it was an honor to participate." But that's the trouble with pretense—once it starts, how and where does it stop?

As soon as I identify myself, Millie Brodie hastens to tell me that she's not sure she can help me. "It was a long time ago, and I don't want to tell you something I don't clearly remember."

I like her immediately.

"I knew your mother. Bertha. She later changed it to Beth, which I didn't blame her for," Millie says.

She's eighty-two now, which makes her seven years younger than Mom, a huge difference when you're growing up. She wasn't a friend of Mom's, she explains, but saw a lot of her because she spent so much time with her cousins, Irene and Sylvia. She had a double tie to Irene and Sylvia's parents: Her mom was Jacob Robinson's sister, and her dad was Kate Robinson's brother.

In 1929, when Millie was five, her family left the old neighborhood for Ypsilanti, about twenty-five miles away from Detroit. They moved back in 1934, when she was nine. By that time, her Uncle Jake and Aunt Kate were living next door to the Cohens in the apartment building at 2205 West Euclid, so she often saw Tillie, Mom, and Annie (she says she's not sure she ever met Hyman) while visiting the Robinsons.

I can feel my pulse racing. Millie's the first person I've found who knew Annie before her hospitalization, and my head is bursting with all the questions I want to ask, but it's important not to skip the basics; I want to have enough information to cross-check her memories later.

"What do you remember about Annie?" I ask.

She pauses, sadness creeping into her voice. "Poor thing. She had braces on her leg. I was a little frightened of her. Intimidated. I don't remember if her problem was mental. Her leg, that I remember."

"She had a brace until she was about sixteen," I say, "and then she got the wooden leg. It was about 1936, according to the hospital records."

"Yes, I remember. I guess that's part of what frightened me. It was foreign to me. Today, of course, they can do a lot more for you, and we're much more familiar with those kinds of disabilities."

She pauses again, trying to come up with the right words. "It's embarrassing to think about how she was treated."

"How was she treated?"

"We all sort of stayed away," she says. "It's hard for me to say that now. But back then we didn't know any better. We didn't say 'disabled' or 'handicapped.'"

"Those were different times, Millie," I interject. "I mean, the school where Annie went was called the Leland School for Crippled Children."

Millie makes no reply. I decide to change the subject. "What about my mom?" I ask. "What was her relationship with Annie?"

"I don't really know. I saw your mom taking care of Annie, but it always seemed to me that it was more out of obligation than devotion."

Such an interesting observation. I underline the sentence in my notes. "What about my grandmother?"

"I remember her carrying around Annie on her back," Millie says quickly, as if the memory had just popped into her head. "Annie wasn't very big, so it must have been earlier."

It's an arresting image, my grandmother, weighed down, her burden on her back. But I'm doubtful. "It seems hard to believe," I say. "By 1932, when my grandparents moved to Euclid, you were eight, Annie was already thirteen. Tillie wasn't very big herself."

"Well, that's what I meant about my memory. It was a long time ago. But

I have this picture of your grandmother, hunched over, carrying that poor child. I don't know how old I was."

Another image floats before my eyes—my grandmother's rounded shoulders. Carrying Annie wouldn't have been easy for anyone, but for my grandmother, with her scoliosis or whatever ailment had left her with that misshapen posture, it must have been excruciating.

"I heard a story," Millie says. "Maybe I shouldn't repeat it. I heard when Annie was born, the doctor knew right away that she wasn't going to be normal." True enough—Mona Evans had written in her Routine History that Annie's leg was bent at birth and couldn't be straightened out. "I heard that the doctor had said, 'I can do something about this right now,' but your grandmother wouldn't hear of it."

Do something about this right now? I stop myself from gasping. I grope for a question, and I'm silent long enough that Millie finally fills the vacuum. "I told you that maybe I shouldn't repeat it," she says.

"No," I say. "True or not—and I find it hard to believe that it's true— even the fact that such a story made the rounds says a lot about how the neighborhood saw Annie."

The child who shouldn't have lived. The child who shouldn't have been born. The sins of the parents are paid for through their children.

Those are the thoughts running through my head as I try to make sense of what Millie has told me. Could this be anything other than rumor, speculation, perhaps some adult's misguided way of describing how much of a burden Annie had become to her family? Why would such a story be repeated or given any credence?

Here's why, I later learn: In the years before and after Annie's birth in 1919, the American eugenics movement argued openly and vigorously for policies that would eliminate "defectives" from society and allow only the fittest to survive and procreate. The movement's tireless campaign resulted in thirty state laws requiring the forced sterilization of those judged mentally or morally unfit, capped in 1927 by an 8-1 Supreme Court ruling in a Virginia case, *Buck v. Bell*, that declared such laws to be constitutional. Justice Oliver Wendell Holmes's majority opinion famously observed that

"three generations of imbeciles was enough." At the time, Holmes's statement fit mainstream thought; only in recent decades has it come to be equated
with all that was wrong with mainstream attitudes toward disability.

A Chicago surgeon, Harry J. Haiselden, championed the next logical
step beyond sterilization. In the four years before Annie's birth, Haiselden
attracted national attention—and widespread approval—with his vocal crusade against intervening to save the lives of "defective" babies. His argument was one part eugenics, one part euthanasia (a word he never used
himself): Infants with serious physical or mental defects posed a danger
to society, he asserted, and the physician had a duty to protect future generations against those destined for lives "without value." Death for nature's mistakes, as Haiselden called these children, was more merciful and
more humane than a lifetime of suffering. "I am sure no jury of sane men
would convict me of allowing a child to die who would be a burden to himself and to the community if permitted to live," he declared in November
1915 when he personally alerted a Chicago newspaper reporter to the plight
of "baby Bollinger," the first of six cases that Haiselden used to gain a very
public platform for his ideas.

Haiselden told the reporter that he had allowed other babies to die, but
always quietly. Now the surgeon wanted to come out of the shadows, and he
had chosen the case of baby Bollinger to make his public stand. The infant,
born on November 12, 1915, at the German-American Hospital where
Haiselden was chief of staff, had a variety of physical deformities, including
a closed lower bowel, misshapen shoulders and neck, a missing auditory
canal, and no right ear. Without corrective surgery to repair the intestinal
problem, the boy would not survive. Haiselden, consulted by the attending
physician, advised the infant's parents, Allen and Anna Bollinger, that their
son faced a life of mental and physical anguish. The Bollingers accepted his
recommendation against treatment, and the surgeon summoned the Chicago press to the hospital for a first-hand look at the baby that he thought
should not live.

"I have no doubt that I shall be called a cold-blooded murderer for allowing this baby to die," the forty-four-year-old Haiselden said in an interview at the time. "I am prepared for bitter criticism. But its death is a
question between me and my conscience. I would not kill the infant. I
would not administer poison or take its life by any active surgical means. I

shall merely stand by passively and let it die. I will let nature complete its bungled job."

When a *Chicago Daily Tribune* reporter asked Haiselden how frequently such deaths were occurring, he openly suggested that some physicians were taking an active role in hastening death. "Many a child marked plainly as an idiot or badly deformed has been allowed to die by not tieing the umbilical cord. If the cord, which must be severed at birth, is not tied immediately after, the infant will die of loss of blood. I do not mean to say that children are permitted often to die by their physicians. But such deaths are not infrequent."

I can do something about this right now.

In the five days between his birth and death, baby Bollinger blossomed into a household name, his misfortunes covered by major newspapers throughout the country. Haiselden and his ideas achieved a longer-lasting prominence; over the next year, Haiselden used a variety of avenues to push his agenda even further into the public consciousness. He invited photographers to the hospital, and urged them to publish pictures of the "defective" babies. The Hearst newspapers, which gave their editorial weight to Haiselden's eugenics platform, published his first-hand account of the Bollinger case in a serialization that began just six days after the Bollinger baby's death and ran for the next six weeks. Haiselden revealed that he had received pleas from anguished parents who wanted his help in finding a merciful way to end their children's ill-fated lives; one such appeal came from the mother of a six-year-old impaired boy. These pleas proved, Haiselden suggested, that it would be better for everyone if these children had failed to live at birth.

Then, in late 1916, the surgeon took his campaign to the nation's newest medium: the movies. *The Black Stork*, an hour-long feature film starring Haiselden himself as a doctor trying to prevent the birth of defective children, tells the fictional story of a husband with an unidentified hereditary disease who ignores the doctor's warnings of the genetic risk of fathering a baby. The rest of the film is a graphic replay of the Bollinger case, with a religious twist: The couple's baby is born with multiple deformities and needs surgery to live, but the mother agrees to withhold treatment after witnessing a horrific vision of the baby's miserable future (as revealed by God). When the baby goes to his merciful death, his soul flies into Jesus's waiting arms. The national advertising for the film, cowritten by Haiselden and a Hearst newspaper reporter, billed it "a eugenic love story."

The Black Stork was no cult film. It played in a variety of mainstream theaters, not just in 1917 but also through the 1920s, outliving Haiselden, who died suddenly in 1919 during a stay in Cuba. But the movie often ran into opposition from local film boards, which found its graphic content too disturbing to be shown, according to Martin Pernick, a University of Michigan professor who unearthed and restored a print of the film while researching his 1996 book on Haiselden and his influence on popular culture.

The Black Stork, one of several dozen films with a eugenics message made during Annie's childhood, was just one part of a national conversation about impaired newborns. "In the wake of Haiselden's campaign," Pernick writes in his book, "death became a widely discussed and often advocated measure for dealing with the unfit." Pernick scoured newspapers in major cities, including Detroit, and found quotes or commentaries from more than three hundred physicians and public figures, many supportive of Haiselden's position (and many others critical of his grandstanding style of advocacy). "Several doctors said they had allowed babies to die," Pernick told me, "and others said they knew it went on."

From time to time, Pernick said, the issue of merciful infanticide came back into the public eye. In the 1930s, when Millie Brodie heard the story about Annie's birth, the euthanasia movement gained new popularity, prompting public opinion surveys to ask questions about the morality of mercy killings. In a 1937 poll, 45 percent of those interviewed agreed that "infants born permanently deformed or mentally handicapped" should be allowed to die.

This was the context for Millie's story. When Annie was born, when her deformed leg wouldn't straighten out, when she was carried around on my grandmother's back, when she boarded the bus to attend the school for crippled children, when she "didn't learn like she should," a significant percentage of her neighbors and other Americans believed that a more humane world would exist if the number of Annies could be reduced or eliminated—and that the nation's doctors had the background, training, and expertise to make the right choices. "You have to remember," Pernick said, "that this was the era when many people believed then, much more than they do now, that science could make an objective determination of who should live and who should die."

I can do something about this right now. There's no way to know if the doctor who delivered Annie ever said that. But does it matter? To live in a neighborhood where people believed that such an offer was made—and to be the parents and sister of *that* sort of child, the sort of child thought to be such a burden to her family and society that, well, maybe she shouldn't have lived in the first place—was that any less disturbing?

And what about Annie? What about her feelings? Surely a girl who could read, who complained to her mother that "normal" activities were forbidden to her, who had enough insight (according to Mona Evans's Routine History) to want independence and yet understand that she would never achieve it, surely this sort of girl would have known something of the ongoing debate about how to deal with the crippled, the unfit, the deformed, the defective, the idiots, the imbeciles, the morons—labels that make us cringe now but were regarded in Annie's younger days as neutral, scientific descriptions of the problem at hand.

As I try to imagine how Annie might have felt, I remember something, something I already knew but perhaps didn't really understand, something that Mona Evans reported about Annie's feelings. I consult Evans's Routine History:

She asked the mother what kind of a casket she was going to buy for her, said that she did not want to die—she wanted to live, commented that everyone laughed at her and wanted to see her in her grave, but that she wouldn't let them "get her."

Paranoia, yes, but eliminate the implied persecution and overstatement, and don't those words just about sum up the outcome that Haiselden and his many supporters would have preferred?

They wanted to see her in her grave.

I've been talking to Millie Brodie for more than an hour now. Her memory of Annie centers more on her leg, and on her being "slow," than on mental illness. Annie's crutches and her bulky brace made her stand out in the neighborhood. Everyone knew Annie, the girl with the deformed leg, the girl who was retarded.

"Did you know she went to Eloise?" I ask.

Yes, Millie says, but she was never sure of the reason. "It wasn't dis-cussed, no one talked about those things, and then I lost track of your mom at some point. I knew she got married, and moved away. I would hear about her from time to time, from Sylvia, maybe. I remember hearing that she had some sort of mental health problem of her own, nothing serious."

Wow. "What did you hear?" I ask.

She doesn't remember anything else. I reluctantly move on.

"Do you think Irene's or Sylvia's families would have photos from back then?" I ask. "I don't have any of Annie."

Millie thinks the chances are nil. "Annie wasn't around. No one played with her." I ask her for names of other people from the old neighborhood, and she suggests I call her brother, Martin. "He's six years older, and he knew your mom better." She gives me his phone number.

"You know," Millie offers, "those years were really hard for your grandmother, raising those kids. She was really poor, and she didn't have any support. I remember that Jacob Robinson tried to help—not finan-cially, because he didn't have much money either. No one had money back then. But maybe through his connections at the court." (He worked at the Wayne County court clerk's office, and eventually became the chief clerk.) "I had the impression he tried to get them some aid through the government."

She sighs. "Hard times. Such hard times."

How hard? Hard enough to make Mom want to escape, no matter what the price? Hard enough to drive a wedge between her and her parents, between what they were and what she wanted to become? Hard enough to see my father—a divorced man with two children, a furniture salesman dependent on commissions for a paycheck—as her "savior?"

Growing up, I often heard Mom's descriptions of poverty's pernicious-ness. Being poor had scarred her deeply, and her fear of poverty was a prime motivator in how she raised us and why she pushed us to excel in school. "Education," she often said, "is what matters. You can't get anywhere with-out an education."

I knew, too, that at some level, she faulted her father—not for the Depression, or their poverty, or the hardships that the family endured, but for not working harder to overcome his shortcomings, for giving up instead of going forward. "I didn't know my father," she had told Hazan at their first meeting in May 1995.

I didn't know him either. I remember Mom taking care of both her parents in their last years, rushing to their apartment to deal with one health crisis or another. Her affection toward her mother seemed genuine and real, but as I think about Mom's attitude toward her father, Millie Brodie's words about Mom's care of Annie resonate in my ears: "She did it more out of obligation than devotion."

The sins of the parents are paid for through their children. I hadn't thought about it before, but now it occurs to me: Tillie probably wasn't just talking about Annie when she said that. She had said "children," plural, and she had two—disabled, disturbed Annie and disappointed, discontented Bertha. If Tillie felt guilty about Annie, about giving birth to a "defective" child in the first place, about her inability to cope with Annie's pain and suffering, wasn't it also likely that my grandmother felt guilty about her inability to protect her older daughter from the consequences of Annie's troubles? Perhaps sending Annie to Eloise, signing that petition calling her daughter insane, perhaps that was Tillie's desperate attempt to save *both* her daughters; getting Annie the help she needed, and releasing Bertha from the nightmare that their life had become with Annie's screams and moans.

What exactly did Tillie tell Mona Evans? *She feels that if her family had money, the patient could have been made well long ago and the present mental disturbance would not have manifested.*

Anger and guilt, the daughters of despair.

Where's Mom? I ask, putting my school books down.
—She's gone away for a rest.
When is she coming back?
—Very soon, just a few days, when she feels better.
Where did she go?
—Not far. Maybe we'll go see her. But if not, she'll be home soon.

When I was about eight, Mom disappeared for a few days.

She didn't vanish. She just wasn't home when I came back from school that day in 1961, and when I asked about her, someone—Dad? Sash?—said that she needed a rest and would be back as soon as she felt better. I was too young to spend much time reflecting on the implausibility of this story. When Mom returned four days later (I think it was four days), she followed the script—she had been exhausted and needed a break. Beyond that, my memory surrenders nothing more. I might have gone to see her at the rest home or the sanitarium, or whatever the place was called, but I don't think so.

Daily life went back to its normal rhythms—school, play, bed—and this strange episode soon faded into obscurity, where it stayed for me until Mom's anxiety attacks in 1995 brought it back. So when Millie Brodie mentioned that she had heard through the grapevine about Mom having "mental health problems," I wasn't entirely surprised—except by the idea that news of Mom's "rest" had migrated outside the family circle and was deemed significant enough for grapevine consumption. By 1961, Millie hadn't seen Mom for years, yet gossip about Mom's mental health had somehow reached Millie's ears, probably through her cousin Irene or Sylvia.

Tough town for keeping secrets.

For Sash, who was twenty at the time and old enough to understand that Mom was more than just tired, this "breakdown" was a scarring experience. Sash came home one day to find Mom in bed, more or less incapacitated, and Dad, sitting in a chair, more or less immobilized. Whatever the cause of Dad's paralysis, she felt she had to take over. "I was twenty, and I shouldn't have been put in that position," she told me during those dark days in 1995 when Mom once again couldn't function and we had to push her to seek treatment.

If history wasn't repeating itself, it was ricocheting, all the way back to Annie.

The envelope from the National Archives branch in Chicago had a promising bulk to it, like the coveted acceptance letter from a college admissions office. I had written away for Nathan Shlien's immigration and naturalization records a few months earlier, on the off chance they might contain some useful information that would lead me to other family members or people from the old neighborhood.

My first thought when I look at the three documents inside the envelope: There's some mistake. I must be reading this wrong.

Second thought: After all I've learned, Mom's secrets still manage to blindside me.

The three documents, all from different time periods in the 1920s, chronicle Nathan's efforts to obtain citizenship, a lengthy process that required several declarations over a period of years. On each form, Nathan gave his "place of residence" as 1026 Medbury Avenue—my grandparents' address, the same address where he was staying when the census-taker came around in 1930.

I had always assumed that Nathan's stay on Medbury was temporary. But based on these three documents alone, it's clear that he lived with Hyman and Tillie (and Mom and Annie) for at least five years. It was suddenly getting quite crowded in my revised image of Mom's childhood. I do a quick reinterpretation: Nathan was living there when Mom turned eight, and still living there when Mom became a teenager. To paraphrase Anna Oliwek, he was *family*.

Yet I had never heard Mom mention his name.

The final count for Nathan Shlien: Ten years. That's how long he claimed a daily presence in Mom's life, according to city directories that I could now mine with much greater precision. A full decade. Most of Mom's childhood.

He came to live with my grandparents in 1922, as Mom was entering kindergarten, and remained until 1932 or 1933, when she was a junior in high school, approaching graduation—just about the time she would be thinking about college.

Why had he come to Detroit? The breakup of his marriage in Chicago, most likely. Anna Oliwek had told me that Nathan divorced his first wife after discovering her in bed with another man. Anna didn't know that he left Chicago, too, as well as his wife.

Maybe Anna was right when she speculated that Nathan was the "uncle from Chicago" who had reneged on his college offer. I had been skeptical:

In my mind's eye, Mom's mysterious benefactor/reneger was a self-made and imperious man who had reached out impulsively from his nicely appointed house in the "big" city (as we thought of Chicago) to bestow a bit of his wealth on a favored niece, but then withdrew his offer in the light of a later day, unaware of how his whims had crushed a young girl's hopes. Nathan didn't fit my image.

But perhaps it was Nathan, after all. He didn't have a lot of money on his Ford Motor Company salary, but maybe he possessed something more valuable than a wealthier man in a distant city—a closeness, an affection, and an understanding of the dreams and desires of this young girl. If Tillie and Hyman had taken their fellow *émigré* from Radziwillow into their family when he needed a fresh start, perhaps he had wanted to return the favor by sending their older daughter to college. But then reality—Alimony? His modest income? The Depression?—caught up with him and he failed to follow through. I'll never know for sure; for now, I'm inclined to believe that he's the one.

Whenever Mom talked about the old neighborhood and her childhood—which wasn't often—her stories carried an undertone of disappointment and resentment. Her family's welfare status deeply embarrassed her; in high school, she skipped lunch to avoid using her government-issued free meal ticket and she walked home, telling her friends that she "needed the exercise" so that they wouldn't know she couldn't afford the few cents of bus fare. Then the most crushing blow of all: her dreams of going to college, of fulfilling the potential that had allowed her to graduate from Northern High School just shy of her seventeenth birthday, dashed by an uncle's unfulfilled promise.

Plenty of immigrant Jews had landed in Detroit and Chicago early in the twentieth century and, within a generation, had made progress from penniless to prosperous. But not my grandparents. Something had gone wrong. Was that why Mom was so determined to flee?

The Cigar Laborer

The casket fascinates me.

No, that's not quite right, it's not the casket itself, it's the entire ritual—the open coffin in the tiny back room, the parade of people going there to say a prayer or say good-bye or just stare. Some people actually talk to him, but why? My grandfather is gone; only his body is here.

I want to see it, I don't want to see it, I don't know what I want—I'm twelve, and that's old enough to see a dead body without getting scared, isn't it? I watch the adults going in and out of the little room, some crying, some not, and I edge myself to the doorway, peering inside at the wooden box. Mom is somewhere with Bubbe, sitting with her, holding her, comforting her. It's just the two of them now that Zayde has died.

I want to see, I don't want to see.

I have to see.

He doesn't look like Zayde, at least not the Zayde I knew. He's smiling almost, which is weird because I don't remember him smiling much. He doesn't look as wrinkled as the last time I saw him. How is that possible? I think about how old he must be—born in the nineteenth century!—and it bothers me that I don't know his exact age. Why do so many people from the old country not know their birthday? Just because you came here a long time ago, and you grew up speaking a different language, why does that make it harder to know when you were born? Mom is telling people that she thinks he was seventy-six or seventy-seven—it's January 1964 now, which means Zayde was born around 1887.

*That's before cars or basketball were invented, that's how ancient that is.
I can only imagine.*

My grandfather first set his Eastern European feet on U.S. soil sometime in 1907. That much I knew from the 1930 census records. But for several months, I could find no hint of how he got here or where he went after making it through the immigration officer's scrutiny. Nor could I find any documentation of Tillie's arrival, which the census listed as 1914. An online search of Ellis Island records yielded nothing, as did an examination of the border crossing records from Canada to Detroit and the passenger manifest lists for Baltimore, Philadelphia, and other ports. I tried every spelling variant I could concoct for Hyman and Tillie and Cohen, without success. Their marriage license proved that both were living in Detroit by July 1915, but their early days in their new homeland, like so much else of my family's history, remained beyond my grasp.

I was looking for the wrong man.

Hyman Cohen did not yet exist when my grandfather bought his ticket for America. "Chaim" was what Anna Oliwek always called him. "Chaim" was the name that David Oliwek had used when he told me that his mother was both a "Korn" and Schlein. It suddenly hit me: I should be looking for Chaim Korn, not Hyman Cohen.

Bingo.

On July 5, 1907, twenty-year-old Chaim Korn, son of Nochim Korn of Radziwillow, Russia, boarded the S.S. *Patricia* in Hamburg, Germany, with a berth in steerage and five U.S. dollars in his pocket. Sixteen days later, after stops in France and England, the *Patricia* steamed into New York's harbor with 160 first-class passengers, 180 in second class, and 2,100 in steerage. At Ellis Island, Chaim answered "no" when asked if he were a polygamist or an anarchist, and he passed a medical examination looking for evidence that he was deformed, crippled, or insane—all conditions that merited exclusion under the immigration acts of 1882 and 1891. He hadn't entered the country yet, but already he had learned something about his new homeland's view of "defectives," at least those from other lands.

After spending four of his dollars to pay the required government "head tax," Chaim made his way to a friend's apartment in Manhattan, disappear-

ing from my view until he showed up in Detroit in 1915. Why had he come?
What attitudes did he bring, and how did they affect his ability to handle
adversity and the birth of a disabled daughter? How did he plan to make a
living?

Eventually, I would assemble enough information to hazard a guess at
the first two questions, but for now, I could only answer the third: The *Patricia*'s passenger manifests, both the one in Hamburg and the one in New
York, list his occupation as "cigar labourer."

Cigar laborer?

I had never heard anything like that. Evans's Routine History, in its
mincingly sparse account of my grandparents' background, reported only
that Hyman hailed from "a family of farmers" and had "very little education," completing just two years in a Jewish school. Was there a thriving
tobacco industry in Radziwillow or its environs? Is that how Chaim (not yet
Hyman) had learned the craft of cigar making, assuming that he had told
the truth about his job skills to the immigration officer? It was common
enough for arriving immigrants to say whatever they thought necessary to
get themselves into the country, and having a means of supporting yourself
was one of those necessary items.

Arriving without money, destination, or job prospects risked rejection
as an "LPC"—a Likely Public Charge—followed by a return trip across the
ocean. But calling yourself a cigar laborer strikes me as an esoteric choice
for a lie; if you had to tell the authorities something, why not just choose
tailor or butcher or the more generic "farm laborer," as so many other passengers on the S.S. *Patricia* did, and be done with it?

Another way to think about it: Perhaps Chaim wasn't describing his
past, but his future. Perhaps he had come to the United States with the ex-
pectation of finding work at a cigar-making company, perhaps a notion
planted either by one of the several thousand steamship company agents
actively promoting the benefits of immigration, or by a fellow Radziwiller
who had preceded him and written home to say, come, come to America,
land of opportunity and cigar making.

Cigar laborer? Is that what brought Chaim to the city where I would be
born? It's certainly possible. Detroit, known to me only as the Motor City,
turns out to have been the Cigar City at the turn of the twentieth century, the
result of good rail connections to the tobacco-growing regions of Kentucky

and further south. No fewer than 189 cigar manufacturers were operating in Detroit in 1907, according to the city directory for that year, employing more than 10,000 workers—many of them women—who produced more than 200 million cigars annually. One news article traced Detroit's tobacco prominence to the pre–Civil War arrival of the first German and Jewish immigrants, "who brought with them the skills and techniques of cigar making from their European homelands."

There's not a shred of evidence that Chaim ever rolled a cigar in Detroit or anywhere else. Reconstructing his work history from various documents, I can describe him as a junk peddler and a janitor, but not a cigar maker. He did get his shot, though, in the brand-new industry that eventually earned many immigrant Detroiters—but not my grandfather—a piston-driven ride out of poverty and into the middle class.

Of all the American cities where my grandparents and other Jewish immigrants could hope to end up in the first two decades of the twentieth century, perhaps none offered more promise than Detroit. Unlike New York, where so many Jews had crammed into the Lower East Side by 1910 that it was home to the densest square mile in the country and perhaps the world, Detroit offered plenty of room for its expanding immigrant neighborhoods. Fueled by the spectacular rise of the auto industry and its related businesses, Detroit saw its population swell more than 60 percent in a single decade, from 286,000 in 1900 to 465,000 in 1910, and then topped that by doubling during the next decade, passing the magic million mark sometime in the fall of 1920. In just twenty years, Detroit had vaulted from the country's thirteenth largest city to the fourth, trailing only New York, Chicago, and Philadelphia.

The transformation happened so fast that it was almost bewildering to long-time residents, not to mention the newly arrived immigrants. The streets, built for the previous generation's horse and buggy, could not handle the polyglot of pedestrians, bicyclists, and junk peddlers with their grimy pushcarts competing for space with the gleaming new automobiles rolling off the assembly lines. No system of traffic signals yet existed; at a dozen major intersections, where traffic engineers counted up to 21,000 cars in a ten-hour period in 1916, the congestion became so bad at peak times that it was "quite impracticable to traverse these streets at all," wrote one historian of the era.

No other U.S. city could claim such a rate of growth during this period. Immigrants from all over Europe—English and Irish, Swedes and Scots, Austrians and Italians, Poles and Germans, Russians and Romanians—flooded into neighborhoods unaccustomed to such a press of humanity. One of those neighborhoods, around the Eastern Market, became a magnet for the thousands of Eastern European Jews streaming into the city—including both my grandfathers, who lived within blocks of each other without ever meeting. Detroit, which had 1,000 Jews in 1880, counted 34,000 by the time Tillie arrived in 1914, many of Russian or Polish descent.

The vicious Russian pogroms of 1881—and harsh new restrictions that went into effect the following year on Russian Jews' right to learn a trade, enter university, or own land outside the so-called Pale of Settlement—triggered an exodus to America rivaled only by that of the Irish and Italians, a mass migration that gained momentum over the next three decades. Between 1881 and 1914, more than two million Jews came to the United States, most of them from the Russian Empire. Between 1903 and 1914, when three of my four grandparents made separate journeys across the Atlantic, an average of 76,000 Jews presented themselves annually to U.S. immigration authorities, more than double the average of 36,000 in the ten years before that.

Some of them returned within a few years, but the vast majority arrived with no intention of ever going back. One of those was Chaim Korn of Radziwillow, Russia.

Barry Moreno spends many days living in the last century. He's a librarian and historian at the Immigration Museum on Ellis Island, which served as a gateway to the future for more than ten million newcomers during its sixty-two years of operation, and I've asked him to help serve as my entree to the past. I want to learn more about the specific factors that might have led Chaim Korn to say farewell to Radziwillow in the summer of 1907.

But first, I can tell Moreno something about the place that Chaim was forsaking: Radziwillow, in 1907, was no sleepy shtetl, no village of the *Fiddler on the Roof* variety. Its location on the border of Russia and Austria had made it a prime spot for the shipment of goods between those two empires since the end of the eighteenth century (and for smuggling operations as well); its inclusion on a major railway line, completed in 1873, guaranteed its development as a bustling town with a flourishing economy.

Radziwillow reaped enormous benefits from its accidental geography. At the time of Chaim's birth in the late 1880s, the town's population had grown to more than seven thousand, including more than four thousand Jews, and signs of affluence were everywhere. The weekly market boasted more than 160 merchants, two two-story hotels played host to traders and travelers, and the nearby farms profited from supplies brought by rail. By the early twentieth century, "the prosperity was felt and seen—doormen in uniforms at important buildings, carriages and majestic horses driven by drivers dressed in an array of shiny uniforms," according to a 1966 memorial book by survivors of Radziwillow's Nazi massacres.

The train station hummed with activity. The railway gauge was a different size on the Austrian side of the border, requiring extra workers to take the Russian goods arriving from Kiev and points further east, and transfer them to cars that could run on the Austrian tracks. Similarly, the crews had to unload and repack imports coming from Vienna and points west. The volume of freight moving through the station led the tsar's government to expand the century-old Radziwillow customs house, one of six such offices then operating in the Russian empire, and to expand the border-crossing brigade already stationed there. Strategically and economically, Radziwillow enjoyed a prominence altogether disproportionate to its small population.

So when some of the town's workers threw themselves into the revolutionary fervor spreading throughout the country in 1905—the year of the failed "first" Russian revolution—54 local businessmen formally requested help, and the government sent additional troops to forestall trouble. Undaunted by the heightened military presence (or perhaps just undeterred), a contingent of Radziwillow's workers—led by tailors and wool hat makers—went on strike in the fall of 1905, demanding a shorter work day, a bigger paycheck, and greater respect from their employers, according to a 2004 history of Radziwillow published in Ukraine. As a town with a Jewish majority, Radziwillow probably attracted additional suspicion; the tsar had publicly described the revolutionaries as a Jewish-led gang, fanning anti-

Semitic feelings that had culminated periodically since 1881 in pogroms—
attacks on Jewish communities, families, and property.

Pogroms had become a staple of Russian life since the imposition of the
anti-Jewish laws in 1881, but there's no documented account of any specific
violence against the Jews of Radziwillow during this period before Chaim's
departure. News of pogroms elsewhere in Russia during 1905—well reported in Jewish newspapers such as the *Chronicle* in London—would have
reached a railway town like Radziwillow at some point, adding to the air of
uncertainty and apprehension that already existed. The 1966 memorial
book by Radziwillow's Holocaust survivors, like many accounts, points to
pogroms as the major cause of Jewish emigration during this period. "Many
Jews fled to America because their homes and small businesses were destroyed, they were attacked, injured and killed, and continued to be perse-
cuted," according to a summary that a translator wrote for me.

Barry Moreno doesn't subscribe to a one-size-fits-all theory of Jewish
immigration. "I think it's a mistake to attribute all Russian emigration to
the pogroms or to say that Jews had 'escaped' them," he tells me. "There's
no question the pogroms were important. But they were isolated, scattered
incidents. Most émigrés had never witnessed a pogrom. I think it's more
accurate to say that pogroms contributed to the more generalized sense of
fear that had spread across the Pale."

This much I know for sure: Chaim and Tillie followed a well-trod path out
of Radziwillow. Before calling Moreno, I did a year-by-year analysis of how
many Radziwillers made it to Ellis Island, based on recently digitized passenger manifests searchable by town name. Between 1900 and 1914, at least
282 passengers listed Radziwillow as their hometown; almost one-third left
in the two years before my grandfather's departure. This matched the trend
in the rest of Russia. Many young Jewish men, after examining their options, were voting with their feet.

Why did the peak come in those years and not earlier? A kind of perfect
storm: In the Russia of 1905 and 1906, Chaim and other young Jewish men
found themselves caught in a vortex of political turmoil, economic depriva-
tions, religious persecution, and military conscription for an unpopular and
ultimately unsuccessful war with Japan. Add the threat of pogroms to this

swirling mix, along with the tension of living in a border town with a large
military presence—a military with a reputation for promoting and sometimes participating in the pogroms—and it's not hard to see why Chaim and
his Radziwillow neighbors might have turned their eyes toward America.

The Russian Jews weren't the only ones hungering to leave their country. From Italy, from Germany, from Romania, from Hungary, from Austria, from most of southern and eastern Europe, emigrants crossed the
Atlantic in record numbers, peaking at nearly 1.3 million in 1907, the year
of Chaim's journey. The steamship companies were not just passive players
in this ongoing drama; their network of agents and subagents operated
throughout Europe, promising cheap transportation to the promised land.
Their tactics drew the scrutiny of Philip Cowen, a U.S. immigration inspec-
tor sent to Russia in 1906 by President Theodore Roosevelt to investigate
the causes of the mass migration. Cowen described how a minority of agents
went beyond propaganda, employing the sort of unscrupulous tactics that
might be expected in an unregulated sellers' market—peddling fraudulent
tickets, extorting bribes to arrange passage, luring customers with the
promise of nonexistent jobs.

Immigration was the talk—pro and con—of Washington in 1907; as
Chaim Korn made his arrangements to leave Radziwillow, a presidential-
congressional commission opened the first official U.S. investigation of
the migration phenomenon, an effort that lasted three years and included
the placement of investigators disguised as steerage passengers on twelve
ships crossing the Atlantic. The panel, chaired by U.S. Senator William
Dillingham of Vermont, reflected the divided politics of the time. Some
members wanted to use the commission as a weapon to restrict immigration, both Asian and European, which they viewed as a threat to the country's stability. Other members, and many more on the staff, pursued a
social reformer's agenda, seeking broader evidence of the kind of exploi-
tation that Cowen had found in his travels to Russia—recruiters prowling
Europe for cheap labor, steamship companies transporting their passengers in inhuman conditions, employers taking advantage of the newcomers upon arrival.

As part of the commission's investigation, two U.S. immigration inspectors visited southern and eastern Europe and found that poor villages
and towns had a surprisingly rich source of information about life in

America. Letters from émigrés arrived regularly, often containing money, and these letters had a powerful effect in encouraging more immigration. "The cottage of the recipient becomes at once a place to which the entire male population proceeds, and the letters are read and re-read until the contents can be repeated word for word," wrote an investigator who had gone to Italy. "When instances of this kind have been multiplied by thousands, it is not difficult to understand what impels poor people to leave their homes. The word comes again and again that 'work is abundant and wages princely in America.'"

Their lines of communication to America gave them some idea of the risks that awaited them at sea and upon arrival. The commission's investigators found that the emigrants had a basic grasp of U.S. immigration law; most were aware that they stood a better chance at admission if they had money, a skill, a place to go, and no obvious physical or mental problems. The rigors of the journey itself tended to weed out many of those who might not pass muster. In the commission's words, "emigrating to a strange and distant country, although less of an undertaking than formerly, is still a serious and relatively difficult matter, requiring a degree of courage and resourcefulness not possessed by weaklings in any class."

Courage. Resourcefulness. Not for weaklings.

I would never have associated these words with my discouraged, defeated grandfather, the rail-thin man who had left so little an impression on me that I can remember nothing of significance that he said from six years of weekly Saturday visits to his apartment. But that beaten man barely resembled the twenty-year-old who surmounted Russia's bureaucratic obstacles to emigration and procured the necessary papers to leave, who then scraped together the money (about $30) for a ticket on the S.S. *Patricia* and negotiated his way to the Hamburg-America line's *Auswandererhallen*, a vast complex of dormitories and dining halls that housed and fed as many as four thousand emigrants awaiting inspection before boarding their ship. He then protected his few belongings in the chaos of steerage, which the commission described as an ordeal that leaves the traveler "with a mind unfit for healthy, wholesome impressions and with a body weakened and unfit for the hardships that are involved in the beginning of life in a new land."

What conditions did Chaim confront on his sixteen days in steerage on the S.S. *Patricia*? I don't have to imagine it, thanks to the detailed report of commission investigator Anna Herkner. The summer after Chaim's journey on the S.S. *Patricia*, Herkner disguised herself as a steerage passenger on another Hamburg-America vessel of the same vintage. Her final report, on that voyage and two others, offered first-hand confirmation of "the disgusting and demoralizing conditions which have generally prevailed in the steerage of immigrant ships."

A one-person backpacking tent has nearly twice as much room as the space allotted Chaim and Herkner in steerage. They slept in iron bunks six feet long and two feet wide, with just thirty inches separating the upper and lower berths. At over six feet tall, Chaim would have consumed most of those thirty cubic feet just by putting himself to bed. With no hooks for clothing or bin for luggage, his thirty cubic feet would have served as bed, closet, kitchen cabinet, towel rack, table, chair, and storage compartment for whatever possessions he had brought from Radziwillow. Most likely, he would have slept in his clothes, not only to conserve space but also because the ship-supplied blanket was too small and too thin to keep him warm. His pillow, if he were lucky enough to get one, would have been stuffed with dried seaweed or perhaps straw, just like his mattress.

If the cramped quarters were bad, the smell was worse. The steamship companies considered their immigrant passengers to be little more than freight, Herkner wrote, and they crammed as many beds as possible in the steerage compartments, row upon row, tier upon tier, hundreds of people breathing the same poorly ventilated air. "The vomitings of the sick are often permitted to remain a long time before being removed," Herkner wrote. "The floors, when iron, are continually damp, and when of wood they reek with foul odor because they are not washed . . . When to this very limited space and much filth and stench is added inadequate means of ventilation, the result is almost unendurable."

An earlier outcry about steerage conditions and the competition for passengers had led some steamship lines to make improvements, but only a small percentage of ships had converted or built "new" steerage by the time Chaim and Herkner went on their trans-Atlantic journeys. Twice Herkner traveled in old-style steerage, and once in new, where the berths had amenities comparable to second class—storage space for hand luggage, hooks for clothing, warmer blankets, a drop shelf for a table, and stewards assigned to clean up seasickness.

Unfortunately, most immigrants never saw new steerage, which was not available on most ships in 1907 and 1908. Rebuilding the steerage quarters meant taking the ship out of service, at least for a few months, and as far as I can tell from available records, the S.S. *Patricia* had no significant inter- ruption in operation between its maiden voyage in 1899 and the 1907 cross- ing that brought Chaim to America. So it seems likely that Chaim would have seen a version of what Herkner wrote of seeing on her first voyage from Bremen to Baltimore: "During these twelve days in the steerage I lived in a disorder and in surroundings that offended every sense. Only the fresh breeze from the sea overcame the sickening odors, the vile language of the men, the screams of the women defending themselves, the crying of chil- dren, wretched because of their surroundings, and practically every sound that reached the ear, irritated beyond endurance. There was no sight before which the eye did not prefer to close."

Eyes shut might have been the preferred mode of travel at sea, but those same eyes grew wide upon entering New York's harbor. A photo of the S.S. *Patricia*, taken just six months before Chaim traveled on that same ship to America, shows the main deck jammed to overflowing with smiling im- migrants eager to get a glimpse of their new homeland. They had plenty of time to gawk; so many ships were arriving in New York during this period that the Ellis Island inspectors were overwhelmed, requiring steerage pas- sengers to remain on their ships or crowd onto ferries while awaiting their turn for processing. Ellis Island's inspectors could handle between two thousand and four thousand steerage passengers on a typical day; the nine ships that appeared on July 21, 1907—the day of Chaim's arrival—carried three or four times that many.

Chaim had made it to America. Now the question was: Would he be able to make it *in* America?

"What did your grandfather do in the Mo-tor City?" my friend Dan Swanson asks soon after we meet at the college newspaper in 1971. Dan likes to play with words,

so he alters the syllable stress, making it "Mo-tor" to resonate with Motown, Detroit's newest nickname in those days.

"He was a junk peddler, mostly," I remember saying, or something like that.
Dan wants details, but I don't have any—I tell him that Mom never talked much
about him, and that we aren't a family that dwells much on the past.

Dan and I are both city boys who went to public high schools and then became
beneficiaries of Harvard's long-running effort to assemble a student body with a
geographic and economic mix. (I wasn't aware until much later that "geographical distribution" began in the 1920s as part of the university president's effort to
counteract the rising percentage of Jewish kids who were qualifying for admission, many from immigrant families in New York and other urban centers of the
Northeast.) I'm also the cliché: two generations after my grandfather left Russia,
where the tsar's laws discriminated against Jews and their educational opportunities, I'm admitted to Harvard.

Dan is a product of Chicago's South Side, and proud of it. He also has a historian's curiosity about the social forces that shape people and their cities, so
getting to know him is akin to submitting to an interrogation—he quizzes me relentlessly about my background, my family, and Detroit, which he regards as
Chicago's little brother.

"How come he never worked for the aut-o companies?" Dan says. "That
scumbag Henry Ford wouldn't give him a job?" Dan's patter is usually colorful
and always anticorporate; he comes from a union town, and he calls himself a
union man.

"I don't know," I say, a little embarrassed. Dan knows a lot about his family
and his city, and his questions make me feel like I should know more about mine.
"I may be from the Motor City"—like many Detroit natives, I disliked the nickname, and rarely used it—"but I don't live anywhere near the auto plants, and
no one from my family ever worked there. It's a part of Detroit that I just don't
know much about."

What happened to Detroit's economy between 1910 and 1920—the decade
when Hyman and Tillie married, set down roots in the city, and started
their family—is staggering to contemplate.

When the decade dawned, General Motors employed 15,000 workers; 10
years later, 50,000 toiled in its plants. Henry Ford's workforce grew at an

even faster rate, going from 10,000 in 1910, to 32,000 in 1916, to 48,000 in 1919. Altogether, 181 auto companies opened shop in Detroit between 1903 and 1926, and their insatiable demand for parts spawned hundreds of machine shops and suppliers, who in turn hired thousands of workers. In the early days of the industry, the suppliers—not Ford or Olds or GM—were king. The brand names that eventually came to dominate the industry were mostly assemblers, dependent on the engines and transmissions of people such as the Dodge Brothers, whose Hamtramck factory rivaled Ford's plant in size and numbers.

Ford and the Dodge Brothers formed an exclusive alliance in 1903 that made all three men—and several other investors—into multimillionaires in less than a decade. Ford and his partners, desperate for cash at the time, gave the Dodges a share of their nearly bankrupt company; as a result, the Dodges secured the dual role of investors as well as suppliers. This profitable arrangement continued until 1914, when Ford declared that he no longer wanted to pay the Dodges twice (referring to dividends and supplies). The Dodges, owners of perhaps the most trusted name in the industry because of their first-rate engines and other parts, struck out on their own. Before the first Dodge Brothers Touring Car came off the assembly line in November 1914, the company found itself inundated with orders, as well as an astounding 22,000 applicants for Dodge dealerships.

Within two years, the Dodge workforce had tripled, from 5,000 to 16,000. Getting a job at Dodge was a coup; while no one would get rich on $3 to $5 a day, it was several steps up from peddling junk on the street. I didn't know much about the auto industry growing up, but I knew enough to wonder why Hyman never managed to get a job at one of the plants, the way so many other immigrants did.

Which is why I was surprised when I obtained Mom's 1917 birth certificate, and under Father's Occupation, it said: "Dodge Bros. employee."

Punching the Dodge clock was no guarantee of stability, however. Like other auto factories, Dodge slowed its production at the end of each model year, resulting in layoffs for a portion of the workforce—particularly the unskilled, like my grandfather.

By the time Annie was born in April 1919, Hyman no longer worked for

Dodge. Annie's birth certificate lists his occupation as "laborer," with no mention of where he was laboring. At some point, he managed to land a job at Ford, but that didn't last long either; Ford's archives show that a Hyman Cohen worked there briefly, in late 1918 and early 1919. When 1920 arrived, Hyman was looking for work and Tillie was taking Annie to the Children's Hospital clinic for the first of many examinations of her deformed leg. With two young daughters, and Annie's worsening health problems, it was not the best time for Chaim to lose his tenuous grip on a steady income.

Detroit and the auto industry, meanwhile, had accumulated so much wealth that its leaders literally could not spend it fast enough. The Dodges built themselves opulent estates in the countryside to complement their mansions near downtown, and Detroit prepared for a series of public works projects and land annexations that would transform the city's character and economy forever. In a space of five years, the city built and opened a new art museum and a new public library; it acquired the privately owned streetcar system; it went on an annexation spree that pushed the city's borders outward in every direction, expanding the city's footprint by nearly 70 percent in just three years, from 80 square miles to more than 134.

A world-class city needs a world-class hotel, so on December 1, 1924, the 28-story Book Cadillac, with its 1,200 rooms, 20 retail stores, and Italian Renaissance grandeur, took its place as the postcard symbol of Detroit's coming of age—and later, for my parents and others in their generation, as the starting point for a downtown date ("Meet you at the Book"). Then, at the close of the decade known appropriately as the Roaring Twenties, privately financed architects, engineers, and construction crews joined forces to complete what others had only dreamed, erecting not one but two routes across the Detroit River to Canada. On November 11, 1929, just thirty months after groundbreaking, the first cars lined up for the 1.6-mile trip across the Ambassador Bridge; less than a year later, the owners of the Detroit-Windsor tunnel opened its lanes—and cash registers—to international traffic.

But for my grandfather and his family, the Roaring Twenties might be better described as the Declining Twenties. Hyman spent the first part of the decade pushing his peddler's cart, while Tillie spent hers at home, caring for one child considered "exceptionally bright" and a second with such a severe handicap that she could not go to school until three years after her age group had started.

When Nathan Shlien showed up from Chicago in 1921 or 1922, Hyman and Tillie probably saw his presence as a boon, or at least a second income; with Nathan contributing a portion of his auto-plant paycheck, they scraped by, renting an apartment on Hendrie Street. Then Hyman returned to Ford for a time, and was working steadily enough to rent slightly larger quarters on Medbury Avenue, for $35 a month.

Hyman stayed with Ford for six years before illness forced him to leave, the Routine History says (although records in the Ford archive could not confirm this second round of employment). By the end of the decade, he was back on the streets, peddling "spasmodically," in the odd phrasing of the Evans report. When the Depression devastated Detroit, the Cohen family lost what little foothold it had. If it was hard for Hyman to get a job when times were good, it became impossible when times went bad. In early 1930, social worker Helen Hall wrote after visiting Detroit, "I have never confronted such misery as on the zero day of my arrival in Detroit." With no federal aid system in place, that misery overwhelmed the city's welfare department, which saw its average monthly caseload soar from 5,029 in the second half of 1929 to 49,314 in the first six months of 1930.

Every day, Hall reported, hundreds of unemployed men lined up at the seven temporary welfare stations established in neigborhoods on the city's east and west sides; after interviewing dozens of them as they waited in the bitter January cold and observing their oppressive sense of gloom, Hall concluded: "The only worse thing I've seen was the look on the faces of a company of French polius [infantry soldiers] who had been in the trenches four years; all hopes seemed to have been wiped out and an intense weariness had taken its place."

Detroit, which had prospered with the auto industry's rise, now died by its precipitous decline. More than 125,000 autoworkers found themselves on the street in early 1930, a third of the industry's workforce; an additional 100,000 lost their jobs in 1931, and most of the rest battled for the part-time work that remained. Many ended up as POGIEs—the Poor Old Guys in Eloise—living in the barracks-like building that the hospital constructed for the city's growing homeless population.

Detroit, so recently the symbol of affluence and progress, now became the standard for scarcity and despair. "Children scavenged through the street like animals for scraps of food, and stayed away from school," Robert

Conot wrote in *American Odyssey*, his history of Detroit published after the riots of 1967. "The attendance department made little pretense of tracking them down . . . Each day four thousand children stood in bread lines. With their sunken, lifeless eyes, sallow cheeks, and distended bellies, some resembled the starving children in Europe during the war."

Mom had just reached her teens when Detroit hit economic bottom, old enough to remember what it was like. Yet she never said anything in detail, perhaps because she could not find a way to talk about those times without talking about Annie as well. So her description of growing up poor had shape but no substance. "It was awful," she would say. "I never want to be poor again. I never want you to be poor."

Reading the city's own records on what happened in that decade, I can finally fathom the depths of my grandparents' despair in those Depression years, as well as the depths of Mom's resentment. Annie's leg, in particular, required more attention, and more treatment, than the family could afford. In 1936, when Dr. Frederick Kidner at Harper Hospital decided to amputate her misshapen leg, the city welfare department paid for the wooden one that went in its place.

If Mom was embarrassed by her father's woeful work history, she was mortified when her family joined the welfare rolls in 1934. The city welfare agency later hired Hyman as a part-time janitor, but his fortunes never turned around, not even after World War II arrived and Detroit regained its place as the nation's industrial heartland. Mom was determined that her parents' fate—impoverished, isolated, still uncomfortable with their English—was not going to prevent her from attaining something better.

THIRTEEN

Invisible

Previous page: *Stepping into Annie's world: Oakman School, 2008*
(Elizabeth Conley photo)

Marty Moss, eighty-two years old and two decades retired from his job selling appliances, lives just a few miles from the suburban Detroit apartment that Mom called home for twenty-three years. When I call him on a June afternoon at his sister Millie's suggestion, he tells me that he hasn't seen Mom "since the war" (referring, of course, to World War II), but he has no trouble remembering the young woman he first knew as Bertha until she made it clear that she wanted to be called Beth.

"I have to tell you—I had a little crush on her." He says the word "crush" with a youthful mischievousness. "We never went out or anything, but we spent a lot of time together. I remember her being worried about getting married. She was a pretty girl, and I used to joke with her that if she didn't find anyone, I'd marry her."

A secret suitor!

"When was this?" I ask.

"Before the war, 1938, 1939."

That's just before Annie went to Eloise. It's taken four months and several false starts, but I've finally broken into Mom's social circle. I ask Marty if the group revolved around the neighborhood or school—he and Mom, I remind him, were close in age, but they had several years on Faye, Sylvia, and Julie, so I wasn't sure what held the group together.

The mention of Faye's name distracts him. "Faye," he sighs. "Everyone was in love with Faye. I used to date her before I went into the service. She

was one of the girls I would have considered marrying, not that I ever suggested that to her."

What about the group? How did they become friends? "I'm not exactly
sure. I think it started with the neighborhood, then friends from school
joined in. I lost touch after I got married, although I would hear about them
from time to time. Most have passed away—Faye last year, Sylvia recently.
I'm not sure about Julie Reisner. I think she's still alive, maybe in California." He paused. "Millie said your mom died a few years ago?"

"In 1999," I tell him. "You know she had a sister, Annie?"

"Yes, but I don't remember seeing her much. She was crippled, right?"

She must have been a striking sight, this young girl with a brace and
crutches, and later with her wooden leg, and yet she moved through the
neighborhood as if she were invisible. Not invisible, exactly—her neighbors, her sister's friends, the people she passed on the street, her fellow
bus passengers, they all saw her, but they didn't see her. She had no presence, no substance, and no impact on their lives.

I think Annie understood this at some level. From the Routine History:
*During the winter of 1939 and 1940 she seemed to be suddenly overwhelmed with
the realization that she would never be able to live a normal life such as other girls
have. She began to display interest in boys and yet could not look forward to marriage . . . She began to lose interest in activities inside and outside her home, no
longer finding consolation in books, in sewing, or attending movies or listening to
the radio, and would spend all her time sitting in a chair, refusing to even go out
of the house.*

By early 1940, she saw hardly anyone outside her family—so hardly anyone saw her. Once merely ignored or shunned, she became isolated and
shut in.

Needing to inhabit Annie's world, I stop by the Oakman School for Crippled Children on one of my Detroit visits. The handsome sandstone-and-
brick building, which opened its doors in 1929, still serves physically
handicapped students, who make up about one-third of its three-hundred-
student population. The word "crippled," however, disappeared from its
name long ago; it's now known formally as the Oakman Elementary/
Orthopedic School.

On the long drive to the school, located on the city's west side, I wonder
if there's any purpose to my visit. It's unlikely that Oakman—the equivalent
of a junior high school back then—has any yearbooks or records of Annie's
six years there, ending in 1937 when she was eighteen, three years older
than the typical ninth-grade graduate. She only got a diploma, the Routine
History said, "because it was felt that it would encourage her, not because
she had actually accomplished this level of work."

As I approach Oakman's front door, I have the impulse to turn around
and head back to the car. What am I going to say when I enter the main office? "Hi, I'm looking for a student who last walked these hallways sixty-
eight years ago . . ." The school's staff is going to think I've lost my mind.
Annie might have been here once, but she's here no longer.

How wrong I am. No written record of Annie exists, but as a kind as-
sistant principal gives me a tour, pointing out the original wooden handrails running the length of every hallway, I have no trouble envisioning
Annie on her way to class, steadying herself as she goes. Amid the school
corridor's usual cacophony—the hum of a hundred voices, the giggles and
shouts and light taps of quickly moving shoes—I can hear the *click* and *thwud*
and *schwush* of crutches, prosthetic legs, and wheelchairs on linoleum. I
can't hear my aunt's voice or ask her any questions, but I can see her phantom figure, the brace on her useless right leg, struggling as best she can
manage with either crutch or handrail, pushing herself forward, a disabled
Sisyphus on her unending journey.

As classes begin and the noise recedes, I stand alone in the now-empty
hallway, vacillating between feelings of anger and sadness—anger that she
had to endure so much pain, and sadness that she was born before science
and medicine could do much for her afflictions.

Mary Greco listens patiently and politely to my pitch, but she's steadfast: If
I want the state of Michigan to undertake a search for Annie's medical file,
she's telling me, I'll need a court order. That's how the Michigan Department of Community Health interprets the law governing mental health
records, she says, pointing me to the specific sections that the department
cites to support its view. My status as Annie's personal representative isn't
good enough.

Another agency, another roadblock in my hunt for the rest of Annie's medical file. After Patricia Waterman informed me that Wayne County had no record of Annie ever being treated at Eloise, I took my search to the state capital in Lansing, where the Michigan Department of Community Health has responsibility for the surviving records of the now-closed Northville State Hospital. Greco works in the department's legal affairs office, and it's her job to handle requests like mine.

As Greco and I talk, I think back to the conversation I had in May 2000, when I naively called the same department to see what I could learn about this secret aunt I had just discovered. *You and five thousand other people,* said the helpful woman who first warned me that I would need a court order to get any information. *What do you tell them?* I had asked her. *I can't tell them anything. State law doesn't let me . . .*

I had come full circle. Six years earlier, Northville was still open (luckily for me, otherwise I might not have gotten either the Eloise records or the 1972 Northville summaries), and I was fumbling in the dark for Annie's medical records. Now Northville was closed (unluckily for me, because closure increased the likelihood that Annie's file had been destroyed as part of a routine disposal of records older than twenty years), and I had specific legal authority allowing me to seek Annie's medical records, but in the eyes of the Department of Community Health, nothing had changed.

Looking at the section Greco cited, I'm even more convinced that the department's response is more or less automatic. One section specifically allows "a court-appointed personal representative" to authorize the release of the deceased's medical records. I'm surprised and heartened. It seems clear—and I make my case in an e-mail to Greco—that I already qualify and that the judge's signature on my Letter of Authority is the equivalent of a "court order," if the department is worried about setting a precedent.

How much of Annie's file had gone with her when Eloise sent her to Northville in January 1972? I didn't know for sure, but it must have been a substantial portion, based on my first forage for Annie's records in 2000. My contact back then had said her friend at Northville didn't feel comfortable sending Annie's *entire* record, so she had photocopied just the beginning and end of the file.

I had to know if the middle portion existed. If it existed, I had to see it.

Who needed to be protected? The patient died thirty-four years ago, both hospitals were now closed, there's a history that needs to be told. What's the harm?

You and five thousand others . . .

Needing to inhabit Annie's body, I pay a visit to Frank J. Frassica, the head of orthopedic surgery at Johns Hopkins University's School of Medicine, a post that makes him one of the leading practitioners in his field. His round face, balding head, and playful wisp of a mustache give him a theatrical air, and he bears a passing resemblance to one of those TV doctors. He has read the Routine History and the court papers on Annie's commitment, which I sent him in advance, so he knows as much as I do about her deformed leg and Dr. Frederick Kidner's decision to amputate in October 1936.

I tell Frassica what I've learned about Kidner—that he was not only the top orthopedic surgeon at Harper Hospital and in the prime of a distinguished career when he operated on Annie, but he had just been elected to a one-year term as president of the American Orthopedic Association. His reputation and renown brought him invitations to deliver lectures at the country's leading orthopedic centers, and made him a major force in the development of Michigan's Crippled Children's Service, one of the country's first such agencies. A 2005 book on major figures in orthopedic history describes the Massachusetts-born and Harvard-educated surgeon as "not one to be carried away by new ideas just because they were new, but was always ready to accept new proposals that had been thoroughly tested by time and experience."

In other words, Annie's surgeon was no slouch. The contrast between his circumstances and his patient's—Kidner lived in Grosse Pointe Farms, one of the city's wealthiest suburbs, in a house staffed by servants, while Annie and Mom shared a bedroom in a four-room apartment—could not have been starker. He was the eminent surgeon, the voice of authority. I doubt that my immigrant grandparents had a clue how to talk with him, question him, or challenge him.

I have to assume, as my grandparents surely did, that Kidner had only the best of intentions in offering to remove Annie's leg. But I don't want to assume. I want to know.

"Go back to 1936," I say to Frassica. "Put yourself in Dr. Kidner's place, if you can. Why does he want to amputate, and what does he tell my aunt and her family?"

To begin to answer my question, Frassica takes me into conference room 5152, the department's gathering place for major discussions. For the moment, I've become one of Frassica's students, although without any of the prerequisite courses I would need to qualify for medical school. He grasps the left leg of a skeletal model that dangles, front and center, in the conference room and he manipulates it to give me a visual understanding of Annie's struggles with her right leg.

"As you know, something went wrong, possibly during pregnancy or birth, possibly inherited, that caused the deformity," Frassica says. The available facts don't lead to a definite conclusion, but Annie's low birth weight—and Mona Evans's statement that the delivery was normal—suggest some sort of genetic condition or some sort of trauma during pregnancy that resulted in damage to the central nervous system and a malformation of her leg and hip (Kidner did a "minor" operation to straighten Annie's hip at the same time as the amputation, according to the Routine History).

"If the problem is neurological, like cerebral palsy, and there's spasticity, then it won't matter how much you attempt to straighten the leg," Frassica says. Annie's doctors did try to straighten it, and kept trying, which probably means they weren't sure of the cause or didn't think it was cerebral palsy. Nothing worked, though, as the Routine History made clear: *She was in casts and braces all the time, but the leg didn't improve much, and failed to develop.*

"If the leg can't function, the muscles don't develop, and that leads to contracture. The leg can't extend and can't bear any weight," Frassica says, pushing up the skeleton's leg so that the model is now balancing—teetering—solely on the other one. Like car engines, legs and knee joints have fewer problems when they're put to work; an unused leg not only contracts, it's far more vulnerable to skin problems and sores. Annie's condition also wasn't static—as she grew to adult size, her limb became heavier to lug around and a greater drag on her ability to walk, as well as requiring a larger brace.

Kidner had started his career at Detroit's Children's Hospital, where he continued to hold a position while working at Harper, so he might well have known of Annie, or known of her case, earlier than 1936. Tillie first brought Annie to Children's in 1921, when Kidner was on staff, and Children's was the place where Annie acquired the cast and brace that, ultimately, failed to work. Kidner would offer amputation only as a last resort, Frassica says, but in Kidner's mind, hadn't Annie more or less reached that point? The Routine History: *Until she was 17 years of age, patient walked with crutches, and at that time she was able to walk a little with a brace.*

For a seventeen-year-old, walking a little wouldn't get her very far; it certainly wouldn't get her to that sense of independence that she craved. To use an expression Kidner had never heard, the surgeon probably saw the amputation as a win-win: Replace Annie's useless limb with a prosthetic one, removing the dead weight that made walking impossible and giving her a chance at a stable gait that, if not entirely normal, at least did not require crutches or braces or handrails.

Even the most resourceful patients, with supportive and wealthy families that can afford the best care and the highest-quality artificial limbs, have difficulty making the transition to a prosthetic leg, which must be maintained daily to perform properly. Annie was hardly the ideal candidate for the task ahead, a factor that Kidner would have taken into account, Frassica tells me. Of course, the ideal candidates—physically fit, mentally acute, psychologically prepared—rarely have to face an amputation. "You would never cut off a limb without a lot of thought," Frassica says on the walk back to his office, "especially since Annie's problems extended to her hip, requiring an amputation above the knee. That sort of prosthetic requires more energy to walk than a person with two whole legs, because of the difficulty of movement without a fully functioning knee joint. Of course, in those days, prosthetics weren't as lightweight as they are now, so it would be even harder."

Even a win-win has its downsides. Annie's life was about to change, and there was no way to prepare her for the unrelenting challenge and exhaustion of life lived with an artificial limb.

Walk a mile in Annie's shoes? No thanks.

Kevin Carroll at Hanger Prosthetics, one of the country's leading makers of artificial limbs, helps me create a picture of Annie and her new leg, the one that the city's welfare department paid for, the one that the Routine History says "never fitted her very well, although it was repaired and changed several times, with the result that patient did not walk well."

Let's start at the beginning: Annie would wake up from the operation, Carroll says, with something approaching grief for her missing limb. There's no good time to lose a leg, but at seventeen, Annie was already too old. "She would have bonded with her leg," Carroll tells me. "If she's like others I've met, she would have seen it as part of her, and losing it would have been a terrible psychological blow." Young children, in Carroll's experience, have the best shot at adjusting to an amputation.

Her artificial leg, standing alone, would have been a work of art, or at least of craftsmanship. Made of wood, covered with rawhide, coated with a lacquer, and finished with flesh-toned enamel to approximate the look and color of skin, Annie's leg represented decades of hard-earned expertise, first acquired in this country during the aftermath of the Civil War, when advances in warfare left more veterans without a hand or arm or foot or leg, and advances in medicine kept them from dying on the battlefield, creating a greater need for a variety of well-made prosthetic limbs than ever before. Union surgeons performed more than thirty thousand amputations of all sorts, with an estimated 75 percent surviving the deadly risks of infection and gangrene; historians put the Confederate numbers, which are harder to document, in the same range.

Titanium alloys and tiny computers are now revolutionizing the industry, offering above-knee amputees such as Annie the chance to walk with a normal gait. (Double amputee Oscar Pistorius of South Africa runs fast enough on his high-tech prosthetic legs to put him in the company of Olympic-class athletes, presenting the overseers of sports competitions with an unprecedented question: Do artificially-powered limbs give athletes with disabilities an unfair advantage over those with two human ones?) But these technological advances are still filtering their way down to the typical amputee; before computers came along to serve as a liaison between mind and body, an artificial limb couldn't simulate the function of knee and ankle joints, and it couldn't absorb the impact of a foot striking the ground, making every step an awkward proposition. For Annie, who never learned to walk properly in the first place, the motion of putting one artificial foot in front of the other would have required weeks if not months to master, as well as large amounts of patience, endurance, and strength.

Learning how to attach the leg wasn't hard, but it had to be done right. Annie would place her stump—or "residual limb," as today's orthopedists prefer to call it—into the prosthetic socket, making sure that it fit snugly, and then tie or strap a leather-covered metal band around her pelvis to prevent the eighteen-pound apparatus from turning on itself. It's likely she had a stabilizing leather shoulder strap as well, which was a common way for above-the-knee amputees of short stature and slight build to better support the heavy leg. Still, there's no way to distribute the extra weight as smoothly and as evenly as a normal leg does. "She would feel the pull on the shoulder with every step," Carroll says.

She would also sweat. The additional energy required to walk with an artificial leg would produce an abundance of perspiration, and the moisture would soak the socket, causing the rawhide there to become wet. If Annie didn't remove her leg once or twice a day to clean it and let it dry, the socket could swell and shrink, losing its precise shape. Then, as Annie walked, the torque would cause her stump to move in the socket, rubbing her skin raw and increasing her chances of getting rashes and infections.

Even if Annie did a perfect job of caring for the socket, the odds were against her. At seventeen, her body was still a work in progress, which meant her stump was likely to change shape. It didn't matter whether it was tight or loose—either outcome would throw off the alignment, making the artificial leg slightly longer or shorter than her other one. "That's when you see prosthetic-wearers swinging their legs around to clear the floor or find a point of contact," Carroll says.

The leg itself could last a decade or even more, but the socket might need adjustment or replacement every year, or every few months, depending on the patient. No wonder Annie had such problems: *This never fitted very well, although it was repaired and changed several times, with the result that patient did not walk well.*

"They're marvelous devices," Carroll tells me. "But they do have their pitfalls."

. . .

Mary Greco's reply to my e-mail makes no reference to the need for a court order. It merely says, without preface, that I should fill out the attached form, authorizing the department to release "protected health information" and providing as much detail as possible about the patient in question. Once Greco receives my signed authorization, she writes, she will "access our record database to see if the information you are seeking is still available."

Greco's e-mail doesn't specifically state that the department now regards me as having the legal standing to seek Annie's records, but logically, there's no other explanation for the turnabout. It's hardly a big victory—after all, I don't yet have a single new piece of information—but I feel like celebrating nonetheless.

Where the form asks for the "identity and type of information," I write a description both broad and precise, attempting to cover every base: "Any and all records, medical or psychiatric, relating to the institutionalization of Annie Cohen, deceased. Records may include Northville State Hospital Case No. 16317 and previous Wayne County General/Eloise Hospital and Infirmary Case No. 17205. See attached supplemental page for specific dates between 1940 and 1972."

I don't have to wait long. A week later, I get a call.

"Mr. Luxenberg? This is Sara West from the Department of Community Health in Lansing." I feel myself gripping the phone a bit harder. "We sent you a letter yesterday saying that we could find no records, that they have been destroyed." If this were a sports event, I would say the crowd just got very quiet. "But we learned today that a record was found, so I wanted to call you before you got the letter."

A record? *One* record? Could she be more specific?

"It's just two pages from 1972," she says. "That's all we have." I pepper her with questions. Why just two pages? How come those weren't destroyed, too? She says she doesn't know, she's only working there for a few months and is calling on Greco's behalf. I apologize for my persistence, explaining that this is my best chance for finding out more about my aunt, that we had only recently learned of her existence. "It's hard to be in this position," I say. "I can't look for the records myself, so I have to rely on the state for a thorough search."

"Your aunt was a secret?" West says. "Wow."

With that one word, I've transformed myself from something other than one of the unseen thousands who write to the government daily, weekly, yearly, seeking information. "I'll see if I can find out anything else about the search process," she says.

On hold, I curse myself for not pursuing the entire file back in 2000. West returns to the line. "It appears that all Northville files older than twenty-five years were destroyed about a year ago, in keeping with the state's records retention policy." She stops. "I'm sorry."

If I were a tire, I'd be flat by now. I persist, though, looking for some sliver of hope. "Then why did these two pages from 1972 survive? They're older than twenty-five years."

I'm asking her questions she can't answer. She suggests that I wait until I see the pages. She's putting them in the mail today.

The surviving record arrives from Lansing, and now I understand why it wasn't destroyed—it's from the state's master index of patients in mental hospitals, a set of cards created to track Annie Cohen's journey through the system after her transfer to Northville. Mostly, it confirms facts that I already know, but two entries stand out, two bits of information that mitigate my disappointment in acting too late to rescue thirty-two years of records from the shredder or incinerator or landfill or whatever the state of Michigan uses to dispose of its history and, in this case, my aunt's.

Fact #1: Commitment date, 6–12–1940. Type of Order: Permanent.

I bring out Annie's court file. My recollection is correct: There's no document describing Annie's commitment to Eloise as permanent, no final order, not even a docket of actions taken so that someone coming along a year or a decade or sixty-five years later might know definitively what had happened to this young woman after three doctors examined her and two had declared her "actually insane." The only hint in the court file is the stamped date, June 12, 1940, and that scrawled notation, "Eloise or Ypsi Public."

This latest piece of the puzzle makes the chronology clear. On April 25, Judge O'Brien sent Annie to Eloise on a temporary order. Two days later, the superintendent of Eloise signed a form letter that states, without qualification, that it would be "improper and unsafe" for Annie to attend the hearing that would determine her sanity. That hearing, set first for May 8 and postponed twice, finally took place on June 12, without Annie in attendance. O'Brien accepted Dr. Peter Bolewicki's tie-breaking conclusion that Annie was actually insane, and made her a permanent patient at Eloise. He stamped the June 12 date on the cover of Tillie's original petition, but otherwise placed nothing in the public file that reflected the change—this momentous, life-altering change—in Annie's status.

Fact #2: A diagnosis, with two codes added by hand, 295.90 and 312.00.

The codes come from the DSM-II—that era's Diagnostic and Statistical Manual, the psychiatric standard now in its fourth edition. Her symptoms fit the criteria for 295.90, a conduct disorder characterized by aggressive behavior, and 312.00, chronic schizophrenia, undifferentiated—both catchall diagnoses.

In other words, Annie left Eloise in 1972 exhibiting much the same symptoms as when she arrived in 1940. Psychiatry and the mental health system had changed dramatically in those three decades, but not much had changed for Annie.

Ed Missavage squints at the 1964 roster of Eloise psychiatrists, photocopied from one of his former colleague's donated papers at the Wayne State University archives. I'm hoping that perhaps one of the young psychiatrists who joined the staff in 1964 might have had Annie as a patient in her later years at Eloise. Missavage studies the list for a few minutes before concluding that it's unlikely I'll ever find any of the doctors who treated Annie. "I don't think any are alive," he says. "But more to the point, I don't think your aunt got much attention from the psychiatric staff after a while."

"Why's that?" I ask.

"She was part of the long-term population," he says. "Her condition didn't change much, so I suspect that the people she saw most often were the attendants and the nurses on her particular ward. And unless we know which building she lived in, there's no way to know who those people were, if they're still alive."

Anonymous and nearly invisible, even at the place where she spent thirty-one years.

• • •

David Oliwek wants me to meet George Barahal, a family friend and professor emeritus of Wayne State University's psychology department. "I've
been telling him about your search and about Annie, and he thinks he can
help," David says. "He's a great guy, and he knows a lot of people who
worked at Eloise. Why don't I take you over there for dinner?"

On a warm May night, too humid for anything more than shirtsleeves,
we spread our deli sandwiches on a table in Barahal's den while he studies
Mona Evans's Routine History and quizzes me about Annie. Barahal's a
man of many interests, one of which is baseball. He's been a fan of the Detroit Tigers since he was a kid in the 1920s and probably owns the distinction (as far as anyone knows) of being the team's longest-running season
ticket holder. He celebrated his ninetieth birthday with a bash at the Tigers'
new Comerica Park. I tell him I'm jealous, and I mean it: Barahal got to see
a few legends play back in his day, including Hall of Famers Hank Green-
berg and Mickey Cochrane—although as a ninety-year-old, he's also had to
suffer through more losing Tiger seasons than either of us cared to count.

"The Detroit Psychological Clinic," Barahal says, looking up at me with
his piercing eyes. "I know the people who used to run that."

I had seen a reference to that office in Annie's records—"the Detroit
Public Schools, Psychological Clinic." I had called the school system to find
out about it, had gotten nowhere, and hadn't tried again. "Is the clinic still
around?" I ask.

"I'm almost certain it is," Barahal says.

"What does it do?"

"Testing, mostly, and social work," he says. "At least that's what it used
to do. Let's see if I can get you Annie's records."

I indulge him. "Sure, give it a try," I say. But what I'm really thinking is:
*Right. I've been making a nuisance of myself at offices and courthouses all over
this state, writing letters and arguing privacy laws and asking gatekeepers to
search for records that may not even exist, and now this retired professor thinks
he can make a few phone calls and presto!, Annie's school records—from the
1920s!—will materialize like magic.*

Which is just about what happens. The following day, before noon, Barahal phones. "Come on over. I've got a fax to show you."

. . .

Barahal is sunning himself on his front lawn when I drive up. He shoves his sunglasses to his forehead, pulls on his shirt, and hands me the fax.

"The director turns out to be former student of mine," he says. "I explained what you were doing, how interested I was in your work, that you were next of kin. We had a nice talk, catching up, and—" he pauses, relishing the punch line "—it didn't hurt that I had given her an A!" He laughs, heartily.

The fax contains a copy of Annie's master card file from the Detroit Psychological Clinic, recording the results of five intelligence and aptitude tests. I'm wary of putting too much stock in IQ figures, but Annie took the tests often enough to provide both a baseline and a comparison over time. I'm no expert on these tests, but I understand the basic concept: IQ is a calculation, not a measurement—the test results would yield an estimate of Annie's "mental" age, which would be divided by her actual age and multiplied by 100 to produce the IQ, or intelligence quotient.

The Detroit Psychological Clinic didn't just administer these tests—it pioneered its own. In the 1920s, clinic experts developed several, including ones aimed at measuring manual and mechanical ability. (The Detroit Tests of Learning Aptitude, now in their fourth edition, are still widely used by psychologists, although no longer by the Detroit public schools.) By the 1930s, the clinic had earned a national reputation as a leader in the field, and it drew visitors from around the country and the world. Seeing itself as more than a placement service, the clinic decided to keep and archive the thousands of test results that it was compiling, a veritable gold mine of data for researchers. Annie's records went into the master card file in July 1953.

On her first IQ test in October 1926, six months past her seventh birthday, she registered a mental age of 5.6, giving her an IQ of 73, or "borderline," between what was then known as mild retardation (69) and the low end of normal (80). On each successive test, her mental age rose, but not at the same pace as her chronological age, so her IQ kept dropping. In November 1930, it slipped slightly to 67, and while that was within the test's margin of error, school officials decided to move her into a special education class for retarded children; in May 1937, she reached her low point—56, still considered mild retardation but trending toward moderate (below 50).

I'm surprised at the decline in Annie's score. "Wouldn't IQ remain relatively stable?" I ask Barahal.

"Not necessarily," he says. "It's not a precise thing. A lot of factors—depression, for example—could account for Annie doing worse as she got closer to being an adult."

I scan the mental ages, looking for the alarmingly low result that Howard Peirce cited in his court affidavit, five years and eleven months in November 1937, which translates to the intelligence level of a first-grader for a young woman six months away from her nineteenth birthday. On the IQ scale, that works out to 32, considered then and now as severe retardation.

I can't find any such result.

The master card shows that Annie took three of the Detroit Tests for Learning Aptitude in November 1937—for intelligence, manual ability, and mechanical aptitude—and on all three, her mental age fell somewhere between nine and ten years old, significantly below her chronological age of eighteen, but significantly better than five years, eleven months.

Academically, that put Annie somewhere in the fourth grade, and as any elementary school teacher would say, a fourth-grader's sophistication level is a big leap over that of a first-grader. Which might explain Annie's insight that "she would never be able to live a normal life such as other girls."

FOURTEEN

One of the Thousands

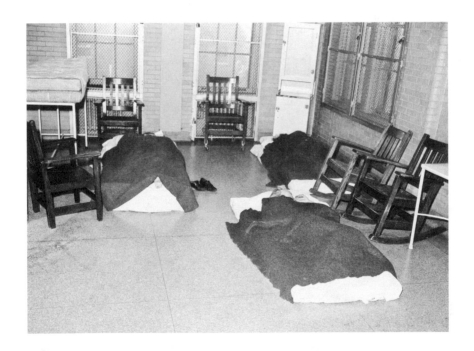

Previous page: *Overcrowded: female patients at Eloise, 1947 (courtesy of the Walter P. Reuther Library, Wayne State University)*

The cars slowed as they made their approach along Michigan Avenue, and fingers emerged from the rolled-down windows, gesturing at Eloise's buildings behind the fences. Often the fingers belonged to parents, and the parents were saying to their befuddled kids, there, that's where the crazy people go, that's where you might end up if you don't behave. If the gawkers arrived at the right moment on some evenings, they might see several small figures clinging to the iron fences, pulling at them, yelling to the startled passengers in the passing cars.

That was a favorite prank of Betty Zimmerman and other children of Eloise employees who lived on the hospital grounds in the late 1930s and early 1940s, when Annie's stay at Eloise turned permanent. "We didn't want them to be disappointed," Zimmerman recounted in a 2007 talk, referring to the gaping motorists. "I'm pretty sure our parents never knew."

Zimmerman's parents were both working at the hospital, her dad as a psychiatrist, her mom as a secretary, when Betty was born in 1926. She describes her childhood there as entirely "normal"—riding bikes on the paved paths, playing hide-and-seek, ice skating on the frozen pond across Michigan Avenue. True, most "normal" children in search of an afternoon snack couldn't hang around an open cafeteria window in hopes of catching a sympathetic server's eye, and most children's Christmases didn't include the annual lighting of a huge tree facing Michigan Avenue while a patients' choir sang carols in the frosty night air. But, she stressed, everyone has a neighborhood, and "this was ours."

What was Annie's neighborhood like, inside the hospital? How did this young woman spend her days? Did she pursue those "normal" activities that had once interested her, such as sewing in the classes offered by the recreational therapy department? Did her previous desire for independence lead her to look for work in the kitchen or the laundry, along with other patients who could handle such responsibility? Did the hospital see her artificial leg as a bar to such jobs? Or was she too bewildered, too depressed, or too overwhelmed by her plight to engage in the world around her?

When Annie arrived, Eloise was just three years into its first attempts at group therapy, a small program that Ira Altshuler had created to reach those patients who had "lost the ability to behave adequately," as Altshuler put it. Individual therapy would be better, Altshuler wrote at the time, but the size of Eloise's mentally ill population—approaching four thousand—made it impossibly expensive to offer one-on-one sessions to every patient. The groups met right on the wards, part of Altshuler's strategy for disrupting the deadening atmosphere he saw there: "The daily sessions . . . not only disperse gloom and monotony but they also destroy the ghastly habit of inertia so prevalent in hospital wards, inertia which tends to wither the few social threads saved during the psychotic process."

Would Annie have been selected for one of Altshuler's groups? Or did her combination of infirmities, as Ed Missavage had suggested, put her firmly into the category of custodial patient, regarded as neither treatable nor curable, one of the many patients destined to live out her days at the institution, a Biddy Hughes of the twentieth century? And then there's this question: How would her destiny have changed if she had been born near the end of the twentieth century, rather than near the beginning?

Before journeying back to the 1940s for his educated guess at what happened to Annie once she settled in at Eloise, Ed Missavage wants a full briefing. He's wearing a camouflage-patterned shirt and pants, his favorite attire these days; I can't remember the last time I saw him in anything else. The Army-style garb and Missavage's gruff demeanor makes me feel like I'm a junior field researcher, reporting to my superior on my latest findings. Missavage's bushy eyebrows knit in dismay at my failure to lay

hands on more of Annie's hospital records, but he grins broadly at my dis-
coveries about Annie's earlier life, especially the interviews with Millie
Brodie and Marty Moss. "Now you're getting somewhere, Stevie." *Stevie.*
Mom would be appalled.

"Let's say that Annie became your patient," I say. "What would you do
first?"

He digs around in the mountain of paper that resides on his kitchen
table, temporarily displacing Supercat, a long-haired feline who regards
the pile as his personal habitat. Missavage finally locates the buried treasure he is looking for, a well-thumbed book called *Outlines for Psychiatric
Examinations*, issued to him upon his arrival at Eloise in 1948. The slim
volume—essentially the forerunner of today's *DSM*, the *Diagnostic and Statistical Manual*—came out of the New York State Psychiatric Institute and
Hospital in 1921, and as the preface states, "was compiled mainly for use of
physicians in psychiatric hospitals." But within a decade, as psychiatry developed a substantial presence beyond the nation's mental institutions,
medical students and private psychiatrists began relying on the 158-page
guide's step-by-step description for examining a patient and collecting the
sort of comprehensive family history that Mona Evans did for her Routine
History.

"First," Missavage says, "a physical exam. But any invasive tests or treatment would have to wait until her legal status was settled and we had a permanent order of commitment. We'd do an extensive interview, with her
and her family, and observe her carefully—her responses, her affect, how
disturbed she appeared."

His copy of *Outlines* is heavily annotated—on-the-job notes of a young
psychiatrist learning his craft as he assessed the expressions, actions,
movements, and moods of the patients under his charge. Flipping to the
pages on schizophrenia, Missavage gives me a brief tutorial on the disorder
and its different manifestations, as they were seen back then. "We were
very pessimistic about schizophrenia in the 1940s," he said. "We didn't
have very good options. Very few patients responded to shock treatment,"
either insulin-induced or electric.

"Would Annie have been a candidate for either?" I ask.

A shake of his head. "Unlikely. Shock treatments were for the manic-
depressives and highly disturbed schizophrenics, and from what I've seen

of her case, she wasn't highly disturbed," he says. "The longer she was there, the more her chances went down. We tended to try it on newer patients."

I nod, but secretly, I'm relieved. From what I've heard and read about these treatments, they were anything but pleasant.

"So what kind of treatment would she get?"

"Not much," he says. "When medications came along in the mid-1950s, she might have been a candidate for one of those." At some point, the Northville records show, Annie did join the thousands of mental patients prescribed one of the new antipsychotic drugs; as a result, she suffered from parkinsonism—tremors or other loss of control over movement—a known side effect from the long-term use of those early medications.

"What about a job?" I say. "There were patients working in the laundry, the kitchen, the cannery. Would she be offered any of those?"

Missavage's wonderfully expressive eyebrows telegraph his skepticism. "Not with her leg. I can't imagine anyone would think she could handle that. She would probably be on a dysambulatory ward."

"Dysambulatory?" I haven't heard that word, a Missavage invention. "What do you mean?"

"Wards for people who couldn't get around very well."

Shock treatments for schizophrenia debuted in the 1930s as more members of the medical world gravitated to the neurological view that there must be a physical cause for mental illness, and therefore, a physical, or "somatic," cure. I had read *Great and Desperate Cures: The Rise and Decline of Psychosurgery and Other Radical Treatments for Mental Illness*, by University of Michigan professor Elliot Valenstein, which recounts how the search for somatic solutions led many U.S. mental hospitals to embrace a series of radical treatments—lobotomies and the various shock therapies (insulin, drug, electricity)—that came out of European laboratories during the 1930s. (Lobotomy, a word that makes us recoil now, won a Nobel Prize for Portuguese neurologist António Egas Moniz in 1949.)

Some in the psychiatric community did express doubts about insulin shock, but overwhelmed by the rising numbers of patients diagnosed with schizophrenia, they were open to any promising treatment. In 1936, one psychiatrist wrote to William Alanson White, the superintendent of St.

Elizabeth's Hospital in Washington, "schizophrenia is so hopeless that anything that holds out hope should be tried."

Eloise raced to the forefront, making plans for a limited insulin shock program two years after the treatment's debut in the United States. It was hard to resist: *Time* magazine wrote, in January 1937, that "the presence in Manhattan last week of a young Vienna psychiatrist, who cures such disoriented wits by means of insulin, created great stir among doctors, great hopes among relatives of schizophrenics." Dr. Manfred Sakel's insulin shock treatment had created these great hopes, *Time* observed, "because U. S. doctors have been able to discover no rational, generally accepted cause for schizophrenia. And they have been generally unable to bring about cures." *Time*'s canonization of Sakel as the man who "cures" schizophrenia proved premature; insulin shock and the other convulsive treatments never panned out as panaceas.

Eloise shelved its shock treatment programs during the war years, unable to find or afford the large number of nurses and doctors to monitor the patients. In February 1947, when Gruber sought approval to resume insulin shock treatments, he told the hospital board that it would require three additional psychiatrists, ten additional nurses, and fifteen more attendants just for a limited program. The board approved a $60,000 budget. In 1948, seventy-four Eloise patients received insulin shock; in 1949, only fifty-eight.

"I did my first insulin shock in 1948," Missavage says, grimacing at the memory. "Fourteen women on D2. I was so glad when it was over. It was physically demanding for the staff as well as the patients. We had to arrive at 6 A.M., five mornings a week, for more than a month. We'd give them a walloping dose of insulin, and then you had to be hypervigilant while the patients were in the comas. Twice, we nearly lost patients who didn't respond at first to the big slug of sugar we gave them to bring them back. Panic would not be too strong a word for what I felt until they finally came out of it."

Electric shock became Eloise's preferred option. The convulsion came quickly, and if done correctly, produced no coma—although broken jaws, from the force of the convulsion, were a risk. Eloise administered 6,617 electric shock treatments to 333 psychiatric patients in 1947, and increased that in 1948 to 7,617 shocks for 474 patients, about 12 percent of the hospital's population. The results were hard to judge; manic-depressive patients seemed to show more improvement than schizophrenics, but over the long term, that improvement didn't hold up.

And then there were lobotomies. Eloise's annual reports, which describe in detail its work with shock treatments, are silent about this discredited procedure, which was tried in many mental hospitals in the late 1940s. "Did Eloise do lobotomies?" I had asked Missavage at an earlier interview.

"We did, for about three or four years, as I recall," he said.

"Why were they stopped?"

"Too many bad results," he said. "Patients urinating on themselves, no evidence of improvement in their illness. We didn't do many, and we abandoned it pretty quickly."

"Would Annie have been a candidate for that?" It seemed unlikely, given everything I knew, but I had to ask.

"I can't imagine why," he said. "No one thought a lobotomy would help someone with mental retardation."

By 1943, Eloise had too many Annies, too many long-term custodial patients, too many patients, period. The rate of new admissions had slowed slightly since the initial boom of the 1920s and 1930s, but the impulse toward institutionalization remained as strong as ever. I reviewed a dozen other Probate Court cases from the month that Annie went to Eloise, and found no other physician's statement comparable to the one from Howard Peirce, who had inserted "not" in front of "actually insane" after examining Annie.

Whether this continuing boom in admissions represented a new enlightenment about the nature of psychiatric disorders or overzealousness by well-meaning professionals with an expansive view of society's obligations—or perhaps a bit of both—it had an obvious consequence: severe overcrowding, and not just at Eloise. The state mental hospitals had hit their limit, too. How could it be otherwise? Michigan's long-held policy toward its mental "defectives" (mirrored in other states) contained an inherent contradiction that led, inexorably, undeniably, mathematically, to a perpetual crisis.

On the one hand, the state had declared as long ago as the 1880s that it had a moral duty and legal responsibility to provide care for its insane and feeble-minded, a commitment restated in 1937 when the legislature over-hauled the state's insanity laws. The standard of "treatment and care" would last until the 1960s, when legal battles led to a new criterion for involuntary commitment: whether the patient posed a danger to himself or others. So every year, more people went to mental hospitals, and every year, more stayed than left. It was only a matter of time before the number of patients exceeded the number of beds—unless, of course, the state was willing to commit itself to a never-ending expansion of its system or change its approach to institutionalization.

From time to time, a public cry went up about the conditions and capacity of the state's facilities. A 1934 survey, ominously titled "Present State of Emergency in Michigan in the State Care of the Insane," reported over-crowding levels of about 16 percent at the six hospitals for the insane (not including Eloise); there were 1,642 more patients than the official number of beds. That was bad enough, but as the report correctly noted, it was nothing new. For years, Michigan's legislature, like others around the country, had been under nearly constant pressure to spend more on its mentally ill and feeble-minded. While these discussions frequently revolved around issues of morality and humaneness, economics often dictated the outcome, and Michigan was no exception.

In 1929, the same year that Gruber had reviewed Eloise's building plans and found them inadequate to meet the hospital's expected growth, the Michigan legislature approved a major new construction program to increase the number of state mental hospital beds by about 25 percent, aiming at an eventual total of 250 per 100,000 population. Four years later, in the depths of the Depression, the legislature rescinded the measure, settling for 182 beds per 100,000. A collective groan went up from the harried superintendents of the state's mental hospitals and three training schools for the feeble-minded, who had envisioned 375 beds per 100,000 as the right number to eliminate overcrowding and handle the growth that they anticipated in the next ten years.

As Michigan's largest county, Wayne had the most mentally ill patients, and the state had always relied on Eloise to take care of the bulk of the Wayne county caseload. Essentially, a partnership had evolved, a partnership that benefited both parties, at least on paper: For decades, Michigan

law had treated Eloise as a state facility for all intents and purposes, subject
to the same regulations, and because Eloise was providing a service that
would otherwise fall to the state, Wayne County received a reimbursement
for patients who remained at Eloise longer than a year. Other counties
weren't taking care of their long-term mentally ill, the thinking ran, so why
should Wayne County?

But the reimbursement never quite matched the cost, and when the Depression hit, Gruber and his staff feared that at the very moment when Eloise needed more resources—for various critical improvements and to take
care of the city's swelling homeless population—money would begin to dry
up. Eloise officials recognized early on that the Depression, as devastating
as it was, could be a boon; the Roosevelt administration was determined to
put the country back to work, and it was handing out money, lots of it, for
public works projects. Eloise and Wayne County set out to capture some of
that New Deal cash, and succeeded. By 1937, Gruber could report the completion of more than three dozen projects, including new water and sewer
lines, an addition to the dairy barn, alterations to the Rouge River to prevent flooding, and repairs to the underground tunnels that ran, labyrinth-
like, beneath much of the complex. The cost of these improvements? More
than $1.2 million, with the federal government picking up nearly 80 per-
cent of the tab.

By the dawn of the 1940s, though, with the national economy improving
and the war in Europe occupying the Roosevelt administration's attention,
the amount of public works money coming from Washington had dwindled
to almost nothing. Eloise needed to look elsewhere for help in paying for
the upkeep of its now enormous campus. Eloise continued to chafe at the
state's reimbursement rate for the 3,500 or so mentally ill patients who had
been at the hospital longer than a year. The rate kept rising—from 95 cents
a day in 1940, when Annie arrived, to $2.35 by July 1945—but it was never
enough to match the actual cost, the hospital contended. Eloise tried to
send more patients into the state system, but those institutions were just as
crowded.

There was one bright spot: Eloise's infirmary and homeless population had declined, the result of the improving economy and a tighter admissions policy, allowing the hospital to convert Ward 106 of N Building
into four hundred psychiatric beds to help accommodate the ever-growing

numbers coming from the emergency psychiatric wards of Detroit's Receiving Hospital. It wasn't enough, though: By 1944, the crisis that had loomed for so long finally arrived in force. Within a few months and for much of the next seven years, psychiatric patients would be sleeping wherever the staff could wedge an extra bed, like steerage passengers on the S.S. *Patricia*.

The disruption brought turmoil to nearly every ward, large or small. Annie could not have escaped it. By 1945, the overcrowding would have impinged on whatever privacy or sense of home she possessed after five years at Eloise. One female ward, designed for 18, had 45 patients; several others, built for 100, had 140. When no more ward space could be found for female patients, the staff began a nightly ritual of clearing the heavy dining hall tables to make way for temporary cots. The next morning, patients had to be rousted from bed early so that the dining tables could be returned in time for breakfast. It was unsafe, and more to the point, it violated the spirit of the state's declared philosophy of providing humane care for society's least fortunate.

With its wards bursting to overflowing, Eloise took the costly step of sending more than two hundred patients to five private psychiatric hospitals. That let a little air out of the bulging balloon, but not enough. On many days, Eloise had to hang the equivalent of a NO VACANCY sign on its front gates, producing a ripple effect at Detroit's Receiving Hospital, which had space for 110 emergency psychiatric patients but, at any given time, found itself with an additional 50 to 150 awaiting transfer to Eloise. When county officials visited Receiving in June 1945, they made sure to bring along the local press for a first-hand glimpse of patients sleeping in hallways.

Something had to be done. The governor, Harry Kelly, had been given plenty of warning about the crisis. Soon after taking office in January 1943, Kelly received a welcome-to-reality letter from Frank L. McAvinchey, a judge from Genesee County and chairman of the Michigan Association of Probate Judges' legislative committee. McAvinchey warned that "in spite of increased facilities for the mental cases of Michigan, our state hospitals soon again will be overcrowded." Two weeks later, the State Hospital Commission chairman, Fred C. Striffler, urged Kelly to set aside money for a new hospital near Detroit, both to relieve the congestion and to reduce the state's reimbursement costs at Eloise.

In the summer of 1943, the hospital commission issued a report remarkable for its candor. "It is a clear, undisputed fact that Michigan has been negligent in providing for the hospitalization of its mentally ill, feeble-minded and epileptic population," the board declared. "This negligence is not of recent origin." But the board's foresight did not match its forthrightness. It blamed the overcrowding on Michigan's tremendous population growth and the state's "sporadic attention" to the problem, without explaining how this could lead to a doubling of the number of institutionalized mentally ill since 1934, far outpacing the state's 10 percent rise in population during that same period.

Kelly promised to act, but he wanted to wait until after the war. Inaction, of course, did nothing to alter the relentless flow of new patients. By 1945, letters were flying back and forth between Wayne County officials and the State Hospital Commission, emergency meetings were hastily convened, and pressure mounted on the governor to act. In the governor's files at the State Archives, there's a June 19, 1945, news photo of the overcrowding at Receiving Hospital. Across the photo, an irate reader wrote in all capital letters that Michigan and Detroit should be ashamed. "How about the GRAND HOTEL for our afflicted?" the reader suggested, a not-so-subtle reference to the famous resort on Mackinac Island in Michigan's Upper Peninsula, a favorite vacation and conference site for the wealthy, the powerful, and the political.

Instead of the Grand Hotel, the State Hospital Commission had secured something approaching the opposite—a recently vacated military barracks on the mainland, in nearby Sault Ste. Marie, leased with the aim of housing five hundred patients there by the end of 1945. The federal government had declared the base as surplus and had offered to rent it cheaply. The makeshift hospital opened to its first patients in March 1945, with the bulk of the patients expected to arrive in the summer.

While the price was right, the location was more than a bit inconvenient. The "Soo," as everyone in Michigan called it (a nod to the city's French origins), was 340 miles from Eloise and so far north that the next stop up the road was in Canada. If families in Detroit objected—and it's not clear from available records whether they had any say in the matter—they would have needed to make their case right away, before the transfer. The distance and difficulties of the trip were too great for the state to shuttle patients back and forth: Getting to the Upper Peninsula in those days required a two-hour boat ride across the straits of Mackinac—if you could get on. The fleet of nine ferries carried as many as nine thousand vehicles a day, but the summer backup could stretch as long as 16 miles, an unavoidable logjam until the Mackinac Bridge opened in 1957.

County officials didn't like the Soo plan. Too far away, too few beds, too little impact on Eloise, which in July 1945 counted 4,612 psychiatric patients as its responsibility, including 255 at private hospitals and those stuck at Receiving. Gruber and Frank E. Kelley, chairman of Eloise's board (and later the state's long-time attorney general), pushed the governor to sign off on a new 3,500-bed state hospital for the Detroit area. The state legislature had authorized $150,000 to buy a site, but had not set aside any money for construction. County officials urged Kelly to call a special legislative session and earmark $2 million immediately.

In the meantime, the Soo would have to do. Charles Wagg, the State Hospital Commission's executive director, asked Gruber to send only "comfortable and tidy patients" capable of caring for themselves. Gruber grumbled at Wagg's request; handing over his best patients would, essentially, raise Eloise's per capita cost by increasing the hospital's overall percentage of difficult cases. But after putting the governor on the spot with their demands for relief and their well-publicized visit to Receiving, the county and Eloise were in no position to resist the Soo conversion.

On July 24, 1945, sometime after 7 A.M., two Greyhound buses left Eloise for the day-long trip to the Upper Peninsula with two doctors, several attendants, and sixty-four patients, all women and all supposedly meeting Wagg's stated requirements.

To my great surprise, Annie was among them.

In her excitement, Jo Johnson almost can't get the words out fast enough. "I found something on your aunt," the overseer of the Eloise museum says over the phone. "A janitor discovered a box of old Eloise records in the

Beard building." That's where I had attended the Friends of Eloise meeting
and heard about the Eloise cemetery; the building also houses several
Wayne County offices. "He called me right away. Mostly financial records
and Gruber correspondence. I was going through the box, and there's a letter that mentions Annie."

A box of old records? It's been more than twenty years since Eloise
closed down. How is it possible this box went unseen until now? I question
Jo about the discovery, but like any good historical commission chairman,
she's more interested in the material itself.

"I put the letter in the mail," she says. "I'm just so pleased to find something for you."

It's quite a find. It's only one sentence of a longer letter, but in context, it
reveals plenty about Annie's status after five years at Eloise and how she
came to board that Greyhound bus. Gruber sent the letter, on July 19, 1945,
to head off any complaints from Wagg and the State Hospital Commission
about Eloise's choice of the first sixty-four patients for reassignment to the
Soo. "There is one other woman, Annie Cohen," Gruber wrote, "who has
only one leg; however, she gets about the institution, up and down stairs,
very admirably with this one leg and is able to take care of herself."

Not just able to get around, not just "comfortable and tidy," but able to
take care of herself. Was that possible? Or was this nothing more than bureaucratic gamesmanship, Gruber saying what he thought necessary to
avert the inevitable questions from the State Hospital Commission when it
learned that the arrivals from Eloise included a woman with a wooden leg—
after Wagg had specifically asked for the easiest patients?

I read on. "There is another patient, Mary Mundy, who has two artificial
limbs; however, she can walk fairly well and can get to and from her meals,
and can look after herself and is not disturbed."

So Annie was the better off of the two, based on Gruber's subtle distinc-
tions: Annie could go up and down stairs—"admirably"—while Mary Mundy
could only walk "fairly" well. Annie could "take care of herself," while Mary
could only "look after herself." Annie's mental condition merited no mention at all, while Gruber took special care to note that Mary Mundy was "not
disturbed." (I suppose that could imply that Annie was disturbed in some

way, but wouldn't that implication create doubt about her ability to care for herself? Gruber had no interest in doing that.)

I marvel at the system's chameleon-like ability to adapt to the circumstances. Five years earlier, Gruber had sent a form letter to the Probate Court, stating categorically that Annie was too sick to attend her own hearing, a hearing not scheduled to take place for several weeks. Now, Annie was climbing stairs and taking care of herself, which made her a suitable candidate for transfer to an impromptu hospital rising on the deserted grounds of a former military base.

What to believe?

I had concluded earlier that Gruber's form letter in 1940 had little to do with Annie's actual condition, that the style and timing of that letter—sent the day after her admission—strongly suggested that it was automatic, part of an overall strategy to control the cost and inconvenience of transporting patients downtown and back. Gruber's letter on the Soo patients had a similar feel: There was no other evidence that Annie's five years at Eloise had transformed her from a frightened young woman too scared to leave her apartment into someone capable of caring for herself. If Gruber's rosy assessment were true, why hadn't she been sent home, at least for a trial period, to see how she might do?

No, I think Ed Missavage had it right, when I asked him earlier why Annie had never been paroled. She had too many strikes against her and too little support from her family. I remember his words: *From our point of view, she's a custodial patient from the outset. She's the type that we don't ever think is going home.*

While there was an undeniable logic to the State Hospital Commission's criteria—the Soo did not yet have the resources to treat the toughest patients, and never would—the stipulations also confirmed that this improvised arrangement favored the state's needs, not the patient's. I can imagine the conversation with Annie:

Annie, you've been a good patient, not much trouble, even with your wooden leg. Your reward? We're transferring you to a rural county, a nice place—no, it's nothing like Eloise, it's actually a converted military barracks, and if your mom had a hard time visiting you before, she probably won't make it to the Soo, it's

hundreds of miles and a ferry ride away. But as soon as we get this overcrowding
crisis under control, we'll bring you back to Eloise, and everything will be just like
it was before . . .

Fourteen months. That's how long Annie stayed at the Soo, fourteen months
and nine days, if she or anyone in Detroit kept count. What brought her
back? Did she turn out to be not so tidy? Did the layout of the Soo hospital
make it difficult for her to get around? Did she miss her family so much that
she regressed and became, despite Gruber's optimism, unable to care for
herself? Did the conversation that Medji overheard in Mom's apartment,
the one about "Chanaleh," have anything to do with Annie's return? Many
questions, no answers.

She didn't come back because the overcrowding crisis was over, that's
certain. The female wards remained as packed as ever, with the sun porches
and dining halls still playing host to the overflow patients. The number of
Eloise patients in private hospitals was still rising, peaking at 477 during
1947. Eloise's 1950 annual report described Receiving's conditions as "inhuman," 330 occupants jammed into the 111-bed facility.

The Soo hospital remained a small and inadequate release valve for another four years, only shutting down in June 1950 because the federal government wanted the base back. Two major developments finally eased the
overcrowding. In 1952, the state completed the new 1,200-bed hospital first
authorized in 1945 (Northville) and in 1954, the introduction of revolutionary new medications for schizophrenia and other mental illnesses allowed
some patients to be treated at home, outside the institutional walls.

For the patients who remained, another revolutionary advance altered
what Ira Altshuler had called "the ghastly habit of inertia so prevalent" on
the wards: the installation of televisions. Instead of staring off into space
for hours, some patients now stared at the TV; Ed Missavage recalls with
some amazement the calming effect that television had on some aggressive
patients. "It was a godsend," he says.

Irene Waryas, an Eloise social worker and graduate student at Wayne University (before it added State to its name), took a look around her in the late

1940s and concluded the obvious: The state could not afford the system that it had created. It was all well and good for the state to assume responsibility for the institutional care of the mentally ill—but, as the thirty-four-year-old Waryas pointed out in her 1950 master's thesis, the reality never matched the rhetoric, nor could it. More institutional patients meant more institutions, and more institutions required a bottomless budget commitment, which had neither political nor public support.

If the state couldn't keep building hospitals, what could it do? Waryas's thesis proposed a major expansion of the state's small "family care" program and the placement of a limited number of carefully selected patients with foster families, much like the current foster care system for neglected children. Her proposal was informed by her own experience; in the summer of 1950, Eloise had assigned Waryas to place up to twenty-five capable patients in private homes. By December, she had placed five. The Michigan Society for Mental Hygiene supported the family care concept as a cost-saving and humane alternative. "We believe that approximately 1,200 of the 29,680 now in mental hospitals could be released to an expanded Family Care program," the society observed in the spring 1950 edition of the "Mental Hygiene Bulletin."

Waryas wasn't challenging the existing system or forecasting the decline of the institutional model that still reigned supreme in 1950. She saw foster care as a parallel program that would complement the work of Eloise and the state hospitals. But her thesis anticipated the rise of group homes and the smaller, community-based model of mental health treatment, and it made me wonder: Would a group home have allowed Annie to thrive, to reach that independence she craved before her commitment to Eloise?

Bill Regenold researches schizophrenia at the University of Maryland School of Medicine, where he's an associate professor of psychiatry, and I've asked him to join my informal group of experts. He's a youthful forty-seven, with an easy smile and hair graying at the temples; his psychiatric training began after the era of huge mental hospitals was ending. Like others I've consulted, he sees Annie's deformed leg and low IQ as evidence that something went wrong, during pregnancy or birth, although he doesn't rule out the possibility of a genetic flaw. He regards her symptoms, as described

in her records, as consistent with schizophrenic behavior, but without evaluating her himself, he's reluctant to classify her initial mental illness as
schizophrenia.

I point out that Annie's commitment papers did not include a specific
diagnosis, so it's not clear when she was diagnosed as schizophrenic. "It
could have been later, after she had been at Eloise a while," I say, as we
settle down at a restaurant near the hospital for a weekday lunch.

Regenold slows me down, offering a mini-seminar on what we do and
don't know about schizophrenia. "I don't call it a disease, because we still
don't know enough about it to connect the symptoms to the cause," he said.
"Schizophrenia describes a syndrome, a collection of signs and symptoms.
We're pretty sure that genetics have something to do with it—at least, there's
a genetic predisposition. The risk in the general population is about one
percent, but in identical twins, if one is schizophrenic, there's a fifty percent chance that the other will be."

I tell him I've been thinking about what might happen to Annie if she
were turning twenty-one now, with the same symptoms as she had in 1940.
He reframes my implied question. "Well, I think—I hope—that she would
have gotten attention at a much earlier age," he says. "We have many more
tools now, and there's more to investigate, and maybe an earlier interven-
tion would have headed off her psychotic break at twenty-one."

Would she have been able to live in a group home, maybe work? I ask.

"That's hard to say, of course, but reading the reports, I kept thinking
that she might have ended up at one of the community-based programs that
exist now, and that she would be capable of holding some sort of job." He
suggested a couple of people who knew more about group homes and what
he called "dual diagnosis" patients—those like Annie who have both mental
disability and mental illness.

I ask him about the alleged sexual assault. If it occurred, could that have
triggered her psychotic break?

He chooses his words carefully. "We don't know what happened that day
that Annie says she was attacked. People with mental illness and mental
retardation tend to be more vulnerable to predators. She may have been
assaulted, and the associated fear could have exacerbated her underlying
psychotic disorder. But it's unlikely that it would have made her chronically
psychotic, if she were otherwise mentally healthy."

I think about Annie's fear of strangers, including Anna, who never saw Annie except in Tillie's company. Real or not, the alleged sexual assault left its mark on Annie's psyche; even a delusion can have serious and long-lasting consequences for someone who has converted fantasy into fact.

As we walk back to the hospital, Regenold reflects on the toll that mental illness often takes on a patient's family. "I wonder," he says, "if your grandmother asked Anna to drive her to Eloise because she wanted to pass the baton to another family member."

I tell him I'm not sure what he means.

"In my experience, parents of disabled children often worry about what's going to happen once they're gone. They want to know that someone will keep tabs on their child. Maybe, perhaps subconsciously, that's what your grandmother was trying to arrange."

Regenold's comment made sense to me. I remember what Anna had said about her first few visits to Eloise—how Tillie had appealed to her daughter; look, this is Anna, your cousin, your family. But passing the baton to Anna couldn't work if Annie wouldn't accept a surrogate—and from what Anna said, Annie didn't want anything to do with her.

I could see how Annie's rejection might have amplified Anna's anger toward my mom, how Anna might feel that, wait, it's not *my* responsibility to accompany Tillie to Eloise, I'm glad to do it, but I wouldn't be making these pilgrimages if Beth—Tillie's daughter and Annie's sister—wasn't so insistent on keeping her secret.

In my many conversations with Anna, I had chosen to maintain a professional neutrality, asking questions rather than making statements or acting as Mom's defense lawyer. Once, however, I did suggest to Anna that there might be another way to look at the facts. "Anna," I said, "I would never compare my mother's life to yours. Nothing compares to the Holocaust. But if you look at the Eloise report, you might see that life for my mom was a kind of personal hell in April 1940."

I read aloud from the Routine History, as I had done once before: "She screamed during the night, kept wanting to get up and seemed to think she would die if she stayed in bed . . . During the week of April 19, patient was so difficult to manage that the family couldn't get any sleep and were all 'going crazy.'"

I waited for a flicker of empathy, an understanding nod. But Anna merely repeated what she told me before. "It wasn't Annie's fault. She's sick. She's still family."

Family. That's the word that Anna kept using. "I am family," she had fumed, when Mom had told her to stop meddling in her family's affairs. To understand Anna's unshakable fury toward Mom, I had to understand Anna's family—not the one she raised in America, but the one she lost in 1942.

I had to understand what had happened in Radziwillow.

FIFTEEN

The Ghosts of Radziwillow

Previous page: *Before the Nazi invasion: Anna Schlajn (Oliwek), age 15, 1939
(courtesy of Anna Oliwek)*

I 've never had any particular interest in writing about the Holocaust. Too painful, I suppose, and more the territory of historians than journalists.

Now, with Anna Oliwek stuck in my head, I had to confront it.

On a gray, windy day in early June, I type "Radziwillow" into the library database of the Holocaust Museum in Washington. Wendy Lower, a professor at Towson University outside Baltimore and an expert on the Holocaust in Ukraine, looks over my shoulder as I begin my research into what the Nazis and their Ukrainian collaborators did to the Jews of Volhynia, the part of western Ukraine where Radziwillow is located.

Most of the Volhynian Jews did not die in the concentration camps of Poland. Most were taken from their towns, their streets, their homes, killed in daylight and in darkness, within earshot and, sometimes, within eyesight of their neighbors and friends. The first wave of executions came within weeks of Hitler's troops seizing control of the region as part of Operation Barbarossa, the multi-pronged Nazi invasion of the Soviet Union launched on June 22, 1941; on July 2, Reinhard Heydrich, the Reich's eager thirty-seven-year-old chief of security, ordered the execution of "Jews in the employment of the party apparatus and the state."

The German Sixth Army had encountered little resistance from the isolated Soviet troops when it flashed through Volhynia on its lightning-quick journey toward the east. Residents of the region describe the Soviet withdrawal in words approaching the supernatural—vanish, disappear, evaporate, rather than retreat or depart. In truth, Red Army tank forces did mount one major counterattack on Nazi forces between Lutsk and Brody, within a few miles of Radziwillow, but after four days of the fiercest fighting to take place in Ukraine during the first week of the invasion, the German panzers managed to overwhelm their well-armored Russian counterparts.

Why a fight there and nowhere else in Volhynia? It's hard to say for sure. Perhaps the Red Army fought the battle primarily to buy time for evacuating thousands of men and shipping tons of manufacturing equipment to safety four hundred miles or more to the east. Perhaps the clash was a test of strength, and the outcome proved the difficulty of defending the land that the Soviets had claimed from Poland only two years earlier as part of an expanded Ukrainian SSR—valuable and fertile territory, but far from Moscow and the usual supply lines. Or perhaps the Soviet leadership was unprepared and quickly abandoned any notion of a full-scale attempt to hold the region. All of these interpretations can be found in the histories. Whatever the explanation, by mid-July, the Nazi forces controlled western Ukraine, and were on their way to conquering most of the vast territory between the Black Sea and the Baltic Sea. There was no opposing force to stop them from imposing their will and their murderous policies on the local population.

I sit at a table in the Holocaust Museum library with Shmuel Spector's book, *The Holocaust of Volhynian Jews, 1941–1944*, and read what happened next. Members of the *Einsatzgruppen*—mobile killing squads organized to carry out executions in Ukraine and elsewhere—asked local Ukrainians for the names of so-called "Soviet activists" and with the assistance of Ukrainian "auxiliary" police, scoured the towns' homes and streets, "arresting" hundreds of Jews and others, and marching them to pre-selected sites where the *Einsatzkommandos* carried out their deadly mission. In Radziwillow on July 15, just seventeen days after the Nazis arrived, twenty-eight Jews were shot as "dangerous Communists" or "partisans." Similar roundups went on throughout the region. By late August, a reported 15,000 Jews—about 6 percent of Volhynia's Jewish population—were dead.

After the winter's thaw made the ground soft enough to dig mass graves again, a second wave of executions commenced in the spring of 1942, first with the herding of Jews into ghettos, followed by systematic "liquidations" throughout the summer and fall. Radziwillow's turn came on April

9, when its estimated 2,600 Jews were divided into a large ghetto for the "unfit" and a smaller one for those considered "useful." Six weeks later, 1,500 were murdered outside town, while about 500 holding "productive worker certificates" earned a reprieve, only to be killed in a second massacre on October 5.

A very few managed to escape. Anna Oliwek—then Anna Schlajn—was one of them.

Impossible. Just impossible. That's the word that comes to mind as I sift through the encyclopedias and histories, the memoirs and testimonies, trying to compose a few sentences to characterize Radziwillow at the dawn of World War II. The town had changed hands so many times since its early days as part of the Radziwill family's many holdings, depending on the year and the map, that it was impossible to give a single identity to the people of Radziwillow. They were Polish, and yet they weren't. They were Russian, but many weren't. They were Ukrainian, except those who weren't, especially the Jews, who weren't Polish or Russian really, they were mostly just Jews, as if they belonged to no nation, and although more than three centuries had passed since the first Jew had appeared in Radziwillow, although the town and the Jewish community had grown up together, although those who called themselves Polish and those who called themselves Ukrainian and those who called themselves Russian could look back on times when all these people, all these religions, all these communities had lived in peace and prospered together, it was their divisions that mattered most when the Soviets, and then the Nazis, changed the map once again.

Not that a single identity would have prevented the bloodshed that followed. That's too simple, too naive a view of European history and the Nazi phenomenon. But the *absence* of that identity certainly made the Nazi campaign easier. It presented the occupiers with the gift of discord, which Hitler's architects of death exploited from the earliest days of the invasion. They preyed on the Ukrainian hatred of the Soviets, age-old antagonisms cemented during a 1919 civil war and inflamed by Stalin's more recent misdeeds in his campaign against Ukrainian nationalism—mass deportations; the confiscation of Ukrainian property; orchestration of a famine that led to mass starvation and the death of millions; and imprisonment, torture, and murder of Ukrainian resisters as enemies of the Soviet state. At the invasion's outset, the Germans allowed the Ukrainian nationalists to dream of another Ukrainian People's Republic, a wisp of independence that ended when the 1920 Treaty of Warsaw returned most of Volhynia to Polish rule while Kiev and eastern Ukraine remained in Soviet hands. The Ukrainians believed that the Germans would be their friends—well, if not friends exactly, then allies, and the Jews, well, hadn't some Jews helped the Russians, and the friend of my enemy is my enemy, and if the Nazis want a list of Jews who aided the Communists, well, we will give them a list and . . .

There is debate among Holocaust historians about the exact nature of the Nazis' extermination plans for the Jews in the Soviet Union, whether Hitler had issued a specific verbal order or whether his strategists knew his wishes and needed no such instruction. There is debate, too, about whether the Nazis planned to kill all the Jews from the outset of Operation Barbarossa or whether, emboldened by early military victories at the front and the apparent willingness of Germans and non-Germans alike to wage a separate "war against the Jews" behind the lines, they then expanded their targets to include every Jewish man, woman, and child.

There is no debate that on July 31, 1941, Hermann Göering, second in command of the Third Reich, authorized Heydrich to prepare a "total solution of the Jewish question" in the territories occupied by the Nazi forces. Invading the Soviet Union was the first step in fulfilling Hitler's dream of extending his Aryan nation all the way to Asia, but it also magnified his "Jewish question"—he could not become master of the Soviet lands without bringing five million *more* Jews into his Greater German empire, the so-called *Grossdeutsches Reich*. Exterminating that many people required an unprecedented amount of planning, logistics, and manpower at a time when the Nazi forces were already overextended and preparing for a final push to Moscow. In the months that followed, Heydrich's SS and security police became determined to find more efficient methods of genocide than mass shootings, which not only tested the stamina and nerve of all but the most hardened killing squad members, but also required the deployment of a significant quantity of German men and ammunition needed for the fight against the Soviets.

Why did the mass shootings take place in the towns themselves, and why did they proliferate? Timing seemed to be a key factor. The death camps in

Poland were not yet constructed, and the Nazis could not yet transport large numbers of prisoners on the Russian railway lines, which were of a different gauge than those in Poland and Germany. The Nazis had to seize large numbers of Russian railcars or modify the tracks, both time-consuming undertakings. So in the months before the Wannsee Conference in January 1942, when Heydrich held formal ministerial discussions of a "final solution," the word went out to the Nazi security forces and *Einsatzgruppen* in Ukraine, Byelorussia, and the Baltics: Kill the Jews where they live.

The German army's primary job was to win the war against the Soviets, leaving the campaign against the Jews to the security forces and local auxiliaries. On August 10, 1941, soldiers in the German Sixth Army received orders from their commander, Walter von Reichenau, forbidding them "from participating in executions as observers, except when ordered to do so by a military authority. The pictures taken of the executions referred to above must be confiscated and destroyed." But the army's support for the coming genocide was essential, as Reichenau and his superior, Gerd von Rundstedt, commander of Army Group South, made clear in an October 12, 1941 directive, "Conduct of the Troops in the Eastern Territories," which said, in part:

> "The most essential aim of the war against the Jewish-bolshevistic system is a complete destruction of power and the elimination of Asiatic influence from the European culture. In this connection the troops are facing tasks which exceed the one-sided routine of soldiering. The soldier in the Eastern territories is not merely a fighter according to the rules of the art of war but also a bearer of ruthless national ideology and the avenger of bestialities which have been inflicted upon the German and racially related nations. Therefore the soldier must have full understanding for the necessity of a severe but just revenge on subhuman Jewry. The Army has to aim at another purpose, i.e. the annihilation of revolts in the hinterland, which, as experience proves, have always been caused by Jews."

It concluded: "This is the only way to liberate the German people once and for all from the Asiatic-Jewish danger."

· · ·

She was eighteen.

Every story, even a Holocaust story, has to start somewhere, and after
going over Anna's account with her multiple times to fill in the gaps and get
the chronology straight, I find myself starting with that simple fact: She was
just eighteen years old when she fled Radziwillow in October 1942 with only
the vaguest idea of where she was going; just eighteen years old when she
walked into a Nazi occupation headquarters with little more than an im-
probable tale and a facility for language; just eighteen years old when she
deceived the Nazis into believing—or at least accepting—her masquerade as
the daughter of a German mother and Ukrainian father. Yet, within a month
of escaping certain death at the hands of a Nazi-led killing squad in Radziwillow, she had secured herself a job as a translator for the *Wehrmacht*'s
military police: a sensitive position, a position of trust, a position reserved
for a member of the German *Volk*, the German nation.

As I examine the documents detailing her deception—including her
Arbeitsbuch, the Nazi-mandated workbook that lists the dates and places of
her employment—I marvel at her guile, her cleverness, her charm. What
part of the family DNA gave her the ability to pull off this subterfuge, and
to maintain this deception not just for weeks or months, but for nearly
three years?

Anna does not start her story with her age. She starts with the warning.

"There's going to be a killing in the morning," said the German woman
who was employing Anna to do domestic chores. "You're too good a worker
to die. I've never seen a Jew work so hard."

Anna, still the interpreter, feels the need to translate for me. "She
helped me not because I was a good *person*, but because I was a good *worker*."
Anna shakes her head. "She told me, 'You can't go home, they're gonna kill
you. Tomorrow, they're going to take all the Jews from the ghetto.'"

Radziwillow, like other Volhynian towns, was rife with such rumors in
the fall of 1942. The killing squad had already executed more than 1,500
from Radziwillow's "expendable" ghetto—including Anna's mother, her
twelve-year-old brother Mendel, and her nine-year-old sister Esther—on

May 29, 1942. Her father's early death in 1934, perhaps from the famine, had spared him the fate of dying in an open pit with the rest of her family.

Before the first massacre, Anna says, she would come to her mother's ghetto before work, and they would talk through the fence, no touching allowed. Then one day, her mother wasn't there. Anna, frantic, went to the *Judenrat*, the council that the Nazis required the Jews to form in the ghetto, and told one of the men in charge, "I usually see my mother before I go to work. She wasn't there today."

What did he say? I ask.

"'Tears came to his eyes," she says. "That's how I knew."

She had to see the gravesite. Soon after the massacre, Anna says, she stealthily made her way before first light to the killing field. It seems incredible to me, not to mention perilous and foolhardy, but Anna says that's what she did, that's what she had to do, she had to see the place where her mother, her brother, and her sister had been executed. She had to say good-bye.

I am family.

No one was there, she says, no guards, no police to keep away the curious. The executioners had coated the pits with lime—Anna uses the Ukrainian word, *"vapno"*—to speed up decomposition and keep down the smell, but there was no way to cover up what had taken place. "There were five big huge, long graves," Anna tells me, shuddering at the image in her mind. "You could see the blood. I hate to tell you this, but it was boiling."

"Boiling?" I say.

"Bubbling, still fresh. I saw a child's hand, sticking out. I was crying and screaming."

Every Jew still alive in the Radziwillow ghetto lived with fear that a second massacre was coming, and that this time, their status as forced laborers would not save them. Before the first massacre, the executioners had had the advantage of uncertainty and deception—they had led the Jews to believe that they were being deported, and that was horrible enough—but this time, the targets couldn't be lulled. Still, how much good would their knowledge do them? Most of them had no place to go, and few places to hide. Some

would flee to the nearby forests, looking for the partisan fighters supposedly operating there, but at most, only two hundred survived. Some would
decide to take their own lives rather than die at the hands of the Nazis; a few
would find families, non-Jews, willing to hide them.

Anna, however, received something more than just a warning; she received an offer of help from the German woman who admired her work
ethic.

The Nazis had sent the German woman and her husband to Radziwillow
so he could work for the *Eisenbahn*, the railway transport serving the Eastern Front via the same train line that gave Radziwillow its prominence as a
border town. If Anna could hide until after the massacre, the husband
would sneak her aboard and take her to the end of the line, 450 miles south-
east to Dnepropetrovsk, an industrial city not far from where the Nazis had
established an *Ortskommandantur*, a local occupation headquarters.

That left the problem of what to do until the transport left. Anna couldn't
go back to the ghetto—if she were there in the morning, there would be no
way out. The local police opened the locked gates only to let the workers
come and go to their jobs, usually under escort. But for all its similarities to
a prison, the ghetto had one huge difference: There was no bed check, no
requirement to sign in or sign out. If someone went missing altogether,
that would draw attention, and if a Jew were caught outside the ghetto after
curfew, the consequences could be deadly. But Anna could vanish for a
night, and her absence would not raise any particular alarm. The German
woman would tell the escort that Anna had already left for the ghetto, and
that was plausible enough for now.

The woman's warning about the impending massacre was sudden, but
Anna's thoughts about fleeing were not. She had been preparing for the possibility, and had even attempted to leave once before, walking the ten kilo-
meters or so across the border to Brody, where her aunt lived. She arrived to
find her aunt's house empty, and when she asked if anyone had seen the family, someone told her, "Don't you know? They were killed a few days ago."

Her flight to Brody (When did she go? How long was she gone? She tries
to remember, but finally shrugs and gives me a weak smile) might have
been brave, but in retrospect, it was mostly rash, the sort of impulsive act
that might be expected of a desperate eighteen-year-old girl. Her other
preparations, however, proved just the opposite. She knew a family whose

daughter had died at age eight. The girl's father was Ukrainian, and her mother was German, which meant that the girl had been a *Volksdeutsche*, an ethnic German of mixed blood—not as good as being pure German, but in Hitler's cosmology, part of the Greater German empire.

"I had to have a new identity and new papers if I was going to leave," she says. "I couldn't be Anna Schlajn any more. I paid that family for hers."

When the Nazi transport pulled away from Radziwillow with its cargo of livestock, clothes, and food, a young girl sat on the floor of one car, surrounded by Ukrainian and Russian prisoners of war being shipped back from German labor camps, deemed too sick to work, their fates unclear. The girl was alone. She had only the clothes she wore, a sliver of bread, and her identification documents.

If anyone asked, she would tell her story and hand over the papers, which said she was Anna Prokopowitsch, age sixteen, born December 1925, *Volksdeutsch*.

The German woman had given her some old clothes, and Anna had put them on, shedding the ones that bore the Star of David that Jews were supposed to wear at all times. The woman's husband had warned her that the transport would be nothing like a passenger train—no seats, no food service, but also no ticket-takers. "He would get me on, but he made clear that I was on my own after that," Anna says.

The presence of the POWs surprised her. She huddled in a corner and waited for the man in charge of the prisoners to approach, as he surely would. Not for the first or last time in her new life, she fought the urge to panic. But instead of a barrage of questions, he offered her some of the soup that he was feeding to the POWs. She took a cup, gratefully.

A passenger train might take most of a long day to make the journey to Dnepropetrovsk, but night came and went as the transport crept slowly through the Ukrainian countryside, stopping frequently, an excruciatingly slow ride that gave Anna plenty of time to practice her new identity, to say "My name is Anna Prokopowitsch" as blithely as she once said "My name is Anna Schlajn." Two or three days, maybe four—Anna doesn't remember how long she stayed on the train, only that it was evening again when the transport ground to a halt in Dnepropetrovsk station.

"This was the night," she tells me now, six decades later, "when I learned to lie."

Several hours ticked by before a man asked her what she was doing there, alone, in the station. "I'm waiting for my sister," Anna told him—or maybe she said "uncle" or "parents," she's no longer sure. He went away, but returned as the station was closing for the night, and told her she would have to leave. She replied, "I'm not going to bother nobody. I'll just sit here quietly until my sister shows up." The next morning, another railway worker asked her why she was still there. She unveiled her concocted story, something about getting separated from her parents, she couldn't find them, she was worried sick. The man took pity on her.

His mother, he said, lived on the outskirts of town, she was old and alone, and she could use the help and the company. He would take Anna as soon as he finished work; he had a car, a broken-down one. Anna, scared and with no place to go, was suspicious but didn't know what else to do. "I go," she says, "and he does have an old mother. Well, not that old, probably in her late fifties, but I was young, so everyone that age seemed old."

Within a few days, Anna came to two conclusions: First, the kind woman didn't have enough food for herself, let alone this uninvited guest, and second, survival depended on finding work. Anna saw a notice that said the local employment office, a branch of the Nazi occupation authority, had jobs available, including one for a translator.

When the woman at the employment office asked about her skills, Anna told her: I speak four languages, I'm a quick learner. She never expected to get the translator job—she was so young, her bogus papers said she was only sixteen—but she thought if she could meet someone in authority, maybe she could impress him enough to land a job cleaning houses. The woman gave her directions to the *Ortskommandantur*, in nearby Novomoskovsk: Go see the major there; he's with the military police, the *Feldgendarmerie*. He's the one who needs a translator.

It was a long walk, more than five miles, and when Anna arrived, the major wasn't in. The building housed all the Nazi security forces—the Gestapo, the SS, the SD, and the military police. While she waited, she rehearsed her story, trying to make it more specific, more convincing. She didn't want a lot of questions just yet, questions that might cause her to stumble. She reminded herself: My name is Anna Prokopowitsch, and I'm just sixteen, but I'm a good worker, and I need a job.

The major's name was Könitzer, a small, stocky man. He listened to Anna's fabricated account and said she reminded him of his daughter back in Germany. Later, after Anna had worked for him for nine months, Könitzer would write her a glowing letter of recommendation, dated July 14, 1943, that reads in translation: "The interpreter Anna Prokopowisch of O.K.I/837, born December 19, 1925, has since November 1942 worked for O.K.I/837 until it closed down. She possesses exceptional language abilities, speaking German, Polish, Ukrainian and Russian. She's enthusiastic, she has a pure, clear sense of judgment and is a fast learner. In translating German into foreign languages and vice versa, she is exceptionally good." He stamped it with the seal of O.K.I/837, military police unit 837 of *Ortskommandantur* I, and signed it with his last name only: Könitzer.

At that first meeting, the major asked her how she had learned to speak so many languages at such a young age, and she told him, "I have a gift, I guess, it comes easily to me." She could have told him she spoke a fifth and sixth language, but now was not the time to brag about speaking Hebrew and Yiddish.

He wanted to hire her; he said he had two interpreters, but both were useless in Ukrainian, something of a liability in occupied Ukraine. There was one problem, the major told her: Regulations require me to hire German citizens for a military job involving matters of security. The military has no authority to issue such identification papers, so you must go to the civilian commissar's office. "I was afraid to go, so I told him, I don't know anyone there, could you please write me a letter?" So the major did as she asked, he wrote the letter that gave her the credibility she needed, a letter explaining that the Soviets had sent her parents away, that her identification papers were gone and she needed new ones.

I'm confused: The Nazis had hired other translators who were *Volks-deutschen*. Did the military police have more stringent requirements? Or was Könitzer trying to protect himself by clarifying Anna's status, while helping her out at the same time? Anna doesn't know. But in retrospect, getting him to write that letter changed everything, it converted her from a runaway with a dubious story into a refugee with the backing of a Nazi military officer.

As she walked to the commissar's office, she says, she tried to calm herself, tried not to show her nervousness about her story, but she underestimated both the power of the major's letter and the lack of curiosity she encountered. The letter was read, and accepted, and the coveted document issued on the spot. She was now a German citizen and a translator working for the military police.

The major looked out for her, she says. As far as he knew, she was just a month shy of her seventeenth birthday when he hired her, this babe in the woods who reminded him of his daughter. He warned her about certain men, telling her, "You're a young girl, stay away from that one." Once, after an officer persisted in his advance, inviting himself to the new quarters that came along with her job, she told the major and he said, categorically, "Don't let him in."

She looks at me sharply when she tells me this, and she says she knows what I'm thinking. We're sitting in the suburban Chicago home where she now lives with Sidney, her old school chum from Radziwillow. I hadn't planned to ask her about sexual favors, whether any were demanded or given; it didn't seem necessary. But she's bringing it up, so I don't cut her off. "Nothing like that happened," she says. "I wouldn't let it, and neither would the major."

I had come to Chicago to go over her story once more, to resolve some of the inevitable discrepancies that dim memory and buried pain have imposed on her account. She wants to be helpful, tries to be precise, but not all the pieces fit together in a seamless narrative. Did you hide one night or two before fleeing Radziwillow? Did you go to Brody just after the first massacre, or was it later? Why does this identification document say *Volksdeutsch*—wouldn't that be a problem, given what the major had said?

At one point, she stops in midsentence, her eyes wide and suddenly misty. She apologizes, saying that she woke up feeling nervous about some family tensions with her children, but confessing that, yes, she sometimes finds it hard to remember such horrific times, that she'll never stop feeling guilty about working for the Nazis. I return the apology, saying that she's such a stoic that I sometimes don't realize how much pain my questions must cause her.

She looks off in the distance, and I wonder whether I'm getting the full story, whether it's even possible to reach that level. Isn't it human nature to wall ourselves off from some parts of our most appalling experiences? She's a survivor, and she survived by lying, by reinventing herself, by taking a job with the killers who had murdered her family, who were bent on wiping out her fellow Jews. Her counterfeit identity gave her a new life, but it also took its toll, requiring her to nurture the deceit, to learn the art of lying—not merely how to *tell* a lie, but how to *live* a lie, because lying was the route to survival, lying was safety. But always, always, she lived with the fear of being discovered. She was a Jew hiding in plain sight, and to make her disguise believable, she had to believe her own deception, she had to make herself appear comfortable among the very enemy that had killed her family. She had to turn herself into a secret. So isn't it possible—no, more than that, isn't it likely—that after the war, when she could go back to being Anna Schlajn, a Jew from Radziwillow, that she would find it hard sixty-five years later to keep it all straight, to help me separate the facts from the fictions, to satisfy my desire for precision when obscurity had been her goal?

Fooling the Nazis turned out to be easier than she had feared. They were strangers in occupied territory; they didn't know the language, the people, or the terrain. The biggest threat to her secret, she says, came from local people who thought she was Jewish. One time, while translating for a prisoner, he looked at her and spat in Ukrainian, "you filthy Jew." He continued his tirade and his German captors finally asked what he was saying. Anna, protecting herself, told them: "He's calling you filthy Germans." They took the man away.

Another time, a German officer hauled in a Jewish woman he found hiding in the nearby forest, calling her a "dirty Jew." The terrified woman saw Anna, who had been summoned to translate, and said in Polish, "Are you Jewish?" Anna, acting quickly, told the woman to be quiet, that she would handle it. She went directly to the major's office and informed him

that the officer was mistaken. "If she's a Jew, then I'm a Jew," she says she
told the major.

I can't help but smile at her audacity in the midst of this life-or-death
confrontation. "You really said that?" I ask. " 'If she's a Jew, I'm a Jew?' "

Anna returns my smile. "The major said, 'Fräulein Anna'—that's what
he called me—'if you say she's not a Jew, then she's not a Jew. Tell the officer
to let her go.' "

Anna's stint with the O.K.I/837 ended abruptly in midsummer 1943. The
Nazi defeat at the battle of Stalingrad in early February had signaled the
beginning of the end for Hitler's vision of a conquered Soviet Union; the
Red Army was pushing back now, pushing to recapture Ukraine from the
German occupiers. Anna's unit would be leaving for combat areas elsewhere, and the major thought it was best if she went to Germany. Anna
wanted to stay in Novomoskovsk, but she couldn't do that—if the Soviets
came, she could end up in Siberia, or worse. For now, she was a German;
going "home" to Germany was her only option.

She boarded the train again, heading west along the same tracks that
had brought her to Dnepropetrovsk nine months earlier. She was on her
way to Memmingen, in Bavaria, armed with the major's letter of recommendation. To her surprise and alarm, the train stopped at the border, in
Radziwillow of all places, something to do with the military needing the
train, so the passengers had to get off and wait for another one.

Suddenly, Anna says, she found herself on the platform, in the town
where she grew up. What if someone recognized her? Sure enough, a man
spotted her, yelled at her, called her a Jew. She had to act quickly. That man,
she told one of the German soldiers, is harassing me just because I'm a girl.
The German soldier didn't hesitate. He confronted the man and told him
that he had better stop or he would be shot.

Fräulein Anna had escaped detection once again.

She spent the rest of the war in Memmingen, primarily working as a
translator for a construction company that was using Allied POWs from a
nearby stalag as forced labor. Within three weeks of Germany's formal
surrender on May 7, 1945, Anna went to the local office and emerged with
a new I.D. card and her old identity. Anna Prokopowitsch, having served

her purpose, ceased to exist; in her place stood the reborn Anna Schlajn, of Radziwillow.

She was just twenty-one.

Her words came back to me, the ones she used in describing her angry reaction when Mom had told her to stop driving Tillie to Eloise:

I'm too strong. I'm too strong. When I want to do something, I do it.

She saw the major in Germany after the war, she says. He was dying of cancer. She told him she was Jewish. He said he always suspected. Whether he did or not, they agreed on this: She was more valuable to him alive than dead.

I had read the history books, but I wanted a first-hand account of what Anna hadn't seen, to hear what she hadn't heard, so I go to the Shoah Foundation's archives at the University of Southern California, repository of 50,000 videotaped interviews with Holocaust witnesses, including one who had survived the Radziwillow massacre of May 29, 1942.

Bella Kron was sixteen when the Nazis came for her and her family. She waited for her turn to die, as the killing squads lined up their victims on wooden planks across the open pits, seven at a time, and shot them. On the videotaped interview, made in 1996, her voice shakes so much from her Parkinson's that she is difficult to understand at times, and when she describes the massacre itself, she sobs so violently that her words become incomprehensible, just like the events she witnessed, until she is unable to say anything at all. She doubles over, presses her fists into her eye sockets so hard that her knuckles turn white. I can hardly bear watching, her pain is so great. She apologizes to the interviewer, saying she rarely speaks about what she saw. "Too hard," she says. "Please forgive me."

She wants to tell her story, though, she wants to be understood, and she knows that the Parkinson's is slurring her words, these precious words that she wants to leave behind on tape so that others will know what happened in Radziwillow that day. As she stood with her mother and her eleven-year-old sister, Rivka, at the edge of the pit, her mother shoved her two daughters, shoved them hard, yelled at them to run. She and Rivka began sprinting, the bullets missed, and the girls kept going, kept running, all the way to Brody. Later, Rivka was shot trying to flee the Brody ghetto. "I had such a big family," Bella said to the interviewer. "I was alone."

Such a big family. I was alone. Anna's words, too.

Bella hid in the cornfields outside town—"like a wild animal," she said—and survived through a series of lucky breaks and lies she told as she made her way toward the Russian front. Eventually, she was captured and ended up at a military hospital, where a doctor suggested that she stay on after her recovery. He put her to work as a nurse. That was just part of her journey, a journey that lasted until the Soviets chased the last Nazi forces out of Ukraine in October 1944.

"To tell you everything," she told the interviewer, "takes days."

Watching Bella Kron reinforces my feeling about the gulf between Anna's life and my mother's. You could say that Mom had escaped the Holocaust because her parents had left Radziwillow a generation earlier, driven away by pogroms and enticed by the prospect of a better life in America. Did Anna, at some level, resent Mom's good fortune? Did Mom, consciously or not, look at Anna and resent her moral superiority?

Despite their differences, though, these two women also shared a bond: Growing up thousands of miles apart, destined to meet, they both had reinvented themselves to survive. Anna shed her deception, but her experience defined her and shaped her worldview. Mom never shed her secret, and it also defined her. She did what she had to do.

I suspect that Mom never intended for her secret to last a lifetime. Most of the time, we make a decision based on the circumstances at a particular moment, in a particular context; we rarely think about the long-term consequences, or if we do, we tell ourselves, don't worry, circumstances change, nothing is forever, I'll think about that later. In this case, however, once Mom created and began keeping the secret, she became stuck with it. Why? What made it so difficult for her to let it go?

SIXTEEN

Abandoned

Previous page: *Mom-in-waiting: Spring 1945, seven months pregnant*

I grab myself a bowl of cereal, and sit down with the morning Free Press. *It's late December 1970, and I'm home for the holidays during my freshman year of college, my first return visit. The night before, Dad went off to bed while Mom and I stayed up to talk, just like the old days. She wanted to know everything—room, classes, food, friends, professors, weather—and it was after midnight when I finally said I couldn't keep my eyes open any longer. Mom always sleeps later than I do, and this morning's no different, but she appears at the kitchen counter in the middle of my second bowl.*

"Have a banana," Mom says, peeling one.

"No, thanks," I say, without lifting my eyes from the paper.

"No banana?" Something odd in her voice makes me glance at her. She looks sad enough to cry. "You always had a banana on your cereal," she says. "I don't even know what you like to eat anymore."

P ain and the mundane often go together.

That's the thought that pops into my head as I pull into the parking lot of Botsford Memorial Hospital on a windblown June morning, my laptop in my backpack and a notarized letter in my pocket, authorizing the hospital to let me examine Mom's medical records. I'm looking for buried treasure, or at least clues as to why Mom decided to mention Annie to Dr. Hazan at their first meeting in 1995.

Walking the path from the parking lot to the entrance gives me this feeling of traveling back in time. The scene outside looks unchanged from that August day in 1999 when I stumbled out of the hospital into bright sunlight after watching Mom take her last breath at the age of eighty-two. There are the unsmiling family members, shoulders hunched, sitting on the same wooden benches, having the same worried conversations; there is the slow procession of cars making their drop-offs and pick-ups at the circular entrance; there is the small knot of smokers, banished from inside the hospital to huddle around the same ugly tan pot, taking one last puff before feeding its long, goose-like throat. I bend down, and yes, there it is, the same stupefying product name: Smoker's Oasis. On that August day, after witnessing Mom's lungs finally surrender after their long battle with emphysema, I wanted to commit an act of violence on that oasis, but now I just wince. Pain and the mundane go together.

I enter the hospital lobby, so familiar after several dozen visits while Mom was alive, and something feels different, something other than the lattes being served at a sleek new coffee stand near the main door. Then it hits me—it feels different because I don't have to worry about how Mom looks or what the doctor is going to say. What's left here is history and memory: This is where the ambulance took her when she had her panic attacks and couldn't breathe. This is where she spent eighteen days in the Botsford psychiatric ward, and this is where I spent hours warding off her anguished pleas to get her out of that den of dementia, to free her from that place where she had to surrender her pencils upon entering so that she couldn't even do a crossword puzzle.

I can't stay here, Steven. Please don't leave me here alone. You don't understand.

After Sash and I said good-bye to Mom on that Friday in May 1995, we took the professionals' advice: Give her your support, but back away, go home, let us do our job. To reassure Mom, to let her know that we loved her, to show her that she might be alone but she wasn't forgotten, all of us agreed to make our presence known through daily phone conversations, consultations with the staff, a conference call with her and Hazan to discuss her progress. But as requested, we did all this long distance, outsiders looking in.

Now I would see what it looked like from the inside out.

The hospital and I had exchanged the necessary letters and legal documents in advance, without debate or dispute, so Mom's records are waiting for me. I'm ushered into a tiny room occupied by two employees entering data into computers, and while they tap, tap, tap, I open the thick folder documenting Mom's stay in the psych ward.

First realization: Mom's pleas to go home didn't stop when Sash and I left her, they just became more indignant and less tearful. The peak came on Day Five, when she told Hazan, "I have been stripped of my dignity. I have been stripped of my freedom." But when Hazan pointed out that she hadn't tried to exercise her legal right to sign herself out, she softened, saying she knew she needed treatment and didn't want to upset her children. By Day Eleven, she had turned almost conciliatory, informing social worker Mary Bernek: "I don't like it here but I'll see it through." On Day Thirteen, she had converted her dislike of the place into proof of her resilience: "I still don't like it here but I am tolerating it. I feel that if I can take it here, I can take anything outside of here."

Second realization: Mom's secret remained as subterranean as ever.

Mom was so terrified when we left that day—*I can't stay here Steven I can't stay here Steven you don't understand*—that I thought she might have said something more about Annie, in therapy sessions or conversations with staff members, to explain her fears about staying there while Hazan switched her to nortriptyline, the antidepressant that he thought would be more effective than Xanax. If the Botsford ward was anything like other psychiatric environments, I was sure Mom would have had ample opportunity during her confinement to discuss her anxiety and her family secret.

No such luck.

The only mention of Mom's sister in the Botsford file comes from me, during an interview I had with social worker Bernek on that first, awful day. I remember thinking that it was important to alert Bernek to Rozanne Sedler's call and the startling news that Mom might have a sister, as skimpy as our knowledge was, in case it might prove helpful in understanding Mom's anxiety. "Pt is reported to have had a sister," Bernek wrote, "who was institutionalized for mental illness and was described as a 'family secret,' which only recently was revealed to Informant."

Informant. That would be me.

At the end of the file, in Hazan's discharge summary, a sentence jumps out at me, like a single illuminated window in a vacant, boarded-up building. Hazan writes that he has had lengthy therapy sessions with Mom "in order to address the patient's extensive anxiety and disappointment and feelings of betrayal at being hospitalized in this unit and then abandoned, she felt, by her family, even though they were very attentive to her."

Betrayed. Abandoned.

Don't leave me here alone, Steven.

When Anna Oliwek stopped driving Tillie to Eloise sometime in the early 1960s, Annie's list of visitors dropped from one to zero. If Tillie were trying to pass the baton, as Bill Regenold had suggested, she didn't have many options. Hyman had never gone to see his daughter, and his failing health left him largely a shut-in until his death in 1964. Mom was keeping her secret, and Annie had already rejected Anna.

Patient has had no visitors in years. That's what social worker Jim Mulherin wrote in May 1972, three months before Annie's death.

Abandoned.

Is it fair to draw this connection between Mom in 1995 and Annie in 1966? I think about it this way: There's nothing fair about fear. As Hazan had noted in his discharge summary, Mom felt "abandoned" even though we were "very attentive" to her. The facts didn't match her perception, but that didn't make her fear any less real. When we left her at Botsford, she could think about nothing other than her fear. Wouldn't her mind focus on the personal experience she knew best, wouldn't her fear conjure up an image of Annie at Eloise . . . *alone*?

Yes, Mom had voluntarily committed herself to the Botsford psych ward, but she also understood this wasn't like checking into a Holiday Inn—she couldn't just check out in the morning after a good night's sleep. I remember Hazan making this clear at the time: Even in a voluntary admission, the hospital's director still would have the right to hold Mom for three days if she wanted to leave—or even longer if the hospital asked the probate court for permission to keep her, and the court agreed. Mom had to trust the system, trust that she wasn't being railroaded into a long-term stay, and trust that her family was looking out for her in case things went wrong. But it's hard to have trust when you're afraid. Fear destroys trust.

Mom loved to read—novels, newspapers, magazines—you name it, she devoured it. Her taste ran to the popular rather than the ponderous, but she loved words and those who wrote them, no doubt one of the reasons why I acquired a reverence for newspapers and a belief that working for a good one was a fine way to make a living.

She didn't leave behind a list of her favorite publications from the 1930s and 1940s, but her letters to Dad from the war often included clippings, mostly from the Detroit papers and *Reader's Digest*, as well as occasional references to the *Saturday Evening Post*. When I was growing up, we had *Look* and *Life* around the house, and I remember Mom saying that when she was younger, she would pick up those magazines if she saw them somewhere, but that her family couldn't afford to subscribe.

Mom's reading habits have brought me to the Johns Hopkins University Library. I want to know what articles about mental illness appeared in popular publications during the late 1930s and early 1940s. I'll never know for sure whether Mom read any of them, but it seems like one way to get a sense of the attitudes that swirled around her before and after Annie's commitment to Eloise.

After several afternoons with articles such as "The Age of Schizophrenia" (an essay bemoaning the ever-growing numbers of patients with that specific diagnosis, a widely discussed trend in the late 1930s) and "But *Is* the World Going Mad?" (an essay arguing that the ever-growing number of patients in mental hospitals was not cause for alarm, but rather proof of psychiatry's progress in identifying and treating mental illness), I come away with a strong feeling that Mom's worries about mental illness in her own family would have centered around two popular notions from that era: First, that psychiatry was a long way from curing the seriously sick; and second, that genetics must be a factor.

For a young woman with a sister thought to be schizophrenic, either notion must have been nothing short of terrifying.

· · ·

The barest sliver of a memory:

*I'm eleven or twelve, and when I don't have a ball in my hand, I have a book.
For the most part, I consume the fictional series aimed at boys of my age: the
Hardy Boys' detective skills, Chip Hilton's jump shot, Roy Tucker's fastball, Tom
Swift's bravery and inventiveness. When I'm not solving crimes or winning the
championship game or hopping around the galaxy, I transport myself to Britain,
where I discover the adventures of a runaway named David Copperfield and the
highlanders of Robert Louis Stevenson's Scotland. I mostly make these trips alone,
but I sometimes ask Mom: Have you read this? Do you think I'd like that?*

*Mom rarely tells me what to read and never suggests that a novel is too old
for me. But when I ask about some of the English classics—Wuthering Heights,
Jane Eyre, Silas Marner—she says she didn't care much for Jane Eyre, that it
was too creepy and maybe too romantic for a boy not yet in his teens. I leave it
off my list.*

*Did she subconsciously steer me away from the book? Did she read the novel
in high school, as so many students did in her day? Did she know then, as I know
now, that the novel's main male character is keeping his wife a secret, that she's
shut away in the attic, that she's insane and that her name is . . . Bertha?*

*And of course it makes me wonder: Did her friends or classmates tease her
about having the same first name as the madwoman in the attic? Was that just
one more reason why Bertha vanished, and became Beth?*

Lisa Hovermale has spent a good portion of her professional life around
people like Annie. She works with so-called "dual diagnosis" patients, those
with both mental disability and mental illness, a relatively new branch in her
field. It's a marriage of disciplines that didn't exist in Annie's day—a patient
was treated as either mentally retarded (a phrase that has been replaced in
the modern lexicon by intellectual disability) or as mentally ill, and the system divided itself that way. There were institutions for the "feeble-minded"
and others for the "insane," but none for patients diagnosed as both. Now,
Hovermale's job exemplifies the changing times: She acts as the liaison between Maryland's mental health and developmental disability agencies.

"Tell me about Annie at the time of her admission," I say. "Do you think she was schizophrenic?" We're sitting at her kitchen table, Annie's records spread in front of us.

"That's hard to know," she says. "Certainly the observations of the court-appointed doctors are consistent with schizophrenic behavior, and she is exhibiting both paranoid behavior and catatonic posturing." She points to the Routine History's description of Annie's long hours sitting in the same chair. "But that's not surprising. Their observations would need to match their conclusion." She wonders whether Annie's condition might now be considered a mood disorder. "In those days, everyone like Annie was called schizophrenic. Bipolar didn't get here until the late 1970s, early 1980s."

Hovermale has taken a yellow highlighter to her copy of Annie's records, and her markings prompt my next question. "Did the report's description of Annie strike you as contradictory?" I ask. "I mean, she has this low IQ score and Dr. Bohn wants to send her to Lapeer, to the institution for the feeble-minded, but at the same time, Annie's insightful enough to say she won't ever have a 'normal' life or be independent."

The same thought had occurred to Hovermale, who warns against relying on IQ test results too heavily. "We know nothing about how they were administered and what was going on with Annie when she took them," she points out. "Besides, IQ suggests how you do in school, not how you do in life."

That's not just a clever line. Those who study mental impairment have concluded that IQ doesn't measure "adaptive ability"—that is, how well someone like Annie might adapt to the complexities of life, including living independently and holding a job.

"What do you think," I ask, "would happen to Annie today? Could she work?"

"Very possible," Hovermale answers. "The intellectual capacity is there, but this"—she points to the page that says the Girls' Vocational School had dismissed nineteen-year-old Annie because she was "too disturbing" to the other students—"could be a significant problem. If she's disturbing to others, her coworkers might not tolerate her. But that may just reflect the onset of her mental illness, not her ability. Today, we might do a better job of recognizing the difference. Back then, it was the Freudian era, and if you were a Freudian, you didn't believe that you could be both MR and mentally ill—a 'true' MR didn't have any inner psychic conflict."

I let that thought sink in. "You mean, Annie's mental illness would be seen as evidence that she couldn't be mentally retarded?"

She smiles. "It was more complicated than that, of course. But as far as the system was concerned in those days, she would be either one or the other."

Even though Annie had exhibited symptoms of mental illness before her institutionalization, I wonder if she ever belonged at Eloise. Howard Peirce didn't think so after examining her at the probate court's request, concluding that her mental retardation and amputated leg played a more significant role in her state of mind than mental illness. Neither did Dr. Bohn, who suggested commitment to Eloise in the first place, but preferred Lapeer. Lapeer's lengthy waiting list—a year, if not more—left Hyman and Tillie with only two choices, either Eloise or home, and for a family that was "all going crazy," Eloise offered at least the illusion of treatment, of doing something rather than nothing. My grandparents—bewildered by the system, trapped by their poverty—did not know where else to turn. "They had no options," is how Gerald Grob, a leading scholar on the evolution of U.S. mental health treatment, put it when I interviewed him. "They had to rely on the system."

Bohn undoubtedly felt that he was offering the better option by advising Tillie to commit Annie to Eloise, and he might have been right, but there's no question that his recommendation defined Annie's infirmity and her future. Sending Annie to Eloise rather than Lapeer was not like choosing the Oakman School for Crippled Children rather than nearby Hastings Junior High. While Eloise would take into account Annie's impairment and low IQ score, the county hospital's mission and orientation, from its examining rooms to its hydrotherapy tubs to its shock treatment units, dictated that once Annie came to Eloise, her symptoms of mental illness would take precedence.

Not that going to Lapeer would have improved Annie's life. Opened in 1895 as the state's first institution for the "feeble-minded," Lapeer grew from two hundred "inmates" that year to forty-five hundred in the 1940s. Many were sent to jobs in the community—girls and women as domestic workers, boys and men as farmhands. Lapeer's superintendents also embraced the state's sterilization law, one of the nation's first and an early victory for the American eugenics movement. Lapeer sought and received court approval, as the law required, for 2,339 of the 3,786 confirmed sterilizations done in Michigan, the fourth highest total in the nation behind California, Virginia, and North Carolina.

Given Tillie's fears about Annie's emerging sexuality, as reported in the Routine History—*It was our impression, as the mother talked, that she was alarmed over the patient's very evident interest in the opposite sex and has done everything she could to repress any expression of these interests*—a stay at Lapeer might well have made Annie a candidate for sterilization.

Eloise, on the other hand, avoided the sterilization practice. A spot check of the Wayne County Probate Court—the place where Eloise would have filed for the necessary legal approval to carry the procedures out—produced no record of any such cases. Ed Missavage recalls no sterilizations during his early days in the late 1940s, and Eloise does not appear in any of the recent newspaper or historical accounts on the state's sterilization policies.

So that's one indignity that Dr. Bohn probably averted for Annie when he suggested a commitment to Eloise "for the interim."

Finding Julie Reisner, the only possible surviving member of Mom's inner circle of female friends from the 1930s, is proving difficult. No one in Detroit seems to know her whereabouts and, unfortunately, her ex-husband has such a common last name that it could take months to run down the possibilities, even if I restrict my research to California. One afternoon, after one more frustrating foray, I console myself by remembering the quip I heard from that researcher at the Library of Congress months ago: *If I were in charge of the world, I would forbid any woman from changing her name when she marries.*

But wait—instead of getting wrapped up in the name change, why not go with the facts at hand? I knew Julie's maiden name—I had confirmed it as Reisner, rather than Reisler. If she had a brother, his name would still be the same.

I check the 1930 census records, and sure enough: Sam, brother, age three. He would be eighty now. Instead of looking for her, I look for him.

When I reach Sam Reisner at his home several days later, he's not inclined to tell some stranger the whereabouts of his sister. But yes, her name
is Julie, yes, they grew up in Detroit, and yes, she's still alive.

"I'd like to talk with her, if I could," I tell him.

"I'll get my son to call you," he says. "He's a journalist. If he says it's
okay, we'll go from there."

The years haven't changed Toby Hazan much at all. He might be a bit more
stooped and a bit grayer at the temples since our last encounter a decade
ago, but his handshake still has the same firm warmth and his eyes still have
the flinty twinkle that I remember. He's read Annie's records, and like Lisa
Hovermale and others I've interviewed, he's convinced that if she were
alive today, her diagnosis and treatment would be "totally different."

"How?" I ask, thinking that he's referring to the events that led to her
involuntary commitment to Eloise.

His answer surprises me. When he says totally different, he means
totally.

"It would have been different from the start," he says. "We know much
more about orthopedic problems, and the emotional effects. Her mother
wouldn't have been alone on this. She would have been in therapy herself
by the time Annie was two or three."

Later, he says, when Annie became morbidly concerned with death,
she would have been treated with antidepressants, perhaps mood stabiliz-
ers. "Institutionalization isn't even on the list" of options, he says, "not
unless she showed herself to be a danger to herself or others." That
phrase—"a danger to herself or others"—has been the legal standard for
involuntary commitment since a 1975 U.S. Supreme Court ruling usurped
the longstanding doctrine that states owed care and treatment to their
mentally ill.

"Institutionalization hasn't been on the list of options for a very long
time," I say. "Some people think we've gone too far, that many of the homeless and many people in jail are the mental patients of the past." I cite a few
books that advance that argument.

He nods. "Trade-offs," he says.

I turn the conversation toward Mom. I tell him about her breakdown in

1960, which she hadn't mentioned to him, and that as far as I knew, mentioning Annie as part of her family history was a first. "I checked with her regular doctor," I say. "When she gave her family background to him, she didn't say anything about having a sister."

He shakes his head, perhaps a kind of half-apology for not exploring these issues with her. "My focus was the present, not the past," he says.

I want to make clear that I think that was Mom's doing, not his failing. "It might have been helpful if she had told you what she had been hiding all these years," I say.

He smiles. "I can't disagree with that."

"Do you remember what you wrote in her Botsford records, that you had lengthy therapy sessions with Mom to deal with her"—I read aloud from his discharge summary—"'feelings of betrayal at being hospitalized in this unit and then abandoned'? That word, 'abandoned,' is a strong word. Is it fair for me to focus on it? Was she thinking that we were treating her just like Annie had been treated?"

He chooses his words carefully, or at least that's how it seems to me. "I think it's fair to focus on it," he says, finally. "Her situation is different, of course. She had plenty of family support. But she certainly felt alone at that moment."

"I only wish we had known the truth about Annie," I say. "It would have been a lot less painful for Mom, and for me."

As I get ready to leave, he says, "One more thing. Be kind to my notes."

I look at him quizzically.

"I'm only giving them to you because you have legal authority." He smiles wanly, and points upward. "I'm not sure whether Beth would want me to let you see them."

Deborah Cohen thinks about the repercussions of family secrets more than most people. She's a professor of British history at Brown University, where she's working on a book with the tentative title *Family Secrets: The Rise of Confessional Culture in Britain, 1840–1990*. She wants to understand how and when the boundaries shifted in that country of the stiff upper lip, what freed family members to discuss publicly what they (or their ancestors) had once viewed as shameful and private. It's an intriguing and original idea, and when I ask Cohen to debate my family secret's place on the confessional spectrum, she readily agrees.

I don't think of my project as fitting the confessional category, I say, but am I fooling myself? Should Mom's secret remain buried? Is it my place to tell it? If Mom were alive, I would hope she would want to tell her story, to kill the secret once and for all by revealing it, but I would not put my hopes ahead of her wishes. Her death, and the secret's reappearance in a form that opened the door to learning about Annie's life, changed that calculus. Disclosing the secret couldn't hurt Mom any longer—at least, that's what I've been telling myself and that's what I tell Cohen when we meet at her house near the university's main campus.

Cohen's thinking mirrors mine, up to a point. "As a historian," she says, "I think secrets shouldn't be allowed to survive the people who kept them. As a historian, I see nothing wrong, at all, with the notion of revealing. But you come along with a particular stake, and that's the complicated part to me. I suppose I started thinking about writing my book because . . . well, why is it that we have a compulsion to reveal? Shouldn't some things be allowed to be secrets? What's the relationship between secrecy and the ability to keep secrets, and the integrity of the family?"

"Do you think it matters what the secret-keeper might have wanted?" I ask.

Cohen has her own stake in that question: If that were the standard, she says, much history would go unwritten. She points out that in my case, only a family member could tell this particular story. "These records are generally impossible for historians to get," she says. "Often, only family members have a right to them."

I tell Cohen about the state's routine destruction of Annie's records and how—in Michigan, at least—being a family member isn't enough, that it takes persistence, determination, and help from other people who see the current laws as unnecessarily restrictive and an impediment to telling stories like mine. But I don't want our conversation to end on that note, so I steer the conversation back to family secrets.

"Do you see what I'm doing as part of the confessional culture?" I ask.

She laughs, then says, "It's not confessional in the sense that you're saying 'I'm an alcoholic, and this is how I came through it.' But yes, in the sense that you, and also historians, have this disciplinary position that it's better for secrecy to be unmasked."

Afterward, I find myself dwelling on what Cohen had said at the beginning of our conversation: *You come along with a particular stake.* That's the heart of it. I'm a writer, but in this case, I'm also a son.

As Cohen said: *That's the complicated part.*

Neil Reisner loves the idea that his aunt has turned up in the middle of my family secret, and he's delighted to play intermediary with Julie, who's eighty-six and living in a Jewish Home for the Aging outside Los Angeles. His dad, as promised, had briefed him about my call, and within a week, Neil has put me in touch with Julie's daughter, Ellen. A family wedding would soon bring Neil and Ellen to southern California, and they suggested that if I could wait six weeks, they would join me at the interview. They seem to think that it will put Julie more at ease.

They set a date with Julie, and I make plane reservations, crossing my fingers that nothing will go wrong between now and then. I think we have a lot to talk about, or at the very least, I have a lot of questions, and she's the only one still alive who might be able to answer them.

SEVENTEEN

Dad's Secret

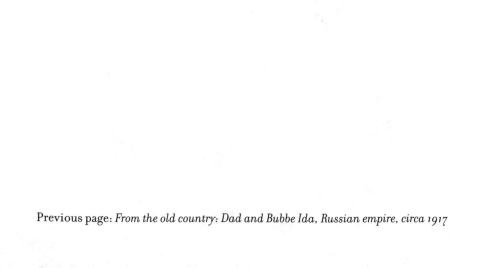

Previous page: *From the old country: Dad and Bubbe Ida, Russian empire, circa 1917*

I'm embroiled in that rite of passage, introducing my girlfriend to my parents, and Mom and Dad have taken us to the Steak & Ale, where Dad can order either of his favorites, strip steak or red snapper. He's in fine form, playing both host and raconteur, still able at sixty-two to turn on the charm that Mom spotted from her perch on that staircase long ago. It's 1976, we're in the Detroit suburb where my parents now have an apartment after nearly a lifetime in the city, and Dad is entertaining Mary Jo with stories from the furniture front lines, explaining how a salesman works a troublesome customer.

As Dad tells the tale, this particular shopper is a bargain hunter, a woman who comes to his store claiming that a competitor down the street will sell her a $300 couch for $150. Can Dad match that? "Sure," he says, nonchalantly, directing her to a row of sofas tagged at $300. She picks one, asks how much of a discount he's willing to give her, and is suspicious when Dad offers the magic number, half price, $150. "What's wrong with it?" she says accusingly, and not waiting for an answer, she's on her knees, examining the legs, tugging at the fabric, pushing here and pulling there, like a car buyer kicking the tires. Satisfied, she hauls herself up and says, "Okay, I'll take it."

Dad says, "Let's write it up." That line often shows up in his furniture war stories; it's salesman code for sealing the deal, moving the customer from oral commitment to putting it down on paper. At the counter, Dad writes on the invoice, "one couch, $150," then "three cushions, $50 each." Total, $300. The bargain hunter explodes, calls Dad a liar and a cheat—those were the nicer words—before demanding an audience with his boss. Dad waits patiently for the

torrent to end, and then says something like this: "Look, lady, you come in here,
asking me to sell you a $300 couch for $150. I can't make any money that way,
and I don't understand why you're here. You already had a couch for $150, and
you didn't buy it, so something made you walk away from that deal. Now, if you
want to buy a good couch, a couch that will last, a couch that will make you
happy, I can sell you one for $300. That's the best I can do."

Mary Jo is in his thrall. "So what happened?" she asks.

Dad waits a beat. "She bought the couch—for $300."

Mary Jo splutters, "You're, you're, you're . . . a con artist!"

Oh, this is going great, I think. No place to run, no place to hide, nothing to
do except remain stock still, smile frozen on my face, and wish that I could disap-
pear.

Dad, ever the salesman, looks at Mary Jo, and a beatific smile forms on his
lips. "A con artist," he says, lingering over the phrase. "Yes, that's exactly what
I am."

T heir marriage wasn't perfect, by any means. The fairy-tale romance—
the carefree, car-loving couple of the old black-and-white photos,
the shared tenderness of those wartime letters, the over-the-top
expressions of affection—gave way to something resembling real life. They
didn't argue much when I was a kid, but when they did, there was a weary
repetitiveness to their disagreements. Dad often brought his work home
with him—that is, he entered the house still steaming about some conflict
with the boss at the furniture store du jour that employed him—and he
would boil over at some point, shouting and red-faced about why I hadn't
taken out the garbage yet or some other small irritation. He made no secret
of his belief that he could do his boss's job better than the boss did, and
after hearing some of his stories, I thought he was probably right.

He certainly could sell furniture. I went with him to work when I was
about thirteen, and came away awed by his ability to win over even the most
sullen customer. I had only the dimmest idea at the time that he wasn't selling love seats and bedroom sets and kitchen tables, that his main product
was himself, that he believed we're all in sales, to one degree or another.

Did my parents love each other? I was sure that they did. I never worried
that they might divorce, although I was aware that Mom treated Dad with kid

gloves, and urged the rest of us to tiptoe around him as well. "Dad had a lousy day at work," she would say, "so don't do anything to make him mad." Sometimes I thought Mom's day revolved around Dad's happiness—making him happy, keeping him happy, worrying about whether he was happy, preventing us from getting into any sort of mischief that would cause him to be unhappy. Mom didn't tell us that we had to be perfect—she didn't place that particular curse on us—but if she had possessed a working magic wand, she would have brought Dad home to a perfect house, a house without troubles.

Of course, the house was hardly stress-free. Money seemed to be the root of most tensions: Dad liked to spend it, and Mom liked to make Dad happy, so she indulged him while lamenting their lack of savings, at times even encouraging him to spend what they didn't have. She understood that, in Dad's well-thumbed book, money equaled success, and with money came status, and with status came respect and admiration. So even though Dad's annual income never topped $18,000, according to his Social Security earning records, he "bought" a new car every two years, because successful people drove new cars and laggards didn't. Dad chose his cars for maximum impact: a Lincoln, a Crown Vic, a royal blue Mercury convertible (my favorite)—statements as much as transportation. We are what we drive, that seemed to be Dad's philosophy; in the Mo-tor City, where grownups loved to talk about their wheels, he fit right in.

It's probably more accurate to say that Dad replaced his old car loan with a new one. He had a Keynesian economist's view of debt: He saw nothing wrong with deficit spending, which made him popular with the bill collectors as well, judging by their frequent calls to our house.

Dad's reputation as a crack salesman made him a hot commodity in the furniture business, but his tendency to tell off the boss occasionally made him a hot potato. He rarely lasted more than a few years at any store, sometimes quitting and sometimes getting fired; at our house, instability became part of the furniture. In 1962, after several months without a job, he took one in Lansing, seventy miles away, coming home only on weekends. My worst fear came true when Dad announced one day that we were all going up to Lansing; they sold the house, but then Dad got into a fight with the new boss and (to my not-so-secret-delight) lost his job. We couldn't get the house back, so we moved anyway. We ended up three blocks away—same neighborhood, same schools, same friends.

The family's finances improved somewhat after Mom went to work, part-time, for the monument company in 1963, but not by much. Their combined pre-tax income inched up slowly from the mid-1960s through the 1970s, peaking at $30,000 in 1978. Mom had taken the bookkeeping job mostly to help with college costs that began taking a bite out of their budget in the mid-1960s. Only through a patchwork of family income, scholarships, work-study jobs, and summer jobs did we all make it through, aided by the astoundingly low in-state tuition at Michigan's schools back then.

I was the first to attend an out-of-state private college, and even with my substantial scholarship, Mom had to add hours at the monument company to make the various ends meet. It was a house of cards that could fall at any moment, and in the fall of 1973, during my junior year of college, it did. Dad had his first heart attack, and didn't work for six months, didn't earn that commission. His earnings plunged, down 50 percent for the year. Until then, I hadn't really understood just how week-to-week they lived; if the university's financial aid office hadn't agreed to increase my scholarship and arrange a student loan, I couldn't have stayed in school.

Mom, of course, was bound and determined to prevent that. Education was king, and once again, I heard about the uncle from Chicago's broken promise. History was not going to repeat itself, not if she had to call the president of the university himself (I, of course, was bound and determined to prevent that phone call from being made).

Mom and Dad chose their roles in this particular family drama, with Mom playing the nurturing, mostly practical wife, and Dad the charming, often moody husband. But Mom wouldn't let their differences divide them, as I found out in 1975 when I learned my first family secret—Dad's, as it turned out.

The two of us were having a casual dinner in Detroit, on one of my occasional visits home after college, when Dad started to spin a long story about a friend who wanted, late in life, to become a U.S. citizen. But the friend had a problem: He didn't have the proper documents to apply for citizenship, nor did he have a green card. Essentially, he was illegal, even though he had lived in the country for nearly his entire life. If his friend fessed up to the government, Dad wanted to know, what would happen?

It took me two or three questions, and maybe ninety seconds.

"This friend . . . is it you?" I asked.

He didn't try to keep up the pretense. "Yes."

My mind raced to grasp the consequences. Not a citizen? What did that mean? I could do no better than blurt something out of my eighth-grade civics textbook.

"But, but, but . . . you told me that you voted for McGovern!" I said, as if voting for president constituted the sum total of what it meant to have citizenship.

Dad smiled, still the salesman. "I didn't tell you I voted *for* McGovern," he said. "I told you I would never vote for Nixon. Which was true."

Truth wasn't the word that came into my head. Nixonian was more like it, a clever dodge. I didn't care one way or the other about his citizenship, but the deception! That I found hard to swallow. I didn't say anything right away, but I didn't have to—my dismay must have shown on my face. Dad looked embarrassed, and only then did I realize this wasn't easy for him, laying himself bare before his son. He had his reasons for concealing and now revealing this long-held secret; it was time for me to shut up and listen.

Like his invented friend, Dad wanted to become a citizen before he died. A second heart attack had crystallized his feelings on that, causing him to think about the might-have-beens and the wish-I-hads, and citizenship ranked high on the list of what mattered most. The irony, of course, was that he only wanted what everyone, including the governments in Lansing and Washington, believed he already possessed.

But that wasn't the point.

The point was this: It galled Dad that he didn't have the same status as native-born or naturalized Americans. For him, for this man who bought a new car every few years (and only American-made cars, to show his support for all things American), status counted. In his own mind, he was as much a citizen as any of them—he had lived here since he was six years old, served honorably in the military, raised a family of five, worked hard all his life, paid taxes, kept on the right side of the law, done everything a good American should do. How was he any different?

I didn't know much about citizenship laws, but I wondered: Why hadn't Dad applied for citizenship during or after the war? Didn't the government make it easy for vets?

I learned that he had tried several times during his Army days, but the immigration service could not find any record of his entry into the country and kept asking him for more information. But he had no more information, nothing on paper to document his arrival from Poland or Russia or whatever that disputed sliver of Eastern Europe was called at the moment he and Bubbe Ida left it. Dad wasn't even sure of the year (1919? 1920?), his age (six? seven?), the name of the ship, or even the port—although it had to be Ellis Island, he asked me, didn't it?

Growing up, I had heard two explanations for Dad's uncertainty: His mother, Bubbe Ida, a bit of a ditz (everyone said), had lost his papers; or Bubbe Ida had smuggled her son in, hiding him under her greatcoat, because he was sickly and she feared that the immigration authorities would send them back to Europe. (This second version had a whiff of intrigue and bravery, so it gained favor over the less interesting story line of beleaguered Bubbe Ida misplacing documents.) No one could get a clear answer out of Bubbe Ida about what exactly had happened, and I wasn't the only one who had trouble imagining how a greatcoat could conceal a six-year-old, or how he could stay there for as long as it would take to pull off such a subterfuge. But immigrant history offers stranger tales than that, so the greatcoat version had a shelf life out of proportion to its logic. Who knew, maybe it was even true.

Either way, Dad was stymied. Whatever options he had to rectify this lack of documentation, he was too discouraged to pursue them. His application went into permanent limbo, along with his hopes for citizenship. Now, in 1975, after a second brush with mortality, he wanted to revive that effort, and he wanted his journalist son's help in navigating the bureaucracy. Sure, I said, I'd do some research, I've never written about immigration law, but I suspected that if citizenship meant as much to him as he had said, he could make it happen. He had a lot going for him, I said—this was the sort of heart-warming story that congressional representatives and newspapers love. The first step would be the hardest; he would need to tell the immigration authorities that he had no green card. Deportation? Out of the question. Come on, I told him, you don't even know for sure where you came from, and wherever that is, the territory has changed hands two or three times since you left in 1919 or 1920, or whatever year it was.

I later learned that I wasn't the first to hear Dad's secret. It had come out a few years before, but only to a limited audience. My brother Mike, a civilian employee in the Navy at the time, was up for a promotion that required a security clearance. Mike asked Dad for details about his background to fill out the required forms, and Dad had revealed the truth rather than cause Mike trouble.

When Dad started spinning his story at our dinner, though, he must have known that I was unaware of the Navy security snafu, or he wouldn't have bothered with the elaborate "I have this friend . . ." gambit. Our dinner ended with an agreement: I promised to find out what he would need to do, and he would decide if he wanted to proceed. I kept my part of the bargain, but ultimately, he could never shake that old-country fear of government authority, and so he did nothing. He died in 1980, a non-citizen to the end.

"Did you know that Dad isn't a citizen?"

Mom showed just a flicker of surprise at my question.

"Of course I did," she said.

I remember nothing else from our conversation. But the overriding impression she left—the one that has stayed with me all these years—was that they were keeping secrets from their children, but not from each other.

So if Mom knew about Dad's secret, wouldn't Dad have known about Mom's?

Maybe a trip to Texas would offer a clue, if not an answer, to that question.

That's where Dad's brother, my uncle Manny, now lives with his wife, Shirley, reluctantly leaving their beloved California to be near their daughter, Sharon, as they got older. (Yes, California—they had achieved what my parents had only dreamed.) Manny and Shirley had topped my original list of people Dad might have told about Annie, if he knew. That list included business associates, but somehow members of that crowd seemed like Dad's least likely confidantes. He worked with them, but rarely socialized with them, and he had changed jobs often enough that most of those relationships hadn't lasted or matured. Besides, as I quickly learned when I started checking, the vast majority of them had died long ago. The men of that generation went long before the women.

No, if Dad had shared the secret with anyone, I think he would have chosen family over business. I had already checked with his younger sister, Rose, who didn't know anything, and I doubted that Dad would have confided in his baby brother, Bill, who was just thirteen when Mom and Dad married. His brother Manny seemed a better bet—he was Dad's junior by eight years, but still old enough to have served in the Army at the same time as Dad, so they had shared that experience. They had corresponded during the war and had even managed to get together in 1944 when they were both stationed in Texas. At family gatherings, the two often hung out together; at least that's the way I remembered those weddings and bar mitzvahs before Dad's death in 1980. No one could doubt the brotherly resemblance when the two men—both salesmen, both known for their charm—stood together, especially as age took its toll on their hairlines. The last time I saw Manny, I thought: I'm looking at Dad, if only he had lived as long.

"I never knew Beth had a sister," Manny is saying. "Never had a clue."

We're having breakfast, just the three of us, with the Austin sun already warming up the room, making the air conditioner cycle on and off, background noise to our early morning conversation. Shirley relies on a walker to navigate their condo, but when I make a move to carry the grapefruit halves to the table, she firmly shoos me away. "As Manny will tell you, I rule in the kitchen," she says. I believe her.

Shirley's physical problems leave Manny with most of the non-kitchen tasks, but he seems almost spry as he hauls out linen for my bed and fetches boxes of old photos from the garage. At eighty-five, he still has the big hands and big ears and wide smile that I remember from my youth; aging hasn't diminished him yet, although he's survived a major heart attack and bouts of colon and prostate cancer. He's my genetic hero, a Luxenberg male who didn't succumb to heart disease at forty-eight, like his father, or at sixty-seven, like mine—living proof that it's possible to make it to my eighties in relatively good health.

By the time I get to Austin, word of my project has reached the extended family grapevine, so I no longer have the element of surprise when I pop the question about Annie. But Manny and Shirley are plenty surprised by the many details and layers, especially when they hear that Annie was twenty-one when she went to Eloise. ("It blew their minds," their daughter Sharon would tell me later.) As we puzzle through the story, Manny reminds me that he didn't meet Mom until 1943, after Annie had been at Eloise for more than three years.

"If Dad knew about Annie," I say, "I was thinking he might have told you. You seemed close. You sent him those letters during the war."

"Your mom's idea," he says of the letters. "She wanted to keep his spirits up." I had brought his letters with me—four to Dad, three to Mom—and he's already reread them. "I don't see any tone in my letters of real warmth," he says. "Your mom was worried about your dad, and she thought letters from me might help."

The mere fact of the letters did not equal the intimacy that I had assumed. What he said made absolute sense: Four letters in two years? Bosom buddies would write more often.

"We really weren't that close, your Dad and I," he says. "You know, we moved from Detroit to Syracuse when he was eighteen. I was ten. He detested it, left after a year, went back to Detroit. I hardly saw him until after the war." He shrugs, almost apologetically.

Now for the big question. "Do you think he knew about Annie?" I ask.

"No," Manny says, immediately. "No," Shirley chimes in a second later.

"Why so sure?" I say.

"Because he would have told someone," Manny replies.

"Even if Mom told him not to?" I ask.

He thinks about that. "Well, I never thought he was all that good at keeping a secret."

We spend the weekend in a family history marathon, ranging over a dozen subjects and nearly one hundred years, back to the mystery of Dad's immigration and the greatcoat incident, why my grandfather Harry left Bubbe Ida and his infant son behind when he left Russia in 1914 ("he had to leave in a hurry—the Russians were going to draft him," Manny says), how Harry's failed bakery ventures in Detroit led him to leave town one step ahead of the bill collectors, the circumstances surrounding Dad's discharge from the Army ("nervous stomach," they both say), Mom and Dad's persistent money troubles in the late 1940s and 1950s ("they had to borrow from us several times," says Shirley, followed by Manny's "but they always paid us back").

Shirley and Mom shared equal status as outsiders to the Luxenberg clan, a bond that might have led them to forge a close friendship. But when I was growing up, Mom seemed closer to Aunt Rose—they kept up a phone relationship, in the days when long-distance costs limited both the frequency and duration of calls—and Rose knew nothing about Annie, so it wasn't surprising that Shirley didn't, either.

Still, Shirley knows as much about the Luxenberg family history as any Luxenberg. She had an academic's love for her subject—she studied it, analyzed it, archived it—so I'm thinking that she might have picked up information about Mom and her family along the way.

"What do you know about my mom's family?" I ask her.

"She never talked about them," Shirley says. "For the first few years after I met her, I wondered if she even had one. I even thought she might be adopted."

I leave Texas no closer to the truth about whether Dad knew about Annie. Manny and Shirley's duet of "No" counted for something, but it didn't settle anything. While I was tilting toward the view that Mom hadn't told Dad—maybe she, like Manny, thought Dad had trouble keeping a secret—I still couldn't rule out the possibility that Mom had enlisted Dad in the conspiracy of silence, and that he had carried off one of his best con jobs ever, not just keeping the secret, but giving off the impression that he wasn't any good at keeping them, which would be the perfect ruse.

Which was it? Unless I could find out more about why Mom had created the secret, I would be stuck in the land of maybes and possibilities and likelihoods.

On the plane back to Baltimore, transcribing my notes, I come across one question I had asked Manny as I was trying to get a handle on how Mom presented herself in the early years of her marriage, as she was getting to know her husband's relatives. We were talking about my parents' money problems, their multiple requests for loans from the Syracuse branch, and I had asked him, "Did you see my mom as self-centered?"

Manny had always liked Mom, from the minute he set eyes on her. He congratulated Dad for finding someone special, someone both lively and nurturing. So I was interested in Manny's answer.

"I saw her as being kind and generous when she could be," he said.

When she could be.

There's something strange about the rest of the letters.

A few days after my trip to Texas, I retrieve the last box of envelopes from a bookshelf to finish what I had started a few months earlier. I grab a bundle, putting them in order by postmark, May, June, July 1945—and I'm confused. Every letter in May is from Dad. The same for most of June. Mom wrote him every day—where are hers?

July is the reverse: None from Dad until the twenty-sixth, and a month's worth from Mom that never reached their destination. They came back to her, bearing a version of the same red rubber stamp: a hand with a finger pointing left and the words "Returning to United States. No Forwarding Address."

No forwarding address? How can the Army not know the whereabouts of one of its soldiers? Was Dad AWOL somewhere in the Philippines?

I flip through the envelopes one by one, day by passing day. Each letter appears well traveled, as the Army Post Office tries in vain to deliver it to Pvt. Julius Luxenberg, #36891866, assigned to the 313th General Hospital somewhere in the Philippines. The markings and cross-outs proliferate as the odyssey continues: "Forward to 132 GH," usually in red ink; "no record at the 132," always in black ink; "126 G.H.," in pencil. In retrospect, it looks ridiculous, but at the time, what choice did the Army postmasters have? Mom faithfully sent a letter every day, and each letter had to travel the same circuitous route, until it finally landed in the hands of someone who seemed to know where the mysterious Pvt. Luxenberg had gone, who wrote: "Evac to USA."

Evac to USA?

The Army had hospitals all over the Philippines. Dad was serving at one. What could have happened to require an airlift to the States?

And why had I never heard even a whisper about it?

. . .

"I'm really beside myself, Duke honey. This is the 8th day without mail.
I'm afraid you're sick . . . I really don't know what to believe."

— July 19, 1945, Mom to Dad, forwarded to 132nd GH on 8/5/45

Frantic. That's the best word to describe Mom's growing fear in July 1945
that some catastrophe had befallen her husband.

Truth be told, she had always worried, ever since Dad had written her
those desperate letters during basic training, telling her that he was heading toward the "insane asylums." He had survived, of course, helped by
nearly a month in the Camp Wolters hospital while doctors ran tests on his
stomach. But Mom's worry never went away; she just learned to manage it,
at least most of the time.

Now, however, she couldn't hold it in. Circumstances had changed,
for both of them. Dad left for the Philippines in late March, taking him
out of mail contact for five weeks while the S.S. *Monterey* made its way to
Manila, and out of telephone contact for the duration of his overseas tour.
They joked that Dad's new assignment would save them hundreds of dollars in long-distance charges, but Mom, six months pregnant, was mo-
rose at the prospect of not hearing his voice, of not having a way to call
him when she gave birth to their child. So in July, when his letters stopped
cold, without warning or explanation, she had no way to reach him and no
real idea where he was. (She sent her letters to an APO in San Francisco,
and Dad, adhering to military censorship rules, only hinted at the 313th's
location in his correspondence.) She was just two weeks out of the hospital, with a newborn turning night into day, and in that vacuum of no sleep
and no news, the dam broke. She did what she had tried hard not to do for
so long.

She let her imagination run wild.

"I must let it out. It's 10 days without mail — there aren't any tears left in
me. I am tearing myself apart I am so worried. I can't stand it . . ."

— July 21, 1945, Mom to Dad, returned, marked "no forwarding address"

"I'm so scared, so worried . . . 2½ weeks without any mail."

—July 25, 1945, Mom to Dad, returned, marked "no forwarding address"

The blackout ended the very next day, a Thursday, July 26, when the phone rang in the Pingree Street apartment and Mom heard Dad's voice. As Dad spun his story, Mom couldn't believe what she was hearing: He had been in the States for two weeks, he was calling from a hospital in Kentucky, but he was fine, really he was, and if all went well, he would have his medical discharge in a month or so, and then he would come home, free at last. Weeks of worry vanished in an instant, and she hardly mentioned his disappearing act. "It was like giving a blood transfusion to a very sick person," she would write him later. "As I have said time and time again, I shall never want for anything when I have you in my arms."

Then it was her turn. She had so much to tell him: First, that he had a son, Michael Don, now exactly one month old, born on June 26. Everyone was being so nice—Hy and Fran had been taking care of her, Sylvia Pierce and her husband had brought over a bathinette, a handy device with a miniature bathtub and storage underneath for clothes and supplies. Mom had written him all the details, of course, but he had never seen the letters, they were still on their Odyssean journey, caught somewhere between the 313th and the 132nd, having not yet reached the man who would stamp them "Returning to United States, No Forwarding Address."

Later that night, after putting their newborn son to sleep, she wrote to Dad's new address, the one he had given her on the phone: Darnall General Hospital, in Danville, Kentucky. "I still can't stop trembling with excitement and joy — I'm walking on air — It's so very odd, but dearest one, I knew you were coming home."

I go through the letter twice, looking for any hint about the reason for his evacuation, and can find none, not even between the lines. Mom merely told him again, as she had on the phone, that he sounded good, and that she had celebrated the news of his impending discharge by going out for the first time since Michael's birth. Dad's brothers were in town to see the baby, and a whole crowd of friends and relatives, including Hy and Fran, had taken her dancing. "I had 2 Calverts and you know what two drinks did to me," she wrote. "I was the life of the party—enjoyed dancing immensely."

She still hadn't recovered from his call. "Imagine you being in the States 2 whole weeks without letting me know," she scolded, "and me knocking my brains out 'cause I got no mail." Why didn't he phone as soon as his feet hit U.S. soil? Well, he said, he knew she had probably delivered the baby, that she would be recuperating and getting used to motherhood, and he didn't want her to worry while she was in the hospital.

Worry her about what? His first few letters didn't say, and Mom let him off the hook, rebuking him only mildly, reminding him that going AWOL from his wife had made her crazy anyway. But she didn't dwell on it. Instead, she entertained him with family and neighborhood news—Julie Reisner was getting married and it looked like Hy and Fran were heading to the altar, too. I had long heard how Hy's decision to marry the non-Jewish Fran had infuriated Tante Hinde, who blamed Mom because Hy and Fran had first set eyes on each other at Mom's shoe store, but now I was witnessing the origins of Hinde's life-long animosity. "Tante Hinde and I had quite a run-in about it," Mom wrote. "It's a long story. I'll tell you about it when you come home."

Dad's first letters only deepen the mystery surrounding his evacuation. "It's sure good to feel relaxed and be able to write to you again," he wrote a few hours after that first phone call. "Talking to you today was worth more to me than all of the medication the U.S. Army could give me . . ."

Medication? Had his stomach finally developed an ulcer? He didn't explain. Dad's letters, usually so straightforward about his failings, now took on an elliptical quality, as if Dad thought that the military censors, who reviewed everything that went out of the Philippines, were still looking over his shoulder.

It was Mom, not Dad, who provided the first clue to the nature of his ailment, an indication that their phone calls were more explicit than their letters. On August 2, she wrote: "Everyone keeps calling up and asking what's wrong with you etc, etc. I just tell them I don't know, so they think it's something wrong with your stomach . . . So I'll wait 'til you get home and you tell them some story yourself."

I could recite the stomach story by heart. I had grown up with it, and that's the explanation Manny and Shirley had offered when I asked them about his discharge. But if that was the cover story that Dad sold us, what was the real one?

Dad had mentioned in one letter that he ended up at Darnall because it specialized in the treatment he needed. I do an Internet search for "Darnall General Hospital." It doesn't exist any longer, but I turn up a 1944 congressional hearing that confirms what I had begun to suspect. "The Army has at the present moment two general hospitals which are exclusively psychiatric. There is one in Danville, Ky. and one in . . ."

So this was Dad's secret.

And Mom: After dreaming of castles in the air, of California paradises and starting their own business, she's left with the reality of a sister permanently residing at a psychiatric hospital in Michigan and a husband who's a temporary patient at one in Kentucky. Does she fear the future, and what it might hold for her and her savior when he finally returns home?

EIGHTEEN

Uncontoured Ills

Previous page: *Undelivered: Mom's letter to Dad, July 23, 1945, "No Forwarding Address"*

"You worry me a little, (or should I say a lot and be truthful) when you said—'you'll see if I'm different when you see me'—for I know you've been thru hell."

—August 5, 1945, Mom to Dad, at Darnall General Hospital

"Without you my life would be empty. I'd be a total loss—and I'm very thankful that I have you to come home to - - - until eternity."

—August 12, 1945, Dad at Darnall General Hospital, writing to Mom

T he letters make more sense now that I know how to read them. The evacuation suggested some sort of breakdown; the medication Dad mentioned must have been for anxiety, or maybe depression; the hospital must have been evaluating him for a psychiatric discharge. No wonder Mom had trouble fending off everyone's questions, but fend them off she did. No, she told them, he's not wounded. No, he's not injured. Yes, he's coming home, very soon, it's just the usual red tape, you know how long everything takes in the Army. In reality, though, Dad had to wait for the Darnall disability board to gather information on him and decide whether he should be discharged.

The waiting tried Mom's patience. The war was nearly over, and she wanted her Duke back, in part so that she didn't have to handle the barrage of questions by herself. "Tante Hinde called — keeps asking me what's wrong with you," she wrote to Dad on August 7. "I always say I don't know — it's rather hard to keep evading the question. Let's decide on something to tell everybody."

Meanwhile, Darnall had sent Mom a long questionnaire as part of its evaluation. "This is what it says," she wrote Dad. " 'In order to arrive at the proper disposition of your relative we would appreciate a summary of his family history, early development, education, habits, character, social and economic adjustment, injuries, illnesses or hospitalization etc.' It was rather difficult to know what to write, but I 'dood' it."

A week later, two days after Japan announced its surrender, setting off the wildest celebration that Mom had ever seen in her hometown, Dad met with a ward officer, and told Mom everything looked good. "I go before the board on Monday morning . . . Then, it's a matter of a week and I hope to be a civilian — the ward officer asked me routine questions, what caused my nervous condition — how do I feel at the present time — what did I do in civilian life — what did I do in the army — how long was I in the service — etc."

His hearing went as he had hoped. The board declared him disabled, and on September 7, 1945, twenty months after he became a soldier and five days after Japan's official surrender aboard the U.S.S. *Missouri*, Pvt. Julius S. Luxenberg put on civilian clothes for the bus ride home. The discharge documents he carried with him did not specifically mention the nature of his disability. When I saw them years later, going through his papers after his death, I assumed that "Certificate of Disability for Discharge" referred to his nervous stomach.

The letters end, of course, just before his return to Detroit, so I have no idea what Mom did to welcome her soldier home. She warned him that she was planning to make a fuss over him, and he warned her that he wasn't the same Duke who had left nearly two years before. Thinking of the future rather than the past, she told him she had decided to take a part-time job in the evenings at $25 a week, selling shoes for Hy. "Imagine, me working for Hy, how times have changed," she wrote. "I wouldn't make a whole lot but it will pull me through on expenses." Dad wouldn't hear of it. "What's this about going to work — I know our finances are a bit low but isn't it too soon my darling? Don't you think it's best to wait a little longer — I know how anxious you are to keep the wolf away from the door – you are one in a million my darling."

Their last letters still talked of dreams, but more modestly than before— no mention of immigrating to California, or owning their own furniture business, or jukeboxes for Evie to jitterbug the night away. Instead, Dad wrote of wanting "a little bungalow away from the turmoil – a large garden in back – beautiful flowers all around . . ." Mom matched his enthusiasm for "a place of their own," but injected a note of pragmatism: "Since housing shortages still exist, I want to start looking around. If we could find an income, how about 5 rooms? It would be nice if we could have a separate room for Michael D . . ."

So much had changed in the two years since his induction. When he went off to war, he left behind a wife working at a shoe store, two daughters living with their grandmother, and few obligations other than his weekly child-support payment. He returned to a two-month-old son, the likelihood that Marsha and Evie would be coming to live with them for good, no significant savings, and no immediate income beyond his $300 mustering-out pay.

Mom told Dad not to worry, to keep his chin up and his spirits high. She had what she wanted—Duke was back!—and they would face the world together. "I do wish you'd stop worrying about responsibilities and going back to work," she wrote him on September 2. "It will all work out."

They would do what they had to do.

More questions for reinterpretation: Did my father's "disability" continue into civilian life? Did it change him, change how he dealt with others, change his family?

I can't yet answer all those questions, but I can say that I don't think it made much difference to the way I grew up. Maybe it helps explain his occasional fits of temper; maybe it provides a context for his restless work history; maybe it helps clarify his paralyzed reaction when Mom had her nervous breakdown. Then again, maybe it doesn't. Having a temper, changing jobs frequently, and not taking command in a crisis doesn't come close to the DSM-I, -II, or -III's definition of psychosis. From my perspective, Dad did what dads are supposed to do: He worked, raised his kids, supported our ambitions. He wasn't around a lot, he wasn't easy to know, he had more anger than was healthy, and his stomach bothered him until the day he died, but he took care of his family and his responsibilities. He was a lousy soldier, but he was a good and decent father.

But a psychiatric discharge certainly does help explain, at least for me, why Mom worked so hard to keep him happy, why she tried to shoo away stress, why upsetting Dad ranked at the top of her list of household crimes. She might have taken on that role anyway, like many women of her generation, but I think something happened in Manila, perhaps not something dramatic, and certainly not something permanently disabling, but something that scared Mom enough to become not just Dad's shield, but his sentry.

What put him on that airlift? Dad's military records would tell that story, if only they existed. Unfortunately, a devastating fire at a St. Louis government archive destroyed most World War II personnel records in 1973, including my father's. His letters, however, made it possible to do a targeted search of a set of documents untouched by the fire: the "morning reports" of each unit, which detail the daily comings and goings of all personnel. Dad wrote his last letter from the Philippines on June 30, 1945, narrowing the timing of his evacuation to sometime during the first two weeks of July.

The morning reports, when they arrive several months later, do more than provide the date. They provide enough facts to piece together the story of his evacuation.

The 313th General Hospital had to build itself. The military, overwhelmed by the casualties from wars on two fronts, had approved a major expansion of the general hospitals in 1944, and it took seven months for the new 313th to collect, train, and transport its staff to the shores of Manila. The S.S. *Monterey* arrived on May 1, 1945; a month later, working in tents and with an insufficiently chlorinated water supply, the 313th accepted its first patient. By the end of June, the hospital had beds for 672, and had treated gunshot wounds, compounded fractures, and sixty-three psychiatric cases. "Psychotherapy and narcosynthesis have been used with good results," the

313th commanding officer commented in his quarterly report. (In narco-synthesis, a controversial technique developed during World War II, a traumatized patient receives a drug such as sodium pentathol to help recall unpleasant or repressed memories.)

Dad had written to Mom about the draining, dirty, debilitating climate. Dehydration posed a constant threat, as did the mosquitoes, which the Army controlled by aerial sprayings of DDT. Dad spent most of May unloading equipment and then wielding a pick and shovel. On May 14, he wrote that he "felt fine"; he was seeing movies every other night, and had loved *Rhapsody in Blue*, the film about George Gershwin. The beginning of June brought "miserable weather," constant rain, "so heavy that it came into the tent, and onto my cot." The heat made everything a steamy mess, and left him wrung out. "Had to change clothes three times today," he wrote on June 20.

His last letter, postmarked July 1, contains no hint of any problems. He said he had just picked up his pay, $5.40 for the month, but the small sum didn't bother him. "I don't go anywhere, and I don't gamble so I can get along. It's enough for my cigarette rations and beer rations."

The morning reports don't give any details about his illness, but they reveal that everything happened in a hurry. On July 2, the 313th admitted Pvt. Julius Luxenberg, patient number 1560, for "psychoneurosis and anxiety, sev." That same day, the 313th transferred him to the 80th General Hospital, the largest in Manila and the best equipped to handle psychiatric patients. The next day, the 313th released Pvt. Luxenberg from assignment, and reported that he now belonged to the 80th General Hospital's Department of Patients. On July 5, the 80th delivered him to Base K at the Philippine island of Leyte, where he remained until an airlift to the States on July 10. On the 80th's final disposition and admission list, an additional diagnosis appeared: "reactive depression."

Lost somewhere in the rush: His belongings, which would include Mom's letters to him for April, May, and June.

Dad, too, was one of the thousands, a different set of thousands than Annie's.

During July 1945, the military evacuated 6,923 "neuropsychiatric"

patients from overseas posts back to the United States, and over the course
of the entire war, 127,660. A battle raged within the military's ranks about
how to handle psychiatric discharges—too liberal a policy would encourage
fakery, too restrictive a policy would place troops in the field at greater risk.
A War Department memo directed draft boards to take time to weed out the
unfit before induction. "These cases are disturbing to the morale and dis-
cipline of a unit," the March 1943 memo declared. "They present a problem
and an unnecessary burden to unit commanders, often requiring that they
be returned to this country after a brief service time overseas." That description pretty much summed up Dad's twenty months of duty, starting
with basic training; he might well have wondered if his draft board got the
memo.

Darnall, which had a capacity of 871 in its psychiatric wards (and fifty
beds for nonpsychiatric patients), handled a substantial percentage of the
evacuees during its nearly five years of operation. Like Eloise during this
period, it faced an overcrowding problem at times; unlike Eloise, Darnall
had no permanent population—patients stayed an average of forty-eight
days before returning to duty, getting a discharge, or going to another hospital for longer-term treatment. So many patients flowed through the facility that the Darnall disability boards could hardly keep pace; in 1945 alone,
they evaluated 5,774 patients, a rate of more than ten a day, granting disability discharges to 4,443 and returning 748 to active duty. Under Army
rules, a diagnosis of "psychoneurosis" required a finding by a three-member
panel, including at least one psychiatrist.

Three months before Dad's case went to the disability board, the Army
surgeon general issued a memo clarifying its criteria for discharge. No patient should be returned to duty unless he can work a full day, the surgeon
general's memo said, and while that standard would undoubtedly result in
discharges for soldiers who could do a full day's work in civilian life, for the
Army's purposes, "their bad attitude and mild residual neurotic disorder
made them ineffectual."

The Army never resolved its ambivalence about psychiatric discharges,
according to its official history of neuropsychiatry during World War II.
Like any large organization, especially one put together in haste and com-
prising career officers and newcomers trained outside the military, the
Army had many voices telling it what to do. Some saw disability discharges

as a quick way to get rid of a problem soldier; some thought such discharges should go only to the clearly disabled, and resisted the idea of using them to improve morale. As might be expected in wartime, the commanders in the field wielded a good deal of influence as to who did or didn't qualify, and the Pacific and European commands eventually adopted different policies. For much of the war, most commanders discouraged the evacuation of psychiatric patients, preferring to treat them at field hospitals, figuring that it would be harder to get them back once they were gone. But the Southwest Pacific command, overwhelmed by psychiatric cases and concerned about morale, ordered airlifts to begin in November 1944.

By July 1945, the airlifts had become routine. On the day of Dad's evacuation, the 80th General Hospital listed ten other psychiatric patients for evac back to the States.

When Mom picked up the phone on that July 26 afternoon and heard Dad's voice, telling her of his sudden evacuation to the States, she might have been thinking about another patient who had just completed a sudden transfer of her own. Two days before Dad's call, Annie had boarded the bus for that long trip to the Soo, to that temporary hospital in the converted military barracks. Mom was still living in her parents' apartment, and Eloise must have notified Tillie and Hyman, so it's hard to believe that Annie wasn't on Mom's mind.

Mom didn't write Dad on July 24, the day of Annie's departure to the Soo. Both of Dad's brothers, Manny and Billy, had arrived to see her and her new baby, and she cooked dinner for them, along with Hy, and Hy's sister Rose. It was one of those unbearably hot, humid Detroit days—so uncomfortable, she wrote to Dad the next day, "that I felt like throwing the dishes out of the window instead of washing them."

That was her last letter before Dad's phone call. After I receive the morning reports and realize that Mom had learned about her husband's psychiatric evacuation within a few days of her sister's transfer to the Upper Peninsula, I fish out her letters from late July and read them again, just to make sure that I hadn't missed anything about Annie.

I hadn't. No hint of Annie, no indication of anything unusual taking place.

Now I knew for sure: If Mom didn't mention Annie in those letters, when she had specific news to pass along, then she never would. Still, the question remained: Was Annie just a forbidden subject between them, or was Dad truly in the dark?

I had plenty of news to share with Manny and Shirley: Dad's psychiatric hospitalization at Darnall, Manny's presence in Detroit on the very day of Annie's departure for the Soo, and a breakthrough that tore a permanent hole—in my view, at least—in the greatcoat story.

Using a genealogy search engine and a Jewish naming dictionary with more variations that I dreamed possible for my grandmother's first name, I had found what Dad had never been able to give the government during his many wartime applications for citizenship: proof of his entry to the United States. "Chaja" was the key that unlocked the door. That variant for Ida, plus the years 1919 and 1920, brought to the computer screen a list of possible hits that included this one: Chaja Feigel Luksenberg, twenty-eight years old, arriving in 1920 at Ellis Island.

Luksenberg, not Luxenberg, which is the name on Bubbe Ida's passport, the one document I have from that era. For months, because of the passport, I had assumed that Luxenberg also had to be the spelling on the passenger manifest. But it appears the ticket-seller had transliterated her name into his own language, Polish most likely, and so she's Luksenberg when she boards the S.S. *Nieuw Amsterdam* for the twelve-day voyage, to the former New Amsterdam, aka New York.

And Dad, the phantom under the greatcoat? He's right there on the manifest, too, Juda Luksenberg, six years old, no question about it. But one part of the tale turns out to have substance: He spent thirteen days in the Ellis Hospital for some unrecorded illness, thirteen days of anxiety for Bubbe Ida, because not only was her son sick, but it was possible that the authorities would say, sorry, you can't come in, you can't join your husband Harry in Detroit, we're sending you back to Europe.

In all that confusion, did Bubbe Ida lose the papers? Is that why she didn't have any when Dad asked her, during the war, to send him any documents that would show how he got here? Bubbe Ida's not around any longer, so I can't present her with these new facts to see what she says.

"Isn't that something?" Manny says when I call. "After all these years."

"Do you think Bubbe Ida made up the greatcoat story, maybe because she felt bad about losing the papers?" I ask.

"Who knows?" Manny says. "People make up all kinds of things, I guess."

That seems like a good transition to Darnall. "Remember Dad's nervous stomach?" I say. "That really was a cover story." I briefly tell him about the evacuation to the States, Dad's eventual transfer to Darnall and his psychiatric diagnosis. When I finish, Manny says, "He faked it."

Faked it? That would be a con artist's triumph. "Why do you say that?" I ask.

"He would do anything to get out," Manny says. "He hated being in the Army."

I consider that. Dad's letters certainly show how much he came to despise the Army—he talked about his superiors much the way he would talk about his furniture store bosses later on. Still, I didn't buy it. I think the Darnall doctors would have their antennas up for outright fakery. Disability wasn't automatic; while most patients left with discharges, the hospital did send about 15 percent back to duty.

No, I tell Manny, perhaps Dad took advantage of what happened in Manila, but I don't think he was faking. He didn't sound like a con artist in his letters to Mom from Darnall; he sounded like a defeated man who wanted to hide what had happened to him. *"Without you my life would be empty. I'd be a total loss – and I'm very thankful that I have you to come home to . . ."*

I have one last question for him. "Do you remember going to visit Mom just after Mike was born? This would have been July 1945."

Now it's his turn to consider. "Only vaguely," he finally says. "Why?"

I tell him that his arrival was on the very day that Annie went to the Soo. "Do you remember Mom saying anything, anything at all, about her family, or family problems? I realize it's a long time ago."

"Too long," Manny says. "I remember going to see the baby, but that's about it. The rest of that trip? Just a blur."

Why would he have any memory of how Mom was acting? He didn't have any context for paying attention—just as I didn't have any memory of Mom

doing anything unusual in August 1972, when she managed to take care of
Annie's burial without raising my suspicions, or anyone else's.

The mountains of paper on Ed Missavage's kitchen table look even taller
and more formidable than during my last visit. I'm asking him about late
1971, the period just before Annie went to Northville. "I know you never
met her," I say, "but you were there in 1971, so tell me what happened when
the transfers began."

Missavage delivers his account with equal doses of disapproval and sar-
casm. For him, the emptying of Eloise had little to do with patients, and a
lot to do with budget-cutters and lawyers who knew almost nothing about
mental illness. "Two things were going on," he says. "First was the move to
get patients out of hospitals. The head of mental health in Michigan had a
$3 million budget problem. He thought he could find the money by trans-
ferring the long-term patients at Eloise, the ones that the state was paying
us to take care of, into the vacant beds at state hospitals."

I pick up the 1982 Eloise history, which I had brought with me. "There's
a section in here about it," I say, flipping to a page I had marked with a yellow
sticker. I read aloud: " 'Transfer of 900 Patients to State Institutions' . . . On
November 15, 1971, the first 238 patients were transferred, with the indication that the rest would be transferred by June 30, 1973.' "

I close the book. "That's a massive number of people to move."

He nods. "We sent patients everywhere—to Ypsilanti, Pontiac, Northville. I helped select the male ones, and I sent the best of mine, the least
problematic, to Pontiac State Hospital, where my wife worked. It went on for
months."

Just as Annie didn't have a say about her commitment to Eloise in 1940, she
had no voice in the decision to uproot her from the place where she had
lived for thirty years. Unlike the overcrowding crisis that put Annie on a bus
to the Soo, however, this upheaval centered on the startling fact that maybe
for the first time since the days of Biddy Hughes, the state of Michigan had
more beds for the mentally ill than it had patients to fill them. The many
competing forces swirling around the country's mental health edifice had

finally collided in 1971, and the impact of that collision reverberated through Michigan's psychiatric hospitals, the state's probate courts, and the state's fledging community mental health system, as well as the wards of Eloise. The expansion that superintendent Thomas Gruber had predicted in 1933 would continue indefinitely? Not just slowed, not just halted, but reversed.

Like a building imploding, the contraction happened with almost breathtaking speed. In 1955, the country's public psychiatric hospitals reached their peak of 558,000 residential patients, or 340 for every 100,000 people in the United States; by 1980, despite a nearly 50 percent jump in U.S. population, the number of in-patients had dropped below 120,000, a rate of just fifty per 100,000, an astonishing turnaround that has yet to end. Today, state and county psychiatric hospitals have an estimated total of 50,000 patients; if 1955 rates and policies still applied, there should be nearly one million.

What happened? In a word, everything. The introduction of antipsychotic drugs altered the very nature of treatment, allowing many patients to go home as long as they "took their meds"; the birth of the antipsychiatry movement called into question the very nature of the asylum approach as well as the very nature of mental illness, even suggesting that mental illness was a myth; the passage of the 1963 federal Community Mental Health Act endorsed alternative settings for treating the mentally ill; the civil rights movement spawned activist lawyers and new legal techniques for challenging the established order; federal and state judges demonstrated a willingness to hear these novel lawsuits, and in some cases, to issue ground-breaking rulings that brought about not just change, but fundamental change. Governors and state legislators, elated at the prospect of reducing costs in a department where expansion had always seemed endless, raised few questions about what the future might hold, although some mental health officials worried aloud about mentally ill patients falling through the cracks of the underfunded and still developing community mental health system.

In Michigan, Gordon Yudashkin, the director for mental health, saw a short-term solution to the state's empty wards and his department's chronic budget problems: reclaiming the state's patients from Eloise. At one time, at the height of overcrowding in 1945, Eloise would have been delighted to

hand over those patients. But now, Eloise needed that reimbursement rev-
enue to stay in business. In the long term, the math didn't work: Just as the
policies of the past had guaranteed the need to build more and more hospitals, the policies of the 1970s guaranteed that Eloise and some state hospitals
would eventually close. There just weren't enough institutionalized patients
to go around.

This time, when Eloise selected several hundred other patients for
transfer, no letter accompanied Annie offering assurances of her ability to
"take care of herself." When she arrived at Northville on January 4, 1972,
she was only fifty-three years old, but she brought with her a host of physical problems and medications—a worsening heart condition treated with
daily doses of digoxin, a fluid buildup that required a diuretic to control,
and a series of recent vomiting episodes that the nursing staff at Eloise had
thought significant enough to note in her medical chart. She remained on
her usual regimen of Serentil, an antipsychotic, and Artane, a drug used to
combat the Parkinson's-like symptoms that often afflict patients on antipsychotic medication for an extended time.

What would become of her? That was entirely up to the Northville staff.
Annie could hardly speak for herself at this point. As the Northville records stated, "At the present time she remains being incoherent and irrelevant most of the time but has been no real ward problem. She tries to
cooperate with the staff as best as she can and follows instructions much
better. The team feels that her condition has stabilized and that she could
be taken care of in a nursing home."

The next day, she was transferred again, for the last time, to Petoskey
Hall, a nursing home run by a private group that, only months before, had
acquired the property from the Jewish Home for the Aged. In one sense,
she was going home. Petoskey Hall was just two miles from the apartment
on West Euclid where she had lived before her commitment to Eloise. In a
more realistic sense, she was going nowhere, to a place where she knew no
one and no one knew her. When she died eleven weeks later of a stroke, a
doctor at Northville took the call from the nursing home and added a terse
note to her chart: "At this time we are not able to obtain any further information regarding this patient or the cause of death."

That's the final sentence, the last words, an ending without a conclusion.

. . .

Lawsuits against mental hospitals spread like wisteria through the nation's federal court system in the early 1970s. Eloise's turn came in 1971, when Gabe Kaimowitz, a young lawyer at the Michigan Legal Services office, took a call from twenty-four-year-old Annette Bell, confined at Eloise on a temporary involuntary commitment that had been extended twice. The clock stood at seventy-five days, and ticking. Bell wanted out.

Although much had changed in the mental health world since Annie's commitment in 1940, not much had changed in probate court procedures. As in Annie's case, two Eloise doctors had certified Bell as mentally ill and in need of "treatment." As in Annie's case, they declared that it would be "improper and unsafe" for Bell to attend her own hearing. As in Annie's case, the probate court judge had complied with Eloise's request to keep Bell at the hospital without a full hearing or the taking of any other testimony.

Unlike Annie, however, Bell had a forceful advocate who saw himself as part of a movement. Kaimowitz interceded on Bell's behalf, requesting a meeting with the hospital's hierarchy and winning Bell's release. It didn't last. Six weeks later, Bell's frantic parents brought her back, saying she was refusing to take her medication, that they didn't know what else to do. Bell agreed to enter the hospital voluntarily, then changed her mind and begged a friend to phone Kaimowitz again.

This time, Eloise rebuffed the lawyer's efforts, asserting that Bell's family was no longer willing to take responsibility for her. Two weeks later, Kaimowitz filed the lawsuit, which like many in its day, used a specific case as a launching point for a broad-based attack on the entire system. It not only alleged that Bell was being held against her will and presented no danger to anyone, but that the entire commitment process was unconstitutional—that Michigan law deprived patients of their fundamental rights, that patients were being confined without a formal diagnosis, and that mental health officials routinely ignored the few protections that the law provided. If the court accepted the premise of the sweeping lawsuit, it would essentially have to shut down the involuntary commitment process and order the Michigan mental health system to start over.

. . .

"Annette Bell was committed simply because she was 'inconvenient,' "
Kaimowitz says from Florida, where he now lives. He's still the tilter at
windmills, well known for his years of civil rights work, his zeal, his dogged
cantankerousness, and his legal crusades against a variety of Florida agencies. After interviewing him, I would add to those qualities a nimble mind
and an encyclopedic memory for Supreme Court cases he hasn't read in
years.

When Bell called him that day in 1971, he was in the middle of a one-
year fellowship at Michigan Legal Services, working mostly on cases involving juveniles. Bell was a "circular" patient, cycling in and out of treatment.
"She smoked incessantly," he remembers. "Paced up and down. Her parents were older, couldn't deal with her, felt guilty about it. One time, they
dumped her on my lawn, said 'You take care of her.' "

Bell v. Wayne County General Hospital turned into an epic legal battle,
requiring three years to resolve and, midway through, merging with a second case from the state's psychiatric hospital in Newberry. The arguments
on both sides embodied the stark extremes of the national debate: Kaimowitz declared that the state had no right to force medication on Bell if she
didn't want it; the state responded that Bell's illness prevented her from
making a rational choice. The state said Bell deserved treatment for her
illness; Kaimowitz alleged that the hospital itself was making Bell sick—
"Who wouldn't be depressed after being subjected to unwarranted confinement?" he asked, rhetorically.

The case also foreshadowed the future. The Michigan Psychiatric Society, fearing that the court might endorse Kaimowitz's argument that Bell
could refuse treatment altogether, warned the court not to go down that
road—a road that other courts would, eventually, choose to travel. Allowing
mental illness to go untreated, the Society said, was itself cruel and inhu-
mane; hospitals and doctors needed discretion to provide treatment—
including medication and shock therapy—to its patients, especially those
too mentally impaired to give valid consent. Otherwise, doctors would be
caught in an impossible position: liable for not treating a patient who
needed it, and liable for treating a patient who didn't want it.

Damned if they do, and damned if they don't, the society's lawyer, William H. Dance, said in court. Is that, Dance asked, where we want our doctors to be?

Annie was still alive when U.S. District Judge Fred W. Kaess ruled against Annette Bell in July 1971, finding no constitutional defects in Michigan law, but she had died by the time a panel of three federal judges declared the opposite in May 1974, invalidating major sections of the involuntary commitment process that, thirty years apart, had sent both Annie and Annette Bell to Eloise. Unlike the Michigan Supreme Court rulings of the 1930s, however, the 1974 ruling was no slap on the wrist, no minor rebuke that could be ignored. From now on, the three-judge panel said, patients would have lawyers, full hearings, and the chance to offer evidence showing why confinement wasn't necessary. The panel agreed with every major charge in the lawsuit, but chose not to throw out the entire law because, it said, "both the Michigan legislature and the Michigan Supreme Court are pursuing efforts to enact new laws and rules." Instead, the panel would be watching to make sure the reforms took the court's ruling into account, and would retain jurisdiction in case the reforms fell short.

What, in particular, seemed to bother the panel about the process, beyond the constitutional question? I'd say the imbalance of power between the system and the patient, especially given the nebulous nature of mental illness. "The Michigan act," the panel wrote, "sets forth a process under which a person whose affliction, in the view of a given court, falls anywhere within a vast, uncontoured description of mental ills, is subject to both temporary and indefinite commitment, whether his particular ill presents a realistic threat of harm to himself or others. In our opinion, the standard of commitment for mental illness is fatally vague and overbroad."

More than thirty years later, Kaimowitz says the country still hasn't gotten it right. "I used to believe it was best to empty out all the hospitals, but I have to agree, I think we went too far, that some portion of the homeless today are the mentally ill of yesterday." Still, he says, he's not in favor of forcing people into treatment. "Confinement changes behavior, and taking someone away from society for a year or two means they miss a year or two of learning and experience. You also can't evaluate patients under duress. Refusal to take medication or accept treatment is seen as evidence of insanity. But wanting to get out of a mental hospital can't be seen as an irrational act. Isn't a desire to be free the most rational act of all?"

Rational, and rarely uncomplicated, in desire or reality.

NINETEEN

Always the Bridesmaid

Previous page: *Here come the bridesmaids: Mom, far left, and Julie Reisner, far right, at the Pierce wedding, 1941 (courtesy of Milton Pierce and Julie Reisner)*

The four women, absorbed in their bridge game and their cigarettes, hardly pay attention to me. It's sometime in 1963 or 1964, and when it's Mom's turn to host the weekly game with Marilyn, Ann, and Ethel, I'm sometimes allowed to observe. I feel important, as if I've been given a special passport to this country of adults. I'm ten or eleven years old, and this is how Mom teaches me her favorite pastime.

They chatter on, but I'm too busy studying the cards and trying to decipher the bidding to follow what they're talking about. Ethel lives nearby and is Mom's closest friend; they play Scrabble together frequently and I know I can always go to her house if I'm locked out. Marilyn and Ann are sisters-in-law, and Mom has just started doing bookkeeping work for the monument company partly owned by Marilyn's husband, Sid. Marilyn is a redhead with the sort of easy, welcoming smile that makes me feel that it's okay to sit at the table while they play. Ann, on the other hand, scares me. Her dark hair frames her long, thin face, and there's an intimidating elegance about her. She's quick-witted and sharp-tongued, unafraid to say exactly what she thinks, and that makes me wonder if I might end up on the receiving end of one of her comments. When she's trying to make her bid, I take care not to say a single word.

After the game, when her friends have left, Mom lets me go over the hands I saw, as best as I can remember them. She's a good teacher, patient and encouraging, and never seems to tire of my questions. If my interest in this adult game seems strange to her, she doesn't show it; instead, she seems pleased, even proud, as if I'm her prodigy and she's the grandmaster. For me, it's just another form of

*competition, like basketball or baseball, my favorite sports; for Mom, it's another
way to be close, although that's not something that crosses my mind, not even for
an instant, as she instructs me on counting cards and the finer points of ruffing
and finessing.*

*Bridge, she explains, is a game of skill, but also of deception. Fool the compet-
ing players into believing that you hold certain cards, and they might make a
mistake that allows you to win.*

That, she says, is what makes the game interesting.

I stare out the restaurant window at the smogless, cloudless California
sky. Los Angeles has outdone itself today, temperatures in the low
eighties on the coast, warmer here in the San Fernando Valley, with
just enough of a breeze to take the edge off the sun's heat. This is the southern California of Dad's letters after his brief visit in 1944, just before
reporting for duty in Monterey; this is the southern California of his
dreams, his castle in the air. *Honey — Hollywood for you and I after the war —
and I don't mean perhaps — it's the most loveliest place — ideal for you and I —
real paradise.*

I'm waiting at the restaurant for Neil Reisner, Julie's nephew, and
we're going together to the Jewish Home for the Aging, where Julie lives.
Driving on the clogged freeways to get here, I found myself thinking that
Los Angeles and its suburbs remind me—seriously—of Detroit and its suburbs. Both exude the car culture, nurturing mythologies that depend on
the style and mobility of the automobile. Detroit built itself by turning out
hundreds of millions of cars, and then L.A. built itself by erecting several
hundred miles of freeways for the cars that Detroit was turning out. It's a
pipeline, from one power center to the other, from the Motor City to the
Mobile City.

Neil's not hard to pick out as he comes through the glass door. Ponytail,
earring, mustache, just as he described himself on the phone when we arranged where and when to meet. He's a journalist with twenty-five years in
daily newspapers, now working as a professor and pursuing freelance projects, so when I briefed him on my quest and told him that I'm hoping Julie
might have specific knowledge of why Mom created the secret, he asked to
come along. "I want to see how it turns out," he said.

It's not a great time for him; he's here for the family wedding, but over the last few days, his dad's emphysema has taken a clear turn for the worse. Last night on the phone, Neil said, "We're moving into the hospice phase." As we ride in his car to the Jewish Home, he warns me that Julie's on edge about his dad's failing health. "She's pretty upset at the idea of losing him," he says. "Her little brother, you know?"

But Julie looks great. A walker rests next to the bed, but when she rises to greet me, she stands tall and erect, her cheeks have a rosy glow, and her white hair frames a face that looks nowhere close to eighty-six years old. She and her daughter, Ellen, were talking about my visit when Neil and I arrive, and I can see that Ellen has been rooting through Julie's closet, hauling out photo albums and other artifacts.

When I explain to Julie that I'm researching a book about my mom's family, she gazes at me, her eyes alert, a little wary perhaps about why someone would fly across the country to talk about the old days in Detroit. If I'm lucky, though, she could be a fount of information: She wasn't as close to Mom as Faye, but she knew Mom longer and better than Fran—and, most important, she knew Mom before Annie went to Eloise, before Annie turned into a secret.

"You're the first person I've been able to interview from my mom's inner circle of female friends," I say, trying to put her at ease. "I wonder how you met. Wasn't Mom a few years older than everyone else?"

"Through Faye," she says. "Faye and Sylvia." Faye, she says, was the group's hub and its glue. I tell her that I've spoken to Marty Moss, and she smiles. "He was a nice guy," she says.

As Julie and I talk, Ellen keeps up her archeological dig; at one point, she brings over Julie's 1938 yearbook from Northern, the same high school that Mom attended, and Julie dons the glasses that hang from a lanyard around her neck, closing one eye to get a better focus on her black-and-white graduation photo. She points to her entry, which unlike most others, shows only her name. "No extracurricular activities," she says. "I had to work in my dad's shop after school." I can hear the resentment in her voice, how this still rankles her, nearly seventy years later.

I ask her about Mom's family. Did she spend much time with them?

No, she says. "She had a little sister who limped," she says. "She was small. Your mom was tall, right?" I press her for more on Annie, but she doesn't remember much more. It was a delicate subject, she says, and when Annie went to Eloise, it became a subject they could avoid.

Either Julie's not a natural storyteller, or I'm asking the wrong questions, because I'm having trouble getting her to relax and just reminisce. I don't think it's a memory issue—she occasionally repeats something she said a few minutes earlier, but her long-term recall seems good, just not very expansive. I'm glad Ellen is there; she chimes in with helpful prompts—"Mom, tell him the story about what you were doing when Pearl Harbor was hit"—that get Julie talking, but I begin to worry that I may have come a long way for very little. This member of the inner circle may know less than I had hoped.

"Other than Faye, what held the group together?" I ask, searching for a springboard rather than a dead end. "What did you talk about?"

"Boys," she says, laughing. "We talked mostly about boys."

That turns out to be Julie's answer to many questions. They went bowling to meet boys. They went to the movies to meet boys. They still lived at home, most of them, and meeting a boy was the first step toward getting away from their parents, away from the possibility—in her case—that she might end up working in her dad's locksmith business.

The guys, she says, were anxious to get married, too.

"Why?" I ask.

She grins. "To stay out of the service."

"What about my mom?" I say. "Was she anxious to get married, too?"

Julie answers with a glint in her eye. "She was worried that she was getting too old. But then she met the boyfriend."

The boyfriend?

"Your father," she says. "That's what I always called him."

I love that she calls him "the boyfriend," that she met him before he was "the husband" or "the father." I dig into my bag and pull out the photo of Mom and Dad at Lake Michigan. "He sure was handsome, and your mom was crazy about him," Julie says, her eyes taking on a faraway look. I try to imagine what she's thinking. Does it conjure up pleasant memories? Or does it remind her of a bygone age she can't revisit?

Finally, she says, "I envied them. So in love."

As we look at several more photos from my collection, Neil suddenly interrupts. He needs to leave. He's been on his cell phone for much of the time, talking to various family members and doctors about his dad, and something has come up. Could Ellen take me back to my car? While we make these arrangements, Julie lapses into silence until, unprompted, she volunteers:

"My feeling was that she didn't want to let the boyfriend know about the sister."

Neil and I both freeze. I hadn't yet asked Julie directly about why Mom had kept the secret, and she had no way of knowing that her "feeling"—*can't tell the boyfriend*—matched one of my working theories of the secret's origin. Later, Neil would tell me that he couldn't believe I didn't show any sign of excitement. But at that moment, all I could think was: Go slow. Find out more. See if she can be more specific, if she can do better than a "feeling." And, don't lead the witness.

Why, I ask, would Mom not want to tell her boyfriend about Annie?

"Your mom was a little frustrated," Julie said. "She wanted to get married. She didn't need him to find out about the sister. That might ruin it."

Neil's gone, and Ellen has accompanied Julie to lunch—served promptly at noon, Julie says, and "if I don't go now, I won't get to eat. So I'm going." I'm left alone with my thoughts for nearly an hour, and I welcome the chance to wrestle with the nuances of what Julie had said: *My feeling was that she didn't want to let the boyfriend know. She wanted to get married. She didn't need him to find out about the sister.*

Not exactly definitive. Certainly not as definitive as "Your mom told me that she decided to keep Annie a secret from your dad because she was afraid, if he knew, that he wouldn't marry her." But perhaps this was as close as I could come, as close as I could expect from a time when friends understood that some things were better left unsaid.

"You're still here?" Julie says, when she returns from lunch.

I like her directness. "Afraid so. Ready for a few more questions?" I try to pick up right where we left off, to recapture the moment. "You told me before lunch about your feeling, about why Mom kept Annie a secret. You said, 'She didn't need him—the boyfriend—to find out about the sister.' "

"Oh, yes," Julie replies, "she didn't want to upset anything."

Did Mom specifically ask you and her other friends not to talk about Annie?

"I don't think she actually did that," Julie says. "It was just my feeling that she didn't want us to talk about it. That was my impression. She was closer to Faye than she was to me, actually, so she and Faye might have talked about it."

Faye. Ah, yes, I'd like to ask Faye, if only Faye were still alive.

I ask a few more questions, but Julie has told me as much as she knows, or at least, as much as she can remember. I'm glad she didn't return from lunch with a more definitive answer; it makes her first memory seem credible. We chat about marriage a bit more—"We all wanted husbands," Julie says—and then Ellen, equipped with a photo of Mom that I gave her so she can look for others, holds up an enlarged picture of the bridesmaids from Sylvia's wedding and says, "Is this her?"

Mom stands at the end of the line of bridesmaids and the maid of honor, all gathered around the groom, resplendent in his white tuxedo. I've never seen the grainy photo before. "That's my mom," I say, elated at the discovery. Julie takes the photo in hand, closes one eye again, and peers at it. "Yes, there's your mom," she says, pointing to the woman on the left, "and that's Faye next to her. That's Sylvia's sister, Irene, she was the maid of honor, and Milton Pierce—it was his wedding, he was marrying Sylvia—and Evelyn— what was her last name? oh, dear—and that's me," she says, pointing to a woman on the far right, who's the same height as Mom.

Hail, hail, the gang's all there—Mom, Faye, Irene, Julie, the names from Mom's letter. I tell Julie about my interview with Milton Pierce, Sylvia's husband, who's ninety now and still making the daily trek to his office at Guardian Alarm, the company that he had built from nothing into one of the largest in the Midwest. His two sons run the business now. "He said he remembered my mom well, but that he didn't know anything about Annie. Do you think there's a pattern here?" I joke. "Husbands in the dark?"

I was still having trouble getting a bead on Mom and Julie's relationship. How close were they? Did Mom confide in Julie? (Then again, did Mom confide in anyone? Certainly not Fran, who slept over at Mom's on many a night in 1943 and 1944, and yet told me she knew nothing about Mom having a sister.) I decide to find out.

Julie, I say, did you ever hear Mom talk about Joe, a guy who wanted to marry her? Or an uncle who promised to help pay for her to go to college, and then backed out?

Julie shakes her head. No, she says, neither one ring any bells.

"I don't think we ever thought about college. *I* never thought about college," she said, emphasizing the "I" and laughing merrily. "We weren't very good students. We were more interested in boys."

I say something about how the world was different then, that women had fewer opportunities than they might today. Julie, who eventually made a career as a marriage counselor and taught workshops on assertiveness training, thinks about that and says, this time without a smile, "Well, my dad never really encouraged us to go to college. We were supposed to help him in the shop."

Ellen hoists another photo. This one I've seen before—no, it's *similar* to one I've seen before, it's from Mom and Dad's wedding day, but a little different. I thumb through my cache, extract a photo, and place it next to Ellen's find.

A match. My photo shows Faye, Mom, Dad, and Tillie. The other shows the same foursome, wearing the same clothes, plus two more people—Julie and a tall man in the foreground I don't recognize.

"Who's that?" I ask.

Julie puts on her glasses again. "That," she announces, "is your grandfather."

It's the only photo I've seen of him in middle age.

"Now," I say, "if only I could find one of Annie."

On a brilliant summer day, the kind that makes me want to cancel my interviews and go for a long walk in the Michigan countryside, I pull into the parking lot of Baker's Restaurant in the small town of Milford. I'm finally meeting Adam Plizga, the trustee for the estate of Irene (Robinson) Doren, Mom's friend and next-door neighbor in the Euclid Street apartment building during the late 1930s and early 1940s.

It has taken several months of serious phone tag to get to this rendezvous. First, I tracked down Irene's son, Barry, hoping that he would let me look through his parents' collection for photos of Mom and—fingers

crossed—Annie. "Sure," Barry had said. "But I don't have them." For reasons that weren't quite clear to me, Irene's photos had remained in Adam's
hands. But Barry had no problem with me looking through them. "Call Adam
and tell him I said it was okay."

I spot Adam as soon as I walk through the restaurant door—he's the guy
with the large box as a lunch companion. But if I had any image of the ac-
countant I had been chasing for months by phone, it wasn't anything like
the man waiting for me. A long gray-streaked ponytail rests neatly on the
back of his polo shirt; the glasses perched precariously on his nose create
the image of an aging professor preparing to show a colleague the fruits of
a year's research.

"Hi," Adam says, pointing to the box. "They're all here."

By the time Adam and I had arranged to meet, I had learned that my mom
and Irene had been more than next-door neighbors, more than two young
women living with their parents in claustrophobic apartments of the kind
that served as home to many Detroit Jews in the mid-1930s. The parents
came from the same part of Europe, immigrated to the United States about
the same time, had two daughters of about the same age. But there the
similarities ended. Jacob Robinson's successful rise in the Wayne County
clerk's office, and later in the local AFL-CIO leadership, contrasted starkly
to Hyman's peddling on the streets and intermittent laboring in the auto
factories.

Whatever had drawn the two families together, it created a bond that
flourished and endured until the end of their lives. And this was no ordinary bond: After Tillie and Hyman moved to another apartment building
several miles north of the one on Euclid, Katie Robinson, by now a widow,
rented the unit right next door.

In my imagination, this long friendship extended to their daughters as
well, and included the sorts of activities typical of two urban Jewish families. If the families spent time together, why wouldn't they go shopping at
Hudson's downtown store, or take a Sunday picnic to Belle Isle, or have
Shabbos dinner together on Friday nights? And perhaps someone had a
camera and took a few snapshots to remind them of these happy times? And
if I were lucky, among the photos would be one that included Annie . . .

That was my writer's fantasy, of course. I could think of a dozen reasons why Irene's collection might not include photos of my mom or Annie. In the 1930s, the camera remained largely the preserve of special occasions: holidays, weddings, birthdays, formal portraits. I had been lucky at Julie's to find the photo of Hyman on Mom's wedding day and the one of Mom as a bridesmaid at Sylvia's wedding. But that wasn't surprising: The camera had a recognized and valued place at marriage ceremonies.

Did Annie ever go to a wedding? I couldn't imagine that she did. That's what other girls did, normal girls, and as the Routine History said, Annie didn't consider herself one of those girls, she didn't live in their world. In that world—a world that called girls like Annie "slow" and "cripple"—how likely was it that someone would raise a camera lens to record her presence?

As my hands reach into the carton on the seat next to Adam, a voice in my head is saying that no matter how long I search, no matter how many of my mom's childhood friends I find, no matter how gracious these strangers are in allowing me to rummage through the very boxes that they would likely grab first if the house caught fire, it was unlikely that anyone had ever taken Annie's photo.

Adam sees the envelope of old black-and-white photos first. He hands them to me. "There may be something in here."

Halfway through the two dozen or so photos, I see my mom. It's another shot from Sylvia's wedding day—this one is just the two of them, bride and bridesmaid posing for the photographer outside an apartment building, their shoulders touching, their veils motionless, their wedding outfits so bright in the sunlight that the camera is having trouble handling the glare. My mom, at five foot six, stands a good two or three inches taller than Sylvia. Over her bridesmaid's dress, she's wearing a full-length white coat; next to the folds and pleats and gathers of Sylvia's gown, the coat's long unbroken run emphasizes the difference in their height.

Adam and I keep looking, and out of another envelope tumbles a shot of Tillie with Irene and Sylvia's parents, the Robinsons. So the families did spend time together! That gives me hope that Annie might turn up yet. It takes us a good two hours to look through every album and envelope, and when we're done, no photo of Annie emerges. "Too bad," Adam says. "I thought for a minute, when we saw that one with the Robinsons and your grandmother, that we might be in luck."

But we find a second one of Mom, again as a bridesmaid, again towering over her companions, two fellow bridesmaids. At the bottom, in Irene's hand, a date: "May 30, 1937." Mom is just nineteen at the time, and she looks a little more gawky, a little more awkward in this shot. I pull out a Ziploc bag containing copies of photos from other family albums that I've tracked down in the past several months, extract two photos of young women in white gowns, and lay them on the table.

"My mom," I tell Adam, "as a bridesmaid at two other weddings."

Love and marriage may go together like a horse and carriage, as Frank Sinatra would croon in the song from the 1950s that Mom liked so much, but in the early 1940s, it was war and marriage that went together. After Congress debated and then enacted the Selective Training and Service Act with a provision exempting married men from a military draft, the country witnessed an unprecedented marriage boom. In New York, so many couples wanted to tie the knot in August 1940 that lines formed as early as 6:30 A.M. outside the marriage license offices in Brooklyn and Staten Island. Draft exemptions weren't the only factor in the surge, but they were the accelerant that produced a record number of marriages in 1941—a record immediately topped in 1942. Manny's wife, Shirley, whose family owned a catering business in Syracuse, remembers working as many as five weddings on some days in 1941. "It was crazy," she told me. "Everyone wanted to get married."

The fever infected Mom's circle of friends, judging by the rising demand for Mom's services as a bridesmaid. What about Mom herself? As far as I know, she had only one brush with a marriage proposal before Dad, from Joe, and I always had the sense that Joe's offer predated 1940. But it didn't matter: Joe wasn't Jewish, so he had no chance. Like many Jewish women of that era, Mom couldn't conceive of marrying outside the faith—not because she was especially religious, but because, as she once said in telling the story, "I couldn't do that to my mother." I grew up thinking that Joe (Mom never used his last name) was a metaphor for disappointment, for dreams unfulfilled, for the road not taken. In retrospect, Joe might have been part of the reason why I didn't identify with observant Jews. If being observant meant that you couldn't marry the man you loved, that didn't seem like such a good deal to me.

I don't know if Mom was as bent on marriage as Julie, but there's no question that Mom was in love with the idea of marriage, head over heels about it. Yes, she had dreams that went beyond finding a man, but none that excluded love, marriage, home, and family. There's certainly evidence that she was worried about her marriage chances: She told Marty Moss that she feared she would never find her soul mate, that marriage would pass her by, and she fretted to Julie that she was too old (at the advanced age of twenty-four, a laughable thought for today's generation, but not for Mom's).

So when she went (where else?) to that wedding in June 1942, that fairy-tale wedding where she looked down the staircase and spotted the stranger with the silver streak in his hair, it's hardly surprising that Cinderella was more than ready to meet her Prince Charming, perhaps even a little anxious, anxious enough to declare impulsively, "That's the man I'm going to marry."

But anxious enough not to tell her Prince about her sister? Julie thought so. I was beginning to think so, too.

The old neighborhood—my old neighborhood, the one where I grew up, in Detroit's northwest corner—looks dowdier than I remember, but I suppose that's inevitable for modest, low-cost bungalows in the depths of middle age. When my parents bought the newly built house on Houghton in 1950, the newly paved street ended at the corner, giving way to the old dirt road on the other side of Fargo, and the newly planted saplings offered no relief from the summer sun that baked the newly planted grass.

Now, as I drive slowly along the well-shaded streets, I'm finding it hard to get my bearings. The field where I played Little League baseball? Still there, but so changed that I stop for a moment, wondering if I've come to the wrong place. Where are the fences? The benches? The huge backstop? No, wait, this must be right, there's St. Eugene, the place where Mom went to the annual Little League banquets, except that it's not St. Eugene any

more, it's a charter school. St. Eugene is long gone, closed in 1989, a casualty of declining enrollment.

But elsewhere in the neighborhood, some things look more or less the
same. There's the driveway (so small!) where my best friend and I chased
our hoop dreams; there's the gravel playground where I once sent a foul ball
through a neighbor's window; there's the house where Mom and Ethel did
battle in Scrabble. Did Mom tell Ethel, her best friend, about Annie? I'd ask
her, but Ethel's gone, too; she died in 2005. Of the bridge game quartet,
only Ann Black is alive, and I haven't been able to find her.

I'm not going to find her here; the old neighborhood yields only
memories.

David Oliwek still lives in the house where he grew up, and with his mom
in Chicago, he has agreed to show me the papers that document her Nazi
deception—her *Arbeitsbuch*, the major's letter of recommendation, Anna
Prokopowitsch's identification card. As we go through the records, I tell
him that this is exactly what I need—names, dates, specifics—to flesh out
the story and confirm crucial details. "It's hard to work off memory alone,"
I say. "Your mom's been really helpful, but she can be vague sometimes."

David hesitates, and then says, "Oh, she knows how to keep a secret."

This doesn't sound like an off-hand remark, or a reference to Anna's
deceiving the Nazis. "What do you mean?" I ask.

And that's when I learn that Anna, like my mother, was guarding a family secret of her own.

Anna wasn't hiding a sister. She was hiding a husband.

Here's how it came out: About ten years ago, as David was trying to chase
down the family genealogy, Anna asked him if he could find someone she
knew from her childhood, a man named Warshawsky. David came up with
information that suggested that Warshawsky had survived the war, and was
living in the Soviet Union. After 1952, the trail went cold. When David reported back to Anna, she urged him to keep looking.

"I said to her, 'Mom, why are you so interested in this guy?'" David
recounts. "And she said, 'Because I was married to him.'"

David doesn't know many details. His mom told him that she and War-shawsky married just before he left Radziwillow to serve in the Russian army, and that she never saw him again.

She was sixteen, maybe seventeen.

"Did your father know?" I ask.

David smiles, aware of certain parallels in the two stories, between his mom and mine. "She says he did know. She just didn't tell her children."

David wasn't sure why his mom was so eager to find out what happened to this man. David's father had died a few years earlier, in 1991, but David didn't think that Anna really wanted to get in touch with Warshawsky after all these years, if he were still alive, which seemed unlikely. She had gone to a few Holocaust survivors' conferences, so maybe that had stirred up some feelings—sorrow or guilt, or a mixture of both. Or maybe she just wanted to . . . know.

Yet more reinterpretation: I would need to go back to Anna, find out what happened, why she left this out of her story about Radziwillow.

Yes, I've become a collector of family secrets.

My cell phone rings as I'm driving home, several weeks later. I can see from the screen that it's Mary Jo. I pull over.

"Manny called," she says. "He talked to your uncle Bill, and he says Bill knew about Annie."

I'm speechless. If Dad's younger brother knew, wouldn't Dad have known? And if Dad knew, then I'm back to square one in figuring out what caused Mom to create the secret.

"What else did he say?" I ask, finally locating my voice.

"He said he didn't want to ask Bill too many questions," she says. "He thought he should leave that to you."

TWENTY

Reinterpretation

Previous page: *Killed where they lived: The mass gravesite near Radziwillow, Ukraine, 2007 (Mary Jo Kirschman photo)*

Mom and I are playing Upwords, her favorite board game, a kind of Scrabble with skyscrapers. It's February 1999, five months after the spill that sent her to a Seattle hospital with a fractured pelvis. Healing took many long and painful weeks, and she's still not her old self. Upwords takes her mind off her problems; I've lost count of how many matches we've had since my son Josh and I arrived yesterday for a weekend visit.

Josh, who's fifteen, bounds over to the table, proposing to play Mom next. He's a novice player, and nervous about whether he can hold his own against the master, so I know that his offer is his way of connecting with her. I'm pleased for both of them; Mom is devoted to her grandchildren, and infinitely patient in teaching them the tricks and strategies that can make the difference between winning and losing. That's why I'm shocked when she looks at him and says, "No. I just want to play with your dad."

I'm irritated at myself for not calling Uncle Bill earlier. He's been on my list, but I hadn't seen any urgency. He seemed like such an unlikely candidate to know about the secret; he was so much younger than Dad, sixteen years younger, and I couldn't imagine why he would know if Uncle Manny didn't. But Bill had lived with my parents for a while during the late 1940s, so maybe like Medji, he had the experience of being there when the unexpected came up. What else could it be?

I reach him in Portland, Oregon, where he and his wife Lil have been living for more than a decade, moving there from California. We don't see each other much, so when Lil answers, I make my apologies for calling out of the blue. Because of Bill's conversation with Manny, he's expecting my call. No reason to tiptoe toward the topic.

"Tell me what you know about Mom's sister," I say.

"It's not something I'd thought about for years," he says. "When Manny mentioned it, I remembered that I knew about it."

"Do you remember how you knew?" I ask.

His memory can't help him on this one. "No."

A lot rides on his answer to my next question. "Did you talk to my dad about it?"

He doesn't hesitate. "I never talked to your dad, or your mom, about it."

That's not the answer I was expecting.

"Do you think you overheard something while you were living with them?" I say. "But if you had, wouldn't you have talked about it with Mom or Dad?"

"It's a mystery," he says.

I have a sudden thought: Maybe the Oliweks are the connection. When Bill and Lil lived in suburban Detroit before heading out to California, they were close friends with Anna and Steve Oliwek, so close—Bill is now telling me—that he and Lil asked the Oliweks if they would be godparents for their oldest son.

"Do you think you might have heard about it from Anna Oliwek?" I tell him briefly about the falling out between Mom and Anna, which happened just about the time that his family and the Oliweks were becoming close.

"That makes sense," he agrees. But making sense doesn't mean it's true, so I ask him to try to remember. I wait, and there's silence. "I'm sorry," he says, finally. "I just don't have any memory of how I heard. I just know I didn't find out from your parents, and that I never talked with either of them about it."

I ask him about my other theory—that the secret was born because Mom feared that if Dad knew, he wouldn't marry her.

"That's very possible," he says. "Your mom was fantastically in love with your father. She wouldn't have allowed anything to interrupt or threaten it."

· · ·

Something did happen in Manila.

Several months after my conversation with Manny, an unexpectedly thick package arrives in the mail from the Veterans Administration. Without much hope of getting anything, I had asked the agency if it had any records on Dad's disability discharge; Army regulations required the VA to get copies of his case, but that didn't mean it had happened.

The VA found the discharge papers, and more—including the handwritten notes of the first doctor to see him on July 2, 1945, the day he fell apart. "Patient states," the notes say, "that ever since joining his present unit last fall he has felt himself working up to a 'breakdown.' States that he has been kicked around from detail to detail and has never been given a regular assignment, and now he felt that he is a detriment to the Army and a liability to himself because he hasn't been able to become a soldier . . . Yesterday morning he went on sick call because of diarrhea. Returned to the dispensary later and there he broke down crying and stated that he might just as well die."

Later examinations, both in the Philippines and in the States, ruled out any threat of suicide. The doctors who saw him seemed perplexed by the cause of his breakdown, but certain that his anxiety was real and that it made him unfit for continued duty. The Darnall board sent him home with a 50 percent disability, allowing him to collect $69 a month in disability pay, subject to periodic psychiatric evaluations of his readjustment to civilian life. Three years later, the VA informed him that "your last examination discloses that your nervous condition has improved to such a degree" that the payments would stop.

Faking it? Was Dad so angry, so miserable that he would feign a nervous breakdown, humiliating himself even more in front of his fellow soldiers? But if he were that calculating, would he then tell an Army doctor that he had not been given a chance to show what he could do? Wouldn't that risk being told, well, we can find a job for you, something that would help the unit?

No, it sounded to me as if Dad had sunk to his emotional bottom, and that his superiors had concluded, this time, that whatever his problems, he was more trouble than he was worth. Send the soldier home to his wife and let her worry about him.

Mom had called Dad her savior, and now, he saw Mom as his: *Without you my life would be empty*, he had written her from Darnall. *I'd be a total loss.*

· · ·

On a single sheet of paper, I draw a line down the middle. At the top left, I write: "Evidence that Dad didn't know." On the right, "Evidence that Dad knew."

Even though I still find it hard to get my head around the notion that Mom kept the secret from Dad, I rapidly fill up the "Dad didn't know" side of the page.

"Photos: None before 1942 except baby pix of Mom and one of Tillie"

"Marriage: As Julie said, telling 'the boyfriend' wouldn't help land him"

"Letters to Dad: No mention of Annie"

"Letters from Dad: No mention of Annie"

"Visits: Explains why Mom didn't take her mother to Eloise. Couldn't go without raising suspicions."

"Mom's argument with Anna Oliwek: Suggests that Mom's real worry was Dad finding out, not the children. Mike too young. I wasn't born"

"Dad's brothers: Manny didn't know (and Manny thought Dad would have said something); Bill knew, but says he never discussed with Dad or Mom"

"Records: Mom saved her parents' marriage certificate (pre-Annie), but no other family documents"

"Dad's psych discharge: If Mom didn't tell him before he went off to the Army, not likely to tell him when he returns. Having not told him, maybe there's never a right time? So she's . . ."

"Stuck with it: Keeping the secret from Dad meant keeping it a secret from us, which meant keeping the secret forever"

On the "Dad knew" side of the ledger:

"Too hard to hide it, Dad would find out anyway: run into an old friend of Mom's, take a phone call from Eloise, something would come in the mail (but if he knew, why no mention in the letters?)"

"They didn't keep secrets from each other (but how do I know that?)"

The pattern seems obvious. The "Dad didn't know" side depended on both evidence and logic, while the other side relied solely on logic; the "Dad didn't know" side accounted for specific facts (no mention of Annie in the letters), while the other side was generic and debatable (it's hard for spouses to keep secrets from each other).

I try to put myself in Mom's place in 1940, after Annie went to Eloise. What would I feel? A stew of emotions, probably: anger at my parents for their poverty and their failure to assimilate better; antagonism toward my sister for making life harder and putting more pressure on me to carry the family forward; fear that I don't have what it takes to deal with my circumstances—and, perhaps, guilt for feeling any hostility at all when I've got two good legs and a sound mind.

At first, after Annie's hospitalization, Mom has no reason to keep her a secret—everyone in her world knew all about Annie, so what would be the point of pretending she doesn't exist? Then, at that wedding in June 1942, Mom meets a reason, and he's standing below her on the staircase, Prince Charming to her rescue. According to Marty and Julie, she's already afraid that marriage has passed her by; she's been a bridesmaid four times at least, but never a bride. She declares her intention to marry this Prince, and as Uncle Bill says, she's so in love (or so infatuated with the idea of love), that she won't let anything get in the way.

So she doesn't tell "the boyfriend," as Julie put it. That requires enlisting her parents in her cause, and while Tillie has qualms about acting as if she has only one daughter, she also has to think about her older daughter's happiness, and so she goes along, at least when Dad's around. Circumstances conspired to make the ruse possible: Annie's prolonged stay at Eloise and a move to a new apartment allow the family to put Annie's physical presence into the past, reducing the chance that Dad might see something that can't be explained away.

Harder, though, to remove Mom's friends from her life or make a blanket request for their silence. But as Julie had said, she didn't need Mom to tell her to keep quiet.

We will never know to a moral certainty why Mom created the secret. I have circumstantial evidence and a mix of firsthand and hearsay testimony from Anna, Julie, Millie, Marty, and others, but the weight of the evidence—

the accumulated facts—makes me feel confident that my reinterpretation comes as close to the truth as memory and history allow.

One final mystery: If Mom chose to keep the secret from Dad in 1942, if she never found the right time or place to tell him, why didn't she reveal it to us after Dad's death in 1980? If she were willing to tell Hazan a doctored version of the truth in 1995, why not tell us that version as well? I was pretty certain of the answer: She had judged herself so harshly that she couldn't imagine that we wouldn't do the same. The longer she kept the secret, the larger it loomed, until it grew to such proportions in her mind that it overwhelmed and paralyzed her.

Support for this thinking comes unexpectedly, when I call the daughter of Ethel Edelman, Mom's old bridge partner. I haven't talked to Natalie Edelman since high school; she was a couple of years behind me, and more my brother Jeff's friend than mine, so I can only imagine her reaction when she hears my message on her cell phone.

We connect a few days later. As usual, I feel a tinge of anticipation as I begin my now-familiar list of questions, even though I'm certain that this particular call will be brief. It's unlikely that Mom had said anything to Ethel, but even if she had, it's even less likely that Ethel would have repeated it to her daughter. Why would she?

As I suspected, Natalie has no idea that my mom had a sister, disabled or otherwise. I'm not surprised; after all, if Natalie had called me after thirty years without contact, I couldn't have said whether her mom had any brothers or sisters, and yet I had spent many an afternoon with Ethel at the bridge table, where gossiping about family life was as much a part of the game as the pad for keeping score.

Figuring that I may as well take advantage of Natalie's training as a therapist and hospital social worker, I ask her a few questions about how today's world compares to Annie's. Natalie's professional side clicks in, and now she's interviewing me—when, where, how long was Annie institutionalized? As I'm sketching the outlines of what I know, Natalie interrupts.

"Was she mentally retarded?" she asks.

I hadn't yet said anything about Annie's difficult birth or her IQ scores or Bohn's recommendation that she belonged at Lapeer. I reflexively begin to answer, thinking that it's part of the checklist of questions that a trained social worker would run through, but then I stop, curious about why she had veered in that direction so suddenly.

"Why did you ask that?" I say.

Her answer takes my breath away. "Because I do recall something now, vaguely."

For the next few minutes, she speaks in short bursts, as she retrieves memories long dormant. "They had been playing Scrabble . . . I was in high school . . . my mom let slip . . ." I keep quiet, letting her grapple with the hazy, half-remembered images.

"I really don't remember too much, and I don't want to push it too far," Natalie warns me, unaware how that reassures me. "I know your mom told my mom something. It was furtive, as if my mom knew she shouldn't be telling me."

Natalie's story, as best as she could piece it together: When she was about seventeen, our moms were Scrabbling and chain-smoking; Natalie was in her room. "Afterward, my mom was very upset," she says. "She came in, almost like she had to talk with someone, and there I was."

"What did she say?" I ask. I'm holding my pen so tightly that the knuckle on my middle finger hurts.

"That they had put your mom's sister away," Natalie says. "My mom was very troubled about it, very pained. She was shaking her head." Ethel couldn't believe that Mom had been keeping this secret from her. But that wasn't all; Ethel had a mentally retarded niece who had been institutionalized, and Ethel had been crushed when it happened. She had told Mom all about it. But Mom, her closest friend, had never said a word about having a sister in the same straits.

That might have upset Ethel just as much as Mom's revelation, Natalie suggests. "They had been constant companions for years," Natalie reminds me. "Sometimes, I thought they were closer to each other than to their husbands."

We try to figure out when this all happened. "It must have been the fall of my senior year . . . The school year had just started," Natalie says. "So that would have been September or October of 1972. When did you say Annie died?"

"August 1972," I tell her.

This is more interpretation than reinterpretation, but here goes: After Annie died, Mom felt free, finally, to let go, tentatively, warily, of her secret. She tested the waters, telling her best friend, and what happened? It backfired. Ethel was sympathetic, but she also felt confused, perhaps even slighted that Beth hadn't confided in her years before. Their relationship survived—at least until Ethel and her husband migrated to Florida in the early 1980s—but as time passed, they talked less and less. I had always thought their relationship had suffered from the distance, but here's another reinterpretation: The distance mattered less than that conversation in 1972.

And if unburdening yourself to your best friend doesn't work out too well, why risk telling your children? So the secret went back underground, until that day in 1995 when Mom mentioned it to Dr. Hazan, for reasons known only to her. Even then, it might have remained buried—if not for a puzzled social worker's phone call and a routine letter from a cemetery asking about the planting of flowers for the spring.

"Do you think your mom ever told your dad?" I ask Natalie, without mentioning the ironic parallel to my question. Her father, Jack, is still alive at ninety, living in Florida.

"I don't know," she says. "His memory's not great, but I'll ask him."

She called back the next day. Her dad had no inkling about Annie, but he did have a number for Ann Black, who had recently moved back to the Detroit area after thirty years in the Maryland suburbs of Washington. She and Mom had lost touch years ago, and I was never sure why. Ann would be my next call.

She's shorter than the woman I remember from the bridge games, but Ann Black's nearly white hair frames the same face that I found both appealing and intimidating all those years ago. Her pantsuit of velvety purple suggests that Ann has maintained her sense of style, as does the handcrafted jewelry on her fingers and around her neck.

She gives me a hug that's more than polite. "How many years has it been?" she asks. "Thirty? More?"

The dining room in the seniors' community where she lives, in suburban Detroit, hums with Valentine's Day activity, as staff members bring in a dozen heart-shaped balloons for an evening celebration. I joke with Ann about Mom's fondness for Valentine's and other "greeting-card" holidays: Mother's Day, Grandparents' Day, and—this was the topper—Sweetest Day, which I learned when I got older was the invention of some candy-maker from Cleveland and unknown to many in other parts of the country. "Your mom certainly was a romantic," Ann says.

I had decided to ask first about Tillie and Hyman, whether Ann had ever met them, and then follow up with an Annie question. As soon as I mention my grandparents, though, Ann shows me that directness remains her hallmark. "There was a big secret in your family," she says. "Your mom had a mentally retarded sister."

No one, not even Anna Oliwek, has described it quite so starkly. "That's not what I was expecting you to say," I say, placing my recorder on the table. "Keep going."

Ann's story starts with an innocuous conversation between new neighbors, playing Jewish geography in one of the many suburban subdivisions that attracted families moving out of Detroit's old neighborhoods in the late 1950s and early 1960s. Marilyn and Sid Frumkin settled into The Ravines just before New Year's in 1964, and Marilyn discovered that she had a few things in common with the woman in the house directly behind hers. One day, Marilyn mentioned her weekly bridge game, and so Mom's name came up.

As Ann tells it, the neighbor said, "I know Beth Luxenberg." They hadn't seen each other in years, but when they were teenagers, their families had adjoining apartments in the old neighborhood around Fourteenth Street. "She told Marilyn about Beth's retarded sister," Ann says. "That's how we knew."

She doesn't remember the woman's name. "It was a family that owned an alarm company."

"You mean Guardian Alarm?" I say. "Sylvia Pierce?"

"That's the one," Ann replies.

Ann's account proved again that the biggest threat to Mom's secret came from the old neighborhood, from the people who knew her before Annie went to Eloise, before Annie became a secret. Nathan Shlien told Anna Oliwek about Annie; Sylvia Pierce told Marilyn; Julie Reisner knew, but she didn't tell anyone; Fran came along after the secret was born, and never found out at all.

What, exactly, did Sylvia tell Marilyn? Ann only knows what Marilyn told her, and even that's fuzzy at this point. When I ask her for details, she says she never knew the sister's name, or that she had gone to Eloise, or that she had a psychiatric illness.

"What did Marilyn tell you about the sister?" I ask.

"She said Beth had a retarded sister who was in a special home and nobody ever mentioned her."

"Did you ever ask my mom about her?"

"Your mother never brought it up, and we certainly wouldn't bring it up," she says, her words tinged with what sounds like irritation or anger. This surprises me—and suggests that Ann's silence flowed from a different source than Medji's and Julie's.

"Did you think about bringing it up?" I say. "Why didn't you?"

"Because it was her job to bring it up if she wanted to. It was her secret." Well, that's more or less what Medji and Julie had said—respect for Mom's wishes. So why the irritation? I'm about to find out.

"Beth knew I had a handicapped brother, Marvin, who's deaf," Ann says. "I also had a cousin who was mentally retarded. She could have told me about her sister. It wouldn't have been a shock to me." She doesn't take her eyes off mine. She's speaking directly, forthrightly, just as she always had. "We never hid Marvin. Wherever we were, he was always my brother. In fact, I went into teaching the deaf because of him. He inspired me to do that. Your mom knew all that, and yet she never mentioned her sister."

I think, *No wonder she didn't tell you. She chose an entirely different path, and she was probably afraid of you, afraid that you would judge her, and judge her harshly.*

"Did Ethel know?" I ask. If she did, that would undermine Natalie's account.

Ann shakes her head. "I don't really remember, but I don't think so. Marilyn told me, because I was her sister-in-law, but I think we decided to keep it to ourselves."

That makes sense, and also preserves Natalie's story. I think about those bridge games, and how strange and strained they must have been at times: Ann and Marilyn, at the bridge table, aware of Mom's secret and yet compelled—by custom, by culture, by circumstance—from saying anything to the other two. Then later, Ethel learns about it, too, but she says nothing to Ann and Marilyn.

Four women, all friends, and all carrying some form of secrecy's burden.

"Do you know her name?" Ann suddenly asks me.

"Yes," I say. "It was Annie."

Ann's eyes show her surprise. "We never knew her name," she says.

That sounds entirely plausible. Memory can play its tricks, but I doubt that Ann would forget that this hidden sister had a first name so close to her own.

"So when you moved away," I say, "there was a reason other than distance that you and Mom fell out of touch. You weren't all that happy with her, although she didn't know that."

Ann's lips tighten slightly as she nods. She brings up Mom's obit. "Someone sent it to me, and when I saw that it called her 'an only child,' it upset me."

The obit. The one I sent to the *Free Press*.

"Why?" I ask, although I had a pretty good idea.

"I don't think handicapped people should be denied recognition. I just felt bad that she was hidden."

I protest. "The obit wasn't Mom's fault. She wasn't around to tell us what to write." I explain the odd situation of having heard that Mom had a sister, but knowing nothing else at that moment—not her name or whether she had lived beyond childhood.

Ann acknowledges the predicament, but says that's partly her point: If Mom hadn't kept the secret all those years, if she hadn't maintained the "only child" pretense, the obit could have given Annie a place in Mom's world.

So many ifs.

. . .

I didn't come to Radziwillow looking for reinterpretation, but it's hard for me to miss. The words are set in granite and tile on polished red stone, and we see it as soon as the three of us—Mary Jo and I and Alexander Dunai, our Ukrainian interpreter and guide—walk onto the massacre site, the same killing field where Anna Oliwek lost her family, the same killing field where Bella Kron ran for her life. Up the hill stands the old Soviet memorial, a concrete obelisk with a bouquet of paper flowers resting on top. We climb the eighteen steps to read the chiseled inscription, which Alex translates from the Russian: "On this place in 1942 there was killed about three thousand peaceful citizens." No mention of how their shared ethnicity had targeted them for death.

Alex had already alerted us to the Soviet habit of describing the Nazi massacres in ideological terms—an assault on the state and its comrades, not on Jews. "The Soviet geniuses managed to write histories of the war without mentioning the Holocaust," he told us, "and I had to read them in school."

The second memorial provides the truth. Erected sometime after the fall of the Soviet Union in 1991, the low circular wall of gleaming white stone offers these words in Ukrainian and in Hebrew, inset in a single contoured line that follows the curve of the memorial: "On this place there are buried 4,000 Jews, inhabitants of Radzivilov killed in 1942 by the Nazis and their helpers during the second World War." A lone Jewish star stands at the wall's central point, reclaimed from the Nazi use of it as a symbol of discrimination and oppression; a burned-out Yahrzeit candle, traditionally lit on the anniversary of a death of a loved one, rests in the tall grass nearby.

I ask Alex about the discrepancy in the number of dead, and tell him that both figures differ from those in the encyclopedias and histories. "The Soviets often manipulated numbers to suit their political agenda, sometimes exaggerating them, sometimes diminishing them," he says. "Whatever the number, it's still unimaginable."

Between the two memorials, an uneven, grassy slope with dozens of slender tree stumps and mounds marks the final resting place of that unimaginable number. There are no names here, no identities. Like Annie's grave, anonymity defines this burial ground. Mary Jo and I debate whether the tree stumps are meant to evoke a field of tombstones, but Alex doesn't think so—the rest of the site doesn't suggest that sort of metaphorical design. No matter, I think; intended or not, the effect is the same.

It had taken us a good hour to find the spot; tall trees make it invisible to the surrounding roads and farms. No signs point the way, and there's nothing at the opening to indicate what lies beyond. Every person we stopped knew exactly what Alex was talking about when he asked for directions to the Jewish memorial, but describing the precise route involved elaborate sessions of waving arms and pointing fingers and torrents of words. As we drove down one dirt road after another, without success, Alex muttered in English, "go here, go there, you'll see it. But I bet they've never seen it."

Alex possesses a hearty laugh, which he lets loose frequently, and a roly-poly physique to match. He has the temperament of a journalist and the practiced eye of a historian, and so hiring him has yielded benefits far beyond his interpreting skills. His years of working with American writers has taken him deep into his country's past, and as we drive the seventy-five miles between Lviv (his home) and Radziwillow on consecutive days, Mary Jo and I exploit our two hours of traveling time on country roads to get ourselves a wide-ranging history lesson.

We spend most of the first afternoon randomly stopping people who look older than seventy, hunting for anyone who lived in Radziwillow before the massacres wiped out the town's Jews or sent them fleeing. "Do you know the family name Schlein?" Alex asks. "How about Korn?" No one does, not even women the same age as Anna Oliwek—women who in their girlhood might have seen Anna on the streets or in the shops. But it's not long before we meet two women whose families protected Jews, including Ludmila Korson, who proudly shows us the Certificate of the Righteous from Yad Vashem, the Holocaust remembrance organization in Israel, documenting that during a two-year period, her grandparents hid at least seven Jewish families in a brick bunker that her grandfather constructed as a shelter.

"Did you know about the mass killings?" I ask Vira Mykhaylivna Pylypchuk after she invites us inside for tea and to hear her family's story. She's eighty-two, and her parents allowed fifteen Jews to conceal themselves in two barns on their property.

"Of course we did," Vira says in Ukrainian, which Alex translates. "We watched them take the Jews by truck. They were crying. We were crying." She's crying now, crying so hard that her words become lost in her sobs.

After reading the accounts of the Volhynian Holocaust, I'm glad to leave Radziwillow having met the descendants of people who resisted the pull of hatred, collaboration, and silent acceptance. That's why certificates and memorials matter; when this generation is gone, how else will the people of Radziwillow remember what happened to its Jewish community after more than three centuries as a vital part of the town's life?

Late in the afternoon, we get directions to one of the town's abandoned flour mills, a local landmark that Anna Oliwek had mentioned. As Mary Jo and I stand outside the wooden building, we notice a lone figure, a young girl no more than ten years old, in shorts and T-shirt, ably and quickly making her way down the street on a pair of purple crutches. She has only one leg. We can't help staring at her, as if she were Annie's ghost.

Back in Alex's car, Mary Jo and I tell him about the young girl. "If Annie had been here in 1919, how would she have been regarded?" I ask Alex. "What sort of attitudes do you think my grandparents brought with them to America?"

Alex says, with some confidence, that a disabled or mentally impaired child in that era would be considered a shame on the family, whether Jewish or non-Jewish. "The family would have taken care of the child, either out of obligation or because there would be no other choice, but if the disability was severe, the family would probably keep the person in the house, away from prying eyes."

If the child were female and the parents had other daughters, Alex says, it would have marked them as marriage risks: Are they okay? Is there something wrong with the family that will show up in future generations?

His words remind me of my grandmother's: *The sins of the parents are paid for through the children.*

I'm showing photos of present-day Radziwillow to Anna Oliwek, in Chicago, a month after our Ukraine visit. Nothing looks the same as when she lived there; the war left so much destruction and damage that the Soviets tore down much of the city center, erecting a massive concrete square that lost its purpose once May Day celebrations went the way of the communist regime.

As we talk about the dramatic changes that the war brought to her birthplace, it seems like an appropriate moment to ask about the missing piece of her wartime narrative. "I understand you were married before the Nazis invaded," I ask.

She smiles, enigmatically, and says, "How did you know that?"

"David told me," I say.

She looks away, retrieving, reflecting, revisiting. "It wasn't much of a marriage," she says. "Here's the story." Warshawsky was twenty and she was sixteen. They knew each other from Hebrew school, and because he worked in a hardware store where Anna sometimes went to pick up packages for a relative. They spent a lot of time together—"teenage love," Anna calls it—but had never discussed marriage. "It was his mother's idea. He got a letter saying he had to go into the Russian army, that he had to leave soon. His mother said, 'You're in love, you should get married, who knows what's going to happen.' She was afraid I would meet someone else while he was away, but if we got married, she told me, then I would be waiting for him when he got home."

They went to city hall. "It took half an hour," Anna says. "I was so young, so stupid. I didn't know what I was doing." Later that afternoon, he boarded a train to join the Red Army.

After the war, from Germany, she tried to find him, to learn his fate. She wrote to people back in Radziwillow, and she accumulated bits and pieces of hearsay and information. "I heard he was dead, then I heard, no, he was wounded, shot in the legs. He had survived, but he had a new wife, a Russian girl. I thought, 'What's the use of pursuing him? He probably assumes I died along with all the other Jews in Radziwillow.' I let it go. I decided to let him live his life, and to move on with mine."

I understand, I tell her. "Why didn't you tell your children? Why keep it secret?"

"It didn't seem important," she says. "All we had was a piece of paper; we had never lived together for one minute. That wasn't a marriage."

"One more question," I say. "Why did you want David to find him after your husband's death?"

"I don't know," she says. "Curiosity, mostly. I wanted to know what happened to him, whether he was still alive."

I understood that, too. Her husband had died, and Anna was reviewing her life, reliving it and the choices she made. This was her version of reinterpretation.

. . .

Mom's last letter, the one she left for us to open after her death, sits on my desk. These are the words that she wanted us to read as we remembered her, and these are the words I'm re-reading now as I reinterpret her recontoured life. *Please do not mourn,* she wrote on May 16, 1996, about a year after her stay in the Botsford psych ward. *You all have given me much love and pleasure . . . Fulfill my final wish, stay close and be good to each other.*

I read her final words with a deeper knowledge and conviction now. Stay close, she was saying, because I didn't have that relationship with my sister. Be good to each other, because I couldn't be good to my sister. Please do not mourn, as I mourned when my family couldn't cope with my sister's disabilities and forces beyond her control.

Or does this go too far? Am I imposing emotions on Mom that she did not feel? I can't know, of course, but this much I do know:

Annie, who arrived in the world with several strikes against her, desired a normal life and was doomed never to have one. Physically deformed, mentally deficient, she met the fate of thousands of people like her, born too soon to know whether the advances in medicine and psychiatry would have given her a better shot at the freedom she so desperately sought. Instead, her world grew smaller, measured by a bed in a psychiatric ward and records that no longer exist.

Mom, desperate to free herself from the depressing world inhabited by her impoverished parents and mentally ill sister, created a secret that turned into a trap. Unlike Annie, she enjoyed the freedom to marry, to raise a family, to achieve a level of comfort and happiness beyond her sister's most imaginative dreams. But like Annie, she also was a prisoner, a captive of her pretense, from which she never escaped and which she endured alone. Loneliness wasn't just her fate; it was her punishment.

I'm more fortunate. My search has allowed me to achieve a freedom of my own; free to see my mother as she was, free to embrace her flaws and accept her choices, free to put aside, once and for all, the pain of not being able to help her, to hold her hand and tell her, convincingly, that, yes, I'm here, I'll always be here, I'm not leaving, I love you, and no, nothing you say, nothing you tell me will make me go away.

Previous page: *Eloise cemetery, 2006 (Martine MacDonald photo)*

T he Eloise Cemetery looks nothing like I thought it would. That's
because it's not a cemetery at all.

I had seen references to that name, always with a capital E and
capital C, so I was expecting gravesites, shade trees, pathways, perhaps
flowers here and there. On my first visit to the hospital, I had passed a large
cemetery on Michigan Avenue, just west of the old main entrance, and I had
thought, there it is, the Eloise Cemetery, the place where the hospital had
buried those patients who died alone, with either no family left or no family willing to bury them elsewhere.

I had thought wrong. That's not the Eloise cemetery. In fact, it's impossible to see the Eloise burial ground from Michigan Avenue, or from a
passing car, or from the site of the main entrance, or from anywhere on
the several hundred acres north of Michigan Avenue where more than ten
thousand people once lived and worked. To see the potter's field that everyone calls the Eloise Cemetery, someone needs to tell you how to get
there and, once you're there, what to look for. Otherwise, you could walk
right over the graves—all 7,144 of them, the first from 1910, the last from
1948—and never know it.

On a wintry day, Martine MacDonald shows me the way. We had kept in
touch after I heard her "Resurrected Voices" presentation at the Friends of
Eloise meeting, and now I wanted to take advantage of the knowledge she's

accumulated in overseeing the artistic project on those buried in the hidden field.

She's the perfect companion for such an adventure, her boundless energy and 150-watt smile warming the inside of her Subaru Outback as we navigate the traffic on this frosty morning. Across from Eloise, we turn off Michigan Avenue onto Henry Ruff Road, heading into history—past the abandoned underground root cellars that once stored up to five thousand bushels of fruits and vegetables from the Eloise farm; past the land where the Eloise cannery once processed sixty-five tons of produce a month; past the place where the Eloise slaughterhouse provided Eloise beef and ham to Eloise's kitchens; past the sites of the greenhouses, the tobacco drying shed, and the last of Eloise's four piggeries.

Martine is forty-seven, and her personal palette includes blue eyes and a head of striking white hair that matches the color of the thin blanket of snow underfoot. Her own artistic contribution for the Resurrected Voices project resonates with her childhood journey. Inspired by the story of two indigent six-year-old girls who died of unknown ailments in the Eloise infirmary sometime in 1920, Martine crafted doll-sized clothes out of death certificates, marrying the innocence of paper dolls with the heartbreak of the girls' early deaths. Martine has first-hand knowledge of abandoned children and institutions: She spent much of her first eleven years in and out of foster homes before adoption gave her a new set of parents and a stable, loving place to grow up.

We park near a chain-link fence, open a gate, and walk along a snowy path that Martine says is a dirt lane in summer. After thirty yards or so, we turn left toward a stand of trees. A picnic table appears in the distance, as if ready to host some ghostly gathering. Martine laughs. "There's a community garden there, and that's a table for the gardeners," she says. "Last summer, when I was on my way to the cemetery, the gardeners asked where I was going. I told them, and they said, 'There's a cemetery there? Where?'"

It's hard to fault the gardeners for their ignorance. No sign marks the spot, either on the chain-link fence or on the gate, and just like the Radziwillow mass gravesite, there's nothing at the narrow entrance to the clearing that says what lies beyond. To my unknowing eyes, it looks like a field, and then I realize—it *is* a field, but unlike the burial ground in Radziwillow, there's no plaque or memorial or stone obelisk, nothing to mark this as final resting place for Eloise's abandoned and indigent.

Martine stoops and points to a cement marker, embedded in the ground, with a number, "300," barely visible in the soil and snow. Just beyond, I spot a second one, 299, and then a third, 804. Only two of the 7,441 graves, Martine tells me, have markers with names on them, and those were placed long after the burials; the numbered blocks, fabricated in one of the Eloise shops, identify the rest of the deceased.

No master list of numbers and corresponding names has ever been found; Jo Johnson, for one, doesn't believe such a list exists. But the earliest death certificates lead her to believe that one was intended. On those, someone took the time to record the burial marker number. But after the first five hundred or so, the notations stopped. Jo and her husband Ernie tried to reconstruct a complete list, figuring that if they put the deaths into chronological order, they could match the numbers to the names on the death certificates.

A logical idea, but it turned out that chronology didn't dictate the order of burials, especially in the winter months. After the ground froze, Martine says, the Eloise grave-diggers would put the coffins into the icehouse to await a break in the weather or the spring thaw. When the grave-diggers went back to work, they understandably put efficiency at the top of their list of concerns, and for all anyone knows, never thought about chronology at all. So there's no way, with any degree of certainty, to match the names, the dates, and the numbers.

Not that many people are asking. After all, these Eloise patients are buried here because no one came forward to claim them at the time of their deaths. Martine and I tromp from one end of the clearing to the other, looking for more numbers in the ground, but we see only deer tracks. I remember a photograph I had seen, with the caption "Eloise Cemetery, 1948," that shows two rows of freshly dug graves, perhaps thirty graves in all, with a neat line of markers jutting one to two feet above ground. But over the years, the cement blocks sank in the sandy soil, so most have disappeared below the surface, leaving only a few visible to unprepared visitors who come with neither trowel nor shovel.

Martine reminisces about her last visit the previous summer. She went with her son, a college student, and he was so taken by what he saw that he later wrote a poem for the Resurrected Voices project. "It was a stunning day, and the field was alive with goldfinches, wildflowers, and blackberries," she says. "I stood there and thought to myself, if you have to be buried somewhere, it's not a bad place to spend eternity."

We stand there silently for a few moments, the wind blowing steadily against us. It's been nearly sixty years since the last burial there. It's quiet, with not a soul in sight; the sixteen-degree temperature and colder wind have permeated our coats, and I suggest that a warm car would feel good.

As we walk back, I think about the growing movement to reclaim the forgotten Jewish cemeteries in Eastern Europe, to treat them as sacred ground and honor the dead buried there, even if there are no Jews living nearby and no family members to tend the graves. Shouldn't the dead at Eloise be treated the same way? Shouldn't the Eloise cemetery have a fence around it and a sign announcing what's here?

"I thought so, at first," Martine says. "I thought it was a crime that it wasn't marked." But we both agree that honoring the Eloise dead isn't as simple as it seems. Abandoned mental hospitals have a history of attracting the curious, and worse. Unless Wayne County is willing to spend money for security or a caretaker, putting a sign on the road or the outside gate might lead to more harm than honor. I suggest that the trees provide a natural shield, and that the county or the state could erect a memorial on the site, or a historical marker, without much fear of causing problems. The irony occurs to both of us: We've fallen into a line of thinking that would keep the cemetery hidden.

We turn around to take a last, lingering look. "So much about these people's lives is hidden, and that history should be told," Martine says. "But maybe the cemetery itself should stay the way it is. It's peaceful, and those buried here didn't have much of that."

I think about Annie and her grave in Section 19, Row J at Hebrew Memorial Park. She, too, is identified by number rather than name, but at least we know for certain that number 19 is her site, her grave, her final resting place. The Eloise dead don't have that. Whatever else Mom did, at least she saved Annie from the fate of permanent obscurity in a cemetery that, like the ghostly Brigadoon, exists more in memory than in name.

. . .

Not wanting to leave any stone unturned, I arrive at the *Detroit Jewish News* offices in suburban Detroit to confirm the obvious: that there was no death notice for Annie in August 1972. I load the microfilm into the reader and scroll through the weekly paper's pages to the issue for August 11.

Yet there she is.

"Annie Cohen, 3378 Richton, died Aug. 7. Survived by one sister."

I'm shocked. Here, in black and white, is the secret. Why would Mom . . .

But wait. No, the secret is intact. Mom's name isn't mentioned, and neither is Annie's true residence. Instead, the notice implies that Annie Cohen, whoever she is, lived out her days on Richton, an address she never knew, on a street she never visited, in an apartment where she never slept or ate or brushed her teeth, at a place she never called home. (Nor did my grandparents, who lived at 3710 Richton, not 3378.)

I look at the other death notices. One catches my eye: "Sanford Bruss, of 30536 Southfield . . . leaves his parents, Mr. and Mrs. Kalman Bruss; a brother, Joel; a sister, Janice; and his grandmother, Mrs. Anna Kass."

A sister, Janice.

Mom must have asked Hebrew Memorial to omit her name. It's the only explanation for why it doesn't follow the form of the others.

Their roles had reversed, preserving the secret: Annie, identified, and Mom, anonymous.

One final stone to turn, this one real rather than metaphoric:

On a blustery April day in 2008, with the grass spongy from the retreat of a recent snow and the buds just beginning to show on the otherwise bare trees, Mary Jo and I approach Annie's grave at Hebrew Memorial Park. The cemetery put the headstone in place a few months ago, and now we have come together to see the memorial for ourselves. Snow flurries had greeted us as we climbed into the car for the long ride over, but now the sun has elbowed its way through the gray skies, the promise of spring replacing the dying wisps of winter.

When I first proposed the idea of a headstone to my siblings, we discussed what words to chisel into the stone. It was important, we all agreed, that the words be true, that they didn't suggest emotions that weren't felt or expressed during Annie's lifetime. Mary Jo and I gaze now at the words we chose:

ANNIE COHEN
APRIL 27, 1919–AUGUST 7, 1972
DAUGHTER, SISTER, AUNT

Simple words that restore in death—for as long as this headstone lasts, anyway—the identities that Annie lost in life.

And the secret? It is now free, free to fade into the past, and into memory.

PRIMARY FIGURES

Beth (maiden name Cohen) Luxenberg, daughter of Hyman and Tillie Cohen
    (born 1917 in Detroit, died 1999)
Annie Cohen, hidden younger sister of Beth (born 1919 in Detroit, died 1972)
Steve Luxenberg, son of Beth and Jack Luxenberg; narrator of the story (born
    1952)

RELATIVES

**The Schlein and Cohen families (Detroit and Radziwillow, Russia/
Ukraine)**
Hyman Cohen (Chaim Korn), Beth and Annie's father, junk peddler and im-
    migrant from Radziwillow (arrived in the United States 1907, died 1964)
Tillie (Schlein) Cohen, Beth and Annie's mother, immigrant from Radziwillow
    (arrived in the United States about 1914, died 1966)
Anna (Schlajn/Schlein) Oliwek, Beth's cousin; a Holocaust survivor from
    Radziwillow who met the Cohen family after 1949, the year of Anna's arrival
    in the United States (born 1923)
Nathan Shlien, Anna's uncle and a boarder with the Cohens in 1930, before
    Annie became a secret (born 1894, deceased)
Bella and David Oliwek, Anna's daughter and son, who as children accompanied
    their mother on a few trips to Eloise; Dori Oliwek, their younger sister

The Luxenberg family (Detroit; Syracuse, New York; and Lomza province, Russia/Poland)

Julius Luxenberg, known as Jack, Beth's husband, son of Harry and Ida Luxenberg (born in Lomza 1913, arrived in the United States 1920, died 1980)

Harry Luxenberg, Jack's father, a baker and immigrant from Lomza (arrived 1913, deceased)

Ida Luxenberg, Jack's mother, immigrant from Lomza (arrived 1920, deceased)

Manny Luxenberg, Jack's younger brother (born 1921)

Rose (Luxenberg) Boskin, Jack's sister (born 1925)

Bill Luxenberg, Jack's youngest brother (born 1929)

Evie (Luxenberg) Miller, Steve's eldest sister, Jack's daughter from a first marriage (born 1937)

Marsha (Luxenberg) Rosenberg, known as Sash or Sashie, Steve's older sister and Jack's daughter from a first marriage (born 1940)

Michael Luxenberg, son of Beth and Jack, Steve's older brother (born 1945)

Jeffery Luxenberg, son of Beth and Jack, Steve's younger brother (born 1956)

OTHER SIGNIFICANT OR RECURRING FIGURES

At Botsford Hospital (general hospital in Farmington, Michigan, where Beth was treated)
Time frame: 1995–1999

Toby Hazan, Beth's psychiatrist

Mary Bernek, psychiatric social worker

Rozanne Sedler, social worker for Jewish Family Service (not associated with Botsford)

At Harper Hospital (general hospital where Annie went for medical care)
Time frame: 1937–1940

Frederick Kidner, noted orthopedic surgeon who decided to amputate Annie's leg

Stephen Bohn, neurologist who suggested that Annie's family institutionalize her

Jean Powell, social worker who first dealt with the Cohen family in the mid-1930s

At Wayne County Probate Court
Time frame: 1940

Patrick O'Brien, Wayne County Probate Court judge who approved Annie's
    commitment to Eloise in April 1940

Benjamin W. Clark, Howard Peirce, and Peter E. Bolewicki, physicians assigned
    by O'Brien to examine Annie and offer an opinion on her sanity

At Eloise Hospital (county institution where Annie lived, Wayne County, Michigan)
Time frame: 1940–present

Mona Evans, social worker and author of a lengthy report on Annie ("Routine
    History") after her admission to Eloise in 1940

Thomas K. Gruber, superintendent, 1929–1948

Edward Missavage, staff psychiatrist for nearly thirty years and former direc-
    tor, male psychiatric division

Jo Johnson, coordinator, Friends of Eloise; chairman, Westland Historical
    Commission

Martine MacDonald, artist and co-originator of "Resurrected Voices: The Elo-
    ise Cemetery Project"

Beth's friends and neighbors
Time frame: 1930s–1942

Faye (Levin) Emmer, a close friend who appears in many of Beth's photos from
    the 1940s (deceased)

Sylvia (Robinson) Pierce and Irene (Robinson) Doren, sisters who lived next
    door to the Cohen family on Euclid (both deceased)

Millie (Moss) Brodie, a cousin of Sylvia and Irene, visitor to Beth's neigh-
    borhood

Martin Moss, known as Marty; Millie's brother and Beth's friend

Julie Reisner (Norton), friend of Beth, Sylvia, Irene, and Faye

Time frame: 1942–1950

Fran (Rumpa) Donofsky, Beth's close friend during World War II who later
    married Jack Luxenberg's cousin, Hy Donofsky

Medji Grobeson, sister of Jack's first wife, Esther; babysitter used by Beth in
    the mid- to late 1940s

Time frame: 1950–1999

Ethel Edelman, member of Beth's bridge group and Beth's closest friend from
   her days on Houghton and Fargo in Detroit (deceased)

Ann Black, bridge game partner

Marilyn Frumkin, bridge game partner and wife of Sid Frumkin, Beth's long-
   time boss (both deceased)

Fred Garfinkel, Beth's coworker and boss

Natalie Edelman, Ethel's daughter

Nonfiction writers face many choices in assembling their accumulated facts and interviews into a cohesive narrative. Here are mine: I have chosen not to reconstruct long-ago events as if I were there; any quotes or dialogue come from documents or from interviews with people who were there. I have used italics to set off those parts of the book that reflect my memories, and I have used quotation rarely and then only when I have some specific recollection of the words that might have been said.

Similarly, I have generally adhered to chronology in describing my effort to discover my mother's reasons for keeping her secret, so that the detective story unfolds as it happened. But reporting a sprawling story like this one cannot be accomplished in a neat, sequential order. I pursued multiple lines of inquiries simultaneously, and they bore fruit in a haphazard fashion, so I occasionally break from the chronology to provide clarifying information that I learned later in the reporting process, but which I could have gained at any time (for example, facts about prosthetic legs). At no time do I alter the time line of my understanding about the secret.

A few words about language and labels: Descriptions of mental illness have changed frequently and dramatically in the past hundred years, almost always for the better. To show that evolution and for the sake of historical accuracy, I have chosen to stick with the language of the time. An example: Michigan and other states had institutions for the "feeble-minded" during the first half of the twentieth century and even beyond, so when I refer to those institutions and that time period, I use the same term.

I hope this offends no one; it is merely part of the story I am trying to tell—the story of a family secret, its origins, and the thinking that led to thousands of hidden relatives in America.

Steve Luxenberg
Baltimore, Maryland
February 2009

$\cdots$ { NOTES } $\cdots$

From the outset, I envisioned *Annie's Ghosts* as part history, part journalism, and part memoir. I spoke with more than 150 people in the course of my detective work, and followed the secret where it led. That route went through archives, libraries, museums, courthouses, and government offices. Often, the narrative itself makes reference to the sources of my material; these chapter notes provide more detailed information on my reporting and research.

PROLOGUE: Spring 1995

3:    *suffering from anxiety attacks* . . . My real-time account of my mother's hospitalization comes from other people's memories as well as my own. Later, for the book, I obtained her medical records, which I had legal permission to see.

ONE: Spring 2000

15:    *It's known as the Patient Protection Act* . . . That isn't the official name. The legislature approved a new "Mental Health Code" (Act 258 of 1974) in the midst of the national movement to provide more legal and medical safeguards for psychiatric patients, which may explain why my contact called it the Patient Protection Act.

TWO: Looking for Mom

31:    *George Eastman's little Brownie* . . . The evolution of amateur photography in the early twentieth century is a fascinating story of technological achievement, as revolutionary in that age as the digital camera has been in ours. Several histories have chronicled the innovative feats of both Kodak and its founder, George Eastman, including Douglas Collins's 1990 volume, *The Story of Kodak* (New York: H.N. Abrams).

35: *Mom's obituary for the local newspapers . . .* Detroit Free Press, M. L. Elrick, "Beth Luxenberg: Work, debate were her passions," Sept. 3, 1999, p. 5B. *Detroit News*, "Beth Luxenberg: Did accounting work for 35 years," p. 2C.

36: *the sixty or so people who had gathered . . .* That's the number who signed the guest book at the funeral.

THREE: The Rosetta Stone

43: *the "Routine History" completed by an Eloise social worker . . .* Eloise opened its social work department in 1923; by 1940, the sort of detailed report written by Mona Evans had become standard practice. The history was an important part of the patient's record, and the psychiatrist assigned to Annie's case would have relied upon it.

45: *just plain heavy, up to eighteen pounds . . .* Kevin Carroll, an executive at Hanger Prosthetics, gave me an education on artificial limbs; I relied on his knowledge here and in Chapter 13.

53: *I consulted a former director of Michigan's mental health department . . .* The former director, Frank Ochberg, served in that job from 1979 to 1981.

54: *Detroit city directories . . .* Published by R. L. Polk, a Detroit company, these compilations of names, residential addresses, businesses, and charitable organizations provide invaluable snapshots of American cities.

55: *I also don't see my grandparents' name . . .* The entire 1930 census is available online through ancestry.com, a fee-based service. Most public and university libraries, as well as the National Archives, have subscriptions to a library edition and offer free access. The ancestry.com database can be searched in multiple ways, a much easier method of locating people than peering at the Archives' microfilm, so I was mystified when I couldn't find my grandparents' listing initially. Once I saw the enumerator's "Hyman Hyman" goof, I understood why.

55: *I peer through this window into the past . . .* My grandparents' listing appears on sheet 3B, Enumeration District 82–131 of the 1930 Census.

55: *Nathan Shlien, boarder . . .* Nathan's last name appears as Shlien, Shlein, and Schlien on various records. Shlien is the most frequent, so I have used that spelling.

FOUR: Unlocking the Door

61: *the muffled voices . . .* I wondered whether Medji was remembering the scene accurately. Why, for example, would Mom and her parents leave the door ajar? But this is Medji's memory, and I found myself trusting it. She didn't have an answer to all my questions, and she willingly said, "I don't remember" when I asked for more detail.

67: *even after the divorce . . .* Esther filed for divorce on May 11, 1942; it was granted on August 13, 1942. Docket 328570, Wayne County Circuit Court.

68: *that honor had gone to Esther . . .* Esther died in 2004 at age eighty-seven.

FIVE: Missing Pieces

75: *one of the worst urban riots in U.S. history . . .* On July 28, 1967, following the Newark and Detroit disturbances, President Lyndon Johnson appointed the National Advisory Commission on Civil Disorders, better known today as the Kerner Commission, after its chairman, Illinois Governor Otto Kerner. The eleven-member panel, after studying twenty-four disturbances in twenty-three cities, found that while there was no "typical" riot, each grew out of social and economic conditions and "constituted a clear pattern of severe disadvantage for Negroes compared to whites." In its most famous single statement, the committee concluded: "To continue present policies is to make permanent the division of our country into two societies; one largely Negro and poor, located in the central cities; the other, predominantly white and affluent, located in the suburbs and in outlying areas."

75: *leaving forty-three dead . . .* Sources abound on the Detroit riots. Like many researchers of Detroit's history, I consulted (and often marveled at) Robert Conot's *American Odyssey* (New York: Morrow, 1974), an epic chronicle of the city from its founding to its emergence as a world economic power to its disheartening decline. Conot documents the conditions leading up to the riots, as well as the riots themselves.

77: *the classical columns of Northern High School . . .* Northern closed in 2007, a victim of the school system's declining enrollment. The building now houses the Detroit International Academy, the state's first all-girl public school.

80: *her life-sized portrait . . .* This is one of two paintings that Eloise's father, Freeman Dickerson, loaned to the institution. One hung for many years in the boardroom, directly behind the president's chair that Dickerson earlier occupied for two years.

81: *the 1982 history of Eloise* . . . No one has written a comprehensive history of
Eloise, but the hospital's overseers twice commissioned employees to com-
pile a record of Eloise's accomplishments. These works are not histories in a
broad sense, but both contain a wealth of information.

    The first, *History of Eloise: Wayne County House, Wayne County Asylum,* by
long-time Eloise bookkeeper Stansilas M. Keenan, appeared in 1913; he updated his work in 1933, and after a delay caused by the economic fallout from
the Depression, a small number were published in 1937. The story of Eloise's
name comes chiefly from the second history, Alvin C. Clark's *A History of
Wayne County Infirmary, Psychiatric, and General Hospital Complex at Eloise,
Michigan, 1832–1982,* published in 1982 by Wayne County on the 150th anniversary of the institution's founding.

    The newest addition to the Eloise canon is Patricia Ibbotson's 2002 pho-
tographic book, *Eloise: Poorhouse, Farm, Asylum, and Hospital,* part of Arcadia
Publishing's Image of America series. Ibbotson, a former nurse at the general hospital, is a meticulous researcher who has mastered the art of writing
fact-filled yet concise captions.

81: *"The name was at once accepted"* . . . When the hospital acquired its more formal name in 1945, it still did not cast Eloise aside entirely, officially calling
itself the Wayne County General Hospital and Infirmary at Eloise, Michigan.
Whether the new name was too much of a mouthful, or whether this was a case
of old habits dying hard, Eloise was what many Detroiters continued to call
it. Meanwhile, the Eloise Post Office, the birthplace of all the fuss, maintained its name until it went out of business in 1979.

81: *"the largest of its kind in the world"* . . . A statistic like this is tough to track down
with any certainty. The 1940 Census records on U.S. mental hospitals, which
do not identify specific facilities, show several with populations in excess of
five thousand. But none had infirmaries with resident populations of substantial numbers, which might mean that Eloise was the largest "of its kind,"
at least in the United States.

SIX: Actually Insane

98: *no transcript or summary of what was said at her hearing* . . . Normally, the
court reporter assigned to the case would only make a transcript for an appeal, or if someone had requested one. As a result, there's no record of
Annie's hearing.

99: *two "reputable physicians," who did not need to be psychiatrists or neurologists* . . .
This provision might suggest that the state relied on people without any particular expertise, but it was intended to protect the patient from overzealous
psychiatrists who might think that everyone could benefit from treatment.

The law also required the appointment of physicians who did not work for the mental institution where the patient was likely to go; based on the several dozen cases I reviewed, that provision was followed. Occasionally, though, the probate judges appointed someone who had a consulting position at Eloise, which could be seen as contrary to the spirit of the law.

99:   *the Michigan Supreme Court ruled in several cases* . . . A 1936 case, *In re Myrtle Davis*, reflects the court's view of the need for a full investigation and the "taking of proofs." The case arose from a petition by Davis's sister. On the same day that the two court-appointed physicians certified Davis, thirty-six, as insane, the probate court held its hearing. The only testimony came from federal probation officer Walter Hoffman, who was asked "What's the matter with her?" He replied: "Insane." On appeal, the Michigan Supreme Court ruled unanimously that Davis had been confined illegally at Eloise, and ordered her release. "In our opinion [Hoffman's] testimony was inadmissible; it is nothing more than an opinion, nothing was shown by the witness upon which such an opinion could be based." The court also rebuked the probate judge for the skimpiness of the hearing, saying "there is no showing that the judge conducted an inquest as provided by law."

99:   *the procedures themselves remained much as before* . . . Case files from this period show that a "full investigation" and the "taking of proofs" rarely took place. The difference for Myrtle Davis was that someone (unnamed in the court's ruling, although it could have been Davis herself) challenged her commitment.

102:   *my spontaneous answer* . . . It was too hard to take notes on my own comments during this part of my conversation with Sandy Ellison, so I wrote down as much as I could remember after the interview ended and checked it with Sandy.

SEVEN: Welcome to Eloise

109:   *Wayne County deputy sheriff John McLean* . . . Annie's court record contains the facts that allow me to describe her trip to Eloise. Other details, such as the grillwork, come from photographs of Eloise during that era.

110:   *Two or three new patients arrived almost every day.* . . . Eloise's annual reports from this era provided statistics on the number of new admissions and parolees, as well as on the institution's yearly food production, the number of employees, and the progress of construction.

110:   *Eloise's herd of cows sent more than 120,000 gallons of milk* . . . The 1937 annual report states that Eloise's farm production—milk, beef, veal, pork, vegetables, and tobacco—had a value of $80,907.99. In today's dollars, that's equivalent to $1.2 million.

110: *1,800 loaves of bread an hour* . . . Clark, p. 114.

111: *a public outcry over the horrifying murder* . . . Police found the body of eleven-
      year-old Lillian Gallaher in a trunk in an apartment rented to twenty-six-
      year-old Merton W. Goodrich and his wife. The girl had been missing a week;
      she disappeared while selling game-of-chance tickets door-to-door, part of
      a fundraising effort for her Catholic school. See extensive coverage in the
      Detroit Free Press and the *Detroit News*, September 27, 1934, and the days fol-
      lowing. A year later, after a nationwide manhunt failed to find the Goodrich
      couple, unsuspecting police arrested a suspicious man for annoying the chil-
      dren at a wading pool in New York's Central Park; his fingerprints turned out
      to be Goodrich's. See *The New York Times*, "Slayer of Girl, 11, Caught by
      Chance," July 4, 1935, p. 1. After his trial in Michigan, Goodrich was sen-
      tenced to life in prison.

111: *Gruber directed the hospital staff to stamp* . . . For an account of Gruber's con-
      cern about the proposed law and his creation of the "Red Star" ward, see Eric
      M. Eisenhardt, "Sexual Deviants in a Mental Hospital," 1954 master's thesis,
      Wayne University, School of Public Affairs and Social Work.

112: *Her name was Bridget Hughes* . . . All the Eloise histories recount the story of
      Biddy Hughes. I relied on Alvin Clark's 1982 history, p. 43. His book is also
      an invaluable source for much of the early history; it includes sketches of the
      first, second, and third Wayne County Houses, as well as photographs of
      many of the dozens of buildings that once occupied the grounds, pp. 1–9.

113: *"that 'awful wilderness'"* . . . Clark, p. 4.

113: *the pioneering efforts of Dorothea Dix* . . . Several good accounts exist of Dix's
      work in Massachusetts, New Jersey, North Carolina, and elsewhere, includ-
      ing the books of Rutgers professor Gerald N. Grob, probably the foremost
      authority on the history and evolution of mental health treatment in the
      United States.

113: *an organization of mutual support* . . . For most of the nineteenth century, the
      Association of Medical Superintendents of the American Institutions of the
      Insane was the voice of the American psychiatric community, for all practical
      purposes. Working with the insane in the nineteenth century meant working
      in an asylum. No specialty known as psychiatry existed (the early psychiatrists
      were known as "alienists," reflecting the prevailing view that mental illness
      was outside our understanding). Private psychiatric practice is a twentieth-
      century development. In 1894, the Association of Medical Superintendents
      changed its name to the American Medico-Psychological Association, and
      then in 1921, it became the American Psychiatric Association, as it is known
      today.

114: *the Kirkbride plan* . . . The American Psychiatric Association's one-hundredth-
      anniversary volume, *One Hundred Years of American Psychiatry*, contains a col-
      lection of essays on the history of the nation's mental hospitals, including the

Kirkbride plan. I have drawn on two in particular from the 1944 anniversary book: "The Founding and Founders of the Association," by Winfred Overholser, then the superintendent of St. Elizabeth's Hospital in Washington, D.C., and "The History of American Mental Hospitals," by Samuel W. Hamilton, of the U.S. Public Health Service.

116: *"sickening circumstances of inhumanity"* . . . The 1878 *Lancet* editorial was written by Dr. H. A. Cleland, the medical journal's editor; it is cited in William J. Kay's essay, "State Psychiatric Hospitals and Medical Establishments for the Mentally Retarded," in *Medical History of Michigan*, vol. 2 (Minneapolis/St. Paul: Bruce Publishing Co., 1930), p. 732. I thought it was significant that an insider such as Kay, then superintendent of the state's institution for the feeble-minded at Lapeer, would choose to take note of such a strong condemnation of the Wayne County Asylum.

Kay's essay also provides a capsule history of institutional treatment for the mentally ill in America. In 1773, before the American Revolution, Virginia became the first colony to erect a separate hospital for the insane; New York became the first state to build one, in 1809. Kay takes special note of the 1823 founding of the Hartford Retreat for the Insane in Connecticut, "the first hospital of its kind to be devoted, exclusively, to the care and treatment of the insane." The State Medical Society of Connecticut contributed money to build the Hartford Retreat, an early example of the medical profession's direct involvement in improving the conditions for treating the mentally ill, Kay asserted. See *Medical History of Michigan*, p. 730. Closer to home, Kay claimed that Michigan's care for the insane "has never come in for serious criticism" (that would come later), lamenting only that the state's facilities, like those "in the rest of the world," have never been adequate to meet the demand, p. 756.

116: *"permanently removed the chains, shackles and dim cells . . ."* Clark, p. 45.

121: the *"Poor Old Guys in Eloise"* . . . Some references offer "Gentlemen" for "Guys." Ed Missavage scoffed at the more polite version, and said "guys" was the word he always heard at the hospital.

121– *construction crews of 350 worked almost around the clock* . . . The project required
122: so much material that local suppliers could not keep pace. One brick manufacturer sent his company's entire daily production to Eloise, more than twenty thousand bricks a day for three months. Meanwhile, twenty gravel trucks formed a kind of continuous conveyor line from Detroit to the hospital grounds, hauling the ten thousand cubic yards needed to mix the concrete. Clark, p. 24.

122: *the largest institutional kitchen in the country* . . . The claim appears in Ibbotson, p. 52.

122: *flow of the brew into a two-hundred-gallon reservoir* . . . Details on the kitchen from Clark, p. 25.

122:   *the infirmary rolls showed 7,441 patients . . .* Clark, p. 25.

123:   *new definitions of what constituted a mental disorder . . .* The difficulty of counting the nation's mentally ill, and how to define a mental "defective," was an
ongoing debate at the Census Bureau. For a brief history of this debate, and
how it reflected the country's changing attitudes toward the mentally ill, see
Atlee L. Stroup and Ronald W. Manderscheid, "The Development of the State
Mental Hospital System in the United States: 1840–1980," *Journal of the
Washington Academy of Sciences*, vol. 78, no. 1, March 1988, pp. 58–69.

123:   *the number of mentally ill residents in hospitals soared . . .* The Census Bureau
made its first attempt at counting the "defective classes" in 1840, and issued
periodic reports on the "Defective, Feeble-Minded and Insane" from 1880 to
1923. From 1938 until 1966, the bureau published *Patients in Mental Institutions.* That publication ceased about the time that the population in mental
hospitals began its steep decline following development of medications that
allowed more patients to be treated on an out-patient basis and the legal/
moral protest that led to the strong patient rights that exist today, particularly
regarding the involuntary commitment process.

EIGHT: I Am Family

131:   *For years, Tillie had been riding the bus . . .* Schedules from that era suggest that
Tillie took a bus downtown and then transferred to the Michigan Avenue
line, which served the Ford assembly plant in Dearborn before continuing
on to Eloise.

136:   *Tillie was one of ten children. . .* My search for Tillie's siblings led me to other
Schleins from Radziwillow, but their descendants did not know my grandparents or the names of Tillie's brothers and sisters.

139:   *the Radziwillow records from that era . . .* The birth records for Radziwillow Jews
born in the late nineteenth century may not exist any longer, according to Alex
Dunai, my researcher in Ukraine. An American genealogy group has compiled
an index of births recorded in Kremenets, a larger nearby town; it includes
some births, marriages, and deaths from Radziwillow, but my grandparents'
names do not appear among the several thousand names in the index.

NINE: Lost and Found

143:   *before comprehensive physicals and lengthy questionnaires replaced the more generic permission forms . . .* I don't remember the medical form. I spoke to John
Johnson of the Michigan High School Athletic Association, which develops
eligibility rules; he said that the card signed by physicians in the 1960s did

not require any statement of specific medical issues as long as athlete's physical condition allowed him or her to play.

153: *In 1915, it was illegal for first cousins to marry in Michigan* . . . Sections 551.3 and
551.4 of Michigan's compiled laws, first enacted in 1903, prohibit marriage
to a "cousin in the first degree." Before 1903, Michigan allowed first cousins
to marry.

153: *one of twenty-four that still prohibit first cousins to marry* . . . Five additional
states have restrictions that prevent first-cousin marriages if the partners
can have children; for example, first cousins can marry in Illinois only if both
are older than fifty, or one is unable to reproduce. See "State Laws Regarding
Marriages Between First Cousins," the National Conference of State Legisla-
tures, www.ncsl.org/programs/cyf/cousins.htm.

153: *risk of birth defects for the children of married first cousins* . . . A 2002 study cal-
culated the increased risk at 1.7 to 2.8 percent above the norm. "Genetic
Counseling and Screening of Consanguineous Couples and Their Offspring,"
Journal of Genetic Counseling, vol. 11, no. 2, April 2002, p. 105.

TEN: Castles in the Air

163: *just as the draft eligibility rules were changing* . . . In the summer of 1942, with
the military's manpower needs becoming more critical, Congress modified
the Selective Service Act to boost the pool of eligible men. That led the Selective Service to create a new rank order for induction. Single men with no
dependents were deemed the most eligible, followed by single men with dependents but who did not have a job that contributed to the war effort. See
"Family Men to Go Last, Draft Rules; Seven Classifications Set Up to Comply
With Changed Law Are Announced," the Associated Press, published in *The
Washington Post*, July 14, 1942, p. 1 and p. 15.

163: *the newspapers were full of talk* . . . One example: "Married Men Face Draft This
Year, Hershey Says," *The Washington Post*, August 22, 1942, p. 1.

163: *ten million able-bodied men, out of the sixteen million registered* . . . Figures from
the Selective Service, cited in William A. Tuttle, *Daddy's Gone to War: The Second World War in the Lives of America's Children* (New York: Oxford University
Press, 1993), p. 32.

ELEVEN: The Old Neighborhood

182: *"no jury of sane men would convict me"* . . . The quotes from Haiselden in this
chapter come from "Doctor to Let Patient's Baby Defective Die," the *Chicago
Daily Tribune*, November 17, 1915, p. 1; available online at www.disability
museum.org/lib/docs/1231card.htm. The Disability History Museum has a

digital archive of newspaper coverage of Haiselden's crusade, largely from the *Chicago American* and the *Chicago Daily Tribune*.

182: *a very public platform for his ideas* . . . The best account of Haiselden's campaign and career appears in Martin S. Pernick's book, *The Black Stork: Eugenics and The Death of "Defective" Babies in American Medicine and Motion Pictures Since 1915* (New York: Oxford University Press, 1996).

183: *pleas from anguished parents* . . . Pernick, p. 5.

183: *an hour-long feature film starring Haiselden* . . . An ad for the movie, published in the *Chicago Daily Tribune* on April 2, 1917, promoted it as "A vivid pictorial drama that tells you why Dr. Haiselden is opposed to operating to save the lives of defective babies." Available online at www.disabilitymuseum.org/lib/stills/501.htm.

184: *"often advocated measure for dealing with the unfit . . ."* Pernick, p. 14.

184: *found quotes or commentaries from more than three hundred physicians and public figures* . . . The doctor who delivered Annie was not among those quoted in the Detroit newspapers, Pernick told me after checking his list.

184: *many supportive of Haiselden's position* . . . A variety of notable figures in American life, including Clarence Darrow and Helen Keller, offered public defenses of Haiselden's actions. Writing in *The New Republic*, Keller drew a distinction between her disabilities (deafness and blindness) and deformities that gave a child no chance at being "useful to itself and the world." She argued that such children were "being spared a life of misery" and that "No one cares about that pitiful, useless lump of flesh." In keeping with that era's growing belief in science as a solution to society's ills, she suggested that a "physician's jury" could be set up to determine whether a deformed baby's life was worth saving. *The New Republic*, December 18, 1915, also cited in Pernick, p. 96, and in Ian Dowbiggin, *A Precise History of Euthanasia: Life, Death, God and Medicine* (Lanham, Md.: Rowman and Littlefield, 2007), p. 74.

184: *a 1937 poll* . . . Dowbiggin, p. 89.

189: *the three documents inside the envelope* . . . These documents were Nathan Shlien's Certificate of Arrival, Declaration of Intention (to become a citizen), and Petition for Citizenship. His typed Declaration misspells his name as "Nathan Thlien."

TWELVE: The Cigar Laborer

193: *it's January 1964 now* . . . My grandfather died on January 2, 1964.

195: *listed his occupation as "cigar labourer"* . . . The passenger manifest in Hamburg uses the German phrase, *"Zigarrenarbeiter,"* or cigar worker. Staatarchiv Hamburg, *Hamburg Passenger Lists, 1850–1934,* available online at www.ancestry .com. The details about Chaim's entry at Ellis Island come from "List or Manifest of Alien Passengers for the United States Immigration Officer at Port of Arrival, *S.S. Patricia*, July 20/21, 1907," microfilm series T715, Roll 948, National Archives in Washington.

196: *One news article traced Detroit's tobacco prominence* . . . The quote and other details come from Thomas L. Jones's report on cigar making in the *Detroit News*'s three-hundredth-anniversary section on the city's founding, accessed online at http://info.detnews.com/history/story/index.cfm?id=24.

196: *home to the densest square mile in the country and perhaps the world* . . . Many writers have cited this statistic, often without the qualifier that I have used and often inflating the number of people per square mile. The claim for the United States is based on the census count for the Lower East Side, which computed to 375,000 people per square mile in 1910, or 585 per acre. But knowing the densest square mile in the world would require comparable data from countries that took no census in that era.

196: *Detroit saw its population swell* . . . The information on Detroit's growth comes from the U.S. Census reports for 1900, 1910, and 1920.

196: *up to 21,000 cars* . . . Conot, *American Odyssey*, p. 193, based on Graeme O'Geran, *A History of the Detroit Street Railways* (Detroit: Conover Press, 1931).

197: *Between 1881 and 1914, more than two million Jews* . . . The immigration statistics in this chapter come from the U.S. Bureau of Immigration and the *Reports of the Immigration Commission 1907–1910*, known as the Dillingham Commission.

197: *no intention of ever going back* . . . Non-Jewish immigrants returned to their native country in greater numbers than their Jewish counterparts, particularly those from Russia, who did not always view the countries of their birth as "homelands."

197: *Radziwillow, in 1907, was no sleepy shtetl* . . . For my portrait of the town, I relied primarily on two histories: *Radyvyliv*, by Ukrainian journalist Volodymyr Yashchuk, published in 2004; and *Radzivilov sefer zikaron*, the 1966 *yizkor* (memorial) book commemorating the lives of the Radziwillow Jews who died in the Holocaust. Alexander Dunai, our translator during a trip to Radziwillow in July 2007, found Yashchuk's account and prepared a written summary for me; Sam Elrom of Baltimore did the same with the *yizkor* volume, which includes a history of the Jewish community in Radziwillow based in part on interviews with the town's Holocaust survivors.

199: *"the more generalized sense of fear"* . . . Several histories, including Ronald Sanders's *Shores of Refuge: A Hundred Years of Jewish Emigration* (New York: Holt, 1988) and Gerald Sorin's *A Time for Building: The Third Migration, 1880–1920* (Baltimore: Johns Hopkins University Press, 1992), support Moreno's description of Jewish emigration from Russia as a multidimensional phenomenon. The twelve-volume Jewish Encyclopedia, published between 1901 and 1906 at the height of the Russian Jewish migration, offers a thorough account of the "temporary regulations" imposed by the tsarist government in 1882 and the impact of those laws on Jews inside and outside the Pale of Settlement. Available online at www.jewishencyclopedia.com.

199: *searchable by town name* . . . A database created by Steve Morse, available online at www.stevemorse.org, makes it possible to search passenger manifests by a town's name, using an exact spelling or variants.

200: *Their tactics drew the scrutiny of Philip Cowen* . . . Cowen wrote two reports on Russian emigration, in December 1906 and January 1907. On the pogroms, he pointed a finger directly at the Russian government, which he blamed for encouraging the attacks by giving promotions and other benefits to officers who participated in the violence. His reports can be found in case files 52411/56, folders 1 and 3, Subject Correspondence series of Record Group 85, Records of the Immigration and Naturalization Service, National Archives.

200: *The panel, chaired by U.S. Senator William Dillingham of Vermont* . . . The Dillingham Commission, created by an act of Congress on Feb. 20, 1907, published its forty-one-volume report in 1911. Nineteen volumes were devoted to statistical charts detailing the impact of immigrant labor on major industries.

201: *"the letters are read and re-read . . ."* Dillingham Commission report, vol. 4, *Emigration Conditions in Europe*, p. 57.

201: *"requiring a degree of courage and resourcefulness . . ."* Dillingham Commission report, vol. 4, p. 21.

201: *procured the necessary papers to leave* . . . In volume 4, the Dillingham Commission included the English translation of a 1909 article in Russian by S. Janovsky, describing the "endless vexations" of obtaining emigration documents from local Russian authorities. Janovsky concluded that the process itself was responsible for opening the door to "a special type of middleman who take upon themselves the task of procuring all the papers necessary . . ." If obtaining a passport wasn't possible, Janovsky wrote, these middlemen arranged to smuggle the emigrant across the border. Text of the Janovsky article in Dillingham Commission report, vol. 4, pp. 251–264.

202: *the detailed report of commission investigator Anna Herkner* . . . Herkner's account appeared in Dillingham Commission report, *Steerage Conditions*, vol. 37, pp. 5–40. She did not name the ships she sailed on, but she provided the specific dates of her voyages in old steerage, enabling me to match those dates with the list of arrivals at Ellis Island. Her report included a grim account of the routine sexual assaults on female steerage passengers: "Not one young woman in steerage escaped attack. The writer herself was no exception." Dillingham Commission report, vol. 37, p. 22.

203: *A photo of the S.S. Patricia* . . . Edwin Levick's 1906 photo appears at the beginning of this chapter.

203: *the nine ships that appeared on July 21, 1907* . . . From the passenger manifests for that day, microfilm series T715, Rolls 947–949, National Archives.

204: *the university president's effort to counteract* . . . Harvard president A. Lawrence Lowell's campaign for a discriminatory admissions policy, protested by prominent faculty members, drew press coverage at the time and has been well chronicled since. See, among others, Marcia Graham Synnott's *The Half-Opened Door: Discrimination and Admissions at Harvard, Yale, and Princeton, 1900–1970* (Westport, Conn.: Greenwood Press, 1979), especially pp. 58–75.

204: *What happened to Detroit's economy* . . . My description of the auto industry's growth between 1900 and 1920 comes primarily from Conot, *American Odyssey*; Charles K. Hyde, *The Dodge Brothers: The Men, the Motor Cars, and the Legacy* (Great Lakes books. Detroit: Wayne State University Press, 2005); and Vincent Curcio, *Chrysler: The Life and Times of an Automotive Genius* (New York: Oxford University Press, 2000).

205: *Hyman no longer worked for Dodge* . . . Personnel records for Dodge, which became a division of Chrysler in the late 1920s, are not among the records that survive from Dodge's early days.

206: *projects and land annexations that would transform the city's character* . . . Based on news accounts and photographs of the building of the Book Cadillac, the Ambassador Bridge, and the Detroit-Windsor Tunnel, as well as the capsule histories that open the 1920 through 1933 editions of the Detroit city directories.

206: *80 square miles to more than 134* . . . From *Manual, County of Wayne, Michigan, 1930* (Detroit: Board of County Auditors), a volume rich in history and facts about the governments of Wayne County and Detroit.

207: *social worker Helen Hall wrote* . . . "When Detroit's Out of Gear," *The Survey*, April 1930.

207: *that misery overwhelmed the city's welfare department* . . . Relief statistics cited in Sidney Fine, *The Automobile Under the Blue Eagle* (Ann Arbor: University of Michigan Press, 1963), p. 19. The Detroit Department of Public Welfare's 1938 "Handbook of Policy and Organization" also recounts the effect on the department.

207: *"Children scavenged through the street like animals . . ."* Conot, p. 283.

208: *the welfare agency later hired Hyman as a part-time janitor* . . . From Hyman's Alien Registration Form, September 6, 1940. On this document, required by the Alien Registration Act of 1940, Hyman reports that he entered the country in July 1910 on the *"Fatherland."* No such ship exists; there was an S.S. *Vaderland*, but my grandfather's name (Chaim Korn) does not appear on *Vaderland* manifests between June and September 1910. Marian Smith, historian for the U.S. Citizenship and Immigration Services, tells me that many immigrants provided incorrect information on the registration forms, sometimes for no other reason than faulty memory. "The form required you to say how you got here," she said, "and immigrants were afraid to leave it blank."

THIRTEEN: Invisible

215: *I tell Frassica what I've learned about Kidner*... The Kidner biographical material comes from newspaper accounts, census records, Detroit city directories, the American Orthopedic Association, and *Who's Who in Orthopedics*, a compilation edited by Sayed Behrooz Mostofi (London: Springer, 2005).

218: *Made of wood, covered with rawhide*... Kevin Carroll sent me a 1958 Hanger Prosthetics marketing brochure, "Keeping Step," from his personal collection of historical information about artificial limbs. Carroll said Annie's prosthetic leg would have been similar in design and construction to the standard ones, made of English willow, shown in the eighty-four-page brochure.

218: *more than thirty thousand amputations of all sorts*... The Union surgeons kept good records, which formed the basis for an 1865 report from the surgeon general's office, "The Medical and Surgical History of the War of the Rebellion."

224: *IQ is a calculation, not a measurement*... Alfred Binet, a French psychologist, developed the first of the modern intelligence tests in 1905 as part of the French Ministry of Education's effort to identify students likely to have difficulty in conventional schools. In 1912, German psychologist William Stern proposed the idea of expressing intelligence as a single number—the intelligence quotient. Standardized intelligence tests, in their early form, were designed to compare students to each other: a ten-year-old performing at the level of a typical eight-year-old would register an IQ of 80 ($100 \times {}^8\!/_{10}$), while an eight-year-old testing at a ten-year-old's level would earn an IQ of 125 ($100 \times {}^{10}\!/_8$).

224: *the clinic had earned a national reputation*... Detroit schools started its first class for mentally retarded students in 1903. In 1911, the Detroit superintendent of schools sought to find more precise methods for identifying students in need of "special education," which led to the establishment of the Psychological Clinic. During the summer of 1912, the clinic's first employee went to New Jersey for instruction in administering the new Binet intelligence tests; the clinic then took over the job of placing "mentally retarded and socially maladjusted" students into special classes, according to a 2003 pamphlet put out by the clinic, now called the Office of Psychological Services.

224: *an IQ of 73, or "borderline"*... The early years of the IQ testing movement coincided with the rise of modern science and the belief, particularly strong in the United States, that it was possible to quantify almost everything. Scientific classifications for various levels of mental deficiency soon found their way into the state laws and the public lexicon. A "moron" in 1925, when Annie took her first IQ test, referred to an IQ between 50 and 69; "imbecile," between 20 and 49; and "idiot," below 20. (These definitions appear in Lewis M. Terman, *The Measurement of Intelligence* [Boston: Houghton Mifflin, 1916].) Those terms, already in disfavor by the late 1950s, disappeared from scientific, educational, and legal use in the 1970s, during the rewriting of nearly all mental health codes in the United States.

FOURTEEN: One of the Thousands

229: *Zimmerman recounted* . . . Jo Johnson, head of the Westland Historical Commission and overseer of the Eloise museum, provided me with a typescript of Zimmerman's talk.

230: *"disperse gloom and monotony . . ."* Altshuler describes his therapy approach in "'Group Treatment' of Mental Patients," an essay in the 1937 Eloise annual report.

232: *prescribed one of the new antipsychotic drugs* . . . The Food and Drug Administration approved the first of these medications in March 1954; within eight months, the psychiatric community had tried Thorazine (chlorpromazine) on more than two million patients, according to Pete Earley's 2006 book *Crazy: A Father's Search Through America's Mental Health Madness* (New York: G. P. Putnam's Sons), p. 68.

233: *"schizophrenia is so hopeless"* . . . Letter from Abraham Brill to William Alanson White, quoted in Elliot Valenstein's *Great and Desperate Cures*, p. 56.

233: *In 1948, seventy-four Eloise patients received insulin shock* . . . Eloise's annual reports routinely reported the number of patients who received shock treatments.

233: *"you had to be hypervigilant while the patients were in the comas"* . . . Elliot Valenstein offers a similarly grueling description in his book, based on his experience of witnessing insulin shock therapy at 1950 at a Veterans Administration hospital in Topeka, Kansas. The thirty patients, he writes, were twitching, tossing, moaning, shouting, and gasping during their convulsions; *Great and Desperate Cures*, pp. 56–57.

235: *A 1934 survey, ominously titled* . . . Fred M. Butzel, a noted Detroit philanthropist often involved in public issues, headed this survey, which can be found at the Library of Michigan in Lansing.

235: *the legislature rescinded the measure* . . . This account of the legislature's change of direction in increasing the number of hospital beds comes from Caroline Jean Whitaker's 1986 University of Michigan doctoral dissertation, "Almshouses and Mental Institutions in Michigan, 1871–1930," p. 296.

235: *the state had always relied on Eloise* . . . In 1934, Wayne County residents occupied only 10 percent of the 10,323 available beds in state mental hospitals.

From Irene Waryas, "A Program of Family Care for Mental Patients at Wayne County General Hospital and Infirmary," 1950 master's thesis, Wayne University, School of Public Affairs and Social Work.

235: *A partnership had evolved . . .* This partnership began in 1897, when state law first granted reimbursement to counties for the care of mental "defectives." In 1903, the legislature made the Wayne County asylum subject to the same rules as the state's institutions.

236: *the federal government picking up nearly 80 percent of the tab . . .* Eloise's 1937 annual report has a detailed description of how federal dollars paid for various improvements at the hospital.

236: *95 cents a day in 1940 . . .* The reimbursement rates come from Eloise annual reports and minutes of Eloise's board, known as the Wayne County Board of County Institutions after 1940.

236: *convert Ward 106 of N Building into four hundred psychiatric beds . . .* Clark, p. 52.

237: *One female ward, designed for 18, had 45 patients . . .* Many of the details in this paragraph come from a letter that Frank E. Kelley, chairman of Eloise's board, wrote to Gov. Harry F. Kelly, June 19, 1945. The letter appears in the minutes of the Eloise board, available at the Westland Historical Commission.

237: *The governor, Harry Kelly, had been given plenty of warning . . .* Kelly's office kept extensive records on the overcrowding crisis, available in the State Archives: Gov. Harry Kelly Papers, RG42, Box 7, File 7, State Boards and Commissions, Hospital Commission, and RG42, Box 39, File 14.

239: *County officials didn't like the Soo plan . . .* Eloise board chairman Kelley suggested, in his June 19, 1945 letter to Governor Kelly, that the state investigate the possibility of buying "several idle summer resorts and converting them into temporary mental hospitals for the custodial care of mental patients."

239: *only "comfortable and tidy patients" . . .* This phrase appears in a Wagg letter to Frank E. Kelley, July 3, 1945. It's clear from the Eloise board's minutes and other documents that Wagg had several conversations with Kelley and Gruber about the state's stipulations. Wagg pointed out that as state hospitals sent some of their patients to the Soo, that would open up beds for transfers from Eloise, implying that Eloise might be able to send more severely ill patients to those institutions.

243: *Eloise had assigned Waryas to place up to twenty-five capable patients . . .* From 1950 Eloise annual report, p. 26.

244: *a mini-seminar on what we do and don't know about schizophrenia . . .* Medical researchers have made progress in understanding this perplexing disorder, but Regenold's comments reflect the continuing uncertainty about its origins. "Schizophrenia is a disease without a diagnostic test," wrote Michael Foster Green, a professor at UCLA's Department of Psychiatry and Biobehavioral Sciences, in his 2001 book, *Schizophrenia Revealed: From Neurons to So-*

cial Interactions (New York: W.W. Norton), which makes diagnosis more of an art than a science. Green's book provides an accessible overview of the latest research, which has focused on neural disconnection and dysfunction, but his larger purpose is to "demystify" schiozophrenia. He argues that popular culture has tended to treat schizophrenia as a "deep and profound" mystery, and thus incomprehensible. Only by demystifying the disorder, he asserts, can we avoid the romanticism and stigmatization that has characterized the disease for so many years.

FIFTEEN: The Ghosts of Radziwillow

249: *execution of "Jews in the employment of the party apparatus"* . . . The full July 2 directive appears in many collections, including *Documents on the Holocaust: Selected Sources on the Destruction of the Jews of Germany and Austria, Poland, and the Soviet Union* (Lincoln: University of Nebraska Press, 1999).

250: *Red Army tank forces did mount one major counterattack* . . . Historian David Glantz has a detailed description of this battle in his paper, "The Initial Period of War on the Eastern Front, 22 June–August 1941," *Proceedings of the Fourth Art of War Symposium, Garmisch, October 1987* (London: Frank Cass, 1997).

250: *twenty-eight Jews were shot as "dangerous Communists" or "partisans"* . . . This figure appears in several books, but most cite the Radziwillow *yizkor* book as the source.

250: *Radziwillow's turn came* . . . There is no precise number for the Jews murdered in the two Radziwillow massacres. The figures in this chapter come from the *Encyclopedia of Jewish Life* and the *Encyclopedia Judaica*, based in part on the Radziwillow *yizkor* book. The 2004 history of Radziwillow, cited in Chapter 12, gives a total of three thousand Jews for 1942, a count that includes all those killed, not just those at the two massacres.

252: *needed for the fight against the Soviets* . . . For the Nazi concerns about the supply of men and ammunition, see Bernhard Kroener, "Manpower Resources in the Area of Conflict Between the *Wehrmacht*, Bureaucracy and War Economy, 1939–1942," in vol. 5, part 1 of *Germany and the Second World War* (Oxford: Oxford University Press, 2003).

253: *which were of a different gauge* . . . Nazi military records show how much the railway transportation problem complicated the German invasion of the Soviet Union. See Bernd Wegner, "The War Against the Soviet Union, 1942–1943," in *The Global War*, vol. 6 of *Germany and the Second World War* (Oxford: Clarendon Press, 2001), p. 879. This ongoing multivolume history, prepared by the German military archives (the *Militärgeschichtliches Forschungsamt*) and translated into English, offers a remarkably detailed view of the Nazi war machine, both in Berlin and in the field.

253: *made clear in an October 12, 1941 directive* . . . For the full text, see "The *Einsatzgruppen* or Murder Commandos," vol. 10 of *The Holocaust: Selected Documents in Eighteen Volumes* (New York: Garland Publishing, 1982). The underlined portion appears that way in the original document.

254: *the documents detailing her deception* . . . These documents provide the specific dates of Anna's work as a translator for the Nazis, and later in Germany; they verified many of the details she had told me. She was uncertain about some dates; in cases of a discrepancy between her memory and the documents, I have relied on the written record.

255: *"You could see the blood . . ."* Anna's account of the scene at the mass gravesite is similar to what others have described in testimony and interviews.

259: *"The interpreter Anna Prokopowisch . . ."* This is Könitzer's spelling of Prokopowitsch. Wendy Lower translated the letter of recommendation.

259: *The Nazis had hired other translators who were* Volksdeutschen . . . Wendy Lower, who has written extensively on the Holocaust in Ukraine, suggested that Könitzer was trying to protect both himself and, perhaps, Anna. "The *Volksdeutschen* were not granted citizenship automatically," she wrote me via e-mail. "Only those who were accepted in the *Wehrmacht* got papers, or so the recruitment posters and decrees claimed." The Nazis needed the translators desperately and often relaxed their hiring procedure, according to Lower, so many local translators working for the Germans in Ukraine did not have citizenship papers.

263: *Bella Kron was sixteen when the Nazis came for her* . . . I gratefully acknowledge the University of Southern California Shoah Foundation Institute for Visual History and Education for allowing me to view and use a portion of Bella Kron's videotaped testimony, which is filed as interview code 14471.

263: *on wooden planks across the open pits, seven at a time* . . . Since 2004, a research team head by a French priest, Patrick Desbois, has worked to establish a full documentary record of the Holocaust in Ukraine, interviewing more than six hundred witnesses and collecting previously unknown documents, including photographs. The Mémorial de la Shoah in Paris mounted a remarkable exhibit of the Desbois team's efforts, called "The Holocaust by Bullets: The Mass Shootings of Jews in Ukraine, 1941–1944." Part of the exhibit, which I saw in July 2007, includes step-by-step descriptions of what the killing squads did at the mass gravesites.

SIXTEEN: Abandoned

269: *she might have said something more about Annie* . . . Mary Bernek, the Botsford social worker assigned to Mom, does not have any memory of talking with Mom about Annie. When I interviewed Bernek in July 2006, she said she wouldn't have asked Mom directly about her secret, but would have waited for Mom to say something about Annie on her own. Bernek's daily notes, part of Mom's Botsford files, don't show any evidence of a conversation about Annie.

271:   *After several afternoons with articles such as* . . . Leslie C. Barber, "The Age of Schizophrenia," *Harper's Monthly Magazine*, December 1937, pp. 70–78, and Farnsworth Crowder, "But *Is* the World Going Mad?" from *The Survey Graphic*, reprinted in *Reader's Digest*, May 1937, pp. 53–57. Crowder intends his essay as a corrective to grim ones such as Barber's, but Crowder's conclusion couldn't have been of much comfort to someone in my mother's position. "Modern psychiatry, by shedding light in murky corners of the human soul, has shown us alarming things, but it has not shown us doom," Crowder writes. "Rather, by giving understanding, by providing humanized, scientific care, by promoting mental hygiene, psychiatry makes us moderns the gainers—not the fated losers—in the immemorial fight for sanity and happiness."

275:   *the state's sterilization law* . . . First passed in 1913, the law was later overturned because it targeted mental "defectives" in institutions, and the Michigan Supreme Court ruled that it had to apply to the mentally impaired in general (in other words, more broadly). A 1923 law restored sterilization as state policy; after the 1927 Supreme Court decision in *Buck v. Bell*, the number of sterilizations began to climb.

275:   *2,339 of the 3,786 confirmed sterilizations* . . . The figure comes from a 1998 lawsuit by Fred Aslin, who was sterilized at Lapeer in 1944 when he was eighteen. Like many such institutions at the time, Lapeer's population included people who were mistakenly deemed mentally retarded; Aslin was one of them. The state had sent Aslin and his eight siblings to Lapeer during the Depression, deciding that their mother was unable to care for them after their father died, according to Aslin's lawyer, Lisa McNiff. Aslin lost his suit on statue of limitation grounds, but the state's director of community health sent him a written apology. "Looking back on it now, it is clear that the treatment you and others received was offensive, inappropriate and wrong," wrote the director, James K. Haveman, Jr. "Man Fails in Lawsuit Over Forced Sterilization," Associated Press, March 10, 2000.

275:   *the fourth highest total in the nation* . . . Thirty-two states had sterilization laws at one time or another, resulting in more than 36,000 involuntary sterilizations, according to Paul Lombardo, a professor of law at Georgia State University. Lombardo's new book, *Three Generations, No Imbeciles: Eugenics, the Supreme Court and Buck v. Bell* (Baltimore: Johns Hopkins Press, 2008), includes a state-by-state breakdown based on work done in the 1960s by Julius Paul, who assembled the data from state records, institutional reports, and surveys of officials in the thirty-two states. In a note accompanying the chart, Lombardo says that the numbers are likely higher than Paul was able to document.

SEVENTEEN: Dad's Secret

287: *Didn't the government make it easy . . .* Congress made it so easy that nearly every military applicant received citizenship. The Nationality Act of 1940 exempted non-citizens serving in the armed forces from all but the most minimal requirements in applying for citizenship; proof of lawful entry (Dad's problem) was one of the few conditions that remained, and the law even offered ways around that. A 1942 amendment to the act went further, creating a procedure for granting American citizenship to applicants on foreign soil, a first in U.S. history. The military had its own reasons for promoting citizenship; a non-citizen, if captured, could be treated as a deserter or traitor rather than as a prisoner of war. By mid-1943, 37,432 applicants had become citizens. Only sixty were turned down. See "Naturalization of Aliens in Our Armed Forces," *Immigration and Naturalization Review*, September 1943, vol. 1, no. 3, pp. 6–11.

288: *he had tried several times during his Army days . . .* Given the tiny number of military applications that failed, it's remarkable that Dad never managed to get citizenship during the war. When he was based in California for a short time during 1944, his commanding officer suggested a brief trip to Mexico so that Dad could come back across the border and thus establish his "arrival" in the United States, a strategy that Dad writes enthusiastically about in his letters to Mom. For some reason, however, the commanding officer never followed through with enough time off for Dad to make the journey. Toward the end of 1944, as the Army's manpower needs mounted, the military relaxed its rules and sent more non-citizen soldiers overseas. At that point, according to Dad's letters, his superiors became less interested in his citizenship problems.

288: *that disputed sliver of Eastern Europe . . .* Dad really didn't know anything about his homeland. Since then, I have learned a few basic facts. In 1913, when he was born, Lomza province was part of the greater Russian empire. After the Soviet-Polish war of 1919–1920, it became part of the reconstituted Poland. Bubbe Ida managed to find a way out of the country in the midst of that war.

297: *"two general hospitals which are exclusively psychiatric . . ."* House Committee on Appropriations hearings on the Labor-Federal Security Agency Appropriation Bill for 1945, 78th Congress, 2d session, April–May 1944, p. 331.

EIGHTEEN: Uncontoured Ills

304: *seven months for the 313th to collect, train and transport . . .* My portrait of the 313th comes largely from Records Group 112, Records of the Office of the Surgeon

General (Army), Box No. 52, 303rd–314th General Hospitals, National Archives II, in College Park, Maryland. The folders contain material that the surgeon general compiled to write the history of the medical component of World War II.

306: *memo directed draft boards to take time to* . . . War Department Memorandum no. W600-30-43, March 25, 1943, cited in *Neuropsychiatry in World War II* (Office of the Surgeon General, Department of the Army, 1966), p. 201.

306: *they evaluated 5,774 patients* . . . Darnall's annual report for 1945, which provides a detailed breakdown of what happened to its patients, can be found in RG112, Records of the Surgeon General, World War II Administrative Records, 319.1 Unit Annual Reports, Box 64, "Darnall General Hospital" folder, 1941–1945. The hospital ceased operation on December 15, 1945.

306: *No patient should be returned to duty unless he can work a full day* . . . From a May 28, 1945 memo, cited in *Neuropsychiatry*, p. 227.

306: *ambivalence about psychiatric discharges* . . . *Neuropsychiatry*, pp. 217–223.

307: *the Pacific and European commands eventually adopted different policies* . . . For a good description of this divergence, see Clarence McKittrick Smith, *The Medical Department: Hospitalization and Evacuation, Zone of Interior. United States Army in World War II* (Washington, D.C.: Office of the Chief of Military History, Department of the Army, 1956).

308: *the name on Bubbe Ida's passport* . . . Her passport contains no stamp showing her arrival in the United States, suggesting that she might have used it to leave Europe but not to gain entry here. Passports were not required for travelers to the United States until 1920.

310: *a $3 million budget problem* . . . Missavage says he traveled to Lansing with an Eloise colleague to meet with Gordon Yudashkin about the Eloise transfers. "There was no way to prevent it," he told me. "It was a done deal."

311: *the contraction happened with almost breathtaking speed* . . . The statistics come from government publications, except for the rates per 100,000, which I calculated.

315: *a panel of three federal judges declared the opposite* . . . In cases involving the constitutionality of a state statue, federal rules allowed the trial judge to convene a three-judge panel. For the panel's full ruling, see *Bell v. Wayne County General Hospital at Eloise*, 384 F. Supp. 1085 (Eastern District of Michigan).

NINETEEN: Always the Bridesmaid

328: *so many couples wanted to tie the knot* . . . Tuttle, *Daddy's Gone to War*, pp. 19–21.

TWENTY: Reinterpretation

337: *certain that his anxiety was real* . . . One doctor at the 126th General Hospital disagreed with a colleague's diagnosis of "reactive depression," but said he would allow Dad's case to go forward to the disability board with that diagnosis included.

342: *if unburdening yourself to your best friend* . . . Mom's thinking also may have been influenced by a major news event that happened just a week before Annie's death: the negative reaction to the disclosure that Sen. Thomas F. Eagleton, the Democratic Party's vice presidential nominee, had been hospitalized three times for depression and had received electric shock treatment. Eagleton decided to quit the ticket after only eighteen days as George McGovern's running mate. In political annals, the Eagleton affair seemed to confirm that the American public was not ready for a vice president with a psychiatric past. For Mom, it might have confirmed the risks of revealing her secret.

343: *an innocuous conversation between new neighbors* . . . Oakland County land records confirm that the Frumkins and the Pierces owned adjoining properties in The Ravines. The Pierces bought their home on December 1, 1958, the Frumkins on November 26, 1963.

346: *"On this place there are buried 4000 Jews . . ."* Several Holocaust references, as well as the Jewish Historical Institute in Warsaw, state that the second Radziwillow massacre took place near Suchodoly, a small hamlet several miles south of the first massacre site. If those killed at Suchodoly are buried there, as seems likely, then perhaps the creators of the new Radziwillow memorial decided to honor the dead from both massacres with the inscription's reference to four thousand Jews.

347: *proudly shows us the Certificate of the Righteous* . . . Yad Vashem confirmed, via e-mail, that on September 29, 1996, the organization had recognized the bravery of Ludmila Korson's family, the Kubits, for hiding Jews during the years of Nazi occupation in Radziwillow.

EPILOGUE

353: *the last from 1948* . . . After 1948, Eloise sent all unclaimed bodies to the Wayne University College of Medicine. Minutes of the Eloise board, Feb. 2, 1948.

356: *could erect a memorial* . . . In April 2008, Jo Johnson told me that someone had expressed an interest in donating such a marker for the site. The idea is still under discussion.

⋯ ⋯ { ACKNOWLEDGMENTS } ⋯ ⋯

A family secret stands at the center of *Annie's Ghosts*; a family's support stands behind it. Mom had asked her children to stay close and look out for each other; my decision to write this book tested that closeness, but my sisters and brothers looked out for me, even when they disagreed with me. I'm lucky to call them my family. Thanks, therefore, to my siblings: Sash, for enthusiasm, guidance, and the insight that we grew up at different times and see our parents differently; Mike, for patience, wise counsel, and giving me that cautious green light to go forward; Jeff, for encouragement, suggestions, and asking, "Who the heck is Annie?" in the first place; Evie, for sharing her memories, saving those wartime letters, and trusting me to do right by them. Thanks, too, to their spouses, their children, and my many relatives; their contributions became cairns on the path to the secret's origins.

Any writer would benefit from having an agent such as Gail Ross, who believed in *Annie's Ghosts* when it was no more than an idea. She never told me what I wanted to hear, only what I needed to do. I now have a firsthand understanding of why she has such a fine reputation in the publishing world. Thanks, also, to her associate, Howard Yoon, whose contributions began with the title and, fortunately for me, didn't stop there.

When Leslie Wells at Hyperion read my proposal for *Annie's Ghosts*, she immediately said she wanted the book. I couldn't ask for a more supportive editor, or a more attentive one. Ellen Archer, now Hyperion's president and publisher, endorsed Leslie's original judgment, which gave me two reasons to believe in Hyperion as my partner. Two years of collaboration have only strengthened that feeling. My heartfelt thanks to copy editor

Anne Newgarden for several sterling catches, and to production editor David Lott and Muriel Tebid of the legal staff for their love of detail.

My friends at *The Washington Post* provided more than I could have asked. Their genuine interest in the secret, and the story behind it, fueled me on days when dead ends outnumbered new leads. Former executive editor Leonard Downie, Jr., and managing editor Phil Bennett granted me the leave of absence that made the book possible. Len's response, when I told him in 2004 about my desire to pursue the story someday, was as sustaining as it was spontaneous: "You have to do this." I regret only that the book took me away from the newsroom at a time of great change, and that I wasn't around to help out. Thanks, also, to Donald Graham, chairman and CEO of The Washington Post Company, whose early interest in the "five thousand" (my shorthand for the many families with relatives once hidden in public mental institutions) gave me confidence in the story's larger significance. At later stages, I profited from both Len's and Don's perceptive reads of the manuscript.

Other colleagues offered encouraging words, sometimes without realizing their importance to me. They include Rick Atkinson, Bonnie Benwick, David Brown, Kathleen Cahill, Glenn Frankel, Bob Kaiser, Kathy Lally, Jeff Leen, Pat Monahan, Steve Mufson, Wendy Ross, Dale Russakoff, Zofia Smardz, and Jane Touzalin. Bob Woodward, my first mentor at *The Post*, has given me an invaluable education over the years, part of what we have called our permanent journalism seminar, but I owe him a particular debt for serving as a role model of how to be a generous colleague.

No writer, at least not this one, can survive without friends who understand the value of forthrightness. Scott Shane refused to let a quarter-century of friendship stand in the way of offering sharp and thoughtful comments; I'm fortunate to count him as a critic as well as a friend. Frances Stead Sellers showed me, not for the first time, why she is a great editor and why I want her to read whatever I write. Mark Reutter, my former *Baltimore Sun* investigative reporting partner, went over the manuscript as if it were his own, and proved again why he's a journalist's journalist. Bill Casey, my former *Post* colleague, offered the kind of critique that any writer craves—specific, smart, and salted with useful suggestions. Laura Wexler, a Baltimore-based writer with a keen appreciation for narrative storytelling, solved the problem of where to place a crucial scene; for that alone, I would pay for her coffee in perpetuity.

Many of the people I interviewed reviewed portions of the manuscript and saved me from more errors than I care to count. Their names appear in the narrative or the chapter notes; I'm grateful to them all. Several people, however, deserve special recognition: Toby Hazan, my mother's psychiatrist, was beyond patient in helping me to piece together those events involving Mom's hospitalization in 1995 that I did not witness. Anna Oliwek, my cousin, welcomed my questions and allowed me to intrude into some of her most painful memories. Jo Johnson, chairman of the Westland Historical Commission and preserver-in-chief of Eloise's history, opened her shelves and cabinets to me. I cannot repay her for her many kindnesses. Marc Manson, a collector of Detroit history and artifacts, spent a day passing along some of his knowledge and introducing me to the Sanborn insurance maps of property and streets, a resource for exhuming information about the city's past that I wouldn't have discovered otherwise. Ed Missavage, the former Eloise psychiatrist, forgave me for ambushing him in the Detroit Public Library; every hour I spent with him was an hour of learning and insight.

I had the pleasure, on my many trips to Detroit, of staying with Sally and Jimmy Rubiner, my wife's relatives. Their spare bedroom became a home away from home, and their knowledge of Detroit was an unexpected bonus. I relied on Jimmy, a lawyer, for help in navigating the Michigan courts, and on Sally for her unflagging interest in the book and her unerring proofreader's eye. Their children, Joanna and Julia, both Californians now, gave me bed, breakfast, and dinner during a research trip to Los Angeles; they truly know how to make a traveling reporter feel welcome.

Credit also belongs to researchers who chased down a variety of elusive facts with persistence and professionalism. Carrie Hagen spent most of a summer reading Detroit newspapers and the *Jewish Chronicle* of London to assemble information about Jewish emigration from Europe and life in Detroit. Lori Berdak Miller plumbed the military records at the National Personnel Records Center in St. Louis, and found both the morning reports and the daily admissions reports of the three army hospitals in the Philippines where my father was a patient in July 1945. Sam Elrom read the Radziwillow *yizkor* book, and wrote a richly detailed summary. Alexander Dunai, our Ukrainian translator and guide, took us to Radziwillow to search for its past; after three days together, I came to value both his friendship and his journalistic instincts.

Zofia Smardz, my *Post* colleague, helped by translating two documents from Polish; Anna Friedman, a longtime friend of my daughter, used her German skills to decipher several other documents. Cora Sellers's careful read of portions of the final manuscript helped to improve it. Dan Meyers, my neighbor and a professional photographer, performed his magic on the book's photos so they could reproduce at the highest possible quality.

Doing the reporting for *Annie's Ghosts* drove home the all-important role that archivists play in preserving history. Governments have an ambivalent attitude about the records they generate, sometimes making them available and sometimes shielding them from scrutiny. Archivists, as a group, have dedicated themselves to the notion that history cannot be told without such records. If I had unlimited space, I would pay tribute to specific archivists and librarians; instead, I'll express my appreciation to the staffs of the following: in Detroit, the Detroit Public Library's Burton Historical Collection and Wayne State University's Walter Reuther Library and its Purdy/Kresge Library; in suburban Detroit, the Rabbi Leo M. Franklin Archives of Temple Beth El; in Lansing, the State Archives and the Library of Michigan; in Baltimore, the Johns Hopkins University's Sheridan Libraries, the University of Baltimore Law Library, the Loyola-Notre Dame Library, and the University of Maryland's Health Sciences & Human Services Library; in Washington, D.C., the National Archives, the Library of Congress, and the United States Holocaust Memorial Museum's library; in Los Angeles, the University of Southern California Shoah Foundation Institute for Visual History and Education.

Several people spent considerable time and energy helping me, even though my requests fell squarely outside any known job description. Roya Hakakian, fellow writer and author of a wonderful memoir, generously gave me how-to lessons. Wendy Lower, professor at Towson University, helped educate me on the Holocaust in Volhynia and then skillfully improved the chapter that delves into it; she also translated many of Anna Oliwek's wartime Nazi documents. Marian L. Smith, chief historian for the U.S. Citizenship and Immigration Services, guided me in obtaining records that I had no idea existed. Loretto Dennis Szucs of ancestry.com, the online genealogy company, shared names from her Rolodex as well as her extensive knowledge of how to find family records. Valerie Cochran at the American Legion's Baltimore office opened the first doors to obtaining my father's World War II disability discharge records. Jamie Soliman helped me navigate the maze of the Wayne County Probate Court; I wish every government office had her clone working there. Alice Pepper at *The Detroit Free Press* pulled together the newspaper's clippings on Eloise and cheerfully put up with periodic phone calls looking for confirmation of one fact or another.

Others who shared their considerable expertise include Robert Bernstein at the Bazelon Center for Mental Health Law; Walter Reich, professor of psychiatry at George Washington University and former director of the United States Holocaust Memorial Museum; Charles Hyde, a Wayne State professor and author of a book on the Dodge brothers; Alexandra Stern, a University of Michigan professor who has done pioneering research on the history of forced sterilization; and Carol Chiamp, a lawyer in Detroit who represented mentally ill patients during the early days of deinstitutionalization.

I'm indebted to the many people who allowed me to comb their family albums in search of Annie's photo. Unfortunately, I never found one. If I had, her image might have been the ghostly figure in the cover illustration. Looking at the arresting stock photo that Hyperion chose reminds me that I won't ever know for sure what Annie looked like.

The last shall be first, in truth and in my heart. My children, Josh and Jill, weren't even teenagers when the secret first emerged; twelve years later, they were reading the manuscript and giving me valuable feedback. The transformation still amazes me. My wife, Mary Jo Kirschman, knows *Annie's Ghosts* nearly as well as I do. She accompanied me on much of this journey, either as a listener or as a witness, and when I needed a sounding board, she was my first choice. It isn't her book, but it reflects her good questions and good judgment. I cannot imagine a better traveling companion.

Page numbers in *italics* refer to photo captions.